Inside
Lincoln's
Army

Brigadier General Marsena Rudolph Patrick. (From the Mathew B. Brady Collection in the National Archives.)

Inside Lincoln's Army

The Diary of Marsena Rudolph Patrick,
Provost Marshal General, Army of the Potomac

Edited by David S. Sparks

New York • Thomas Yoseloff • London

Thomas Yoseloff, *Publisher*
8 East 36th Street
New York 16, N. Y.

Thomas Yoseloff Ltd.
18 Charing Cross Road
London W.C.2, England

6023
Printed in the United States of America

19541

Acknowledgments

ONE OF THE ENDURING PLEASURES of historical study is the unfailing courtesy and co-operation one meets at the hands of fellow students and searchers. In the course of preparing the Patrick Diary for publication I have been fortunate in the good advice and assistance I received from many very nice people. I am particularly indebted to Ralph Happel, Historian at the Fredericksburg and Spotsylvania National Military Park, for the answers to a host of questions as well as for a personally conducted tour of General Patrick's headquarters and camp sites in and about Fredericksburg, Virginia. George Harrison Sanford King, also of Fredericksburg, kindly shared his very extensive knowledge of the early families of that part of Virginia.

In the Manuscripts Division of the Library of Congress, where the manuscript of the Patrick Diary is now located, I enjoyed the good fellowship and assistance of Dr. Percy Powell and Mr. John dePorry.

At the National Archives Mrs. Sarah D. Jackson of the Civil War Branch was a great help on more than one occasion.

The staff of the Theodore McKeldin Library, at the University of Maryland, and particularly Miss Virginia Phillips and Miss Betty Baehr, met my innumerable requests with their usual kindness and equanimity.

I also want to thank the General Research Board of the University of Maryland, which provided funds for typing the manuscript.

I trust that Phyllis Bate Sparks will not be embarrassed by

5

a public acknowledgment of her contribution to the completion of this project. I know, even if she does not, how important that contribution has been. My thanks, finally, to Hugh G. Earnhart who prepared the index.

DAVID S. SPARKS

University of Maryland

Contents

List of Illustrations

Introduction

I.

THE APPOINTMENT OF MARSENA RUDOLPH PATRICK to the post of Provost Marshal General of the Army of the Potomac was the result of a stroke of luck or the touch of genius too rarely felt in Mr. Lincoln's favorite Army. The job of chief policeman called for a hard and harsh disciplinarian who could deal with the thieves, murderers, and deserters who were swept into the army by the offer of bounties or a fear of the draft. It also called for a man of absolute integrity, for the opportunities for the sale of influence or favor were many and the rewards would have been high. Further, the post required a sense of justice and a high degree of tact, for it involved dealing with a civilian population that was both enemy and friend in the manner peculiar to civil wars.

It is clear that General Patrick possessed these virtues in abundance. It is equally evident that he was a hard man to work with or for. Soldiers who wrote to their home-town newspapers, associates who recalled Patrick in their reminiscences, even official army dispatches reflect the General's industry, honesty, courage, and piety, but the note of cordiality or affability that softens the portraits of Generals Grant, Meade, and even Sherman, is wholly lacking.

There was, however, a gentle side to General Patrick. As his Diary testifies, he enjoyed feminine company. Undoubtedly he considered himself something of an old charmer, particu-

11

larly with the good Secession ladies of Virginia. His sympathy for the innocent victims of the war was proverbial. As a matter of fact, Patrick was frequently suspected of pro-Southern sentiments, particularly by Radical Republicans who distrusted his Democratic proclivities. Ultimately he was removed from his duties in postwar Richmond because of his reputation for being too soft on ex-Confederates.

Marsena Patrick was born on March 11, 1811, the tenth and last child of a moderately successful farming family which lived near Watertown in upstate New York. Running away from home at the age of ten, allegedly seeking freedom from the domineering Puritanism of his Mother, Patrick knocked about for several years. He worked on the Erie Canal, taught school, and acquired one or two influential friends in the process. It was through the intercession of one of these, General Stephen van Rensselaer, that Patrick was appointed to the Military Academy at West Point in 1831. He scraped through, graduating forty-eighth in a class of fifty-one, in 1835. His career, after graduation, consisted of duty at the usual round of northern and western posts, followed by active service in the Seminole War in Florida, and with General Wool in the Mexican War. In 1850 he resigned from the Army and returned to the Finger Lakes region of New York, settling first at Geneva and then near the village of Ovid. There, in one of the garden spots of the world, on the high tableland between Lakes Seneca and Cayuga, Patrick became a successful farmer who sought to interest his neighbors in a variety of agricultural experiments and reforms.

His interest in scientific farming led to his selection as President of the New York State Agricultural College, established at Ovid in 1859. The college, subsequently absorbed by Cornell University, had barely opened its doors when the outbreak of war closed them.

The family that General Patrick left behind when he went off to the war, which occupied so much of his thoughts and filled so much of his Diary, consisted of his wife Mary, two daughters, and three sons, and it is clear that he ruled it as though it were a military command. Mary McGulpin Patrick was a Michigan girl whom Patrick met, courted, and married during his first tour of duty after graduation from West Point, while he was stationed at Fort Mackinac. In her husband's Diary she frequently appears as "Mrs. Patrick" and one has the feeling that she was similarly addressed in the intimacy of the family circle. The Patrick first-born was a daughter and they named her Mary. She was just eighteen when the firing on Fort Sumter turned the Patrick household upside down. Mary's religious life, her health, and her handling of money seem to have given her father constant concern. The Diary suggests that General Patrick was deeply disturbed by the possibility that Mary contemplated breaking with her father's Presbyterianism. Apparently this possibility was roughly equivalent to man's original fall from grace, in the eyes of the old soldier.

Julia, aged fifteen in 1861, seems to have been a constant source of comfort to her father. Brayton, twelve years old in 1861, is the "Bucky" of the Diary who visited his father at City Point in 1864. "Renie," or Irenecus, was nine when the war began and George Benjamin, or "Geordie," was the baby of the family at six. Normally the household also included one or two girls who served as either the "hired girl" or as a teacher for the younger Patricks. Mary and Alice Hogarth, daughters of a tailor in nearby Geneva, served in these capacities throughout most of the war years.

Upon receiving the news of Fort Sumter Patrick immediately offered his services to his native state. In May of 1861 Governor Edwin Morgan gave him a commission as Brigadier General in the state militia and appointed him Inspector-General of the rapidly growing New York forces. In this capacity it became Patrick's duty to keep track of the fast growing list of laws, orders, regulations, and administrative directives which governed the organization and outfitting of state troops destined for Federal service. Under the leadership of the very able Morgan, New York was soon raising a veritable host. It was arming, equipping, and feeding the new soldiers at state expense, but with the understanding that the state would be reimbursed by the Union government for expenses incurred.

General Patrick soon wearied of what quickly became largely a bookkeeping assignment. He thought he saw in the post he occupied an opportunity for greater service to both the men in the ranks and the people they left behind them. He proposed that he be permitted to follow the state troops into their camps around Washington to act as a liaison officer between the state organizations and the national government. He felt that in this way he could insure that state forces remained under New York officers, that New York regiments would not be brigaded with "foreign" troops from other states, and that he could, in a thousand small ways, remind New York troops of the continuing concern of the state authorities for their welfare while they served their country so far from home.

Whether Governor Morgan saw the political possibilities in the mission that Patrick proposed and feared the General's use of the office of Inspector-General or whether Patrick's political ineptitude simply alienated the Governor cannot be known, but the upshot was that Patrick's authority to speak for the New York organizations was withdrawn in the fall of 1862, and the Major-Generalship which Patrick claimed had been promised him was not forthcoming. Patrick then determined to resign as Inspector-General just as soon as he could find a suitable appointment in Washington. He was engaged in that search when the portion of the Diary which still survives and is reproduced here begins on January 1, 1862.

After what proved a long and embarrassing delay Patrick's appointment as a Brigadier General of Volunteers was confirmed by the Senate and on March 21, 1862, he assumed command of James S. Wadsworth's Brigade in King's Division of McDowell's First Corps of the Army of the Potomac. The Brigade consisted of the 20th New York State Militia (80th New York Volunteers), the 21st, 23rd, and 35th New York Volunteers. Patrick was convinced that Wadsworth's gentle treatment of his Brigade had spoiled the men and that sterner measures were required. Within a few weeks he had antagonized virtually every man in his command and won the undying enmity of some. Prompt punishment of even the most minor infractions of regulations, long hours of drill in everything from mud to dust and snow to searing heat, and a demand for the punctilious observance of military etiquette combined to raise questions about Patrick's capacity for effective leadership.

When General McClellan moved the Army of the Potomac to the Peninsula between the York and James rivers for his attempt on Richmond, President Lincoln detained General McDowell's Corps to cover Washington. Moving slowly down the Orange and Alexandria Railroad during the first weeks of April, McDowell's command, including Patrick's Brigade, arrived on the Rappahannock, opposite Fredericksburg, on April 19, 1862. The Federal forces soon occupied the town and Patrick was placed in command as military governor. It was Patrick's introduction to the manifold problems of an army operating in semihostile country.

As military governor Patrick promptly made clear his determination that no civilian would suffer needlessly. Partly out of his deep deligious convictions, partly out of his belief in what constituted a wise occupation policy, and partly out of his inability to watch innocent bystanders suffer the barbarities of war, Patrick sought, in every way open to him, to meliorate the lot of the civilians caught in the tides of conflict that were sweeping over Fredericksburg. He was quick to post guards at the homes of unprotected women and children. He tried desperately to curtail the raids of Federal soldiers on smoke-houses, horse barns, henhouses, and sheep flocks, albeit without much success. No lover of secession or disunion, Patrick was as firm with the soldiers as he was lenient with civilians. He was convinced that good order in the Army would go far toward returning Virginia to its former loyalty. In his frequent sermons to his assembled troops, as well as to the endless line of terrified soldiers who were hauled before him for individual offenses, Patrick sought to impress upon them that, but for the grace of God, the people they were robbing and plundering might be their own fathers, mothers, or sisters. This conservative and more civilized view of a proper occupation policy became a casualty of the Civil War but there were many, like General Patrick, who sought to maintain it as long as possible.

Patrick's first tour of duty as military governor of Fredericksburg was ended by Stonewall Jackson's thrust down the Shenandoah Valley, in May of 1862, which forced the recall of McDowell's command. The Patrick Brigade participated in the fruitless attempt to trap Jackson at Front Royal and Strasburg. By mid-June, however, Patrick was back in Fredericksburg, where he again took up his duties as military governor of the town.

Six weeks later the Union forces were again withdrawn from Fredericksburg as General Pope sought to hold off the Confederates until McClellan's forces could be moved from the Peninsula to the Washington front. Patrick's Brigade became part of Pope's Army of Virginia and fought at Second Manassas. When Lee sought to capitalize on his victory over Pope by his invasion of the North in September of 1862, Patrick's command, as part of McClellan's revitalized Army of the Potomac, was heavily engaged in the battles at South Mountain and Antietam Creek. In this fighting Patrick's officers and men learned the value of some of the lessons in discipline and drill that he had been teaching. A new respect and affection for the old man began to be felt in his command.

One of the most touching scenes described in the Diary is the presentation of a silver service to Patrick by the departing members of his Brigade.

General Patrick's combat record, however, was one of competence rather than brilliance. This, coupled with his successful record as a military governor in Fredericksburg, led to his appointment as Provost Marshal General of the Army of the Potomac in October, 1862. General Orders No. 161, dated October 6 at the Headquarters of the Army of the Potomac, Berlin, Maryland, and signed by McClellan, did not specify the duties of Patrick's new post. In spite of numerous orders and circulars issued in subsequent months, the precise scope and duties of the Provost Marshal General of the Army were never fully defined. McClellan's report, written some months later, is probably the best statement of what he had in mind when he appointed Patrick to the post. His report lists the following duties which "indicate the sphere of this department."

Suppression of marauding and depredations, and of all brawls and disturbances, preservation of good order, and suppression of disturbances beyond the limits of the camps.

Prevention of straggling on the march.

Suppression of gambling-houses, drinking-houses, or bar-rooms, and brothels.

Regulation of hotels, taverns, markets, and places of public amusement.

Searches, seizures, and arrests. Execution of sentences of general courts-martial involving imprisonment or capital punishment. Enforcement of orders prohibiting the sale of intoxicating liquors, whether by tradesmen or sutlers, and of orders respecting passes.

Deserters from the enemy.

Prisoners of War taken from the enemy.

Countersigning safeguards.

Passes to citizens within the lines and for purposes of trade.

Complaints of citizens as to the conduct of the soldiers.

General Patrick thus became responsible for the interior economy of the Army of the Potomac. Normally he could count on having a brigade of infantry, several detachments of cavalry, and a battery or two of artillery under his command to assist him. He preferred regular Army or New York troops and usually managed to trade around until his command reflected this preference.

A perusal of Patrick's official correspondence preserved in the National Archives in Washington makes it clear that two areas of responsibility became increasingly important and absorbed more and more of his time and energy. The first was the gathering of information about the enemy, and the second was the problem of trade between North and South through and around the military lines. The need of the Army for better information than that provided by Allan Pinkerton and his detectives led to the creation of the Bureau of Information under Patrick's jurisdiction. The problem of trade, and the entire question of the treatment of civilians within the lines of the Army, which was inextricably bound up with it, was never solved to the satisfaction of anyone. Patrick, however, was in daily contact with the problem and must be credited with injecting an uncommon note of common sense and humanity into the whole messy business. Certainly a great many civilians, caught in the holocaust of war, owed their livelihood as well as their lives to General Patrick.

Appointed by McClellan, Patrick continued as Provost Marshal-General of the Army of the Potomac under Generals Burnside, Hooker, and Meade. In December of 1864 his responsibilities were enlarged when he became Provost Marshal General of the Armies operating against Richmond, as well as of the Army of the Potomac, and moved his offices to Grant's Headquarters at City Point, Virginia.

A final evaluation of Patrick's services as Provost Marshal General must await further study, but a telegram of General U. S. Grant to Patrick's immediate superior, General Henry W. Halleck, on June 1, 1865, when Patrick was Provost of the Department of Virginia with headquarters in Richmond, is certainly pertinent. Grant wired, "Do you not think it advisable to relieve General Patrick? The machinery kept up in his duties is represented as heavy, and his kindness of heart may interfere with the proper government of the city." It would appear that Patrick was too kind, too civilized, too much the Christian gentleman to hold an important position in the Confederate capital after Lincoln's assassination had loosed the Northern desire for vengeance. On July 7, 1865, Brigadier General Marsena R. Patrick was relieved of all command in the military forces of the United States.

II

General Patrick's manuscript Diary is in the Manuscript Division of the Library of Congress. It fills one small volume and two large journal books plus a few sheets torn from a fourth volume. Time has taken a toll only in the first volume. There a few words have been obliterated by the effects of water or mold working its way into a few pages. For the most part the hand is clear and firm, although there is occasional evidence of fatigue, illness, or haste. With rare exceptions, Patrick wrote in his Diary nightly, just before retiring. Occasionally the pressure of field operations or a trip to Washington forced him to skip a few days, but he invariably filled in these gaps from pocket memoranda he kept for the purpose. There are about half a dozen days for which no entry was made and for which no explanation was offered. The Diary covers the period from January 1, 1862, to June 16, 1865, making it much the most complete Diary kept by any Union commander or staff officer.

The Diary stands today just as Patrick wrote it, with two exceptions. At some date subsequent to its inditing the General, one of his family, or some subsequent owner, has underlined a few passages in pencil and starred a few pages where some major event is described. The other change is more serious. In about seventy different places, passages varying in length from one to twenty-five lines have been marked out. The great majority of these deletions involve one or two lines. The The deleted passages have been heavily covered with either blue ink or black crayon. In a few instances the black crayon was added to a passage already inked out. Approximately 375 manuscript lines have been crossed out in this fashion. In a few instances where the ink is not too heavy it has been possible to read the original entry with the aid of special lights. Invariably the entry deals with Patrick's eldest daughter, Mary, and usually it reflects Patrick's momentary displeasure with her handling of her money or her growing independence in matters of religion. Whether these deletions were made by the General, by Mary, by some other member of the family, or by some other person cannot now be known. It is apparent that the General was deeply attached to all his family and the Diary itself is evidence of his continuing love for Mary.

The manuscript of the Patrick Diary was given to the Library of Congress in 1955 by Mr. S. F. Adams of New York City. He had inherited it from his father, Professor Ephraim Douglass Adams of Stanford University, who will be remembered for his two-volume study of *Great Britain and the American Civil War*. Professor Adams reported obtaining the Patrick Diary from a resident of a veteran's home. Whether or not it was the Central Branch, National Home for Disabled volunteer Soldiers, in Dayton, Ohio, over which Patrick presided from 1880 to his death in 1888, is not known. This gap in the provenance of the Diary would be disturbing if it were not for the fact that corroborating evidence for literally hundreds of Patrick's statements, drawn from every page of the Diary, is available and has been examined by the editor. The Diary, from first to last, is an authentic historical document.

The great importance of the Patrick Diary stems from its author's unique opportunity to observe the internal operation of one of the great armies of history. While commanding generals and their staffs came and went, Patrick remained. Too low to arouse the envy of the more ambitious generals, but high enough to be privy to most of the opinions, hopes, and plans of the commanders, Patrick has provided the modern student with a priceless view of the inner councils of the Army of the Potomac.

Perceptive students of the Civil War have long suspected that many of the policy decisions credited to Lincoln or Davis, the cabinets, the Congresses, or one of the army commanders were actually made at a lower level. Patrick's Diary offers much new evidence in support of this hypothesis and a fine opportunity for the close study of the process of policy formulation on the complex problems of trade with an enemy in time of war, army and civilian morale, conflicting loyalties and interests in areas occupied by military forces, and a host of lesser questions.

More specifically, the Patrick Diary offers the student of military history an unparalleled opportunity to observe the day-to-day operation of the staff departments and personal staffs of the army commanders. The comings and goings of this second level of the military hierarchy will help to solve a hundred little puzzles that have long intrigued the special student of particular campaigns or individual officers of the Army of the Potomac. The social life of Army headquarters in

Washington, as well as that of the army in the field, is also
sketched with a sure hand. Patrick's portraits of the successive
commanders of the Army of the Potomac are fresh and reveal-
ing, his estimate of Secretary of War Edwin M. Stanton is
most judicious, and his references to such men as E. R. S.
Canby, Peter H. Watson, and Charles A. Dana serve to recall
the immense contribution to the war effort made by some
Washington bureaucrats who have been too long kept in the
wings.

In spite of the fact that Patrick's judgment was a bit erratic
and his perception not all that it could have been, the special
student and the general reader alike will long be indebted to
him. He once against reminds us that the fabric of our history
is made of threads of a thousand hues; it requires the telling of
a thousand tales of heroism, cowardice, and everything in
between. It is possible that he has provided us with a new
sense of pride, humility, and shame: pride in what was
achieved, humility at what was suffered, and shame for what
was inflicted in the course of a great civil war.

III

General Patrick's manuscript Diary is approximately
260,000 words long. Considerations of size and cost prohibit
publication of the entire Diary. Further, it has its share of
the trivialities and repetition that characterize all but the
greatest of diaries. In making deletions the editor has been
governed by the following considerations:

1. In common with the vast majority of soldiers, both
North and South, General Patrick suffered a good deal from
a variety of intestinal disorders. His difficulties were aggravated by a serious case of hemorrhoids, which flared up

several times during the war. Patrick was also troubled by a persistent pain in his shoulder, which he attempted to cure with a variety of treatments, including a "galvanic" battery. The almost daily references to his physical disorders have been deleted except where they seemed measurably to affect his work or state of mind.

2. Patrick kept up a very extensive correspondence with a large number of personal friends, business associates, and his family. For the most part he mentioned only the fact of sending or receiving a letter and made no reference to its contents or purport. When these references make no mention of persons known to history and when nothing is indicated of the contents of letters to or from the family, they have been deleted from the Diary.

3. Patrick's morning routine was unvarying, and he invariably described it. It included a reflection on the quality of the previous night's sleep, note of a time spent in reading Scripture, and mention of breakfast. Patrick's daily description of this almost inflexible routine has been deleted for the most part.

4. Patrick frequently described the process of moving the Headquarters Camp and invariably mentioned it when such a move deprived him of his supper. When his descriptions of this process dealt exclusively with trivia they have been deleted. No move of the Headquarters Camp itself has been ignored, however.

5. In August of 1863, Patrick took leave and visited his family in Geneva, New York, and then visited friends in Rhinebeck, over in the Hudson River Valley. Mention of the details of this leave have been deleted.

In matters of form the editor has made no change in General Patrick's punctuation, paragraphing, sentence structure, or capitalization. The spelling of a few place names and one or two surnames gave Patrick continuous trouble. He preferred to spell Fredericksburg, Virginia, without the "k."

He spelled nearby Aquia Creek with an extra "c," making it Acquia, a common error even today. He almost invariably spelled Culpeper, Virginia, with a third "p," making it Culpepper. He was also rather consistent in his misspelling of the name of General William W. Averell. In order to reduce the number of square brackets and "*sics*," Patrick's most consistent spelling errors involving places have been noted in footnotes the first time they appear. All other corrections and additions supplied by the editor also appear in square brackets. Patrick normally used a two-em dash in place of a period, but occasionally he used the latter. His usage has been preserved here. Chapter divisions have been made by the editor.

The editor is fully aware of the risks he has run in reducing the length of the Patrick Diary. The inevitable result of the deletion of material that was either trivial or repetitious is to make the past more interesting than it was to those who lived it. The long stretches of time when nothing of interest was happening, so familiar to all of us, are substantially reduced. The result is a subtle distortion of the past which, however lamentable, is inherent in all study of history. Similarly, the deletion of the names of persons with whom Patrick corresponded or visited while on leave emphasizes the military portion of his wartime career, and leaves us with the impression that he spent a greater proportion of his time with men of rank and importance than was the case. The risks, however, were unavoidable and the editor can only hope that his necessary intrusion between General Patrick and his readers will be forgiven by both.

DAVID S. SPARKS

Chapter I

Seeking a Commission and a Command

JANUARY 1, 1862, THROUGH MARCH 21, 1862

In May of 1861, General Patrick had accepted a commission as Brigadier General in the New York Militia, to serve as Inspector General of the state forces. In this post he had divided his time between New York and Washington. In the fall of 1861 he had been unofficially attached to General McClellan's staff with the understanding that he was to perform liaison duties between McClellan's headquarters, New York troops, and state officials in Albany. Patrick thought his activities had the approval of Governor Morgan and he was under the impression that Morgan had promised to make him a Major General. By January 1 Patrick had learned that he did not have the support of the Governor and he was seeking a staff position or a field command in McClellan's Army of the Potomac before submitting his resignation as Inspector General to Morgan.

This was the winter of "all quiet along the Potomac," when McClellan, busy with the tasks of organizing, training, and outfitting the Army of the Potomac, refused to be moved by demands of press, public, or even the President, for an advance. Finally, on March 10, 1862, unable to withstand the pressure longer, he took the Army down to Manassas, only to be met by empty trenches and wooden "Quaker" guns left by the retreating Confederates. In marked contrast were the successes of A. E. Burnside at Roanoke Island, N.C., those of U. S. Grant at Forts Henry and Donelson, and S. R. Curtis at Pea Ridge in Arkansas.

25

Washington [,] *1' January* [,] *1862, Wednesday Night*——

This has been one of the most beautiful days I ever witnessed, even in this delightful climate. . . . Took some Tea & a griddle cake for Breakfast & went over to the Office. . . . I left for home just as the Officers were going over to pay their respects to the President—— I believe there were the usual operations of the day and a great many were drunk at night. . . .

Washington, *Thursday Night* [,] *2' January, 1862* [.]

. . . After 9 o'clk. I went to the Office. . . . Maj. [William P.] Wainwright of the 29' came over . . . then I went to the Ordnance Office, Saw [Brig. Gen. James W.] Ripley, [Col. William] Maynadier & [Capt. James J.] Benton,[1] got 2 manuals, . . . then had a long talk with [Lt. Col. Edward McK.] Hudson.[2] McClellan is said to be mending & [Col. Randolph B.] Marcy, too. . . .[3]

Rhinebeck [,] *Saturday Night* [,] *4' January* [,] *1862* [.]

I rose at the usual time on Friday & went to packing for travel to Albany. . . . McClellan was too ill to see any but [Brig. Gen.] Seth Williams;[4] . . . Made arrangements about my horse, Orderly, Fuel, etc. etc. . . . After dinner I mounted & rode to the cars— 5 o'clock train, paid $8.00, came off, riding

---

[1] Gen. Ripley was Chief of the Ordnance Department; Lt. Col. Maynadier and Capt. Benton also served in Ordnance.

[2] Hudson was a Captain in the Fourteenth U.S. Cavalry and an additional aide-de-camp on McClellan's staff.

[3] Both General McClellan, General-in-Chief of the Army, and Col. Marcy, his father in-law and Chief of Staff, had been seriously ill. McClellan's typhoid fever had struck him on December 20.

[4] Seth Williams was McClellan's Adjutant General.

all night, with discharged soldiers etc. Smoking & drinking &
cold. . . . It was an uncomfortable ride last night, . . . The
weather seems as cold as Greenland.

Albany [,] *Monday Night, 6' January* [,] *1862* [.]

Yesterday was a *very* cold day. About 0 at Sunrise & not very
high in the day. . . . We were near two hours behind on reaching here, on acct. of snow. [Silas W.] Burt[5] had taken rooms
for me, at the Franklin House—— So I came [,] took my dinner, finished my Report [as Inspector-General New York
State Militia] & went to the Capitol—— Carried in my
Report, but Gov. [Edwin D. Morgan] was absent at the
funeral of Gerrit Lansing. . . .[6]

Albany, *Tuesday Night* [,] *7' January* [,] *1862.*

Went to bed rather late last night. . . . I reported to the
Governor who recd. me with "distinguished consideration" &
talked about his Inaugural, which he then read to me. It was
not possible to talk of our own affairs, as every body was
waiting to see him—— . . . I recd. a Letter from Col. Hudson,
just in time—— He had seen & talked with McLellan [*sic*] &
Marcy—— All is ready for me. . . . Since Dinner I have been
at the Capitol & Offices, have been in the Governor's room
talking with him on all sorts of subjects Except that which
brings me here. . . .

---

[5] Major Silas Wright Burt, Jr., was the Assistant Inspector General
for New York and was in charge of the Albany office.

[6] Gov. Morgan was also Chairman of the Republican National Committee. In addition he held a commission as a Major General of the
United States Volunteers, serving as commander of the Department of
New York—altogether a man of considerable power in national as well
as state councils. Gerrit Lansing, a longtime New York politician, had
been president of the Albany Insurance Company at the time of his death.

Albany, *Wednesday, 8' January, 1862*——

. . . Was in the Assembly & heard the Letter of Gov. Morgan
to transmit my Report, without comment. . . . I wrote to
Williams & [Lt. Col. James A.] Hardie[7] for [Cuyler] Van
Vechten,[8] who goes to New York & Washington tonight for
money. . . . Recd. several Letters, including one from Gen.
[Christopher C.] Augur[9] about appointment of his Aides des
Camp. . . .

Albany, *Thursday Night, 9' January* [,] *1862*——

Slept pretty well & rose this morning at the usual hour. . . .
Was in Governor's Room with Prof. Jackson about the 18'
[Regt.] and then with the Governor alone—— Had a very
stormy time with him, he denying the statements I made in my
Letter to [Senator] Preston King,[10] but eventually admitting
all excepting the *time* & *object* for which I was to be appointed a Major General—— He thinks my pay is quite
sufficient and on the whole thinks I have not done much.
Sometimes he was very angry, sometimes behaved better than
I expected under the circumstances—— . . . He has desired
this quarrel in order to repudiate his obligations & get rid
of me. . . .

---

[7] Col. Hardie was an Assistant Adjutant General on McClellan's staff.
In time he became an Inspector General in the United States Army and
part of Secretary of War Stanton's personal military staff.

[8] Col. Van Vechten was the Quarter Master General of the New
York Militia.

[9] Brig. Gen. Augur, a Regular in the 13th U.S. Infantry, commanded
a Brigade of New York Volunteers in King's Division of McDowell's
command.

[10] King, a Republican, was the senior senator from New York.

Saturday Night, 11' January –1862 [.] Washington
   City [.]

On Thursday Night I went to bed late & room very warm. . . .
Quiet ride to New York—— . . . An uncomfortable ride to
Philadelphia—— Two Courtesans near me, attended by men
who call themselves Gentlemen—— Then came a drunken
3 months Volunteer. . . . We reached here at about 6 $\frac{1}{2}$
o'clock—— Got Breakfast unpacked trunk & cleaned up——
. . . Saw Hudson—— McClellan not so well—Marcy not so
well—Marcy going to New York. . . . Went to dinner & then
to see Preston King. . . . Spoke to King about *my* nomination—— Says it is all right.

Washington, *Sunday Night 10.20* [,] *January 12' 1862.*

. . . This morning, day & evening, *very* mild. . . . Did not go
to Church—— My cold makes me cough. . . . Called to see
[Maj. Alexander Eakin] Shiras—— then to see [Maj. Henry]
Hal Prince, close by——[11] Went over to [Brig. Gen. Samuel
P.] Heintzelman's[12] & staid till 10 o'clk. . . .

Monday Night, 13' January——

. . . At the Offices & all about until 11$\frac{1}{2}$ o'clock, then started for
[Brig. Gen. Edwin V.] Sumner's[13] Division, to see about

---

[11] Maj. Shiras was an "Old Army" friend of Patrick. An 1829 graduate
of West Point, he was an Assistant Commissary of Subsistence in the
Washington office of the Commissary General. Maj. Prince graduated
in Patrick's 1835 class at West Point and was now serving in the Paymaster's Office.

[12] Gen. Heintzelman commanded a Division in McClellan's Army. A
West Point graduate of 1826, the gruff old Pennsylvania Dutchman kept
a kind of open house for "Old Army" men in Washington.

[13] Gen. Sumner, whose booming voice had earned him the nickname
"Old Bull," was a divisional commander destined for corps command
in McClellan's army.

Enright's Regt[14] [.]————... The Regt. was at the front & did
not see it. ...

Washington, *14' Jany. '62* [.] *Tuesday Night.*

Slept well last night———— Snowy morning. ... Cold tonight &
indications of further storms. Sec. [Simon] Cameron resigned
yesterday & [Edwin M.] Stanton of Pa. was appointed in his
place————[15] My ... business after Bkft. was ... to see Marcy,
who leaves for New York tomorrow. I talked with him about
business & he says that McClellan [now?] wants me to take a
Brigade, rather than a Staff position; that he has few who
understand how to control men & command them [,] that
Staff Officers seldom succeed in it. ... There is a Bill for
reducing the pay of the Officers of the Army about one half,
& it is likely to be passed———— Congressmen, however, do not
touch their own pay———— There appears to be much exultation over the forced resignation of Cameron, by almost all I
hear speak of it.

Washington, *Wednesday Night, 15' Jany. 1862.*

... [Brig. Gen. John Henry] Martindale[16] came to see me &
went to dine with me———— He is full of business, as usual,

---

[14] Col. Richard C. Enright commanded the 63rd New York Volunteers.

[15] Secretary of War Cameron had become an embarrassment to the
Lincoln administration. His administrative bungling had combined with
his endorsement of abolitionism and advocacy of the idea of arming Negro
soldiers to make him a political liability among the conservatives Lincoln
was seeking to win over. Cameron was sent as Minister to Russia in
the hope of retaining his powerful political support. In an effort to
preserve the nice political, economic, and geographical balance of his
Cabinet, Lincoln on January 13 appointed Edwin M. Stanton to succeed Cameron.

[16] Gen. Martindale commanded a brigade of Maine, Massachusetts,
and New York volunteers in Fitz John Porter's Division.

spread Eagle, but withal, very able & devoted to his profession—— From [Charles G.] Myers, who has been here two or three times today, I learn that when Gov. Morgan presented the list of salaries of his Staff to the Military Board, Myers & [Col. Duncan] Campbell[17] both proposed to increase mine, but the Governor objected, on the ground that it would make ill feeling with the other members of the Staff—The Liar!

Washington, *Thursday Night* [,] *16' January, 1862.*

Last night the weather changed, becoming quite cold & freezing hard. . . . Mounted and started for Upton's Hill. . . . The horses were sliding . . . in the mud. Some of the ground was broken up & some frozen hard, on the roads—— . . . Went to [Col. Henry C.] Hoffman's Regt.[18] between the Depot & Bailey's—or Munson's Hill—— The Regt. was on picket, but I looked through the tents—— Called to see [Brig. Gen. James S.] Wadsworth——[19] The day was such that there could be no drill, or parade—— Dined with Gen. Augur & Mess at 4 o'clock. . . . There will be a move soon, I presume.

Washington, *Friday Night, 17' July*—— *no January* [,] *1862.*

Slept well last night & up at usual hour this morning—— After Breakfast Dr. Weston of Trinity came to see me about Schools in New York for Children of Volunteers & I made him a list of New York Regiments. . . . Was at Head Quarters

---

[17] Myers was a former attorney-general of New York and Col. Campbell was the Assistant Adjutant General on Gov. Morgan's staff.

[18] Col. Hoffman commanded the 23rd N. Y. Volunteers, a "Lower Tier" outfit from Elmira and Owego, New York.

[19] James S. Wadsworth was a wealthy upstate New Yorker whose convictions had carried him from the Democratic Party, through the Free Soil Party, and into the ranks of the Republicans.

& casually saw McClellan—— He looks very much pulled down, pale & thin—— I said nothing to him. . . .

Washington, *Saturday Night* [,] *18' January, 1862*——

Last night about 10 o'clock I was called down to Mr. [Ransom] Gillette's [Gillet] room to see a Mr. S. [amuel] J. Tilden[20] of New York on business. Came up & wrote late. . . . Slept well. . . . Wrote Mrs. Patrick to send me a Box with Blankets & bed clothes. . . . I had to go & see [Brig. Gen. George] Stoneman.[21] He desires to overhaul all the Cavalry, & a Bill is introduced to that effect. So the day has passed, in rain and mud & slush generally—— . . .

Washington [,] *Sunday Night, 19' January, 1862*——

Last night Wainwright came in here after I had laid down my pen & staid till near ten. He says the mud is 6 inches deep in their camp & about the consistency of treacle. . . . I have been reading "Golden Fruit" or the Trees mentioned in Scripture. . . . Since Dinner I have written a long letter to Buck & a short one to his Mother—— . . . I am feeling very lonely & very uncomfortable in regard to many things—— Am filled with forebodings of Evil to befall the Country & involving me, my family & those I love in ruin.

Washington, *Monday Night* [,] *20' Jany, '62.*

. . . I did intend to see McClellan today, but he was with the new Secretary [Stanton], who took his seat today & recd. the Army Officers—— . . . Was intending to have looked over

---

[20] Tilden, a conservative New York Democrat, was destined to lose the presidency to Rutherford B. Hayes in the celebrated election of 1876.
[21] Gen. Stoneman was McClellan's Chief of Cavalry at this time.

Tactics this evening, but [Rev.] Dr. [John] Van Ingen has been here until about ten o'clock.

Washington, *Tuesday Night, 21' January* [,] *1862*——

. . . Had a long talk with [Col. T. T.] Gantt & the Orleans Boys—— The Duc d[e] Chartres I have often met, but see little of the Compte de Paris——[22] Nice young man—— Hudson said the General wanted to see me after 12 o'clock—— . . . Sent my Orderly over to watch for McClellan & waited & waited, until McClellan went home & I missed him—— . . .

Washington, *Wednesday Night, 22' Jany. '62* [.]

. . . Went to see McClellan & had a talk—— He is able, he says, to put me where I will not be obliged to serve much, under my juniors—— Will see the President & have my name sent in—— Then talked of New York affairs generally. . . .

Washington, *Thursday Night, 23' January, 1862.*

. . . Telegraph from Stonehouse[23] saying "Ten Regts. of Maximum Strength will be sent forward in 3 weeks["]—— Letter from Governor about Treasury Notes—— Went to see [George] Harrington[,] Asst. Sec. Treasury & then Telegraphed & wrote the Governor—— . . . After dinner met

---

[22] The Duc de Chartres and the Comte de Paris, the latter a pretender to the French throne, were the "Captain Chatters" and the "Captain Parry" of McClellan's staff who did so much to enliven Washington society during the first winter of the war.

[23] This is an error. Major Thomas *Hill*house was the Adjutant General of New York.

Dennis [Hart] Mahan[24] & had a very pleasant talk with him about War, [Maj. Gen.] G. [ustavus] W. Smith,[25] McClellan & others—— . . . I am not well, my bowels being out of order & I must again take a dose of brandy.

Washington, *Friday Night, 24' January, 1862.*

. . . After Bkft. I . . . took horse for [Brig. Gen. Winfield Scott] Hancock's Brigade.[26] The roads are horribly muddy—— From Georgetown I took the towpath to near Chain Bridge & got along quite well. . . . Brig Gen. [W. F.] Baldy Smith was absent——[27] Rode over to Hancock's—— It was too late when I started home to allow me to see [Brig. Gen. George A. J.] McCall.[28] The day has been raw chilly & cheerless. . . .

Washington, *25' January, 1862*——*Saturday Night*——

. . . Office early—— Came back with letters & went to writing, which I kept up till night. . . . This morning, . . . the sun made his appearance for the first time in some 11 or 12 days. . . .

---

[24] Prof. Mahan was for many years the Professor of Civil and Military Engineering at West Point and had taught a great many of the general officers in both Union and Confederate service. Father of the naval-power advocate, Alfred Thayer Mahan, Dennis Mahan's influence over the tactics, strategy, and military politics of the Civil War has been too little understood.

[25] Gen. G. W. Smith was eighth in the class of 1842 at West Point and a great favorite of Professor Mahan. He followed his native state of Virginia into the Confederacy and was quickly commissioned a Major General.

[26] Gen. Hancock commanded a brigade of Wisconsin, Pennsylvania, New York, and Maine volunteers in W. F. "Baldy" Smith's Division.

[27] Gen. W. F. Smith, a strict disciplinarian, who was cordially hated by his troops, commanded one of the largest divisions in McClellan's Army.

[28] Gen. McCall commanded a Division of the famous Pennsylvania Reserve.

Washington, *Sunday Night, 26' Jany. 1862*——

. . . Up late, Breakft. late, toilet late and then too late for Church—— Wainwright came in & I had only time after he left to dress & go over to Col. [Joseph P.] Taylor's[29] to eat my share of a haunch of Venison sent him from Penn. Heintzelman, [Brig. Gen. John] Sedgwick, Clark[e?],[30] [Col. Charles P.] Kingsbury[31] & Hancock Taylor, with the Col. [,] Wife, Bell & Eva, constituted the dinner Party—— It was very quiet, very pleasant & homelike. . . .

Washington, *Monday Night, 27' January, 1861* [2.]

. . . After Breakfast this morning I came to my room, to wait for the Mail, when who should be ushered in but Mrs. Thad. Kendrick of Albany, with letters from [Tom] Arden,[32] Gov. Morgan & every body, *to* every body, bent on going over to Gen. [Brig. Gen. Daniel] Butterfield's Camp[33] & to have me go with her—— She is determined to get her husband into the Army—wants him on Staff & does not know what all——. . . At Butterfield's, at [Brig. Gen. George] Morell's[34] —with [Brig. Gen. Fitz John] Porter & all! We have got back

[29] Col. Taylor was the Commissary General of Subsistence.

[30] Gen. Sedgwick commanded a brigade of Maine and New York volunteers in Heintzelman's Division and was one of the stalwarts of the West Point coterie in Washington. This Clark is probably Colonel Henry F. Clarke, Chief Commissary of Subsistence for the Army of the Potomac.

[31] Col. Kingsbury spent his days trying to keep McClellan's army supplied with guns and ammunition as Chief of Ordnance for the Army of the Potomac.

[32] Tom Arden was an assistant adjutant general on Governor Morgan's staff.

[33] Gen. Butterfield commanded a Brigade of New Yorkers, Pennsylvanians, and a maverick outfit of Michigan boys in Fitz John Porter's Division.

[34] Gen. Morell's Brigade, with those of Martindale and Butterfield, comprised Fitz John Porter's Division.

alive & I have written to Tom Arden *how* to provide for him at home. . . .

Washington, *Tuesday Night, 28' January, 1862.*

. . . I have had [Francis B.] Spinola[35] after me today, wanting me to go into business, cloth & clothing for the Army—— . . . Saw McClellan today & have agreed to see him again tomorrow. He thinks . . . it morally certain that I will take a Brigade.

Washington, *Wednesday Night* [,] *29' January ,62* [.]

This has been a mild, half misty, muddy day—— . . . At 12 o'clock I went over to the Office of the General—— He says my name has gone to the Senate—— I am now anxious to be off—else I may not have time to do what I wish at home. . . . Wainwright was here & I wrote to [Brig. Gen. Joseph] Hooker,[36] introducing him—— He goes there as Chief of Artillery.

Washington, *Thursday Night, 30' January, 1862.*

Slept well—— Wrote letters to [ex-] Gov. [Hamilton] Fish[37] & after Bkft. went down to see him, but he had got out of the way, somewhere. . . . Wrote Letters to Senator [Judge Ira]

---

[35] Francis B. Spinola became a Brig. Gen. of Volunteers in July of 1862, which would suggest either a goodly success or a dismal failure in his cloth and clothing venture.

[36] About half of Gen. Hooker's Division were New Yorkers and he had strong family ties with the State.

[37] Hamilton Fish, scion of two wealthy and aristocratic New York families, had been Governor and Senator. He was currently active in raising troops and money for the war effort in New York City.

Harris,[38] . . . asking him to look to my nomination, if it should come up. I sent it to him at the Capitol. . . . Went in to see Mr. [Erastus] Corning[39] for a few minutes—— I talked to him of my nomination & he will watch for it.

Washington,—*No! New York, 31' January* [,] *1862* [.]

. . . Get all packed & take Hack for depot—— Uncomfortable sort of ride, cheerless & no one to talk with, except as [sic] the Young Compte de Paris, Robert d' Orleans, who was on his way to New York with some Lady friend, to meet the Prince de Joinville, Duc de Penthrivre [sic] & Duc de Chartres[40]—— He talks well : is modest & intelligent. It was quite late, (near 11) when we reached New York & I went into the Dey St. House. . . .

Albany, *Saturday Night, 1' February, 1862.*

Slept rather late—— Up & breakfasted, very stormy—— . . . Bought cheap straps as Brig.—Bought 6 shirts (under) & drawers. Inquired about saddles, Rubber Cloths etc. . . . At 3 :15 started in the storm for Albany—& were $\frac{3}{4}$ of an hour behind time in leaving the City . . . arriving in Albany at 11 $\frac{1}{4}$. I came to the Delaven & got a room. . . .

---

[38] Ira Harris, a leader of the Albany bar and longtime justice of the New York State Supreme Court, was the junior Senator from New York from 1861 to 1867. A Republican, he was addressed as either Judge or Senator by his associates.

[39] Erastus Corning was a wealthy iron manufacturer and President of the New York Central Railroad. He had been Mayor of Albany and was now serving his second term as a Congressman. A Peace Democrat, he had attended the Washington Peace Convention of 1861, and while he generally supported the Administration's war efforts, he regularly protested its more arbitrary acts of censorship and intimidation.

[40] The Prince de Joinville kept a watchful eye on his likable nephews. The Duc de Penthrevre was his son.

Albany, *Sunday Night, 2' February, 1862.*

Awoke with a headache—— Bkft. & removed to a better room—— . . . Doctor [James P.] Kimball[41] has accepted [a] position on my Staff, as A. A. Genl. & we have talked with each other fully, in regard to outfit, mess arrangements etc . . . [Tom] Arden came in just after I laid down my pen & we have had a long pleasant talk over my affairs, & he will arrange with the Governor about *time* of my resignation & some incidental matters of Expenditure etc. . . .

Albany, *Monday Night, 3' February, 1862*——

Night cold—— Had a fire made in good season & got up—— . . . I recd. a note from Arden in the morning, who had seen the Governor and seemed to think all was fair. This also is confirmed by [Silas W.] Burt, who says the Governor was delighted at my not fighting him—— . . . Dined at $3\frac{1}{2}$ o'clock & then went up to see the Governor, who received me with "very distinguished consideration," but as he was going out I agreed to meet him at 9 tomorrow. . . .

Albany [,] *Tuesday Night, (9 o'clock) 4' Feby. 1862* [.]

Rose & breakfasted early . . . went to see the Governor & talked over all our matters of business, saying nothing *outside* of business—— Went to the Comptroller's & settled up by business with that Department. . . . I shall go off at 11:15 this evening.

---

[41] The good doctor was commissioned a Captain and served as an Assistant Adjutant General on Patrick's staff until the end of 1863.

Wednesday Night [,] *9 o'clock, 5 Feby.* Ovid——

. . . After reaching the cars I found no berth unoccupied——
Subsequently, however, a Mr. Wilbur of Batavia, to whom
Gen. Scroggs introduced me, gave me part of his berth, to
Syracuse. . . . I came up, getting home just at dark, in the
Stage Sleigh—— They were not looking for me before morn-
ing—— I find all well and we have had a nice time tonight.

Ovid [.] *Thursday Night* [,] *6' February* [,] *1862* [.]

. . . After Breakfast & prayers I had to unpack my Trunk &
take it up to town . . . to have it repaired. . . . Did not stay
longer than to pay Pew rent & some other little things &
come home. . . . I have spent the day at home entirely, as I do
not wish to go out much until I know what I am to do. . . .

Ovid, *Friday Night* [,] *7' February* [,] *1862*——

. . . Troubled about my affairs. Get the Blues awfully sometimes of late. . . . When the mail came down it brought a
Letter from Preston King of 3' Inst. saying that my name
not having come to the Senate, he had asked the Adjt. General
about it & found that it (*or* I) had not been nominated——
I wrote McClellan enclosing that from King. . . .

Ovid, *Saturday Night, 8' February* [,] *1862* [.]

. . . Up & breakfasted at the usual hour, then I sat down to
settle up small matters in the way of accounts—— Wrote
to Horticulturist, Missionary, Herald, Home Missionary,
Country Gentleman to send their Bills & discontinue their

papers—— Wrote to Child's Paper, Merry's Museum &
Mother's Magazine, enclosing to each $1.00 for 1862—— I
have paid for New York Reformer & Northern Journal &
Senaca Co. Sentinel up to 1' April & ordered them
stopped—— Have also ordered Ovid Bee stopped. . . .

Ovid, *Monday Night, 10' February, 1862* (10 o'clock) [.]

Yesterday . . . I read Dr. Sprague's Thanksgiving Sermon to
the Family—— . . . Talked with Mary & Julia freely in regard
to my property before going to bed on Saturday Night, telling
them how I stand as to debts, receipts etc. I hope it will cause
them to act more reasonably. . . . Have been all day engaged
in writing, endeavoring to get all my accounts settled & in
such condition that my Wife & daughters may understand
them. . . . I have had my Clyde Colt shod today, ready to
take to the field. . . .

Ovid. *Tuesday Night, 11' January, 1862 (February)* [.]

Slept rather uneasily last night. . . . I took up all my papers &
made a general arrangement of them, reading My Will to
Mrs. Patrick & the Girls, & then putting it, with my Deeds
etc. into the safe. . . . Gen. [Brig. Gen. Charles P.] Stone has
been taken to Fort Lafayette, as a prisoner—— Why is not
stated—— I do not believe he is disloyal, but no man can
say that.[42]

---

[42] Gen. Stone, an 1845 graduate of West Point, with a fine record in
the Mexican War, had commanded the Union forces which were routed
at the Battle of Ball's Bluff in October of 1861. Arrested by Stanton, he
was held without charge for 189 days in Fort Lafayette and Fort
Hamilton in New York. When the charges, which stemmed from the
Committee on the Conduct of the War, were finally presented in
February of 1863, Stone easily disposed of them. Never officially charged,
tried, or convicted, Stone was returned to active duty in 1863.

Ovid [,] *Wednesday Night, 12' January——February,*
1862 [.]

. . . I went down to the Farm House & got out the Farm Books
to look over my account. . . .No Letters from Washington for
myself. . . .

Ovid [,] *Thursday Night, 13' February, 1862.*

Went to bed at 12 last night & slept well. Have packed two
boxes today. . . . I get nothing from Washington & feel quite
uneasy. I do not know what it means—— . . .

Ovid, *Friday Night, 14' February, 1862.*

This has been a stormy day & yesterday was so too—— The
New York Mail failed today, on this account, probably——
. . . Have packed a good part of my Books and the springs
(of Beds) & all my loose papers—— . . .

Ovid, *Saturday Night, 15' February, 1861* [2].

Did not sleep well last night, The fact is I have slept alone so
much I do not sleep well "double"—— Besides Geordie was
uneasy & has been quite unwell today. . . .

Sunday Night—9 o'clock, 16' February [.]

. . . Weather cold—— . . . Have been at Church & heard a
wonderfully longwinded sermon from Dr. Lounsberry. . . .
Tonight I have been reading to the Children, "Golden Fruit,"
talking & praying with them.

Ovid [,] *Monday Night* [,] *17' Feby. 1862* [.]

Up at the usual hour this morning. . . . No news from Washington & I am in much anxiety. I must go there. . . .

Ovid, *Tuesday Night* [,] *18' Feby. 1862*

Sleep disturbed last night. I am getting very nervous at hearing nothing from Washington and becoming doubtful of my appointment. . . . Fort Donelson is taken & 15000 prisoners—— [Gen.] Johnston (A.[lbert] S.[idney]) & [Brig. Gen. Simon Bolivar] Buckner are prisoners. [Brig. Gen. Gideon J.] Pillow & [Brig. Gen. John B.] Floyd[43] stole off with 5000 men—— . . .

Ovid, *Wednesday Night, 19' February* [,] *1862* [.]

. . . I went to town this morning & posted Letters for [Alexander S.] Diven[44] & Shiras in Washington, asking them to see what the matter is about my appointment. . . .

Ovid, *Thursday Night, 20' February, 1862.*

This has been a gloomy day—— Stormy & drifting, so that the roads are all filled up & no Mails from New York. . . .

---

[43] Gen. Johnston was not present at Fort Donelson. It was Brig. Gen. Bushrod R. Johnson who was captured at Donelson, but he subsequently escaped by the simple expedient of walking away from his captors at mid-day, a few days after the surrender. The Confederate commander at Donelson was Buchanan's Secretary of War, John B. Floyd. When the crisis came on the night of February 14, Floyd turned the command over to Gideon J. Pillow, who immediately passed it on to Simon Bolivar Buckner. Floyd, Pillow, and Col. Nathan Bedford Forrest escaped before Buckner surrendered the fort to U. S. Grant, on February 16.

[44] Representative Diven, schooled at the Academy at Ovid, was a Republican Congressman representing the Elmira area in the Federal Congress.

Friday Night—— 10 ¼ *o'clock* [,] *21' February* [,]
    1862 [.]

. . . Wrote this morning to Preston King, Col. [J. P.] Taylor &
[Lt. Col. Albert V.] Colburn,[45] that I should leave on Monday
for Washington. . . . I have received. no Letters & only the
World of Wednesday came today. It brought no news, except
that . . . Alex. H. Stephens has resigned the Vice Presidency
of the C.S.A. & come out for the Union——

Ovid, *22' February, 1862*—— *Saturday Night* [,] *10 ½*
    o'clk [.]

. . . I slept better than usual last night. . . . I read Washington's
Farewell Address aloud this evening—— Have been reading
[General Henry Wager] Halleck on War.[46]

Sunday Night, 9 ½ o'clock, 23' February [,] *1862* [.]
    (Ovid) [.]

This has been a pleasant day, Mild & thawing . . . went to
church with the Children—— . . . Have read Observer &
been hearing the Girls sing—— This is my last night at home
for the present, I suppose—— What is in [the] future is
known to God only——

Ovid, *24' Feby.* [,] *Monday Night*—— At home——

. . . I sent my trunk to the Boat, intending to go down in the
cutter at night, but a violent storm arose—the most violent of

---

[45] Col. Colburn was an additional aide-de-camp on McClellan's personal staff.

[46] *Elements of Military Art and Science* (New York: D. Appleton &
Co., 1846).

the season & has raged the remainder of the day, preventing the Boat from leaving Geneva—— . . . Have spent the day in an attempt to be employed, so as to keep my mind from eating itself up—— Have read Halleck almost exclusively. . . .

Washington (405 New York Avenue) *Thursday Night* [,] 27' *Feby.* '62.

I am once more in my old room & ready to make a few notes—— On Tuesday the . . . mail brought a note from Mr. [William] Kelly[47]—— Also from Diven, asking me to hold on & he would write again—— President's affliction[48] prevented him from being seen. . . Took leave of the Family at 5 and drove to the Boat—— There was deeper feeling when I left than there has been at any time before & I felt very badly myself—— . . . It was about 2 o'clock when we reached Elmira—— . . . Arrived at Baltimore after a tedious ride at 6.30 P.M. & at 7.30 left for this City. . . . It was cold & I was tired & without fire—— So I went to bed at 11. . . . After Bkft. I saw Hardie, from whom I learned that McLellan [sic] was up with [Maj. Gen. Nathaniel P.] Banks[49] & would be for a day or two—— . . . After seeing [Brig. Gen. Irvin] McDowell[50] a moment saw Marcy just a moment—— He knew not how

---

[47] Hon. William Kelly shared Patrick's interest in agricultural reform. He had been a member of the Board of Trustees of the New York State Agricultural College when Patrick was its President. He owned "Ellerslie," an eight-hundred-acre estate just outside of Rhinebeck overlooking the Hudson River.

[48] Lincoln was deeply affected by the death of his son, Willie, at this time.

[49] Gen. Banks, the former Massachusetts Congressman and Governor, had been Speaker of the House in 1856 and 1857. He was refurbishing the dispirited Army of the Shenandoah which the Confederates under Jackson and Johnston had so neatly outmanuevered before the Battle of 1st Manassas.

[50] Gen. McDowell, in spite of the rough handling he received at 1st Manassas, retained command of a division in McClellan's Army of the Potomac.

things stood, & as Meigs & others were with him on business about the Upper Potomac, I went over to see [Alexander E.] Shiras, who had seen Adjt. Genl. & written me——— Thought [Gen. Lorenzo] Thomas[51] believed I was not nominated because no more were to be made except by promotion——— I saw Thomas, however, who said that McLellan's [sic] influence was good for nothing & if my friends would see the President, that would be the only course I could have any confidence in——— So I went directly to the Capitol & saw Senator King who said he had just written to the President——— Senator said he would see the President tonight, Diven & [Robert Bruce] Van Valkenburg[h][52] would see the President tonight or in the Morning——— . . . Saw Mr. Corning, who says he will consult the other Gentlemen tomorrow & do what they think best in the case——— . . . From Hardie I learn that Stanton is running a jealous opposition to McClellan —sold out to the [New York] Tribune & thwarting McClellan in every possible way——— Others say they think his brain is a little affected, he acts so very strangely——— . . . Government has taken possession of the Rail Road, so that but 2 Trains run for Citizens per day. I saw Pete [Henry M.] Naglee[53] today, for the first time since we graduated & he looks remarkably well. . . .

Friday Night, 10 o'clock, 28' February [,] *1862*, Washn.

. . . Went to Breakfast at 8 o'clock & then came back & wrote a Letter to my wife——— While at this, Diven & Van Valkenburg[h] came in, on their return from the White House, where they had been to see the President, but missed him. . . .

---

[51] Gen. Thomas was The Adjutant General of the United States Army.

[52] Rep. Van Valkenburgh was a Republican Congressman from the "Lower Tier" counties of New York.

[53] Classmate Henry M. "Pete" Naglee commanded a brigade in Hooker's Division when the Army of the Potomac moved to the Peninsula.

I went to Head Quarters & saw Marcy, who says that McClellan will be home tomorrow & that he will attend to my nomination at once, for he wants me—— . . . At 6 I went down to see Diven who came up & saw [Senator Ira] Harris, who did *not* see the President, tho' he went for that purpose. . . . A long talk with McDowell who believes McClellan to be very insincere.

Washington, *Saturday Night, 1' March, 1862*——

Last night I slept well & today have felt well. . . . After Breakfast I sat down & read Cavalry Tactics until 10 then . . . mounted & rode up to the Review Ground east of the Capitol, where I found [Gen. William F.] Barry reviewing [Col. Henry J.] Hunt[']s Artillery Reserve. There were about a dozen Batteries out, including two or three Light Batteries—— Horse Artillery—— There were a good many of my old associates there—— [William A.] Nichols & [Lt. Col. George W.] Getty & Hunt & Barry[54]—— I staid an hour & came home. . . .

Washington, *Sunday Night, March 2' 1862.*

. . . Decided not to go to Church, as I do not wish to meet my friends, or to have it known that I am here. . . . When I came back [from tea] Major [Silas W.] Burt came with me & has been in my room ever since—— It is now 10.45—— He has been talking of his past Associates—public men—— With Wm. H. Seward to whom he is, politically opposed, he has had a life long acquaintance, having slept with him a year, as a School Boy, boarding at his Father's—— He has no

---

[54] Gen. Barry commanded McClellan's artillery. Col. Hunt commanded the artillery reserve. Col. Getty commanded an artillery detachment. Nichols, a West Point graduate of 1838, was serving in the Adjutant General's office in Washington.

respect for him whatever—— It is said that Seward smokes
& snuffs incessantly before Dinner & drinks from that
time—— . . .

Washington, *Monday Night* [,] *3d March, 1862.*

. . . Went over to Hd. Qrs. Army of Potomac, but did not find
out enough to please me very well. Went over to Hd. Qrs. &
Colburn started off to get all the facts in the Secretary's room,
but the Sec. being engaged "publicly" today does no business
for Officers—— The facts are these. On the 28' or 29' January, McClellan applied, with the Authority of the President,
to the Secretary, for my immediate Appointment—— The
Sec. directed Asst. Sec. [Peter H.] Watson to write the letter
of appointment—— He wrote it & laid it before the Sec. for
Signature—— He supposed it had gone to the Senate & so
reported, but no letter can be found, and although I lose more
than 1 month's rank & pay, the general has, tonight, made a
new application & by tomorrow the thing will, probably be in
the Mill—— There is trick somewhere [sic]. . . .

Washington, *Tuesday Night, 4' March, 1862*——

. . . Went over to War Office—— The Adjt. Genl. had taken
my nomination to the President this morng. . . . I have been
down to see Senator Harris & Mr. Corning. . . .

Washington, *Wednesday Night* [,] *5' March*——

. . . Went to the Capitol & saw King, who told me that my
Name had just been before the Committee, dated 4' March,
& that he had tried to call it up at once, but those who had

friends opposed it & I was obliged to take my place on the
Calender. I came to Hd. Qrs. saw McClellan accidentally——
A request was written, forthwith, to Senator [Henry] Wilson,[55]
asking, if possible, to let my name come up, as I am wanted.
What the result will be I cannot yet say. . . .

Washington, *Thursday night, 6' March, 1862*——

Slept pretty well—— Up & Bkft. Bowels deranged—— Taken
pills & *shall* take Brandy on going to bed—— [Diven] came to
say that he desired me to let McClellan know that he, Diven,
knew there was a powerful cabal that will overthrow him if
he does not move within a few days—— They are exulting
over the bad weather, & their hope is to prevent a re-union of
the States—— I went over & told [Seth] Williams the Sub-
stance & to tell the General if he wanted to see me, to send for
me. Hardie says that McClellan is perfectly aware of it—that
he knows there was a Cabinet meeting called 3 or 4 days (or
nights) ago, for the purpose of removing him, & that the
President (so Clark[e] says)[56] has sworn, that if McClellan does
not move in [blank] days he will move him. . . . I feel greatly
troubled about our public affairs & think, with Diven, that the
radicals are getting the control of both Congress & Executive.

Washington, *Friday Night, 7' March* [,] *1862* [,] *(10
o'clock)* [.]

. . . Went over to Hd. Qrs. Marcy called me up to his room
& we talked over our affairs & how much McClellan knows
of the plots against him. He knows them all, evidently & this

---

[55] Sen. Wilson, an old political professional from Massachusetts, was
Chairman of the powerful Senate Committee on Military Affairs.

[56] Again probably Col. Henry F. Clarke, Chief Commissary of Subsistence for the Army of the Potomac.

very day has done something, I suppose, to bring matters to a
head. I told Marcy to tell him that I would go with him as
Volunteer Aid if my nomination is not confirmed. . . . Saw
Preston King & Old Col. [Josiah] Sanford at [Brig. Gen. Silas]
Casey's[57] Office. . . . Mrs. Casey is thought to be dying. She
was out yesterday and paralyzed today.

Washington, *Saturday Night, 8' March, 1862* [.]

This has been the most pleasant day we have had in a long
time. . . . Went over to Head Quarters—— Nothing new——
It has been as I supposed—— A rowe [sic] last night & this
morning—— It is said that Stanton asked McClellan to
resign—— He probably will not do it, and the President will
Sustain him—— . . . I took the saddle at 1 o'clock & went
down to see Preston King—— Senator Wilson left my name
off the Calender [sic] & yesterday the others were confirmed—— King is disappointed and so am I—— . . .

Washington, *Sunday Night, 9' March, 1862*——

. . . Saw Hardie & had a talk with him—— Learned that it
is not & never has been McClellan's plan to attack Manassas;
that he intends to take Richmond—but that he has not intended to move here until we had possession of Tennessee——
This has been his plan & so [Gen. Don Carlos] Buell[58] is
instructed. . . . After Tea I went over to Heintzelman's &
there met quite a number—— There is news tonight—— The
Merrimack destroyed 2 of our frigates with a loss of 800 men

---

[57] Gen. Casey, a crusty West Pointer in Heintzelman's class of 1826,
also kept open house for the "Old Army" in Washington.

[58] Gen. Buell commanded the Army of the Ohio at Nashville and was
McClellan's favorite candidate for over-all command of the West.

on our side, at Norfolk, but was finally driven back by the
Monitor—— . . .

Washington, *Monday Night, 10' March, 1862*

This has been an exciting day. After 11 o'clock last night
McClellan ordered a forward movement. At Daylight the
Divisions on the other side moved & Gen. Keyes on this side
crossed—— Then came the other troops which have been
pouring through all day—Artillery, Cavalry, Infantry, Volunteers, Head Quarters & all. There was a tide of soldiers moving
until 3 or 4 o'clock—— I have just seen Senator Harris who
says nothing has been done & that there will be a fight over
[Col. Isaac F.] Quinby & myself,[59] on the Ground that New
York has had more than her share of Generals—Very Likely.
I feel tonight like selling out my horses & going home—— I
was at Head Quarters—— Saw Marcy & the Staff—— Hoped
then to be with Casey, but it is doubtful—— His wife
died today at 5 o'clock. This is a sad time for him to be a
Mourner—— . . .

Washington, *Tuesday Night, 11' January* [*March*],
   1862——

Slept none—— Utterly disgusted & disheartened—— After
Breakfast went down to see Diven & told him about matters—— He asked me to see Senator Wilson—— I did so &
was disgusted with him—— He pitched into McClellan & all
connected with the War—— I came home satisfied about *him.*
Subsequently I mounted & went down to see King. The hope
was to have an Executive Session but it was not held. Came

---

[59] Col. Quinby, a West Point graduate of 1843, commanded the 13th
New York Volunteer Infantry.

down & hunted all about Saddles & an outfit of Traps. Then
called at Casey's about 2 or $2\frac{1}{2}$ o'clock—— Saw Capt. Tom.
Casey only—— They had sent me a note to act as Pall
Bearer. I came back & after dinner got a Barber to trim me up
& reduce my Beard some. . . . It is thought that all is over
with McClellan, as the Rebels fled before he had a chance at
them—— They had burned everything at Manassas. . . .

Washington, *Wednesday Night* [,] *12' March, 1862*——

. . . I was in the Saddle until $10\frac{1}{2}$ o'clock then came home,
dressed and at $11\frac{1}{2}$ was at Casey's Dr. [Phineas D.] Gurley &
an Episcopalian officiated. Prof. [Joseph] Henry, [John P.]
Gillis, [Dr. Septimus] Tuston [Tustin], Archy Campbell, Dr.
Warren & myself Pallbearers. Remains taken to Georgetown
Cemetery. All the Family behaved with great calmness &
propriety, but the blow is heavy upon every one of them. . . .
There will be a Democratic delegation here to see the Presi-
dent, probably tomorrow. Their efforts may give the President
Conservative Strength—— The Radicals are in the Ascendant
& McClellan is degraded to the position of a Department
Commander, Halleck & [Gen. John C.] Fremont being his
Equals—— The President assumes the Chief direction himself
& issues "War Orders." There has been no Executive Session
today & I am here two weeks, this evening—— I am very
uncertain about my fate, yet.

Washington, *Thursday Night, 13' March, 1862*——

Slept well last night, up at 7 & Bkft. at 8. . . . We . . . went to
the Navy Yard, (no to the Arsenal) where I met [Maj. George
D.] Ramsey & he took us through the Yard——[60] Looked at

---

[60] Major Ramsey commanded the Washington Arsenal.

the Guns & Carriages & Pontons[61] & Train etc. . . . [I went] to see Seth Williams, to whom Marcy had telegraphed from the front to know if I was confirmed, but the Senate did not reach me today. This evening I have been at Mr. [William] Kelly's room & went with him to see Stevens, the Battery man & to look at his Model of a Steam Battery——[62] . . .

Washington, *Friday Night, 14' March, 1862*——

. . . Marcy said the General had telegraphed for me, if confirmed. He then told me that there would be an attempt to take one up today out of his place on the Calender [sic] & for me to ask my friends to do the same by *me*. As he urged it I . . . saw [Senators] King & Harris with Mr. Kelly. Came back & had a long talk with Marcy. Learned all about our Affairs—— . . . The Senate did not reach my name, as I learn, & I hang over another week.

Washington, *Saturday Night, 15' March, 1862*——

Went to Head Quarters of Potomac—— All will be removed from there tonight, Head Quarters being at Alexandria—— McClellan is there & the impression is that we are to advance on Norfolk—— Others say, on Richmond—— Casey has orders to move with his command—perhaps Monday—— [Col. Edmund] Schriver[63] is detached as McDowell's Chief

---

[61] The French spelling of "ponton" was regularly used in Army publications and Patrick vacillated between "ponton" and the more familiar spelling of "pontoon."

[62] This is Edwin Augustus Stevens, brother and heir of the Robert L. Stevens who had designed the great ironclad "Stevens Battery." E. A. Stevens was in Washington seeking a Congressional appropriation of approximately a million dollars in order to complete the ship which had been begun by his brother at Hoboken, New Jersey.

[63] Patrick was mistaken. Col. Schriver remained McDowell's chief of staff through the subsequent campaign.

of Staff—— Staff Corps are being made up—— I went down
to Willard's with Schriver, after Dinner & found President
King[64] there & his Son Rufus etc. etc. [Gen. Lorenzo] Thomas,
too, was there & is very indignant that I am still left behind—— He says he shall see Wilson & tell him it *must* be
done—— . . . I am becoming very sick of Washington. . . .
The destruction of all my plans connected with the College
[New York State Agricultural College at Ovid] & of course
the destruction of all my plans for the remainder of my life,
are great disappointments. . . . My religious life has been
unsatisfactory to me & I presume to others— Certainly it has
been to God—— . . . God is merciful or I should despair——
I would give much to be at home & in peace with my Dear
Family.

Washington, *Sunday Night, 16' March, 1862*

. . . This evening I have been at Heintzelman's[.] He was
absent, but I found the Family—— The jealousies among the
Commanders of Divisions & Corps d' Armee is making bad
work—— McDowell appears to be insatiable in his Ambition
& now that he is a Major General he is taking airs upon himself—— But for McClellan he would never have been
confirmed—— That is said by all—— It shows great Magnanimity in McClellan.

Washington, *Monday Night, 17' March, 1862*——

. . . I saw McDowell a while this morning & he was very
earnest that the Wadsworth Brigade should be given to me.
He went to see McClellan who was in town for a few hours

---

[64] Charles King, President of Columbia University. His son, Rufus,
commanded a Division in McDowell's Corps.

about it, but I don't know the result—— ... Tonight I learn
from Senator Wilson that my nomination was confirmed & I
am now to date from the—When? I have written a note to
Marcy informing him of the fact & desiring him to let me
know, as soon as may be, where I am to go. ... Came home
& wrote Gov. Sprague[65] in behalf of Casey, the [sic] he may
be a Major General. ...

Washington, *Tuesday Night, 18' March, 1862*——

... I was up at 6 o'clock & overhauling my trunks, sending
off Tables etc. Took Clothes to Tailor's to be altered, bought
Cloth to alter my Flan. Coat, bought Cassimere shirts for campaigning—bought all needful little things, ordered a saddle &
hunted up bedsteads, etc. etc. etc. ... About noon I learned
from Casey that I was assigned to McDowell's Corp[s], King's
Division, as Commander of Wadsworth's Old Brigade—— ...

Washington, *Wednesday Night, 19' March, 1862*.

Up early this morning—— Did considerable work before
going to Breakfast; returned & mounted for a ride—— Took
Long Bridge road to Alexandria, Thence to Head Quarters
at the Seminary, and thence to [Brig. Gen. George A.]
McCall's where I found [Brig. Gen. John F.] Reynolds &
McCall[66]—— Thence to McDowell's where I found [Brig.
Gen. Rufus] King & got information—thence to Augur's but

[65] Patrick here underlines the very important powers retained by the
state governors in their control over promotions in the Volunteer service.
William Sprague was the millionaire boy-Governor of Rhode Island.

[66] Gen. McCall had just assumed command of the Second Division of
McDowell's First Corps of the Army of the Potomac, and Gen. Reynolds
commanded his First Brigade. Franklin's First Division and King's Third
Division completed McDowell's Corps.

missed him——[67] Thence to Col. [William F.] Rogers of 21'
Comdg. my Brigade—— Talked with him and his Staff, rode
back with Capts. [James M.] Sanderson & [Edward A.]
Springsteed to King's[68]—then back via Bailey's Cross Roads,
calling at the 35' 20' & 23' Regts. Was detained at the draw-
Bridge both ways losing nearly or quite an hour. . . .

Washington, *Thursday Night, 29' March, 1862*——

. . . My first business was to pack & repack Trunks, so as only
to take with me what I want, actually, & nothing more. . . .
My commission *ought* to be made out tomorrow, but I don't
know that it will be—— Since Dinner I have been down &
purchased a Talma, to keep the rain off me—— Am now
very well provided—— Bought a Bible, as I had to turn in
my large Edition—— . . .

Washington, *Friday Night, 21' March, 1862.*

This has been a busy day for me, as I have been on my feet all
day, in mud, compelling me to wear Rubbers, whereby my
feet are made very uncomfortable—— . . . Went to War Dept.
& found Sec. had my Commission but wanted to see me——
So I had to call on him & make my bow, but found Gen.
[Ethan Allen] Hitchcock, who is to be his mentor & guide,
I trust. At all events I pressed it strongly on Hitchcock to do

---

[67] Gen. Rufus King was now Patrick's Division Commander. Gen.
Augur commanded the Third Brigade of King's Division and became
Patrick's next-door neighbor.

[68] Col. Rogers commanded the 21st New York Volunteers. Capt.
Sanderson was the Brigade Commissary Officer and Capt. Springsteed
was an Assistant Adjutant General on the staff Patrick was inheriting
from Wadsworth.

so.[69] Met McDowell who told me that Stanton had talked to him last night about me & that I had not talked—no, *called,* on him. As my Commission did not come from the White House, McDowell went up & started the President—— So I got it, was sworn in, & had Kimball nominated A.[ssistant] A.[djutant] General. . . .

---

[69] Major General Ethan Allen Hitchcock, a West Point graduate of 1817, had retired from the Army in 1855 after a long and honorable career, which had included service on the Indian frontiers in Florida and the West, in the Mexican War, and on the Pacific Coast. In spite of feeble health and advancing years, he responded to Stanton's summons to Washington, where to his astonishment and consternation he was offered command of the Army of the Potomac. Refusing that, he reluctantly agreed to stay on and give Stanton whatever advice his military experience might provide. Stanton, however, normally ignored Hitchcock's advice.

Chapter II

Training Troops and Placating Citizens

MARCH 22, 1862, THROUGH MAY 26, 1862

THE PERIOD FROM March 22 to May 26, 1862, was a trying time for General Patrick. Most of his troubles stemmed from his efforts to "get thieves, skulks and political scribblers to become soldiers," but they did not end there. The movement into Virginia placed the Federal army in a position for which nothing in its experience had prepared it. Neither officers nor men were quite clear about their own status, to say nothing of the position of the Virginians. Elementary questions had not been asked, much less answered. For example, no one was certain whether the Federal army was liberating the people of Virginia from misguided rulers, or simply occupying enemy territory. Was the Union government trying to restore law and order or was it trying to conquer a peace? Was it suppressing rebellion or fighting a war? Patrick's instincts and training, in common with those of most of the "Old Army," called for conservative measures, for the protection of persons and property, and the maintenance of law and order. Inevitably there was conflict and confusion, which Patrick's account brings it into sharp focus.

In the West the first major conflict, and the biggest battle Americans had ever fought, took place between Shiloh Church and Pittsburg Landing in Tennessee on April 6 and 7. The death of Albert Sidney Johnston was perhaps a greater loss to the Confederacy than the defeat suffered by southern arms on the second day of the battle. In late April the Federal Navy captured New Orleans, and on May 8 Stonewall Jackson opened his Valley Campaign with a victory over Milroy at the little village of McDowell in the mountains to the west of the Shenandoah Valley. The confusion caused in Union councils by Jackson's rapid movements in and out of the mountains and up and down the Valley is vividly illustrated in Patrick's Diary.

Washington, *Saturday, 22' March, 1862*——

. . . After paying my Bill at the Ebbitt House and getting a
Team, I got a pass from the Provt. Marshal for my Servant,
started him off to Camp, to remain until I get there. . . .
Have had a long talk with Marcy at his own request, about
Matters. . . . McDowell does not yet act firmly, even according to his own showing & his wife is the rallying point for all the
Abolitionists & Anti-McClellan men, who are exceedingly
intemperate in their language—— [Adam,] Count Gurowski[1],
speaks violently & publicly, that McDowell—no McClellan is
a Traitor & a Secessionist—— . . .

Upton's Hill, Fairfax Co. *Sunday Night* [,] *23' Mch.*

This morning the Sun showed himself nicely & gave promise of
a fine day—— I . . . came off, Capt. Springsteed with me,
over long Bridge, waiting a long time, & out to the Camp,
where I found Col. Rogers & officers. From there I went over
to Gen. King's . . . & then home to a very late dinner. Cold &
raw. I am in Wadsworth's Old Quarters at Upton['s]
Hill—— . . .

Upton's Hill, Fairfax Co. *Monday Night*[,] *24' Mch. '62.*

A cold & uncomfortable night—— Slept little. Rose early——
. . . The house is cold and smoky, & wood poor—— . . .
Have sent into town for a Cook—— . . . Went down to
King's & as the order placing me in Command has not been

---

[1] Adam, Count Gurowski, a Polish revolutionary who had lived in the
United States since 1849. An inveterate gossip and given to wild ex-
aggeration, he had found a haven as a translator in the State Department.
When not carrying tales he was pouring them into his copious diary.

recd. there. I did Some General business & returned—— . . .
There is quite an effort made to get persons on my Staff, as
usual. . . . I make no promises whatever but think I shall
take a young man of Philadelphia for my aid, name [Lt. John
V.] Bouvier. . . .

> Upton's Hill, Fairfax Co. Va. *Tuesday Night*[,] *25'*
> *March.*

. . . Was off before 7 o'clock for Camp to inspect the Regts.
of the Brigade at Bailey's Cross Roads—beginning at 9 o'clock.
I got through at ten, with Roger's Regt.—& took up [Col.
George W.] Pratt's.[2] I had got well along with it when an
order to appear at McDowell's Head Quarters for Review of
the Army Corps arrived. . . . We had out the whole of
McDowell's Army composed of all sorts of troops, numbering
about 35,000 men—— McDowell reviewed them but
McClellan was on the ground a part of the time. I saw &
shook hands with him & [Brig. Gen. Philip] Kearney,[3] Bailey
Meade & a host of others. My Brigade was as good as any I
saw except Kearney's, I think. . . .

> *Wednesday Night, 26' March,* Upton's Hill Va.

. . . Went down to Camp at 9 & remained there until 4 or 4½
o'clock & came home—— Had all the Colonels of Regts,

---

[2] Col. Rogers commanded the 21st New York Volunteer Infantry, and,
as senior regimental commander, had commanded the Brigade in the
interim between Wadsworth's transfer and Patrick's assumption of command. Col. Pratt commanded the 20th New York Militia (80th New
York Volunteer Infantry).

[3] Gen. Kearny spelled his name without a second e. More to the point,
he commanded a fine brigade of New Jersey volunteers in William B.
Franklin's Division.

together & gave them some general ideas of business. . . . I staid to see the Regts. of my Brigade on Battalion Drill & watch their movements—— Rogers does very well. . . . I feel rather annoyed tonight by hearing that we are to be reviewed again tomorrow whereas I intended to have had a Brigade Drill.

Thursday Night, 27' March, Upton's Hill, Va.

. . . After Orderly hour and the signing of Morning Reports etc. I went down to Head Quarters of Division & found a Review to come off this Afternoon at 2'30" on the same ground as before—— I also received a note inviting me to lunch at 1 o'clock at Gen. McDowell's, to meet Lord [Richard B. P.] Lyons & several Officers of the British Legation & Army. . . . After waiting a long time the Distingue arrived & we were presented & Lunched—— All the General Officers of this Army Corps were present—— Henrietta King, the daughters of Secretary [of the Treasury] Chase,[4] Mrs. Ricketts[5] & Mrs. McDowell were there—— We were late of course—— The Review was a good one. . . . After it was over I remained a while with these Ladies I named & Gov. Sprague. . . .

Friday Night[,] *28' March,* Upton's Hill, Va.

A bad night. . . . It was a pretty hard business for me to go down to Battalion Drill at 2.30 but I had ordered it out. . . . I made bad work & so did they—— Difficult to say which was

[4] Secretary Salmon P. Chase had two remarkable daughters. The regal and ambitious Kate, who was destined to marry Gov. William Sprague, and the more retiring Janette.

[5] The ubiquitous wife of Brig. Gen. James B. Ricketts, who appeared on nearly every field the Army of the Potomac trod.

the worst—— However, we got through & I came home, very
slowly. . . . I feel badly tonight & must take medicine left by
Dr. [Francis M.] Wilcox & some Brandy. . . .

Saturday Night, 29' March 1862, Upton's Hill——

Slept quite well & was up in good season. . . . Was off before
8 for the Camp—— . . . I remained there till 10 or 10½
o'clock & came home. . . . It [soon] began to snow, sleet, rain,
& be very uncomfortable generally—— . . . I went down,
however, to the Camps, to see how the men were getting on. . . .

Upton's Hill, Va., *Sunday Night, 30' March, '62.*

. . . Storm still in progress. . . . After reading my morning service
I sat down to write a Letter to my Family—— Dr. Hough
(Sanitary Commission)[6] & Col. Pratt came in & I sent it off,
by them, to Washington. . . . Although this is the Sabbath, I
have been obliged to look over Tactics, Regulations etc. etc.
The day is gloomy & the men feel gloomy. . . .

Upton's Hill, Va., *Monday Night, 31' March, 1862.*

I . . . got up early this morning, breakfasted before 7½ & went
to Camp. Every thing was behind in the way of Guards,
Reports, etc. on account of the Storm—— Although it had
cleared off this morning, finely, the men were slow, Officers
Do. . . . Went down to Drill—— Men behind times in arriv-

---

[6] The United States Sanitary Commission, a private, nonprofit organization, was modeled after a British Commission sent to the Crimea in
1855. It raised its money through voluntary contributions and fund-
raising "Sanitary Fairs" and spent it in alleviating the hardships of the
sick, wounded, and convalescent Union soldiers.

ing—— Formed in Mass—then into Column—then deployed
by Battalion—in 4 lines, opened Ranks & rode through——
Marched around & to the best grounds and then handled them
in masses almost exclusively. . . .

Upton's Hill, Fairfax Co. Va. *Tuesday Night*[,] *1' April,
'62.*

This has been a lovely day—just cool enough to be bracing——
. . . Got off quite early for Camp, riding the Mare. Got there
early and remained until ten o'clock, waiting for the Morning
Report of 35'—— Sent for [Col. Newton B.] Lord & his Adjt.[7]
Gave them both to understand that such a matter must not be
repeated—— I was most thoroughly disgusted with him——
His object is to make himself of consequence by being troublesome. . . . Drilled my Battalions in Mass Movements some 2 or
3 hours, on confined grounds—— . . .

Upton's Hill Va., *Wednesday Night*[,] *2 April, '62.*

. . . Got down to Camp by $8\frac{1}{2}$ o'clock. . . . I was out, by invitation—to see the drill of the Ambulance Men under the
Surgeons. . . . Had Brigade Drill in a high wind & just as I
closed up Kimball arrived. . . . Since Supper have been writing
& had Orders for loading our Stores on the transports tomorrow. . . .

Upton's Hill, Va, *Thursday Night* [,] *3' April '62.*

. . . Up soon after dawn of day & got off soon after Breakfast
for Camp. . . . Went down to Gen. King's—— Thence to Gen.

---

[7] Col. Lord commanded the 35th New York Volunteer Infantry.

McDowell's—— Both these Generals were in town. . . . King & his Aid called here to see me & say " Division Drill tomorrow." . . . McDowell at old Point [Comfort].[8]

Bivouack beyond Annandale, *Friday Night*[,] *4' April '62.*

I went to the Head Quarters of Gen. King on business & just as I rode up he recd. an Order to move his entire division, with all speed to the Front—— He was, like all the rest of us, taken by surprise and his Officers were scattered in all directions. Instead of our getting off at 3 o'clock it was nearer $4\frac{1}{2}$. Every thing was in bad shape. The Quarter Masters & Commissaries were in town, packing Stores on the Barges, for the Division to move down the River—— Our teams were over there & we had trouble enough. Our Teams were overloaded & stalled and our men overloaded with Traps also, so as to string out & make bad work. . . . It was long after dark when we bivouacked beyond Annandale 2 or 3 miles. . . .

Camp 1 Mile from Bull Run, towards Manassas, *Friday —No—Saturday Night——— 5' April, 1862——*

. . . We were marched through the rain, after we *had* started, until it stopped about $1\frac{1}{2}$ o'clock. . . . Were to have been off at 7.30 but it was nearer 9 when I got under way—— First Gibbon's Battery, then Augur's Brigade[,] Then Monroe's Battery & My Brigade, then [Capt. George W.] Durrill's [Durell's] Battery & Cutler's Brigade—— The March has been good today, considering all things & the men have not strolled

---

[8]Fortress Monroe was at Old Point Comfort on the tip of the Peninsula between the York and James rivers below Richmond and just across Hampton Roads from Norfolk. It was becoming a major base for McClellan's advance up the Peninsula.

as I expected. . . .[9] We are in Bivouack one mile from Bull Run, on the Manassas Road—— We passed through Fairfax C. H.[,] Centerville & the defences of the Rebels which were very strong. We saw, also, the almost countless huts & Quarters of Secesh. Scattered over the Country—— The rebels must have been very strong.

Camp 1½ Mile S. W. Bristoe, Warrenton Road[.] *Sunday Night*[,] *6' April, 1862*——

. . . Manassas Junction is one of the most miserable places I ever saw, and is now thronged with Troops—— We came on through there, however, passing [Brig. Gen. Henry W.] Slocum's Brigade[10] just this side & then came over through a long Muddy road, crossing a stream which I think they call "Broad Run" & are now encamped 1½ miles S. W. of Bristoe Station, on the Warrenton Road—— . . .

Camp Wadsworth near Bristoe, *9' April 1862*[.]

Two nights have passed without any record of operations——
On Sunday Night I went to bed expecting we should remain only a day, or so—— Next morning (Monday) I was up early, got Breakfast, arranged for Dr. Kimball to go to Washington. . . . I went out & made arrangements for a Brigade Guard around the Camp. . . . then turned out & went over to Gen. King's. . . . I found that no subsistence Stores were in Depot, that [Gen. William B.] Franklin had seized upon the Forage Train at Manassas & only faith could keep my men alive——

---

[9] Patrick soon dropped the term "strolled" and adopted the more widely used "straggling."

[10] Gen. Slocum commanded the 2nd Brigade of Franklin's Division in McDowell's First Corps.

Stores, however, *did* arrive before night. . . . I spent 2 or 3 hours in the saddle in the Afternoon about Guards, Rounds, etc. . . .

Camp Wadsworth, *Bristoe, Thursday*[,] *10 Apl. '62.*

I went to bed last night in thick smoke, after trying to get a fire in my Tent, in which I was not at all successful. . . . I spent the forenoon in looking through the Camp & Camp Guards, in fitting up my stove, which is now very comfortable and in attending to business generally—— . . . We *hear* that McClellan is in Washington & is not disposed to brook this interference with his plans—— It seems probable that there will be a rupture—— I expect it. . . .

Camp Wadsworth, *Friday Night, 11' April, 1862.*

. . . After breakfast I inspected the Guards, both old & new—— Both very tardy & dilatory in all their operations. . . . Tonight I had a Lieut. arrested for forcing the Guard & treating a Sentinel with disrespect—— I wrote a Letter this forenoon to Julia & after dinner took it to Gen. King's Head Quarters—— While there I learned that Gen. McDowell had left there about 12 o'clock, for Warrenton, with the expectation of having Franklin's Division there tonight—or at Catlett's [Station],[11] but an Order came on about 2 o'clock to recall the Division of Franklin; & it has *re*passed us on its way to Alexandria this evening. . . .

Camp Wadsworth, *Saturday Night*[,] *12' April '62.*

. . . Had a time with the Guard, before I could get them broke in—— I took off the belts of one Corporal & One sentinel for

---

[11] Catlett's Station was approximately 30 miles south of Washington on the Orange and Alexandria Railroad.

neglect of Guard Duty—— Had notice sent me that one of my men, of the 23' had been shot by a Sergt. of Augur's Brigade, for refusing to halt, when ordered, repeatedly, by the Provost Sergt[.]—— He was shot dead—— The Sergt. is fully justified in the Act & I took the opportunity to address the 21' Regt. in regard to these matters, & also the Guard. . . .

Same Camp, Prince William Co. *Sunday Night, 13' April '62.*

. . . The Order of the Sec. of War was read at the head of all the Regts. Thanksgiving for victories offered & petitions for Divine favor—— . . . I passed from one Regt. to another, saying a few words to each according to circumstances—— I talked to the 20['] of home & the Hudson, & the bad taste displayed in the habits they formed here—— To the 23' of their loss, of the reasons for it and the lessons it has taught—— To the 35' of their Obscene & profane language, of my associations with their friends etc—— To the 20' [21'?] of our dependance upon the Lord of Hosts, the God of Battles. . . .

Camp Wadsworth, Va. *Monday Night, 14' April, '62*[.]

. . . I learn that McDowell went down this morning to Washington to ask for permission to go down the River, to join Gen. McClellan—— . . .

Camp Wadsworth Va., *Tuesday Night, 15' April '62.*

. . . Was variously engaged until about $3\frac{1}{2}$ o'clock when I was sent for by Gen. King to Augur's Brigade. . . . It seems that

McDowell ordered Augur, forthwith to Catlin's [Catlett's Station] so as to leave there tomorrow morning, prepared for two days march. . . . Augur did not move until about 6 o'clk. He will have a night March of it—— I am punishing two prisoners of the 20' for stealing, plundering & marauding.

Camp 1 Mile N.W. from Catlin's [Catlett's] Station, *Wednesday Night*[,] *16' Apl.*

This morning rose in good season & had Bkft. at 7 o'clock. . . . Then rode over to the Head Quarters—— Whiskey & Water still flowing freely. . . . Just as I was leaving an Order came for me to move to this place. . . . We found the roads in terrible condition & almost impassable. . . . I am established near an Old Overseer's House of Mr. Quesenberry, who has been a Union man but Franklin's Division killed 600 sheep for him, & other animals in proportion, for which Franklin refused to give him any Receipts, or make any acknowledgement.

Same Camp, *2 o'clock, Friday Morng.*[,] *18' Apl. '62*.

. . . Rode to McDowell's Head Quarters, expecting to find him there. He had left, but a little while before, for Washington. I saw only [Col. Edmund] Schriver & his Staff—— Came back to King's & there found Orders for me to establish a line of Pickets along "Cedar Run"—— Said to be $2\frac{1}{2}$ miles forward —— I did go on 4 or $4\frac{1}{2}$ miles before finding it, with Lieut. Col. [Nirom M.] Crane & 4 Companies of the 21' Regt. I crossed the Run & bivouacked the men—— We had quite a visit with a Mr. McCormick & Family—Wife & Daughters—— They are Union people, but of course feel for their State. It was night when I got back. . . . Mr. [Josiah]

Blancard [Bankerd] came down & warned me for Fredericksburg—— Gen. Augur moved there today (Thursday). I
support him with my Brigade & two Batteries. . . .

This is *Sunday, the 20' day of April, 1862*—— (Camp
near Frederic[k]sburg, Phillips House)[.]

. . . Since my last entry in this diary I have made a good March
& got pretty well settled. . . . We turned out on Friday Morning at 4 o'clock intending to be on the March by 6, but it was
7 o'clock before we got into the Road—— . . . We came
down to Catlett's, where I found a part of the Teams loading
with Stores—— We came past them, intending to pass Cedar
Run with the Troops & halt for the Waggons—— We found
the roads for the Teams & Troops diverged from each other,
but were told that they came together at about 3 or 4 miles
from the Ford—— I was with the Teams & found after having
gone some 2 or 3 miles, that we were wrong. . . . It was dark &
in a heavy rain when we halted, having marched nearly or
quite 20 minutes [miles?]. I took possession of a house owned
by a man named Briggs—— They were frightened, but we soon
reassured them & got supper at the house, inasmuch as our
Teams did not get up until very late—— It was a hard night
& the troops were perfectly unmanageable, I suppose. They
burned fences & ran riot. . . . I found both Officers & men
running into private homes & playing the mischief generally
—— . . . I directed the Colonel of each Regt. to have a detail
of reliable men, to march at the head of each Regt. one of
them to be posted at the door of every house, to shoot down
Officer or man who should attempt to enter—or go any where
about the premises, except to the Wells, or Springs—— It
had an excellent effect upon the Troops. . . . We came on down

to Falmouth[12] & found Augur posted on the left bank of the River, his guns commanding the town. A deputation was there from town. The troops had cleared after [Capt. John] Gibbon sent a few shell into them & the people agreed to surrender the City whenever we send over a force to take possession of it, which we cannot do before other Troops arrive. . . . I am satisfied that the Rebels are dealing double with us—— If they can muster force enough we shall be attacked in our present position. . . . Have been at Gen. Augur's Head Quarters & all about, stopping at the Lacy place, where I will hope, we may have our Hospital. . . .

Monday Night, 21' April 1862, Before Fredericksburg.

. . . Men demoralized from this long inaction from Rain & are Strolling in all directions—— They, or some of our Command, have been plundering houses, insulting women & committing depredation for miles around the country—— . . . I am almost discouraged in my efforts to get thieves, skulks and political scribblers to become Soldiers. . . .

Tuesday Night [,] *22' April 1862*[.] (Fredericksburg).

. . . McDowell rode up about 10 or 11 o'clock, but could not dismount, being on his way to Belle Plain, to establish the Depot *there* instead of Acquia Creek,[13] that being only 9 miles,

---

[12] Falmouth proper is a small village across the Rappahannock River and about a mile north of Fredericksburg, but the name is applied locally to an area of several square miles.

[13] Belle Plain, on Potomac Creek, and Aquia Landing on Aquia Creek provided landings for Potomac River shipping. In time both Aquia Landing and several points on Potomac Creek became major bases of operations for the Army of the Potomac. Patrick's error in spelling Aquia with a c is a common one. It has been neither corrected nor marked with a *sic* for that would have involved an unnecessary intrusion by the editor.

against 15 to Acquia. I rode out with him, perhaps a Mile when a Rain came on so strong that I turned back, getting wet through. . . .

Same Camp[.] *Wednesday Night, 23' April '62.*

. . . Up early this morning. . . . Rode out to a Mr. Pollock's, where the house was rifled. . . . Had a pleasant call and returned, to find ourselves overrun by Gen. King's Staff, who had taken possession of the house & premises in a very rude manner. . . . This P. M. I have been down the River looking for new Grounds to encamp upon. . . .

Camp at Wallis' [Wallace] House[,] *Thursday Night[,] 24' April '62*[.]

Last night just as I had fallen asleep, the Paymaster of my Brigade arrived & had to be provided for in the rain. . . . I had the Paymaster & his Clerks to Breakfast with us, & then went out, after 8 o'clock, to the Camp. Then I went all through the grounds for miles around, looking for a Site to encamp——— Concluded, finally, to take up my own Quarters at a house near ($\frac{1}{2}$ a mile) the Phillips place & owned by a man named Wallis [Wallace]. . . .

Saturday Night, 26' April 1862———Frederic[k]sburg———

Slept well last night & rose early this morning. . . . At 11.30 was at Gen. King's Hd. Quarters to talk with him & Augur. We agreed that it would not be well to send a Brigade over the River without hearing from McDowell. Also that we would

advise protection to Union People there as soon as possible——
Secesh are carrying them off every night—— . . .

Camp before Frederic[k]sburg, *Monday Night, 28' April
'62*[.]

. . . Took a look with the Cols. of 20' 21' & 23' at the ground
south & west of Camp, selecting a new place for bivouac, about
a mile from the old site. . . . The difficulty was, to find a place
where there is plenty of water near dry ground, & where there
is shelter. . . .

Camp before Frederic[k]sburg, *Tuesday Night, 29' April
'62*.

. . . The Bridge of Boats is in progress, under Capt. Robinson
& a couple of Howitzers are sent down to protect them; also
a Company of Infy. (Capt. Wedell's) to protect the Guns. . . .

"Wallis [Wallace] House, Little Whim, *30' May [April,]*"
1862, Wed. Night[.]

A very unsatisfactory day in every respect. . . . After Breakfast
I . . . rode down to the Camp with Kimball & [Lt. William W.]
Beckwith,[14] to look at the Troops under Muster—— They
behaved, or were allowed by their officers to behave, in a very
shockingly unsoldierlike manner—— Then I visited the
Guards, Sentinels etc. and came home utterly disheartened——
The Officers are a set of drones, generally & do not care a fig
for discipline or duty—— . . .

---

[14] Lt. Beckwith was Patrick's Assistant Adjutant General.

Little Whim, *Thursday Night, 1' May, 1862*——

Last night was rainy & the day has been cloudy. . . . This Afternoon I went over to Head Quarters—— . . . Gen. McDowell has been there some 24 hours & had left but a short time before I reached there—— Some British Officers were with him & he had reviewed Augur's Brigade—— He does not say anything of the Movements—— . . . It is believed that there are Rebel Officers, disguised as Citizens, around our Camps at this moment—— . . .

Little Whim, *Friday Night, 2' May, 1862*——

This has been a busy day. . . . I . . . went down to see if a Battery, or rather a Gun or two, could be so placed as to protect the Rail Road Bridge beyond Frederic[k]sburg—— We could destroy the Bridge but cannot protect it—— Then came down, & while about crossed the River to Frederic[k]sburg to find a place to put a Comp. which are to act as a Guard for the Bridge of Boats—— I returned & detailed Capt. Todd's Compy. of 23' for that duty—— Home & worked till 4, then went down, with Cavalry Escort, & after some delay crossed the Bridge & rode through several of the Streets with Gen. King, his staff & mine—— *I* remained until almost dark, attending to matters there. . . . After the Bridge of Boats was completed, Gen. King & Staff concluded to go through town, with my escort—so we started off & rode through Caroline & Princess Anne Streets, looking at the points to be guarded by sentinels, & property to be secured. The Secesh people were very indignant at the profanation of the Sacred Soil by Yankees—— It was amusing to see the manner in which the Secesh women showed us their Backs—— They were all looking until about the time the Cavalcade would get opposite their doors then, with a grand air they would throw back their Crinoline, as Stage Ladies do—— It was quite refreshing to see the two daughters of a Mr. Clark, a Northern man, wave their white Kerchiefs to welcome us & in one house a little Union Flag in the hand of the Ladies. In general every body was disgust[ed].

Little Whim, *Saturday Night, 3' May, 1862*—— (Frederic[k]sburg).

. . . Rose at the usual hour & breakfasted. . . . Sent notice to the Colonels that they should join *me,* at 3 o'clock, say, in Camp if they wished to see Frederic[k]sburg. They did so & we went over into town, quite a Cavalcade, with my escort of Cavalry ——We went out to examine the Railroad Bridge, which we found intact, then examined to see if it had Combustibles around it—— Gave a charge to the keeper of the Bridge, who agrees to report to Mayor [Montgomery] Slaughter any thing that goes wrong in his domain—— Came down & saw the Mayor about it, then rode on & met Augur & [Brig. Gen. George G.] Meade[15] & [Col. John N.] Macomb, with their "Cohorts" parading the town & took them along with me—— . . . Went to Gen McDowell's Head Quarters. . . . I only saw Schriver & the Staff, McDowell having been to the River & Crossed over, while I was at the Bridge, with the Secretaries of State [Seward], of War [Stanton] & Treasury [Chase], staid there a few minutes & then returned with them to Acquia Creek, where he now is, or rather to Belle Plain—— I called at Gen. King's when I came home, to say, that if a Regt. goes over, I prefer sending over *Companies,* as I choose to control them myself—— I do not wish to trust a Colonel over there. . . .

---

[15] Gen. Meade, destined for command of the Army of the Potomac, was at the moment commanding the 2nd Brigade of McCall's Division in McDowell's Corps.

Little Whim, Wallis' [Wallace.] *Monday Night, 5' May 1862.*

Yesterday Morning I rose in good season. . . . Attended to business until 10½ o'clock. . . . We had Jeff. Davis' Coachman up, who left Richmond the Sunday before—— He gave valuable information. The Leaders are preparing to evacuate Virginia. Of this there is no doubt—— At one o'clock we heard of the evacuation of Yorktown—— . . . This morning I was again at work early. . . . Office work done I went to Camp & thence across the River & over the Ponton Bridge which I had sent a Company over to protect. . . . We then followed my route of yesterday & after examining the heights I took a part of the Cavalry & gave chase to the Rebel Pickets on the Telegraph Road, catching one—— . . .

Tuesday Night [,] *6' May, 1862*—— Wallis [Wallace] House, Little Whim.

. . . Attended to business until about 9 & then went over the River. . . . Spent the time until noon & long after, in reconnoitering. . . . Went over the Hill to the former Rebel Camp and where our men are cutting timber for a Block House, or Block Houses—— . . . From there we came down, in rear of the Camp, by Mr. Howisson's [Howison], where I found that some of the men had been, already——

Wednesday Night, 7' May 1862, Little Whim——

. . . After I had breakfast, early, I managed to get up a buggy & went over to town in it . . . feeling quite unable to ride on horseback—— There I had work enough to do—— Getting a truck over the River, fitting up other trucks & sending over, or

to the River Bank a quantity of heavy lumber, for the Bridges.
About 12 o'clock I met McDowell, as I was returning who
halted & had a long talk—— The result of it was that being
very much dissasisfied with operations of Provost Marshals,
Aids of Division Generals etc. he directed me to take the
entire charge remove my Head Quarters to the other side &
take charge of all matters in the city. I have taken the Farmer's
Bank at the solicitation, or request of the Mayor & remove
tomorrow. . . .

Banking House, Frederic[k]sburg, *Thursday Night*[,] *8'*
May '62.

. . . I have been overrun with business all day & have been
assured, over & over again, that the Rebels are within 3 miles
& 2 miles of me, in force. Gen [J. R.] Anderson, Gen.
[Charles E.] Field, & Gen. [Maxcy] Gregg are in command,
Anderson on the Telegraph Road, Gregg on the Rail Road &
Field on the Bowling Green Road—— I think there cannot be
over 15000 men, all told—— Deserters have come in, & Flag
of truce came to our outposts, bringing 2 prisoners of War,
just Exchanged. . . .

Banking House, Frederic[k]sburg, *Friday Night, 9' May*
'62[.]

Took a Tod at 10½ o'clock & went to bed with my clothes on
for a Snooze, giving orders to be called at 1 o'clock & horses
to be saddled—— I recd. messages thru' all the hours, so that
I did not get any good sleep at all & at 1 o'clock I was in the
Saddle—— Had Beckwith & Bouvier with me & some
Orderlies—— Was over the River & all among the Regts.

then about the Depots, Bridges etc. It was after 3 o'clock when I got in & gave myself again to sleep—— The night passed without an attack & this morning I was again at work quite early—— Have had a very busy day—— . . . In the Afternoon I got into a Buggy & drove all over the town & suburbs—— Visited all the outposts—— Had several Citizens arrested & brought into town—— Are under Guard today & tonight—— It is *expected* that there will be an attack tonight—— Gen. McDowell left here about 11 o'clock—— He came in about 9—— He hangs on terribly.

Banking House, Frederic[k]sburg, *Saturday Night, 10' May, '62*.

. . . There has been no trouble—— The enemy made no movement last night nor has he at this hour (7 o'clock) today—— We sent out & brought 2 women, Mrs. Smuck & Daughter from some 5 miles out—— They were captured under fire from the pickets of the Enemy & brought to town & placed with their daughter—— I have also had the 2 men captured last night placed in a fair prison, & 2 Coxes, having given their pledge, are left in their house under a sentinel—— I had another *long* call from McDowell, [Brig. Gen. James B.] Ricketts & Augur—— They take up time. . . .

Banking House, Frederic[k]sburg, *Monday Night '12' May '62*[.]

. . . Yesterday morning I was up & about business until Breakfast. . . . Officers became very devotional all of a sudden & swarmed over here for Church—— I had intended to go to Mr. Lacey's [Lacy] Church [Presbyterian] myself——

McDowell came over, with all his tail & the other Generals with their tails. . . . I was interrupted by a call from the front, on the Bowling Green Road—— Went out & found My Cavalry had taken a Lieut. & a dozen prisoners—— . . . While examining the prisoners, an hour after, I found a Courier dashing in, to say that they were being driven by the enemy in force—— . . . On arriving at Deep Run, where I proposed to hold the enemy, the troops were placed in position & I directed them to hold the ground, without pushing, as McDowell was dreadfully afraid I might frighten them—— I rode up on the height when *whiz* went a Minie by my horse's neck & lodged in the shoulder & neck of a horse behind me— killing him—— Soon as we could move forward our Skirmishers, we cleared the ground, leaving their pickets—$\frac{3}{4}$ of a mile in front—— Their main body had retired—— Came home & found the town all excited & Generals had their commands ready— . . . This morning I found a regular stampede of the Union women from out on the Plank Road—— They came early & were in fear of their lives from Rebel pickets—— They wanted me to protect them. . . .

Farmer's Bank, *Frederic[k]sburg, 13' May, 1862*——

. . . Breakft. Then go to a Barber Shop & get my head & face sheared—— . . . I then, (in the Street) met [Col. Herman] Haupt, for the first time since graduating—— He & McDowell, with his tail, came over to my Office & the latter *Staid,* as usual—— Then came [Brig.] Gens. [Christopher C.] Augur, [John J.] Reynolds, [George G.] Meade, Augur [sic], [Edward O. C.] Ord & [James B.] Ricketts were here & had their usual sit.[16] . . .

---

[16] Gens. Reynolds, Meade, and Ord commanded the three brigades of McCall's 2nd Division of McDowell's Corps. Gens. Ricketts, Patrick, and Augur commanded the three brigades of King's 3rd Division of McDowell's Corps.

Farmer's Bank, Frederic[k]sburg, *Wednesday Night, 14'*
May '62.

. . . The usual amount of all sorts of business *early* in the
day, but as it came on to rain the business fell off——
McDowell was the only General from the other side. He is
troubled greatly because they do not hurry up the bridges etc.
that he may get supplies for his Army—— His Generals
think he should move—— Yesterday I had quite a time with
a Daughter of Dr. [Abram B.] Hooe & her Aunty, & some
of her friends but survived. . . .

Farmer's Bank, Frederic[k]sburg, *16' May, '62, Friday*
Night.

. . . After the morning business was completed, or so that I
could leave [Capt. Charles] McClure & Bouvier accompanied
me out to the front. Found the pickets of the enemy at Salem
Church firing at our pickets at the Toll Gate & altho' they
did not hit any one, still it was unsafe—— Col. Rogers crossed
with me from there along the picket to the Mill & Camp,
from which I went to the Bowling Green Road & home——
Found here my successor as Inspector of New York, Gen.
[Chester A.] Arthur [in pencil, "later President"]. He ran
down on his way to Fort Monroe, via Washington. . . .
Arthur has friends here, his wife having been born in this
very house, I think—— He is out visiting her uncle, Dr.
[Brodie] Herndon—— McDowell was over here at 2 & while
here was called to Washington—— . . .

Farmer's Bank, Frederic[k]sburg, *17' May, 1862,*
Saturday.

. . . Was overrun with business until 6 o'clock allowing no
time for Dinner before. . . . Mrs. Rickets came over to

return my call and the Staff with the General—— [George] Guest & some others were here—especially the Mayor & Dr. [William S.] Scott—— Then came Dr. Rose's Brother from the Warrenton Road & Herman Briggs—both arrested & brought in as Guerrillas—— Col. Biddle of McCall's Division arrested them, the object being to steal their horses—— It has been done & they are here to prove their property. I managed to get dinner at 6 & then came off for a Buggy expedition to [John L.] Stansberry's [Stansbury] to see about an Examination of his house by some Officers. I think the search was made by the Tribune or Times Reporter & somebody else. . . .

Farmer's Bank, Frederic[k]sburg, *Sunday Night, 18'*
   May[.]

Slept well & rose early. . . . Haupt came in here to see me & sat a short time—— His cars are running today from Acquia Creek to this place—— I do not know whether they will cross the Creek (Rappahannock) or not, tonight. . . . The Churches were attended by many of our Officers & men—— The day has been beautiful but I have had a number of things to vex and disturb me. The final one was a flag of truce being led into town by Maj. [Charles W.] Drew instead of being recd. at the outposts, as usual[.] He had been all thro' town before I knew it & I sent him on for General McDowell to detain, but he thought it not advisable—— He came over here & showed me the despatch & answers.

Farmer's Bank, Frederic[k]sburg, *Monday Night*[,] *19'*
   May, '62[.]

. . . I have had ladies & Gentlemen & all sorts of people to deal with, including Reporters & Deserters—— Two deserters

came in this morning, having left Hamilton's Regt. at 2 o'clock
this morning—— From them I obtained valuable information—— . . . Two Flags of Truce have come in today,
(properly) bearing messages to McDowell & myself—from
[Gen. J. R.] Anderson, with Ladies on their way to this place
& further North—— . . .

Farmer's Bank, Frederic[k]sburg, *20' May, Tuesday, '62.*

. . . A Mrs. Grymes, a Miss Snowdon, & Miss Hooe, all came
to see me—Very condescending ! . . . Rode down, after
Dinner after 6 o'clock—to examine the premises of Miss
Fanny Mayo, who has been over-run with Soldiers—Bridge
Builders—— I gave orders in relation to them and then went
over to the Bowling Green Road. . . .

Farmer's Bank, Frederic[k]sburg, *21' May
   (Wednesday)*[,] *'62*[.]

. . . Had some time with the Mayor, Marie [Marye] &
others—— It is beginning to be feared, very much, that I am
about to leave the Command in Frederic[k]sburg—— They
are in trouble—— A Flag came in from Anderson, with the
Consul from Bremen & Wife, which afforded me an opportunity to write to Anderson, explaining the matter of the Flag
of Truce Yesterday, about which I had no knowledge until
this morning—— . . .

Farmer's Bank, Fredburg, *22' May, Thursday Night.*

. . . After Breakfast I was all over town, in every direction.
. . . Gens. McDowell & King have been here & I now know

much of Gen. McDowell's plans—— [Brig.] Gen. [Abner] Doubleday relieves me in command of Frederic[k]sburg—— We shall soon move, I presume, as [Maj.] Gen. [James] Shields has arrived today, and we are preparing to March, rapidly. . . . I find that it will be a hard thing to get our Brigade in motion—— The trouble is now about Teams.

Farmer's Bank, Fredburg. *Friday Night, 23' May* [,] *'62.*

. . . At 10½ o'clock McDowell sent over for me to meet the Prest. & Sec. of War. I went over & found them there & all the Generals, including Paddy Shields & his Irishes. Staid longer than I desired, returned & prepared to receive the Prest. & Cortege at the Bridge—— Took them through town to my Camp, saw the men under Arms only at the Guard, but the others only turned out—— We came back to my Quarters staid half an hour, when I escorted them to the Bridges & said Adieu—— Doubleday has arrived & made a fool of himself before he had been here an hour. There is a feeling of sadness in the whole community & I feel sad myself, at the thought that these helpless families are to be left to the tender mercies of an Abolitionist. . . .

Farmer's Bank, Fredburg. *24' May '62 (Saturday)*[.]

. . . Rained till noon, tho' not hard—— Mrs. Alsop went out to meet her daughters, on the Bowling Green Road, under a flag, according to an greement made with me—— I had a time with a Mrs. Temple who wanted to send shirts & comforts to her Son an Officer in the Rebel Army. She was very pious & very insolent, but Mr. Marie [Marye] took her in hand & got her out of the way. . . .

Farmer's—No—Downman House, *25' May '62*[.]

. . . Contrabands & pickets reported the enemy fled——
Reconnaissance ordered—— At 10.40 moved with 4 companies of Cavalry on the Plank, the 35' on the Telegraph &
4 Companies of Cavalry on the Bowling Green—all to meet at
Alsops, on Telegraph [Road]—— I had got 5 miles out & was
recalled by an order to March this P. M. with my Brigade, to
Acquia. Shield's [sic] & King's Divisions to Catlett's, Reynolds
to relieve me—— I had everything in readiness, & Reynolds
on the spot, when an Order was issued, countermanding &
sending Ord instead of King, to Catlett's, leaving me in
town So I sat down—— An hour after King came in town &
said Augur was to come over & take the Telegraph[,] Gibbon
the Bowling Green & I the Plank. So I packed up again & came
off, taking possession of the Downman House, which was
placed at my disposal—— We got here between 5 & 6——
The cause of our stampede is the reverse of Banks, or something of the kind & a fright in Washington. . . .

Downman House, *Monday Night, 26' May, 1862.*

. . . [I] went off about 8 o'clock, to town. Gen. King could
tell me nothing about business, so I went to Genl.
McDowell's—— He had left just before for the front—— I
got a map & returned to King's. . . . We took the Telegraph
Road, following Augur, & came up with him near Wm. Alsop's,
at the old Camp of Gen. Anderson—— There was Gibbon
from the left, & soon after Augur returned, with McDowell.
We decided that I should move forward, tomorrow, to the
Telegraph Road—— I started back, sending Orders to the
Colonels to come forward—— Had a long ride thru' the
woods & found Reynolds here—— He is to relieve me & went

into town to get my Sentinels relieved & sent up to their Regt. . . . I expect to be off tomorrow morning, early—— We are to go directly to Hanover Junction & Richmond if we can get there.

Chapter III

Contending with Stonewall Jackson

MAY 28, 1862, THROUGH AUGUST 13, 1862

IN LATE MAY OF 1862, Stonewall Jackson's celebrated Shenandoah Valley Campaign was coming to a climax. Jackson, in overwhelming force, pounced on elements of Nathaniel P. Banks' command near Winchester, Virginia on May 25. Banks retreated northward down the Valley with Jackson in close pursuit. Lincoln thought he saw an opportunity to trap Jackson. He determined to bring Federal forces under Fremont from the mountains to the west of the Valley and a portion of McDowell's force from the east side of the Blue Ridge together in a pincers movement which would catch Jackson before he could retreat southward up the Valley. The trap was to snap shut at Front Royal and Strasburg. King's Division and Patrick's Brigade were part of the eastern arm of the pincers. Why Lincoln failed to catch Jackson is apparent in Patrick's Diary.

June 26 to July 1 is the period of the Seven Days which climaxed McClellan's campaign on the Peninsula below Richmond. When the fighting was over the new Confederate field commander, Robert E. Lee, had driven the Federal forces from the gates of Richmond and into a defensive position at Harrison's Landing on the James River.

In July, Lincoln brought Henry W. Halleck, architect of victory in the West, to Washington and placed him in command of the Army. Halleck's first move was to try to combine McClellan's Army of the Potomac and John Pope's new Army of Virginia. While McClellan was moving from Harrison's Landing to join Pope in Northern Virginia, Lee struck. The battle of Cedar Mountain (or Slaughter Mountain, or South-west Mountain, or Cedar Run) between Lee's van under Jackson and the leading elements of Pope's Army under Banks took place on August 9.

May 28 [,] *Wednesday Morning,* Massaponax Creek,
   6 miles from Fredsburg———

Yesterday we left the Down Man [Downman] House at about
10 o'clock & came on via Salem Church, to Wm. Alsop's———
We crossed the Creek & came on the heights to encamp. . . .
Towards night I took a ride, with my Staff, through a
beautiful Country, 2½ miles, to Massaponax Church, a
Brick Structure like most of the Country Churches of Old
Virginia——— The Valley of the Massaponax is very rich,
indeed & most of it well cultivated by the Alsop family[.]
Gen. McDowell is called again to Washington, & we understand that he is ordered to make his Head Quarters at Alexandria——— His Staff went down last night——— We very much
fear that we shall be ordered back as [Brig. Gen. George D.]
Bayard[1] has been recalled already & Several Militia Regts.
have again been ordered out for the protection of Washington.
. . . We hear that none of the enemy are within less than 35
miles of us, but that they are returning, in small numbers, to
burn up the Bridges. . . .

May 29' [,] *Thursday Morning*——— Still at the same
   place this morning [.]

I rode over with Augur & Gibbon, about 4 o'clock, Yesterday,
to Gibbon's Camp——— . . . We found nothing new in the way
of Orders, save that the fright in regard to Washington has so
far abated that Gov. [Andrew G.] Curtin [Pennsylvania] has
countermanded the Order calling out the Militia for three
months.

---

[1] Gen. Bayard commanded McDowell's cavalry force.

Thursday Night, 29' May, at Hartwood, Irwin's place,
   7 miles from Frederic[k]sburg———

I mounted my horse at $7\frac{1}{2}$ or 8 o'clock & took a turn among
the pickets & Rebel Camps so lately deserted, returning about
9 o'clock, just in time to receive the Order for breaking up to
March for Catlett's, with all despatch——— To my consternation I found that my teams had been sent into town for Forage
& Subsistence [,] that issues of Beef were going on, that said
Beef must be cooked—etc. etc. etc. We did get off, however,
following Augur's Brigade closely——— We had to halt, however, in town & close up before crossing and I was there some
time——— The Mayor & many others called while I was halting & paid their respects——— I sat down on the steps of the
Gordon House, (as I was told) a very Aristocratic Mansion,
to watch the movement of my Troops, near the head of the
Bridge——— While there Servants came from that house &
another, bringing nice pie & cool milk, with the compliments
of their Mistresses to Gen. Patrick, & say that "Although we
are Southern Ladies, we wish to show our regard for Gen.
Patrick & to express our thanks for the kindness he has shown
us, the protection he has given us & the perfect quietness &
order he has preserved in the Town." The refreshments were
very acceptable & the spirit of the ladies still more gratify-
ing——— After leaving town we were delayed & our Teams
blocked up at Falmouth——— We came on & reached Irwin's
rather late, so that I did not have my Tent pitched, but thrown
upon a Tree. Augur's Brigade, as usual, had taken up the
whole country & I had to do as I could. . . .

Friday Night, 30' May, Camp at Elk Run, $4\frac{1}{2}$ miles from
   Catlett's———

Tried to move at 7 but did not get off until $8\frac{1}{2}$ o'clock. . . .
Settled with Irwin's son by giving a Certificate, which Augur

& King failed to do, tho' it was asked of them—— . . . Irwin's property is nearly destroyed by the Troops who have passed & repassed & he himself arrested, at Catlett's—— A hard case, truly—— We had a fair march to a place $3\frac{1}{2}$ miles from here, where we halted. Gen. King overtook us there, with a despatch from McCall, via Frederic[k]sburg, saying that McDowell had directed him to hurry us up to Catlett's, where we would find immense Trains to carry us to our destination—— . . .

Saturday Night, 31' May, at Catlett's Station, In an Orchard, heavy rain.

At ten o'clock last night a despatch from McDowell, hurrying us forward. [Gen. Thomas J. "Stonewall"] Jackson, [Gen. Richard S.] Ewell & [Gen. Edward] Johnson, re-enforced by [Gen. Joseph R.] Anderson, are in the Valley & we are to cut off their retreat. We move at 6 in the morning (by Order) to take Cars at 8 for Front Royal. . . . Owing to various delays we did not get off as soon as we intended. It was 9'30" when I reached Cadett's & no Train—— Hunted up Gen. King, who was at Quesenberg's [Quesenberry], whose property is nearly all destroyed by the Wadsworth Guards—— As vile a set of brutes as can be found—— They all fled like sheep the other day, burning & destroying everything, including 1000 BBls. of Flour at Bristoe, tho' they did not see a Single enemy—— No Train having arrived I went back to Cedar Run & had some Cattle butchered, went into Camp, as it rained & waited for the Train—— . . .

Sunday Night [,] *1' June*—— Still in that vilest of vile places—Catlett's[.]

. . . Up early & made arrangements for sending off all our property, Tents etc. (excepting what is absolutely necessary) by the Waggon Train, that goes by land, to Front Royal, At 11'15" Gibbon & I went up to see King & proposed to March across to Haymarket, but after waiting 2 hours it got too late & we came off—— I had Tents for 2 or 3 of us put up & stretched myself out for a snooze. The Stench of this place is insupportable—— It is vile & wretched in every respect.

Monday Night [,] *2' June*—— Camp 2½ Miles from Haymarket——

Rain, Rain, Rain! . . . At about 11 o'clock we decided to wait no longer, & I succeeded in getting one Waggon to carry our Luggage—— I had then to issue a day's Subsistence to the men and that kept us until about 1 o'clock——It was terribly hot when we started & Gibbon's Brigade, which started ahead of mine straggled badly & threw away their Blankets, coats etc. before they were three miles out—— I rode on, without waiting for the Troops & overtook Gibbon at Greene's place (Greenwich) 8 miles out—— . . .

Tuesday Night [,] *3' June, 1862*—— Camp at Bull's Run, near Haymarket——

Rain again last night that almost drowned us out, & rain this evening—— I had Reveille beat at 4, hoping to get off, pass Gibbon, take the Cars by 7 or 8 o'clock & join the others at Front Royal, but the rain delayed. . . . But it was just as well, for on reaching Haymarket we found that all our Troops had been sent back from Front Royal, Jackson having escaped down [up] the Valley on Saturday night—— So they were here, having arrived last night & this morning. . . . McDowell is at Front Royal, the Telegraph wires between us, cut, the Rail Road Bridge impassable & no communication—— . . .

Wednesday Night, 4' June, 1862, Camp near Haymarket,
   Bell's or Grayson's Farm——

. . . The ground is saturated with water & fairly springs up in
our Tents—— Have done nothing, today, but try to keep
dry. . . . Several of the Officers have been over to see
me & there is great despondency expressed in regard to our
Division—— Gen. King amounts to nothing & his Staff are
worthless—— McDowell has lost the confidence of his men,
entirely—— They speak very strongly against him. . . .

Thursday, 5' June, 1862—— 12'30" P.M. At the same
   Camp, Bell's House——

. . . Since Breakfast I have spent most of my time in talking
with the Officers & correcting opinions, though I find my own
opinions yielding to the current. . . .

Friday Night, 6' June, 1862—— Camp near Warrenton [,] Fauquier County, Va.

An unexpected change—— I went to bed at ten o'clock last
night & had my nap till 11'15" when I was interrupted by a
despatch from Gen. King directing me to have my "Brigade
in readiness to march early tomorrow morning——" . . . We
had a slow march in consequence of the time taken up in
fording streams—— They are swollen to torrents by the rain
& difficult to cross—— . . . We are on very good ground,
and in beautiful country—just on the border of the Blue
Ridge——. . .

Saturday Night, 7' June 1862—— Camp one mile from
  Warrenton.

. . . Breakfast at 6 & at 7'15" I . . . rode into town—— Found
Gen. King had taken possession of a Hotel & was living there
in fine style—— I took a survey of the town & found it full
of quiet old homes—— The people did not seem to be so full of
spite as those of Fredsburg—but were not very much pleased
to see our [sic] Streets full of Yankee Soldiers—— . . .

Sunday Night, 8' June, 1862—— Eastern View, Fauquier
  Co. (Randolph House). [.]

. . . We were quiet & I had time to read an hour, nearly, in
the Gospel of John—— Then came inspection & I had, also,
to look at my own Guard etc. etc. . . . Called on a Maj.
Saunders, who was very polite & then upon a Mrs. Campbell
& her Aunt, Mrs. Horner. They too, were very polite & gave
me Strawberries & cream—— Then I rode over to see the
Carters, but had just arrived when an Orderly reached [me],
saying that I was wanted in Camp—— Arrived there I found
that Gen. McDowell had ordered the Division forward; that
we would move, at once, to Frederic[k]sburg, via Catlett's. . . .
The Carters were down there—— The Young Widow, more
talkative than her Sister, seemed to have some curious feelings—— Intensely Virginian, strongly prejudiced & very
proud, I took a great deal of pleasure in talking with her. She
was disappointed that the Yankees appeared so well, & behaved
so well—— Said it did not seem to her that these Soldiers
were her enemies etc. etc. When I prepared to Mount, in
taking hands, she said " I cannot wish you success, but I do
hope that no evil will befall you." Our Course was a little
to the right of Catlett's, going to the Junction, tho' *I* was
obliged to halt about $2\frac{1}{2}$ miles short of there. . . . It is *now*

expected that we move on directly, to support McClellan, at
Richmond—— It is said that other Troops are also following,
from Rectortown—— probably [E. O. C.] Ord's & [George
D.] Bayard's—— . . .

Monday Night, 9½ o'clock, 9' June '62—— At Elk Run,
  say 4½ M. from Cattl [ett's].

. . . We had Breakfast at 6 & while eating it an Express arrived
saying that we would move out as far as Elk Run & await
Orders. . . . I expect[ed] to be joined here by the 21' via
Catlett's, which place we left some 2½ miles on our left, . . .
but on reaching here I found the cause of the delay, in a
Telegram from McDowell—— It seems that Shields' extreme
advance had met with a repulse & been driven back, with a
loss of 2 guns—— McDowell waits to see whether this repulse
is the result of rashness on the part of our Troops, or whether
we must really return to the Mountains to assist Shields, Fremont & Banks—— We therefore halt until Shields can be
heard from.[2] . . . I think it probable that we shall move
tomorrow, but perhaps not quite so soon.

Tuesday Morning, 9 o'clock, 10' June '62——

Same Camp, at Elk Run.
Last night was cold, & this morning rainy, since 5 o'clock——
It appears like a settled rain. . . . There was trouble about
sheepstealing & hog killing[.] I have about 21 men arrested
last night & I know not how many carcasses of sheep have
been found—certainly as many as 12 or 15—— This matter

---

[2] The Battles of Cross Keys and Port Republic, where Jackson turned
on elements of the commands of John C. Fremont, Nathaniel P. Banks,
and James Shields, were fought on June 8 and 9.

of Guards for property, patrols for Rogues, etc. kept me up a good part of the night. . . .

Wednesday Night, 11' June, 1862——— Same Camp———

I was in hopes to have found myself well on my way to Frederic[k]sburg by this time, but no orders have yet arrived & I am in doubt if we shall move tomorrow, judging from present appearances——— The day has been very fine for marching, but no one has tried it, save Gibbon, who, as I suppose stretched off this morning from the place where he encamped yesterday morning, but on account of rain, went into camp not many miles from here——— . . . I have been engaged in this sheep stealing operation, having had the Captains of the Companies before me——— Have discharged all but 4 of the 17 men, on their agreement to pay $5. each, on the next Muster Roll— The 4 refuse——— I shall ask for a military Commission to try them——— . . .

Thursday Night, 12' June, 1862——— Same Camp, on Elk Run———

. . . I rose soon after daylight, as I had to send off Mandeville to Washington, to procure clothing & other property for Brigade[.] I sent also, for a Box of paper collars, some postage Stamps & stove pipe——— These matters delayed me, until 9 o'clock, then came other matters and I did not get to the Creek, where I went to wash me until near noon. This made it rather a hot bath, for the sun was very powerful indeed———

. . .

Friday Morning, 11 o'clock, 13' June, 1862. Same Camp,
   On Elk Run——

. . . This morning, after our usual Hd.Qrs. duties, I took a
turn thro' the Camps, looked out about building bridges that
have been destroyed, etc. etc. winding up at Augur's Head
Quarters, from which I have just returned—— . . . We shall,
probably, soon be moving—— . . .

Saturday morning, 9 o'clock, 14' June, 1862. Camp at
   Tullis' near Town Run——

. . . Gen. Augur moved by here this morning, en route to
Frederic[k]sburg— —It seems that Gibbon wrote, supposing
either Augur or myself to be on the road, and urged us to
hurry up, having no confidence in Doubleday, who is now in
command—— Both Gibbon & Doubleday are on the Frederic[k]sburg side—— . . . King writes that Shields was worse
handled by Jackson than is reported—— . . .

Sunday, 2'15" P.M., 15' June, 1862—— At the Same
   Camp, Town Run——

. . . Until within a few minutes the day has been intensely hot,
but a refreshing shower is now in progress & the atmosphere
is comfortable. On account of the heat, I presume, there was
no service in any of the Regts. I think—— I sent for Col.
[Charles W.] Drew this morning, as he had just arrived from
Frederic[k]sburg. He says the pickets are all driven in & that
only a Provost Marshal & his Guard are on the Frederic[k]s-
burg side—— The Troops are all drawn up on the Lacey
[Lacy] side hill—— 2 Brigades—— Doubleday is in com-

mand—— Maj. Lacey [Lacy] has been captured and is a Prisoner. The people are very hostile & their demonstrations very disagreeable. . . .

Monday Night, 16' June—— Same Camp——
　　8 o'clock——

. . . The day has been cool, first rate for Marching; but we can get no order, nor hear of Gen. McDowell's whereabouts. . . . Sickness is not increasing, but a great many are unfit for duty. . . .

Tuesday Night, 9 o'clock, 17' June, '62. Same Camp, on
　　Town Run——

. . . The Regts. have Drills, some by Compg. & some by Battalion, but there is no ground, hereabouts, proper to drill on. . . . I sent Beckwith over to Catlett's, to Telegraph McDowell, asking for any orders they might be pleased to send me—— He got for reply a request to know my "exact position," which was given but no other communication followed—— . . .

Wednesday Night, Tattoo, 18' June, '62 Camp at Tullis,
　　on Town Run——

. . . In our present disordered state, hanging, as we do, by the Gills, upon the whim of the Comdg. General, there is very little to be accomplished in the way of discipline & instruction—— The men are indifferent & feel that they are acting without an object, or a purpose; consequently they behave badly, strolling over the country, stealing, destroying fruit trees loaded with partially ripened fruit etc. etc. The Regt. Officers, as a general rule, are of the opinion that property in Rebeldom is, or ought to be, free to all who are in arms against them. . . .

Thursday Night, 19' June, Same Station——

. . . This morning . . . the Regimental Commanders gathered here for the purpose of talking over our position, the condition of our troops & in what manner we could best insure a little better discipline etc. The fact that there is no ground, within a long distance, on which we can drill, is all against us, but we concluded to do what we could in that respect. . . . Col. Davies is here this evening & says that [Col. Alfred N.] Duffie[3] told him, that Gen. McDowell had a *very* bad fall, yesterday, his horse having reared & fallen backwards, pressing the pummell of the saddle into his stomach, so that he lay insensible for a long time after. . . .

Friday Night, 20' June, 1862, Still at same Camp, on Town Run, Tullis Mill.

. . . I sent Bouvier out to visit all the Families that have Sentinels at their houses & take a list of them. He was absent all day & must have travelled some 35 miles. . . .

Saturday Night[,] 21' June, 1862—— Camp near Spotted Tavern—— 5 miles from Catlett's.

. . . As I intended to make a move today, I sent out & recalled the Guards established at the various houses in the neighbor-

---

[3] Col. Duffie, a Frenchman, commanded the 1st Rhode Island Cavalry.

hood, but *some* have concluded, I think, not to come
in—— . . .

Sunday Night, 22' June, '62. Camp at Spotted Tavern,
   Forbes Plantation—— (Embry's)[.]

. . . I was busy all the forenoon about stolen horses—— Have
recovered two horses, stolen by men of my Regts. but am
unable to fix the guilt upon either of the *thieves*, though I have
one in custody. . . .

Monday Night, Tattoo. 23' June, '62—— Camp at the
   Spotted Tavern[.]

. . . It came on to rain, most violently about 5 or 6 o'clock
& continues to rain heavily—— Of course, under any such
circumstances, a March is perfectly certain—— So I have just
recd. orders to March, with all the Troops, early tomorrow.

Thursday Night, 24' June, Headquarters, Wallis
   [Wallace] House, Little Whim[.]

One of the most rainy nights of the season. . . . so that the
Troops were not drawn out until $7\frac{1}{2}$ o'clock. . . . The road
was *very muddy,* of course, but the day was not so hot as to
oppress the men & they got along very well. . . . I came on,
thro' Falmouth, & up by Augur's Camp to the Rail Road,
thence across to my old Camp, between the Wallis [Wallace]
House & the Mill Dam. After getting the Regts. into Camp
I went down to Gen. King's, at the Lacey [Lacy] House——
He seemed to know very little about business connected with
our movements. . . . I find no Bridges left. & nothing but a

Ferry is now to be had for the crossing to Frederic[k]sburg. . . . I do not think we shall remain long at the camp where we now are, the ground has become so filthy from the frequent encampments of Troops thereon, that I shall find a new place as soon as I can——

Wednesday[,] *25' June*—— *9 o'clock P.M*. Wallis [Wallace] House, Stafford Co.[,] Va.

. . . After attending to a little business I rode into Camp & then went down below with Beckwith, to hunt new Grounds—— After a while I sent him to Gen. King's, on business, & then went down to Strother's, where they are shipping a Pennsylvania Regt. of Cavalry to join McCall. . . . I did not go into Strother's house, or call there, but I did call on Mrs. [John] Seddon[4] & was recd. as a *friend*. I was recd. in the same way by the [John Bowie] Grays [of "Travellers Rest"] & Mrs. Strother came over there to see me—— I feel that there is a great deal of real kind regard for me all through this part of the Country—— . . .

Thursday Night, 26' June '62—— Little Whim, Wallace House, Stafford Co.

. . . I was engaged in Office business all the forenoon writing, examining etc. etc. Had calls for help, in all directions & attended to all sorts of duties. . . . Capts. Springsteed, McClure & Kimball went on to Washington, also the two latter to purchase Horses for themselves—— Beckwith purchased, the day he was down, a *very* nice little horse at $115—— . . .

---

[4] Mrs. John Seddon of "Snowden" was sister-in-law to James A. Seddon, the Confederate Secretary of War.

Friday Night, 27' June, Wallace House, Little Whim,
Stafford Co.[,] Va.

A very hot day & the closest night I have yet experienced. . . .
The Troops moved from their old ground to the new, soon
after 8 o'clock. . . . Felt very unwell & did not go to Camp
until about 5 o'clock. Found them pretty well settled & the
grounds full of all sorts of Peddlers, Dealers and Ambrotype
men. Had to arrest some & break up others. Got back to
Quarters at dusk & met an Express calling me to Gen. King's.
. . . King had just recd. a despatch from Secretary of War,
directing him to report in person, prepared to assume command of Fremont's Army. The Departments of Banks,
Fremont & McDowell, have been merged in the Army of
Virginia & Gen. [John] Pope[5] assigned to its command. It is
said that [James] Shields has resigned because the Senate
refused to confirm his nomination as Major General—— I
hope it is true.[6]

Saturday Night, 28' June, 1862[.] Wallace House,
   Little Whim—— Va.

An exceedingly restless night, followed by a very uncomfortable
day—— My Liver, Stomach & Bowels are all out of order.
. . . Fremont has not resigned, but has asked to be relieved.

---

[5] Gen. Pope was brought east after some highly publicized victories on
the Mississippi at New Madrid and Island No. 10. Frémont, more concerned with questions of rank than with future reputation, refused to
serve under a subordinate and asked to be relieved. Lincoln obliged
Frémont but the initial decision to give Frémont's German troops to
Rufus King fell through. Franz Sigel, a German revolutionist who had
migrated to the United States in 1852 and spent the intervening years
as a school teacher and superintendent of schools in St. Louis, was given
Frémont's command. It became the 1st Corps in Pope's new Army of
Virginia.

[6] Patrick was to be disappointed. Shields did not resign until the
following March.

Monday Morning, 30' June '62, Wallace House, Stafford
Co.[,] Va.——

. . . My Staff Captains returned this evening——Capts.
Kimball & McClure with horses & Equipage for them-
selves—— . . . They say that McDowell is in Washington, very
much downcast—that this Division was ordered to join
McClellan, but he succeeded in sending off Shields instead——
Shields was leaving Alexandria yesterday. . . .

Monday Night, Tattoo——

. . . There is a general foreboding of ill luck to McClellan——
Rumor says he has been repulsed & driven from before Richmond with heavy loss—— Telegraph is silent, which is
ominous—— . . .

Tuesday Night, Tattoo, 1' July, 1862, Wallace House,
Stafford Co.[,] Va.

. . . Had my breakfast. . . . Beckwith & I then rode to the
Lacey [Lacy] House—— Gen. King had arrived but was
asleep—— I Saw his brother, William, who came down with
him—— We then rode over to Gen. Augur's—— From him
I learn that this Division is, probably, destined to Gordonsville, there to meet with Banks & [Gen. Franz] Sigel. . . . The
telegraph wires from McClellan's army are not working——

Wednesday, 2' July, 1862——*Tattoo*—— Still at
Wallace House, Little Whim——

I did not sleep well last night. . . . The State of the country
was anything but cheering & I felt very little like sleeping. . . .

Nothing was done with troops on account of the weather &
after attending to the usual morning business, I went down to
Gen. King's at about 10 o'clock—— They have little more
that is definite, from Richmond—— . . . Gen. Reynolds is
taken prisoner & some other Generals—— A great many
prisoners have been taken by the Rebels & we have lost a great
many killed. From our own side we have few particulars. All
we know is, that on Tuesday McClellan commenced his change
of Front forward, & carried out his plans [his "change of base"
to the James River], tho' attacked by the concentrated forces
of the Rebels, after their reinforcement by Jackson & Beauregard.[7] He is, *now,* in better position, as is believed, than
heretofore & with [Gen. Ambrose E.] Burnside & [Gen. Joseph
K. F.] Mansfield near by,[8] to re-enforce him, the fall of
Richmond is regarded as certain—— . . . There appears to be
very heavy firing, far away to the South of us.

Thursday Night, 3' July '62—— Still at Wallace House,
Little Whim——

. . . The papers have given us but very little that is new today,
but Capt. Springsteed telegraphs me, that at 5 P. M. Yesterday Gen. McClellan sent a very favorable despatch to
Washington. . . .

Friday Night, 4' July '62. Wallace House, Little Whim
——

. . . At about $7\frac{1}{2}$ o'clock I rode up to the grounds of the
Brigade & visited the Colonels Rogers & Pratt, to whom was

---

[7] The rumor that troops from Gen. P. G. T. Beauregard's command in
Mississippi had arrived in Richmond was widely believed in the Federal
Army, but it was only a rumor. Jackson's troops, however, had most
emphatically reinforced Lee.

[8] Gen. Burnside had a force of about 10,000 men centered on New
Berne, N. C. Gen. Mansfield had a small observation force at Suffolk,
watching the south side of the James River.

committed the Execution of the Programme for the '4' of July'
—— I remained & saw it carried out, the Regts. forming
squares on the Brigade grounds, where the prayers, Declaration,
etc. were disposed of, the Music by the Bands etc. etc. as usual
—— I was called out, of course, but I could only wish them
a good time & a few words in relation to McClellan, which
brought down the cheers. . . . Then followed Horse & Foot
Races. . . . Then took Tea, went to Gen. King's, saw the fire-
works & came home——

Saturday Night, 5' July, 1862—— Wallace House,
    Little Whim——

Last night I went to bed at ten o'clock, taking my little toddy
like an old toper & it gave me a right good sleep. . . . Gen. Buell
is on his way from Baltimore, to McClellan, with 25000 men
——[9] Gen. [Winfield] Scott is in Washington & is talked of
as Secretary of War,[10] with Banks as Assistant, but the more
prevalent idea is, that Halleck will be Secretary of War——[11]
Stanton is doomed! McDowell is using every effort to keep
this Division under his own Command, but Marcy[12] is in
Washington trying to have us ordered down, forthwith——. . .
I have seen Richmond papers of Thursday—— They are in
the best possible spirits & look upon the ruin of McCellan as
perfectly certain. *We* regard him as perfectly *safe,* but unable

---

[9] A wild rumor. Maj. Gen. Don Carlos Buell had his hands full
trying to find the key to Chattanooga and on this date was actually in
Huntsville, Alabama.

[10] The rumors were flying thick and fast. General Winfield Scott was
in retirement at West Point. The basis for this rumor was probably the
fact that Lincoln had, on June 23, made an unannounced trip to West
Point to confer with Scott.

[11] Lincoln's order making Henry Wager Halleck the General-in-Chief
of the Army, not Secretary of War, is dated July 11, 1862.

[12] Marcy was still McClellan's Chief of Staff.

to act on the aggressive until he is reinforced with 50, or 60,000 men—— . . .

Sunday (5½ o'clock P. M.) 6' July 1862, Wallace House[,] Little Whim——

. . . *I have shaved off all my beard* excepting my Moustache & hardly know myself, not having seen my own face for the last ten years—— Went to the field, with all my staff at 7:30 & found the Regts. in line, on their own grounds—— Brought them into the large field & had a fine Review. It took only an hour & three quarters—— . . . Called up all Extra duty men & had DeForest read Paragraphs of the Regulations to them in regard to their general conduct & bearing towards their superiors—— . . . The Brigade is very deficient in this kind of discipline. . . .

Monday Night, 7' July '62—— Wallace House, Little Whim[.]

Hot, Hot, O how hot! . . . After dinner rode over to Frederic-[k]sburg. . . . On the way a Teamster was very abusive to me, for some cause, wherefore I jumped down upon him, took him by the throat & gave him a sharp cut or two with my riding stick, which shut him up. Came home via. Gen. King's—— Found that Augur had been ordered to the Command of a Division with Bank's Corps—— This evening we have all (my Staff) been over in the Ambulance, to bid him Good Bye—sorry enough to part with him, too——

Tuesday, 8' July, Head Quarters, Wallace House, Little Whim.

. . . After about 7'30" went to Camp & Staid until 10, though not for Drill—— My object was to ascertain the condition of the Regts. as to discipline & Police, which I found to be bad enough—— I had learned yesterday in Fredsburg that passes were forged, that my Guard was good for nothing, that Officers & men were playing the mischief in town & that several must be court martialed. . . .

Wednesday Night 9' July. Headquarters, Wallace House, Little Whim[.]

. . . This morning I was up early, breakfasted in good season & prepared for Brigade Drill. . . .Took carriage for Gen. King's Head Quarters. . . . Mrs. Col. (or Gen.) Steuart ["Maryland" Steuart] of the Rebel Cavalry—Hunter's Niece was there, on her way to Charlottesville, to meet her husband, wounded—— I was glad to see her—— Had seen her at her Uncle's, just as the war was breaking out. . . .

Head Quarters 1' Brigade, Camp Rufus King, *Thursday Night, 10' July, '62*[.]

. . . Had Breakfast & got our men out at 7 o'clock on their Color Lines—— This I followed up with Brigade Drills—— Did not do very much except measure our own *Strength,* or rather, our *length.* Our Battalion Lines were increased by more than 150 men, by the Stringent orders of Yesterday. . . .Orders came from Gen. Pope, via Gen. King, to be ready to march at an hour[']s notice, with 10 days['] provisions. . . .

Friday Night, Tattoo, 11 July, 1862—— Camp Rufus King——

. . . An Order was sent me this evening to call in all persons on Guards, those at the Bridges excepted tomorrow Morning, which looks much like moving very soon. . . .

Saturday Night, 12' July '62. Camp Rufus King, Stafford
    Co. Virginia[.]

. . . Breakfasted & did business until 1'30'', then rode . . . to
the Lacey [Lacy] House, to see McDowell—who had just
arrived & sent for me—— Had quite an interview. He says
that Doubleday has been the cause of more evil to him than
any one else, having made the matter of his guarding rebel
property a test of his loyalty——

Sunday Night, 13' July, '62——

. . . I rose early & at 8 o'clock the Brigade was out for
Inspection & Review. . . . The Review was good—— I then
had the Battalions stack arms, close in Mass on the Hill side in
front of my Brigade Head Quarters & there talked to them
for about half an hour—— They understood me—*as a
Brigade,* for the first time, I imagine—— That is, they understood the principle by which I am governed & it will, probably,
be more easy to govern the whole Line. . .

Camp Rufus King, Monday Night, 14' July '62, Stafford
    Co.[,] Virginia—

One more hot day— . . . Went over the river, with Col.
[Nirom M.] Crane, in boat, near pontoon Bridge & went to
the Farmer's Bank, where I saw most of the prominent
Citizens—— They learned, one after another, of my being in
town & called to see me—— Those who went to Richmond I
saw. [Provost Marshall of Richmond, John] Jack [Henry]
Winder played Tyrant *there* just as he did down at Vera
Cruz—— They could not see Reynolds & he is now in

Prison.[13] . . . We shall stop all passes, for Frederic[k]sburg, except on public service. . . .

Tuesday Night, 15' July, 1862—— Camp Rufus King

. . . I slept pretty well, after having given a very severe talking to one of the Capts. of the 23' for Intemperance—— He is a man of 35 & wept like a child. . . . After Breakfast I prepared for and had a fine Brigade Drill—— . . . Since the Shower came up several men have got drunk, knowing there would be no Drill this afternoon. I have sent for Capt. [Henry] Rich & put him on the trail—— The Liquor Sellers had better look out. . . .

Wednesday Night, 16' July—— Still at Camp Rufus King Stafford Co. Va.

. . . I had the Brigade out from 7 to 9, when it became very hot—— . . . A storm of wind, thunder & a little rain, came up about 3 o'clock blowing things about my tent at a great rate —— I ran out, having my glasses on, stumbled & threw my spectacles—— We must have looked an hour before finding them— —I cannot see to read, at night, without them & my eyes are now failing, somewhat rapidly. We have just found our men get their Whiskey from Captain [John H.] Coales [Coale] the Depot Commissary—— He is a very miserable subject. . . .

---

[13] On July 4, Mayor Slaughter and Jack Marye had carried to Richmond a petition, signed by twenty-seven of the most influential men of Fredericksburg, seeking the exchange of Gen. John F. Reynolds. Fredericksburg's high regard for Reynolds stemmed from the brief period when, as one of Patrick's successors, he had been military governor of the city.

Thursday Night, 17' July, '62—— Same Camp——

. . . There has been a deal of Whiskey drinking through the Regts. both among the Officers & men. . . . I am sorry to see Pope getting up such a Staff—— He has got Ben Welch, [Jr.] Commissary General of the State [of New York] on his Staff as Colonel! A spy of Gov. Morgan! A boot lick & toady! I see, however, that little Charley [Lt. Charles R.] Suter, who has just graduated in the Engineers, is also assigned to duty with his Staff. . . .

Friday, 18' July, '62——

. . . I was up, this morning, in good season & spent the time until drill in the usual manner—— . . . The Drills, for some time back, have been very interesting, as the men are beginning to see the value of them, & in the formations against Cavalry they are pretty well posted. . . . I suppose that we shall soon move, as Pope has published his Address to the Army of Virginia, which seems, to me, very windy & somewhat insolent. With such a Staff as he has gathered, politicians & rowdies among them, who are any thing but Soldiers, I shall feel little disposition to cultivate his acquaintance. . . .

Tattoo, Friday Night,

. . . Tonight Gen. Pope's Orders have been recd. giving the Authority to lay contributions on every town & village thro' which we pass—— Contributions in Forage & Subsistence—— I do not like his orders—they are the Orders of a Demagogue!

Saturday, 1 o'clock P. M.[,] *19' July, 1862,* Camp Rufus King, Stafford Co.[,] Va.

. . . The Orders of last night were discussed [at King's Head-quarters] & I was shown the despatch of Pope, directing King to cut the Virginia [Central] Rail Road, between Hanover Junction & Gordonsville, by getting the Cavalry off at night, crossing the River & forcing a march of 35 miles, which could be done easily & the men return in 36 hours—— The River, however, was rather high & the Boat Bridge in a bad condition, so he did nothing—— While I sat there another despatch came, *expecting* he had done it ! . . . I have been eating Black-berries, & some cake, & some cucumbers & have put a cup of chocolate over all—— If I am not sick it will not be my fault.

Sunday Evening, Parade, 20' July '62——

. . . I reviewed the Brigade at $7\frac{1}{2}$ o'clock this morning & it really looked right well—— . . . I got through at a little after 9 and concluded that I would go to Church . . . went over to the Presbyterian Church in Frederic[k]sburg—— The side pews are set apart for the use of the Soldiery & were quite well filled by a quiet Auditory—— It *did* seem good to meet to-gether with those who keep holy day—— Mr. Lacey [Lacy] is a man of fine abilities & gave no offence, that I could see, to the Soldiers of the U. S. his discourse being eminently consolat-ory & specially intended for those who have friends in prison. . . . His prayers were fervent & discreet [sic] & appropriate—— . . . After dinner I had a long interview with Dr. Van Slyek, of the 35', who has been making use of a good deal of intemperate language about Rebels & Rebeldom etc. etc. He will not do it again. . . . It seems to be understood that Gen. Halleck is on his way to Washington, to become General-in-Chief of the

Army—— Neither [Randolph] Marcy nor [Stewart] Van Vliet were confirmed as Brigadier Generals; nor were [Gustavus Adolphus] Scroggs, [Henry L.] Burnett & several others.[14] The feeling is very strong against McClellan in very many places. . . . Our men know every house in the whole country, and . . . they now believe they have a perfect right to rob, tyrannize, threaten & maltreat any one they please, under the Orders of Gen. Pope.

Monday, 9¼ o'clock P. M. 21' July—— Camp Rufus King, Stafford Co.[,] Va.

. . . This Order of Pope's has demoralized the Army & Satan has been let loose—— I have been sending out Guards, again, as the only mode of keeping up discipline in the Army, but this evening Gen. King has sent me an Order to withdraw my Guards from all Rebel Property & houses—— He is frightened at the attacks of Newspaper writers & the Tribune, & Pope's Order for political purposes—— . . .

Tuesday[,] 22' July—— 7 o'clock P. M.

. . . I attended to about 35 or 40 Contrabands, who have on the outskirts of my Brigade, living by stealing & plundering —— I have captured & sent them to Washington. . . . I sat down at 7 to write a Letter . . . & had just closed it when

---

[14] Both Marcy and Van Vliet had been serving under commissions as Brigadier Generals, which expired on July 17, 1862. Marcy was subsequently confirmed but Van Vliet did not regain his star until March of 1865. Gustavus Adolphus Scroggs, a Brigadier General of New York Militia, was a Buffalo political figure. He was subsequently appointed a Brigadier General and assigned to New Orleans to organize a regiment of Negro troops for service in Texas. Henry L. Burnett, a Judge Advocate, was finally confirmed in March of 1865.

summoned to meet Gen. King, on important business. It was
to make a list of 4 out of 8 names, in Frederic[k]sburg, to
arrest as Hostages—— I took out [Thomas B.] Barton,
[Charles C.] Welford, [Thomas F.] Knox & [Beverly T.]
Gill—— They will be arrested tonight & sent to Washington
by the early train, tomorrow.

Wednesday, 12 o'clock M.[,] *23' July*—— Camp Rufus
  King, Stafford Co. Va.

. . . Barton & Co. were sent off this morning, greatly to the
disgust of Barton.

10½ o'clock P.M.

. . . I was called over to Gen. King's quite late—say 8 o'clock,
to organize an expedition for tomorrow—— King, Gibbon &
myself made it up—— [Col. Judson] Kilpatrick returned
from his raid upon Hanover Junction & tells enormous stories
—— My belief is they stole more horses than they captured.
. . .

Thursday, 9½ o'clock P. M. 24' July, 1862—— Camp
  Rufus King——

. . . Went to Gibbon's & looked over the Expedition with him.
. . . Came home & was busy until about 4 o'clock, when I followed the Expedition up to near [George] Guest's house,
Plank Road—— It is intended to go 7 or 8 miles tonight &
tomorrow about 20—— We re-enforce tomorrow. . . .

Friday Night, (Tattoo) 25' July '62—— Camp Rufus
   King—— Stafford Co.

. . . After dinner I was sent for by Gen. King—— Pope has
overhauled King about affairs at Frederic[k]sburg & King has
answered him that communications with the enemy cannot
be prevented without sending a Brigade over, & *that* is in
violation of his orders—— He has asked leave to send over
such command & I am asked if I will go, if such order be
given—— I have replied that I will think of it & that if I can
have full powers to act, I would do so. I drove over to take a
look at the points where I thought of placing the different
Regts. . . . I . . . called at the Provost Marshal's Office. . . . His
conduct has been very strange, undoubtedly & the probability
is, that he has been completely under ' Secesh ' influences——
Elated at the consequence he possessed as the Provost Marshal
of Frederic[k]sburg, he took airs upon himself & accepted the
hospitalities of the Citizens & was hand & glove with them——
. . . The town is full of Brothels & Prostitutes & drinking
saloons & all sorts of vile institutions, all [of] which he understood perfectly well. . . .

Saturday Night, Tattoo, 26' July—— Camp Rufus King,
   Stafford Co. Va.

. . . Gen. King sent for me & I rode down in the Ambulance
—— He had recd. orders for me to send over, (or somebody)
2 Regts. . . . I accordingly drove over to select for two Regts.
camping grounds—— . . . After dinner I sent out the Officers
of the various Regts. to look for themselves & lay out their
camps. . . .

Sunday Night (10 o'clock)[,] Camp Rufus King, 27' July '62.

This has been a busy day—— . . . I went over the River & arranged with the Surgeons for Hospital Sites—— Came back & had an interview with the Mayor and Jack Marie [Marye], in regard to matters within the City & what I wanted done by them, etc. . . .

Monday, 9 o'clock, P. M.[,] Tattoo, At the Old Farmer's Bank[,] Frederic[k]sburg——

This is the 28' day of July, just about two months since I left here, to a day—— And now I am back, in the same old room, with the same cares & anxieties as before—— Less force & more duty required of me—— . . . A Mrs. Duvall, near Spotsylvania, came in this evening not to re-capture 12 negroes, but to allow her property to be returned to her, in the shape of Cart & oxen etc. stolen from her, last night——

Tuesday Night, 10 o'clock, 29' July—— At the old Farmer's Bank[,] Fresburg——

. . . I have given passes without number, rejected still more, organized the Guards & store houses & Bridge Companies & patrols etc. . . . The Cordon around town has been so very close that nobody can get in or out—— . . . I believe there has been a Mail smuggled out of town this evening, by Miss Roy Mason. Had I known it earlier I should have overhauled her—— . . .

Wednesday Night, 10 o'clock, 30' July, '62. Farmer's
　　Bank, Frederic[k]sburg——

. . . I have done up a deal of business today—— . . . The loose
population is scattering in all directions—— A great many have
cleared the course & gone to Washington & elsewhere—— . . .
Have captured a quantity of Whiskey—some 15 BBls. and
also a quantity of Wines & Liquors in boxes & cases—— . . . I
had Tattoo beaten here, at 9 this evening, by the Drum Corps
of the 23' & through the streets of town, followed by a patrol,
with directions to take up either Officer or man found out, after
that time—— . . .

Thursday Night, 31' July, 1862—— Farmer's Bank,
　　Frederic[k]sburg, Va.——

. . . I feel very much troubled indeed, today, about several
things—— *One,* is very galling! The "Chief of Police" as he
styles himself, has been here, from Washington, Since Yesterday. He has been making himself generally busy about our
affairs & has telegraphed to Washington that all things are
in very bad condition here—— Nobody here is doing his
duty——

Friday Night, 1' August, '62, Tattoo——— Farmer's Bank,
　　Frederic[k]sburg.

. . . Having received a Telegram from Gen. McDowell to
Gen. King, to the effect that Richmond is reported from the
James River & from Sigel, as being evacuated & desiring me
to send Scouts & Scouting parties to the front to ascertain the
exact state of affairs—— . . . Have established negro

quarters where fugitives can remain a day until sent forward to Washington by Rail. . . . I have given the "detectives" & "Chief of Police," a lesson in military usage today.

Saturday Night[,] *2' August, 1862—— Tattoo——*

Farmer's Bank, Frederic[k]sburg——
. . . I have several topics of interest for the day—— One of them is the hegira of Negroes—— Today I have sent off the slaves of Flipper [Flippo] & Gravitt [Gravatt]—some 50 or more—— They came over here in the family coach, loaded as never before, even in Old Virginia—— . . .

Sunday Night, 3' August, 1862 (Tattoo)[.] Still at
     Headquarters, Bank——

This has been a day of hard work, notwithstanding that it is the Sabbath. . . . The ferry Boat that went down the River, brought up a great many Small boats—— She brought up a prisoner named Gouldman who was taken with articles crossing the River below Port Royal. . . .

Monday Night[,] *4' August—— 9'30"*[.] Head Quarters,
     Farmer's Bank——

. . . I have had a large number of these calls today from ladies—calls of the most objectionable character—or rather, for the most objectionable objects—— There were quite a number of prostitutes arrested & to be sent off in the eleven o'clock run, but Burnside's Advance of 6000 men arrived at Acquia & the Cars were sent for—— So I could not send them on—— . . . It is believed, now, that we shall join Gen. Pope the latter part of the week & Burnside occupy this entire line——I do not want to serve under Gen. Pope—— I have not a particle of confidence in him.

Tuesday Night[,] *5' August, 1862*—— Head Quarters, Farmer's Bank, Frederic[k]sburg[.]

A repetition of yesterday—— Intensely hot—Melting—— My reputation in Frederic[k]sburg is lost, completely, I expect, as I have caused a number of persons to be searched, & it has raised a great row—— Well! It was necessary. . . . We shall probably move from here, Gen. Pope says, about the last of this week, or first of next—— We will, probably, take the Plank Road to Orange Court House, & thence to Culpepper [Culpeper] to join McDowell.

Wednesday Night, 6' July—August, I mean—— Head Quarters, Farmer's Bank——

This has been a busy day. . . . I am prepared for a move. I believe & Gen. King tells me, that as soon as the troops return from the front we shall all be ordered to join Gen. McDowell—— . . .

Thursday Night[,] *7' July* [*August*], *'62.* Head Quarters, Farmer's Bank[.]

. . . The business of closing up & preparing the Office for turning over to a Successor, has occupied me most of the day——

. . . Gens. Burnside, [John G.] Park[e], [Jesse L.] Reno & King were over, about 11 o'clock, to see me and the result was, a decision to send over Gen. [Isaac I.] Stevens to relieve me—— . . . [Gen.] Stevens came over, dined here, looked over all matters & ordered over certain Regts. He is staying here with me, until tomorrow, when I turn over the Command to him. After 5½ o'clock I went over the Wire Bridge, on Horseback to Gen. King's & as I was coming off Burnside called me to his Tent, where I remained some time. . . .[15]

Saturday, August 9' 1862—— Head Quarters, Downman House, Va.

Yesterday was a very busy day. . . . I recd. the good people who came to call upon me. . . . then rode with Stevens in a Waggon for 2 hours, to look for a place to put his Troops etc. as well as to examine the lines of defence etc. etc. Then we went over to see Burnside & King—— I then went back & arranged an Expedition for Col. Pratt to go down the River to Taylor's & Dickinson's, capture them & their animals & bring them in—— . . . This morning I was up early and prepared for work . . . Messrs. [John L.] Stansberry [Stansbury] & Hayes have been here to see me & talk about the operation of Pope's Order—— Gen. Burnside holds about the same views upon the treatment of these people that I do—— Gen. Stevens is pursuing my course, thus far, precisely—— I am glad he concludes to do so.

---

[15] Burnside had brought the Ninth Army Corps to the Rappahannock line with a view to shielding the movement of McClellan's forces to the Northern Virginia line. Stevens commanded the 1st Division and Reno the 2nd Division of Burnside's command. Parke was to hold Falmouth. Rufus King remained in command of McDowell's 1st Division under the Army command of Pope.

——*5 O'clock P. M.*

Quite a busy 3 hours—— Recd. a note from Gen. King to see him, in all haste. Went down & found a telegram from Pope, calling us all forward, [Gen. T. J.] Jackson having crossed the Rapidan towards Culpepper. I move up on this side & cross at Ely's Ford, go out 4 or 5 miles & wait for [John P.] Hatch & [John] Gibbon. I am to be followed by [Abner] Doubleday, & joined by Gen. [Rufus] King.

(Memoranda kept in my pocket Book)

On *Saturday night* I marched, with my Guard, to Aldrich's— 8 miles on the Plank Road & slept in a house—or *staid* there, all night—— . . . Monday—no, *Sunday* morning, at 3 o'clock, Reveille sounded & at 5 the order was given to March—— We took the road to Chancellorsville & thence to Ely's Ford, on the Rapidan—— It is a fine ford & we crossed without difficulty—— From there we went on about 4 or 5 miles, to the junction of this road with that from Falmouth, over which Hatch & Gibbon were to come & at 10'30" A. M. halted at the house of a man named Humphreys —a Baptist preacher then absent at a funeral—— After waiting a long while, sending messages both ways, to Doubleday in my rear, & Hatch on my right, an Officer of McDowell's Staff, Capt. Merritt, with a strong Cavalry escort arrived, to hurry up Gen. King, saying that Jackson had taken a strong position on Slaughter's Mountain & was cutting Banks to pieces—that Augur was severely wounded [Gen. John S.]

---

[16] Brig. Gens. John P. Hatch, Abner Doubleday, and John Gibbon commanded the 1st, 2nd, and 4th brigades in King's Division. Patrick's was the 3rd brigade. Augur commanded the 2nd Division of Bank's 2nd Corps of Pope's Army of Virginia and Geary and Prince commanded the 1st and 2nd brigades of Augur's Division.

Geary the Same, & Donnelly also—and Gen. [Henry] Prince taken prisoner.[16] Under the circumstances I concluded to run the risk of being cut up myself & gave orders to move forward at 6 o'clock—— Before that hour, however, I recd. Orders from Gen. King, saying that he would be up by 8 or 9 o'clock with 2 Brigades & Harris Cavalry, & that we would all move forward together—— I lay in expectation of his arrival, but did not see anything of him, or any portion of his command until early *Monday Morning*[,] *11' August* when the Column made its appearance about 7 o'clock, followed by King—— It was about 8 o'clock when I followed Hatch. . . . We halted about 4 o'clock at Stephensburg [Stevensburg], got supper & came on, again at 6'30" or 7 o'clock. We marched until within about 1½ or 2 miles of the battle field, leaving the road a little & turning into a field about 11'30"[.] It was 12 when I lay down upon the ground to get some sleep, expecting to go into the fight next morning—— . . . Got some Coffee & sent our Train to Culpepper[17] Court House, to remain there & await the issue of the action expected to take place.

Tuesday Morning, 12' August——

About 9 o'clock came notice that the enemy had fallen back & that we would remain in position—— I immediately went to an Old House, to avoid a Thunder Storm & remained there during the day, doing nothing but trying to sleep[.] . . . All sorts of Statements were afloat during the day with reference to the fight—— Gen. Augur has gone to Washington, under charge of Mrs. Ricketts—— His wound may not prove fatal—— . . .

---

[17] Patrick's error in spelling Culpeper with an extra "p" is a common one. In the hope of avoiding unnecessary intrusions, it has not been corrected by the editor.

Wednesday Morning 13' August.

. . . Towards night [Benj.] Welch, of Pope's Staff, came down
here & staid some time—— . . . McDowell, King & all
others who command Troops have just the same difficulty
about this order of Pope's which gives a general license to
pillage, rob & plunder—— It has completely demoralized my
Brigade—— On their way here the 21' robbed, all the way—
stole Horses under Col. Rogers['] order—in fact every body
robs & plunders by Order—— I am so utterly disgusted that
I feel like resigning & letting the whole thing go—— I am
afraid of God's Justice, for our Rulers & Commanders deserve
his wrath & curse—— There has never been such a state of
things before, in any command—— I have never seen anything like it——

Chapter IV

The Patrick Brigade under Fire

AUGUST 14, 1862, THROUGH OCTOBER 6, 1862

BY EARLY AUGUST OF 1862 Stonewall Jackson had become something of a Nemesis to the Federals. Patrick and his friends had been too late at Strasburg when Jackson escaped up the Valley and they had been too late again for the battle around Cedar Mountain (or Slaughter Mountain). They would not be too late for Jackson's next appearance in the holocaust of Second Manassas. Patrick's Brigade, which gave a good account of itself in the fighting on Pope's left flank against Jackson and then against Longstreet, did even better against the Confederate rearguard at South Mountain. It was in the van of McClellan's attempt to force the pass and get at Lee's army before it could reunite. The pass was forced but Lee was able to retreat to a defensive position along Antietam Creek. Patrick's Brigade was again in the thick of the fight, this time on the right where the musket fire on the morning of September 17 harvested men, as well as corn, to produce the bloodiest day in American history.

In the middle south the Confederacy made a major effort to regain control of Kentucky when Braxton Bragg and E. Kirby Smith set out from Chattanooga and Knoxville in a drive for the Ohio River at Louisville and Cincinnati. In the Mississippi Valley Confederate efforts to halt the Federal push down the River resulted in the battles of Iuka and Corinth in Northern Mississippi. At Iuka on September 19 and 20, Federal forces under William S. Rosecrans repulsed Sterling Price's Confederates. At Corinth on October 3 and 4 Rosecrans held off a second Confederate effort.

Thursday Night, 14' August, Camp near Culpepper, Va.

. . . [Gen. Rufus] King's Division took the field to be reviewed
by [Gen. John] Pope,[1] nominally at 9, really at 10'30". . . .
We massed our Battallions, [sic] then flanked to move out——
The ground was very inconvenient & much too small—— We
passed around in quick time & then got out of the way as
[best] we could with our Battalions, after which we called our
Field Officers to the front & presented them to Gen. Pope. . . .
Many of the Officers of our Brigade have been up there [the
Cedar Mountain battleground] today—— It was a bloody
battle, fought without object & in its results disastrous to us,
our loss being very large & the condition of the Armistice for
burying the dead being that no interference should be offered
to the Rebels securing *all* the Arms lying on the battle field——
In this way they obtained from us over 1000 stand of
Arms—— Yet the lying reporters and interested parties call it
'Our Victory.' . . .

Friday Night, 15' August, Camp near Culpepper Court
    House Va.

. . . After Breakfast I was engaged in business until 8'30"
then got into an Ambulance with Beckwith & rode to Head
Quarters to see [Gen. Irvin] McDowell before issuing Brigade
Orders. Pope kept me a half hour & seemed glad to have a
talk with me. I broached the subject of my visit & he put in
my hand an *Order* published last night, not yet issued,
of the most stringent character—— It is stronger even than
McDowell's—— With this in my hand I can fight any
thing—— . . .

---

[1]   Brig. Gen. Rufus King's Division had become 1st Division, Third
Corps, in Pope's Army of Virginia.

Saturday, 3 o'clock P.M. Side of Slaughter's Mountain, Culpepper Co. [,] Va.

. . . At 8¼ o'clock the Regts. were in line & I read to them Gen. Pope's order, then read my own Order of this date——— It is a sweeping Order, but I mean to have it obeyed——— The Officers & men were taken aback, but they could say nothing——— We then began the March & it was but little after 9 when I reached Gen. [Rufus] King's Head Quarters, where I learned that instead of leading as I had been told on Thursday, I would march as the 3' Brigade——— So I had to halt & wait until the other Brigades came up & passed me——— . . . I have encamped my Brigade by Regts. & taken a House close by, as it is offered me for the sake of protection[.] Gen. King has gone higher up the Mountain, to Parson Slaughter's House———

Sunday Night, 17' Augt. '62. Camp on Slaughter's Mountain, [ ] miles from Culpepper.

After attending to my Camp duties last night, or afternoon, I mounted my horse & rode up the valley to the North of the Mountain, then up to Slaughter's House, now deserted & every thing about it broken up by the Marauders & pillagers of our Troops——— . . . I slept pretty well & got up in pretty good time this morning——— Breakfasted & started off before very long, with my Aids. . . . [Gen. Zealous B.] Tower[2] joined us & we went to the top of the mountain from which we had a glorious view in all directions except the North——— The enemy's pickets (or a reconnoitering party) were on a hill, upon the opposite side of the River, 5 miles away, while two Corps, supposed to be those of [Gen. Jesse L.] Reno & [Gen. Isaac I.]

[2] Gen. Tower commanded the 2nd Brigade of Rickett's 2nd Division of McDowell's Third Corps.

Stevens were on the left about an equal distance—— we were joined by Generals [Robert C.] Schenck, [Adolph] Von Stein-wihr [Steinwehr], [Robert H.] Milroy & [Abram] Duryea, also on the lookout—— While there a Messenger came in to say that Gen. [Samuel S.] Carroll, while out with the Pickets near the River had been shot through the breast—probably mortally wounded.[3]

Monday, 2'30" P.M. [,] *18' Augt, '62*—— Camp on
Slaughter's Mountain [,] Va.

. . . Got up at about 6 o'clock & after the usual duties & business, took a run off on the left. . . . I found [Gen. George L.] Hartsuff,[4] quite sick, Tower & Ricketts encamped together & Ricketts in a fury almost; at a Letter from McDowell, censuring him for the manner of his movement last night, very unjustly—— He came with me, on his way to see McDowell. . . . We met Gen. Pope & his Cortege, returning from [Gen. Jesse L.] Reno's—— He halted me & told me I had better ride back with him to my Brigade, as we were on the eve of a movement—— I did join him & learned the idea—— It is this—— So soon as the movements of McClellan from Richmond was known, the entire Richmond Army left to join [Gen. Thomas J.] Jackson, who now has 150,000 men within 6 miles of us & we must skedaddle—— . . . An order came at 5 p.m. to start the Teams all off & [Capt.] Springsteed moves on—— All our wheels go on & of course this Book goes on with the rest of the Baggage[.]

---

[3] Generals Reno and Stevens commanded the two Divisions of Burnside's Ninth Army Corps. Schenck and Von Steinwehr commanded the 1st and 2nd Divisions of Franz Sigel's First Army Corps, while Milroy had an independent Brigade in the same Corps. Duryea commanded the 1st Brigade of Rickett's Division. Gen. Carroll, who commanded a Brigade in Rickett's Division, was not mortally wounded.

[4] Gen. Hartsuff commanded the 3rd Brigade in Rickett's Division.

Wednesday Morning, Augt. 20' [.] Ford of the Rappahannock, Fauquier Co. [,] Va.

After the Teams were off & we had waited the entire day for
Orders, notice came a *little before dark,* that the Command
(Division) would move at *one* o'clock, following Ricketts
Division—— So we could do nothing but lie down and wait
till *one.* Gen. Ricketts *began* to pass in proper time, but the
road was blocked at the forks by [Gen. Franz] Sigel's train (as
all Trains were ordered to precede the Troops) & we waited &
waited & waited. . . . until daylight, and 10 o'clock A.M. arrived
before we were fairly on the March—and *Such* a March!
Halting & moving—moving & halting, without system. To
march 16 miles we were in *motion all* day. . . .

Sunday [,] *3 o'clock* P.M., *24* ['] *Augt. '62.* Sulphur
Springs Road [,] 1 mile from Warrenton [.]

To resume my pen—I might say, that on *Tuesday Night,* by
the help of [Lt.] D. [avid] O. DeWolf, I got over the [Rappa-
hannock] River & found a couple of Tents up, at 9 P.M.—
that I went into one & the Staff into the other & had just fallen
asleep when Gen. King & Staff came up—without where to
lay their heads—— So we took them in & on *Wednesday* I
had a sick day—scarcely able to be out of bed, but did bring
up a little writing & took Medicine—a great deal of opium
to check the violent pain in my bowels—— . . . About 4
o'clock I got permission to establish my Camp about a mile
from my former position—— . . . On *Thursday Morning* I
rose late, got some Breakfast, prepared for action & sat down
to write. . . . The Artillery commenced playing about 10
o'clock apparently at the Ford in our front—— I put the
men under Arms & waited Orders—— After [Gen. Irvin]
McDowell had been gone but a few moments, he sent me

word to draw out my Brigade & move forward—— I did so—— Battery was just coming up & reported to me—so we put it in position & I put 3 Regts. behind it, & threw out the 21' to Skirmish on my right—— [Gen. John] Gibbon's Brigade was ordered out to support me but did nothing until almost night, when [Col. Edgar] O'Connor got his Regt. down to the River as Skirmishers but only after mine & the Sharpshooters had led the way—— The Rebels appeared to have a Battery, divided into Sections & 2 small Brigades or about 5 or 6 Regts. of Infy—with a Regt. of Cavalry—— The Cavalry had crossed the ford & our Object was to drive them back & secure the crossing—— For this we worked— much of the time very badly, for the want of any head, or System—— McDowell, Pope & King took a hand in & fizzled—— About 5 o'clock the matter was turned over to me & we put forward our Batteries, supported by Strong columns & preceded by Skirmishers—— We drove them across the River, but their Sharp Shooters and Battery at the Ford being masked & protected, we could not drive them out as it was becoming dark & we were not in a position that could safely be held by Artillery, over night—— Indeed we were obliged to get out as [best] we could, under a shower of shells so well thrown that the wonder is we were not destroyed—— In the course of the day the Battery & Skirmishers drove the enemy from their positions 5 times but we only took 2 or 3 prisoners, as those on this Side were Cavalry & escaped by the fords—— . . . We went back to our first position, planted our guns & posted our men behind them, except the 20' which I left to guard the front & the crossing. It was very dark & the Men & Animals had nothing to eat—the shelling had driven away all & every thing from our old camp to a place two miles away & the Supply train had preceded it, to Catlett's the night before—— I sent for something to eat, to be brought out in the Ambulance, which I could sleep in—— . . . At one & half came an Orderly directing me to withdraw my Command

before Sunrise—no word as to who was to relieve me—or
that any body would do so—— When the time came for the
movement I knew that [Gen. John P.] Hatch⁵ was to take my
place & went over to see him—— His Regts. had not yet
turned out—— I sent back word to delay the movement until
they should get up but it was too late—— My men were on
the move—— I halted them as soon as I could reach the
ground & held the ground until Hatch could relieve me——
All day Friday was spent in cannonading all along the line—
[Gen. Nathaniel P.] Banks, [Gen. Franz] Sigel & ourselves,
with [Gen. Jesse L.] Reno below—— Hatch did not succeed
in driving the enemy from the fords, however, though preventing his crossing. . . . We were ordered to be ready to move
at a moment's warning, but it was after 9 o'clock before we
were ordered on the Warrenton Road—— . . . While at Head
Quarters for instructions, Gen. [Rufus] King had a [epileptic]
fit (to which he is subject) & the command devolved on
Hatch—— The day was excessively hot, the men straggled—
the orders were conflicting & everything went wrong. Sigel got
on the wrong road & cut our line, delaying us for 2 hours——
Our March, however, continued & we reached Warrenton just
at dark. . . . This Morning (*Sunday*) . . . I was overtaken by
Bouvier, with an Order from McDowell, not to go into Camp,
but to March on the Sulphur Springs road, at once—— I
obeyed & got about a mile out of town when McDowell,
himself, directed me to halt & receive Subsistence, which the
men were entirely destitute of, having made their supper &
breakfast out of the porkers & corn & potatoes in the fields &
gardens—— Their Haversacks had nothing in them at all.
That *halt* has continued until now & I propose to have the
men prepare for the night, as it is now almost 6 o'clock. . . .
McClellan's Army is coming up on the Rappahannock, from
Frederic[k]sburg to Barnett's Ford—— Heintzelman's [Third]

---

⁵ Gen. Hatch now commanded the 1st Brigade in King's Division.

Corps [Army of Virginia] is arriving at Catlett's today,
[Capt. Charles] McClure having been down there for
Rations—— [Gen. John] Pope has made a disgraceful, shame-
ful retreat, from Cedar Mountain—wanting only an attack
upon our rear, on Tuesday, to have made it a perfect rout——
As it was the Teamsters Stampeded—— A good thing
occurred on Friday night—— [Gen. J. E. B.] Stuart's Cavalry
made a dash on the Train, at Catlett's. Captured Pope's
Quarter Master, 3 or 4 of his private waggons & 274 prisoners[6]

Sunday Night [,] *7 o'clock, 24' August*—— Camp 1 Mile
    west & South of Warrenton [.]

This morning it is said that there was a big darky dressed up
in Pope's captured clothes & paraded through the streets——
He seems to be universally detested by the Citizens & our
Troops are loud in their expressions of disgust. [Gen. Irvin]
McDowell is equally despised—not despised—but disliked by
all—— His policy towards Citizens humane & just, towards
troops very faulty—— [Gen. Ambrose E.] Burnside seems, as
I learn, likely to have a large force under his command——
[Gen. George B.] McClellan is no longer heard of & it is said
will be superseded. All the line of the Rappahannock will be
the scene of operations & this becomes the battle ground, for
some time yet to come—— I am so thoroughly disgusted with
the management of *this* Corps, that I am anxious to leave
it—— I feel that disgrace *here* is inevitable. Orders are
conflicting—— If I obey, I ought to be punished, If I *dis-
obey*, I *may* be. This is the State of things—No Order—No
system—— All is confusion. . . .

---

[6] The redoubtable Stuart did more than that. He captured Pope's
dispatch book and a file of incoming letters. And, having lost his own
cloak and plumed hat to some Federal Cavalry on Aug. 18, he was
gratified to find among the booty of his raid Gen. Pope's cloak, dress
uniform coat and full dress hat—plume and all!

Monday Morning [,] *12 o'clock, 25' August, '62* [.]
Same Camp, near Warrenton———

Last night was cool——— . . . I sent an Officer, for Orders, to
Head Quarters, but did not get any until near 10 o'clock.
Then, I was ordered to remain in position, ready to move at
short notice——— . . .

Monday, 25' August,

After dinner I mounted & rode into town to see Gen. [Rufus]
King who was quartering at the Hotel & get instructions———
I could get none from him & left, but was recalled by
McDowell, who said he wanted to see me & to have me go
with him to the top of the hill (Watery Mountain)——— I
waited for & with his Magnificence until disgusted, then rode
with him to the top of the Signal Mountain from which the
whole country, for a vast distance, was spread out, in full
view. There we staid & staid & staid for his Magnificence to
expatiate, until near dark after which we descended the
Mountain by a different route——— . . .

Tuesday, 26' August, ['] *62*———

At about 3 o'clock I was aroused by a Staff Officer directing
me to . . . (move to) Sulphur Springs——— About an hour
before McClure had arrived, bringing provisions, which had
to be issued before moving & it was 6 o'clock before we were
finally in the road, followed up by the whole Division——— . . .
On arriving at the Springs I found the Hotel had been burned
the day before, (as we supposed on the Hill) & passing it I
went down, with Staff & Orderlies to see about crossing———
Riding about there, very carelessly, supposing Ricketts ahead,
I did not notice the rebel Pickets, until the Staff called out, 3
or 4 times, "Gray Coats"——— Then we put spurs to our

horses & cleared, with a volley of balls whistling by us from 20 or 30 pieces—— The Officer had ordered me to surrender, before firing—— . . . Fire was soon opened on us by their Batteries & we put our own in position—— Several times certainly, we compelled them to change the position of their Batteries & putting two of our Regts. on the left, & the 21' in front, we kept up sharpshooting thro' the day—— We killed & wounded a great many of their skirmishers—— Towards night a white flag came in & while it was at the crossing, their Skirmishers took the opportunity to withdraw & to carry off their wounded & dead—— That done, they commenced firing, even in sight of the flag—— I went down & ordered it to clear out—— The ostensible object of this flag was to send in a woman in man's dress, taken prisoner & belonging to Sigel's command—— She came in—— . . .

Wednesday Morning [,] *27' August,* Still at Sulphur Springs——

Our Troops did not get into any engagement, the enemy having retired during the night, as we learned from a prisoner, up to Waterloo—— . . . At 3 o'clock P.M. the Division was ordered to move to Warrenton & on arriving there found everything in the utmost confusion & our Teams, with supplies & every thing else, ordered out of the road—— We kept on for Gainesville, altho' I told [Gen.] McDowell that our men were out of provisions—— He said we had "got to have pinched bellies & a Hell of a fight before we could eat or rest"—— We went on & encamped about 10 o'clock some 5 or 6 miles from Warrenton—— . . .

Thursday Morning [,] *28' August*

(Marched at Sunrise for Gainesville . . . & found the Army halted—— Its advance had been shelled at the point where

the Manassas & Centreville roads came together—— We
halted there until about 3 o'clock & moved on about a mile—
where we again halted & a reconnaissance made by McDowell
[in pencil : (?)] who fired a few shots to which no reply was
made & he rode on. The Command attempted to follow &
had passed two Brigades when a Battery opened on my Line
& shelled it, but by putting the men completely under cover
we lost none—— The Teams, however, of the whole command were thrown into the greatest confusion & smash up——
The Brigade under Gibbon, however, under whose order I
know not [in pencil : (?)],[7] sailed into the wood & made [a]
fight—— They were met by a large force & a terrible musketry
fight ensued. Darkness came on & only by the sheets of flame
could we know the position—— I immediately threw out the
35' & 23' Regts., but the 20' *had fled* & I could not get their
whereabouts for more than 2 hours. After some 2½ or 3 hours
all firing ceased & I withdrew my skirmishers—at the same
time sending in the 21' & 23' to the battle ground to guard
it & secure the wounded, where they remained all night——
. . .

Friday Morning [,] *29' August*——

At about 3 o'clock we marched, in silence, on the Manassas
Road, the 21' & 23' having been recalled—— We had a fine
March. . . . We reached Manassas early in the morning &
prepared for such rest as we might get—— Our object was to
get Subsistence, also; but the enemy had come in & broke up
& burned every thing—— It was some time before we got
supplies, but we succeeded after some delays—— At about
12 M. [in pencil, changed to 10 A.M.] [Gen. Fitz John] Porter's[8]

---

[7] Gen. Patrick went back over his Diary in 1866 at the request of
Fitz John Porter. These penciled questions marks and inserts probably
date from that review. They appear to be in Patrick's hand.

[8] Gen. Porter commanded the Fifth Corps of the Army of the Potomac.
It was just arriving from the Peninsula via Aquia Creek.

Corps having passed on towards our lines of yesterday, we
were ordered to follow him & did so, for 3 or 4 miles (or about
¼ or ⅛ mile beyond Milford road [)]—when we were met by
McDowell, turned about & ordered on a shorter road to the
scene of yesterday's operations (Groveton) where it was said
that Sigel was engaged with the enemy—— On arriving near
the field (Sud. [ley] Spring[s] Road) we were halted & by
direction of Gen. McDowell took position, which was afterwards changed by [in pencil : (by him & sent by)] direction
of Gen. Hatch. I was [in pencil : (then)] ordered to support
the Penn. Reserves, on the left, ([Gen. John F.] Reynolds)—
I did so—— I was then ordered to march across to the Right
& support Sigel, by Gen. Pope—— Got two thirds of the way
across & was met by a Staff Officer of (Gen. Patrick's Friend)
[Irvin] McDowell, directing me to return, instantly to my
former position—— I returned but had not been able to get
the last Regt. in position before I was ordered to join the
Division. . . . I obeyed the order & went to the top of the Hill,
by the House, [in pencil : (Dogan's)] where the action had
been most severe an hour or two before—— . . . Darkness was
again coming on & when I learned that Hatch's [1st] Brigade
was giving way, I went forward, in two lines to sustain
them—— We got up to the Corn field & off to the right——
The 35' charged the South Carolina (23 ?) & drove them off.
After the darkness was such that we could not distinguish
friend from foe—I changed & withdrew my lines to the low
ground, the left resting on the road—— While at this, a
Rebel Column filed into the Road & challenged me, ordering
me to halt—supposing from their position, that they were
friends I answered, at the 2' Challenge, "Patrick's Brigade,
King's Division," ["] Surrender or we fire"—It was
Ricketts Rebel Brigade [in pencil : (John B. Hood's Texas
Troops)]⁹—[Lt. John V.] Bouvier was with me—— I think,

---

⁹ Gen. John B. Hood commanded a Brigade in Evans's Division of
Longstreet's Command.

too, that my Orderly, Honesty, must have been near me——
We turned & struck spurs to our horses—— Instantly a shower
of bullets whizzed by us—— Poor Bouvier was shot & fell, his
horse at the same time being killed under him—— Perhaps
Honesty was killed too, as the Harris Cavalry report finding
him dead with 7 Balls in him but I still hope that he is a
prisoner——I rode rapidly through the Orchard, warned the
Batteries of their danger & then rode down the Road, to see
what supporters were in my rear—— Knowing that my own
men were safe, lying *perdu* in the darkness. I found pickets in
the road, of Cavalry belonging to Sigel, but could get no one
to ride up the road to reconnoitre—— I then rode over to
Gen. [Julius H.] Stahel[10] for some Cavalry & finally, to Col.
McLane [McLean],[11] Comdg. Brigade on my right & rode with
me to my own Camp, where arrangements were made in
regard to Picketing for the night—— In the mean time
Bouvier had been brought in by the 35' & though supposed
to be mortally wounded, was cared for by the Surgeons &
carried on a Stretcher to my Head Quarters—— I remained
at the Van Pelt House [at bottom of page: in Patrick's hand
(John Dogan's place—so Mr. Van Pelt told me 25' June '63)]
until day began to dawn, when I ordered the Batteries & their
supports to be withdrawn to cover, a few rods, supposing the
enemy's force *might* still be opposite, on the other side of the
road—— Fortunately they had withdrawn & nothing was
visible in our front, save pickets & stragglers of the enemy. I
rode over to Gen. McDowell's & reported, by whom I was
directed to send out Skirmishers to the front & examining the
fields & woods on both sides the road—— On arriving at the
Dogan House,[12] however, I discovered a column of the Rebel

[10] Gen. Stahel commanded the 1st Brigade of Schenck's Division.

[11] Patrick is referring to Col. N. C. McLean of the 75th Ohio, who
commanded a Brigade of Ohio troops in Schenck's Division and fought
beside Stahel and Patrick.

[12] The Dogan House stood on a small rise just to the North of the
Telegraph Road about midway between Groveton and the Manassas-
Sudley Spring Road,

Troops in the Warrenton Road, moving to the rear & large
numbers straggling in the fields to the right of the column &
moving to the rear——— Sending a few shells into the column
its movements were hastened & finally hidden by the intervening hills——— The skirmishers on the left of the road had
not reached the wood, however, before the ground was occupied by the Penn. Re.[serves] & they were withdrawn———
This was about 7 o'clock A.M. & about the same time I was
relieved from duty at the Dogan House by Gen. [Fitz John]
Porter's [Fifth] Corps & ordered by Gen. McDowell to take
post on the right of Sigel——— I did so, placing my Brigade in
2 lines——— I remained in that position until about 1 o'clock,
when I was instructed by Gen. Hatch to join the Division,
near the Hill I had left at 8 o'clock prepared to advance on the
Warrenton Road, supporting Porter. This was done & the
Brigade rejoining the Division, was ordered to support Hatch's
own Brigade, commanded by [Col. Timothy] Sullivan. Our
first position was in the low grounds & on the swell, in front
of the Dogan House & on both sides of the road——— From
that position we were ordered to the right, the Brigade forming
two lines, about 50 paces apart & stretching over to the right,
as far as the recess in the wood——— At the fence, by the
wood, the 1' Line halted a few minutes, when the order was
given for both lines to advance preserving an interval of 150
paces——— This was about 2 o'clock P.M. [in pencil: (after 2
perhaps)]. From the moment of entering the wood a heavy
fire from the front was poured in & much confusion prevailed
from contradictory orders as to the designation of lines. . . .
The 21' & 35' Regts. . . . moved steadily forward, the left
being impeded some 5 minutes by a retiring Regt. or Brigade,
until the whole had reached the farther edge of the wood, the
left (35') having in its front a strong body of the enemy in a
Cornfield & behind a R.R. Bank with a Battery pouring shell,
Grape and canister upon it with great fury, while the right
(21'), in its advance, on passing the first line was thrown into

temporary confusion by the rising up of that line, but thro' the exertions of the Officers order was restored & the Regt. pushed forward under the direction of Gen. Hatch, crossed the fence into the open field beyond the woods, where it sustained a most galling crossfire from the enemy, which was returned & the Regt. moved forward to the ditch, about midway between the fence & the R. R. embankment, used by the enemy as a parapet—— From behind this embankment a continuous discharge of Musketry was kept up, which it was impossible to return as the enemy was perfectly protected—— Here the loss of the first line was very heavy & the 2' having been ordered to extend still further to the right to prevent the enemy's left from turning Gen. Hatch's right, pressed forward towards the R. R. embankment—— From this cover a fire was poured into the 20' Regt. which cut it in two, the Col. [Geo. W. Pratt] was carried from the field [mortally wounded] & this Regt. . . . attempt [ed] to advance, fell back & formed on the left of the 19' Indiana, with which it again advanced only to fall back as before—— During this time the 23' Regt. . . . went forward to the edge of the wood and there remained, until ordered to withdraw—— From the time we entered the wood a shower of shot & shell were falling around us, but both Officers & men, so far as I could see, & I was at different times & repeatedly along the lines, behaved with coolness & courage—— Gen. Hatch having been wounded, left the field, which I did not know until some time after—— Seeing our lines on the right & left falling back, I rode to a point where I could see that the movement was general & then sent an Aid to inquire of Gen. [Abner] Doubleday[13] by whose order the Troops were falling back & on learning that it was by order of Gen. [Fitz John] Porter, I immediately ordered my own Troops to form in the edge of the wood, under the fire both of the enemy's & one of our own Batteries which had been

---

[13] Brig. Gen. Doubleday succeeded to command of the Division when Gen. Hatch was wounded.

playing upon us for the last ten or fifteen minutes—— [Foot-
note, by Patrick: "Honesty & I went over this ground 25'
June '63."] The Brigade . . . retired in good order to a position
on the Right of the Sud. [ley] Springs [s] Road, near the rear
of the wood adjoining the Head Quarters of Gen's Pope &
McDowell where I found one of Sigel's Batteries without support & stragglers fleeing in great numbers to the rear from
the field—— Throwing in a part of the Brigade to support
the Battery & the remainder across the roads & thro' the
woods, every man was halted & sent back, or retained in the
wood, until order was restored. The Brigade remained in this
position until all Guns were withdrawn from that part of the
field when it crossed over to the Centreville road, took the
New York Battery of Capt. [John A.] Reynolds in charge,
reported in person to Gen. McDowell & then marched, at
dusk, with the Battery to Centreville—— Our Total Loss this
day, Saturday, was 54 killed, 312 wounded, 221 missing,
several of whom are known to be prisoners—— The night
previous (30') the 35' Regt. lost 12 killed & wounded, in the
charge upon the Rebels—— We reached Centreville at about
10 o'clock P.M. . . .

Sunday Morning [,] *31' August*——

Found my Staff & Brigade near me when I rose & after getting
some coffee went to see Gen. McDowell—— Found all the
Generals there & recd. orders to move out a mile or two on the
Fairfax Road—— . . . We got the Brigade in motion about 9
o'clock & moved off—— Went into bivouac on the North of
the Road, with the Division—— Here we remained, cooking
& preparing for a good sleep, though obliged to detach some
companies for Guards, etc. . . . About 3 o'clock came an order
for my Brigade to open the Fairfax Road.

Monday Morning, 1' Sept. '62.

We packed our kit & at daylight the Train, [Capt. John A.] Reynold's Battery, & my two remaining Regts. were in the road and the march began—— We passed the 'shelling' position in safety & reached Fairfax, where I spent some 3 hours. . . . Before putting out my pickets, I recd. an Order from Gen. McDowell to give up the business & return to my Division—— . . . About 11'30" we started off. We had marched about half way when Joe Hooker,[14] now a Maj. General[,] met me & said he had orders to turn me back, as the enemy were making an attempt to get between us & Washington—— So I countermarched & pushed my men back, in all haste to near Fairfax then took the Leesburg Road & went to Germantown, then struck off to the left, to the Rebel Rifle pits & seized them—— [Brig. Gen. Darius N.] Couch's Division soon after came in & other Troops—— The 20' amounting now to about 180 or 200 men, I detached at Hooker's request, & marched them up the Leesburg Pike, to aid the Cavalry in holding a position until re-inforcements could arrive—— They arrived just in time to save it, & (though not long under fire themselves,) a severe engagement took place there [in pencil ("Chantilly")] in which [Gen. Isaac I.] Stevens & [Gen.] Phil Kearney [sic] were both killed—— A violent thunder storm came on just before dark & the rain poured in torrents. I was drenched before I could get my rubber suit & being obliged to remain on the field, in constant expectation of an attack, I passed a wretched night, in the darkness, rain & cold—— I may here say in relation to [Lt.] Bouvier, that [Capts.] Kimball & McClure, on Saturday found a nice place for him near Bull Run, with a *very* neat family

---

[14] Maj. Gen. Hooker, acting under orders from Pope, was gathering odds and ends of troops to try to hold off the Confederate attack down the Little River Turnpike at Chantilly.

of free negroes & leaving two of our Guard with him, they
left him doing well. McClure did not leave him until Sunday
Morning—— On Monday we heard that the Rebels had put
Hospital badges on our two men left with him & still having
charge of him, & that he was doing well. . . .

Tuesday Morning, 2' September,

I reconnoitered, from Daylight & met [Gens.] Hooker & Couch
& [John] Buford——[15] Went to Breakfast & then ordered
teams to the Ground to remain. Went down to town & met
all the Generals in Council—Pope, McDowell, [William B.]
Franklin, [William F.] Smith & [Samuel P.] Heintzelman——
Went back & about 11 o'clock, or 12, was ordered to join
the Division & go to Falls Church, as the enemy were turning
our right—— Moved off & had gone ¾ of a Mile when I
was ordered to hurry back to resume my position & hold it——
Went back, Battery & all, & staid until 4 o'clock[,] all the
other troops withdrawing & leaving me to cover the retreat.
Orders came, however, for me to march before Couch &
follow Franklin on the Alexandria Road—— . . . We did so
& after getting near Annandale, exhausted by want of sleep, I
got into the Ambulance & crossed over by Bailey's X Roads,
to Upton's Hill, reaching there between 11 & 12 at night. . . .

Wednesday Morning, 3' September, '62.

We slept, or snoozed, quite late, but finally got up & breakfasted, then sought for ground to encamp on—— The other
Brigades of the Division having arrived early in the day yester-

---

[15] Brig. Gen. John Buford commanded the Cavalry for Bank's old
Second Corps of the Army of Virginia, which would soon become the
Twelfth Corps of the Army of the Potomac.

day succeeded in getting their old grounds, but *we* had to take up with a very poor position. . . . Some few alarms were prevalent, but we were not called out, as a Brigade——

Thursday Morning[,] 4' September, '62——

This morning, after a fair sleep, I got up & made the rounds, to see what would be the Order of the day—— Orders for clothing yesterday & today were being acted on, but great delays with reference to our Regts. & other Teams [sic], in getting up with Knapsacks & Baggage. . . . [Alexander S.] Diven, now a Lieut. Col. of a new Regt. came to see me—— [Robert B.] Van Valkenburg[16] is the Colonel of it—— Just [at] night reports came in that the enemy were driving in our pickets and making an advance in force, on the Leesburg Pike—— . . . We took up *our* position to defend both this & the Fairfax Road—— These arrangements made & my own convictions being that the demonstration of the enemy was only a reconnaissance, I lay down in the Ambulance & slept.

Friday Morning, 5' September——

Was interrupted during the night by all sorts of calls, reports etc. . . . About 9½ o'clock I moved down & reported for instructions to Gen. [John P.] Hatch—— He concluded, or rather Gen. Cox, that only one Regt. would be required to remain. So I left the 35' & brought the others back to Camp—— . . . An Order came in the evening to establish

---

[16] Alexander S. Diven and Robert B. Van Valkenburgh, Republican Congressmen from New York, were taking time from their recruiting and Congressional activities to lead the 107th New York Volunteers in the field. Van Valkenburgh maintained his dual role through the remainder of the war. Diven resigned his commission on May 11, 1863.

our Old line of Pickets & the 35' being already on the ground, was the Regt. first detailed. . . .

Saturday Morning[,] 6' September——

Last night I was much interrupted by picket reports etc. This morning, early, I put my Report in DeForest's hands for copying. As it was impossible to get certain data here, I rode over to Head Quarters of Gen. McDowell, at Arlington, to obtain it—— He was absent, but I saw (Col. Edmund) Schriver & [Gen. James S.] Wadsworth & got some portion of the information[.] I also learned . . . that McDowell is to be relieved from all command, the public feeling against him being intense, & that [Gen. John] Pope, also, will be relieved from all command in the Army, here. McDowell (Schriver says) did not want to fight the enemy on Saturday, but I cannot see how that can be, after his gratuitous remark to me that morng. McClellan is in command of all the forces about Washington— in other words, of his own Army, Burnside[']s & Pope[']s. There is a general feeling that the Southern Confederacy will be recognized & that they deserve to be recognized. I returned from Arlington somewhat fatigued. . . . I was, soon after, taken with vomiting & purging. . . . Expecting to keep quiet tomorrow I went to bed, only to receive Orders to move in all haste thro' Washington, up 7' St. & out to Leesboro, 8 miles from Washington—— I sent for Col. [Wm. F.] Rogers [of the 21'], turned over the command to him, had an Ambulance prepared to ride in & got myself into it very soon after dark.

Sunday Morning——7' Sept. '62.

It was daybreak when we reached, or crossed the Acqueduct [Aqueduct] Bridge. . . . We came to a halt about 2 miles out

of Washington & remained there several hours, broiling in
the Sun—— A Mr. Lewis came out to see me & asked me to
go into his house & lie down on the Sofa—— . . . There I
remained . . . until towards night. . . . The Brigade moved
on at a Snail's pace about 11 o'clock & finally reached its
Camp—— . . .

Tuesday, 9' Sept. '62——

An order having come requiring us to turn in all transportation, nearly, we reduced our Baggage to the least possible
quantity & sent our trunks & all other *un*necessaries to be stored
in Washington—— . . . We had nearly reached the Camp
of the Division when we learned that it was moving & we
followed, on the Pike. We marched slowly, with many interrup-
tions, until night, when we encamped & I got some Chicken
Soup, which I very much needed & highly relished. . . .

Wednesday[,] 10' September 1862——

. . . [Gen. Joseph] Hooker came over to see me, having been
placed in Command of McDowell's [First] Army Corps. . . .
[Gen. Ambrose] Burnside is in command of the Right Wing
Army of Virginia——[17] About noon Orders came to move to
Cooksville & we packed up—— . . . We got in motion after
a while & after repeated halts & rests & delays we reached a
place called Unity, or near there, where it was decided that
we should encamp for the night—— About 1½ miles before

---

[17] Gen. Gibbon remained in command of the 4th Brigade of what was,
for the moment, Hatch's Division in Hooker's First Corps. Burnside did
act as a kind of "Wing" commander but the Army of Virginia had disappeared on September 5th in the reorganization that marked McClellan's
return to power,

reaching there, we passed the large Homestead of Hon. Odin Bowie Davis, one of the most prominent Union men of Maryland—— He had applied for a Guard, & on hearing that I was sick, sent a very pressing invitation to have me stay with him over night—— . . . When I got there I found the Family in a state of Excitement which my presence in some respects served to alleviate—— One son & 3 daughters, with himself & Wife constituted the Family—— They live on an estate that has belonged to them for Generations—— The tombs of the Grandfather & Father of the present proprietor are in the home ground—— . . . *He,* like many others, feels that the Government has repudiated all its pledges, that the Constitution is sacrificed & the War is carried on for party & personal purposes.

Thursday Morning, 11 Sept. '62.

. . . I did not sleep any last night & believing that we should not move today, concluded to lie in bed—— . . . but finding that an Order to move had been given the Division, I got up, had some milk porridge . . . mounted Snowball, & attended by Tom, went forward to the Division—— . . . I rode in the Ambulance, on leading the Brigade & Col. [W. F.] Rogers rode a part of the way with me—— We went to a place near the Great Turnpike, known as Lisbon & encamped for the night. . . .

Friday Morning, 12' Sept. '62.

. . . Orders for Inspection were recd. but by ten o'clock we had orders to move. . . . We had the most tedious delays on the March, halting without any apparent reason, until rain came on & with it darkness, long before we arrived at New Market, where we bivouacked at about 9 o'clock—— Train was all behind & we all went supperless to bed——

Saturday Morning[,] 13' Sept. '62.

. . . We marched to the Monocacy, 3 Miles from Frederic & went into Camp. . . . The whole valley of the Monocacy was covered with our Troops, the rebels having only left Frederic yesterday—— We are to pursue & give battle, I understand, wherever we meet them—— As I am disgusted with Hatch & have no confidence in King & regard Gibbon as a despicable toady, I have written, this Afternoon, to Burnside, to know if any probability exists of my being transferred from this command—— . . .

Sunday[,] 14' September, 1862[.]

. . . We passed, with the great body of Troops, through Frederic, the citizens waving their flags & giving us water & welcome—— Gen. King rode in front (my Brigade leading) having come up last night & assumed command. Gen. Burnside passed us, on his way to the front & told me that he had recd. my note of yesterday—that as soon as these few days of work were over, there would be early attention to what I had written. On arriving at Catoctin Creek we halted for lunch. . . . While here Gen [Rufus] King, was relieved from the command & ordered to report to the Adjt. Genl. in Washington—— Genl. Hatch was ordered to the command of the Division. . . . Reaching the Stone Church a mile, or mile & a half to the right of the road (pike) we found Gen. Hooker & staff awaiting our arrival—— He ordered forward one Regt.

(& I sent the 21' Col. [William F.] Rogers[)] which was ordered to ascend the ravine on the Mountain side, deploying skirmishers on the right & left—very soon after Hatch ordered the other Regts. forwd. & I suppose all had started together, as I led up the 35' & ordered it to deploy its whole line connecting on the right with the 21' & extending its left clear over to the National Road.

(Battle of South Mountain)

From some cause the 20' & 23' did not follow & some delay occurred in getting them up to support the 35' but by dint of hurrying & pressing they got up—at least the 23' did, but the 20' as usual on such occasions, hung back—— We all ascended the mountain rapidly, & after much trouble in placing the 20'[,] I found that the 35' had left a wide space between its right & the left of the 21'—— Leaving Orders to swing the left forward & the right back, upon the lower crest of the Mountain, I started off, with an orderly, to find the right of the 21' but while doing so, got too far to the front, between the Skirmishers of the 21' & of the enemy—— My orderly gave me warning of "Gray Coats" & I plunged down the Mountain Side followed by a volley from the enemy which passed over my head—— They, having revealed their position by this fire, I brot' over the 35' & connected, followed by the 20' which I placed under the orders of Col. Rogers, to act with him & strengthen him on the right. This operation had scarcely been completed when Gen. Hatch arrived with his Brigade to support me & the whole again moved forward—— Firing commenced almost immediately & increased in intensity on our right & front—— Finding their force to be on the top of the Mountain, I drew in all the 23' & 35' from the left & merged them in the general line of battle—— The action was hot & heavy, the position of the enemy being a very strong one, on the hill, behind the rocks & fences & in the Corn-field—— The 21' & 20' moved up to the fence on the right & silenced the Guns by picking off the cannoniers—— Still further on the right Meade['s] & Ricketts' Divisions were engaged & by the time it was dark, a most terrific engagement was going on, [Gen. Abner] Doubleday had joined us [and assumed command of the 1st Division] & Hatch had gone off with a ball hole in the calf of his leg—— We drove the enemy from the field, but a most disgraceful scene ensued, the men firing all their ammunition away after there was nothing to shoot. I withdrew a part of my men, only, at about 8 o'clock & went down the Mountain—— . . .

Monday, 15' Sept. 1862. Camp, or Bivouac near Boons-
     boro, Maryland——

I slept well last night in the Ambulance & rose only for Break-fast, at 6'30"[.] Immediately afterwards I started off to get my Brigade together, on the pike. I found the 20' & 21' and ordered them into position, then found the 23' & 35' on the Mountain Side & ordered them to the same place—— Return-ing to the Brigade I made arrangements to fill up their boxes with Ammunition & obtained provisions. The Order finally came to move on, but it was done very slowly, [Gen. Edwin V.] Sumner's whole [Second] Corps having come between me & the other Brigades of the Division—— . . . We reached Boonsboro & turned to the left towards Sharpsburg, but could not proceed more than a mile before we were obliged to halt, the road being blocke[d] up—— Turning the Brigade into a field thro' which ran a nice stream, I rode on, thro' one or two little villages, until I reached the front where I found our Batteries drawn up to operate against the Batteries of

the Rebels placed on the hills this side of Sharpsburg——
Finding [Gen. Abner] Doubleday I reported to him & as the
road was so blocked all the way, it was decided that I should
remain all night in my present position & move up early in
the morning—— . . . I saw Gen. McClellan this morning for
a few moments, on the road. He looked well—— Wherever he
goes the Troops cheer him enthusiastically—— That he is
their man no one can doubt who sees him pass along the
lines—— Can't say that I like to serve under Hooker.

Tuesday, 16' Sept. 1862——

Rose at 4 o'clock & turned out the command, but it was
6 o'clock, nearly, before we moved— the road had been pretty
well cleared & we got up to front in good season—— The
enemy remained in much the same position & I placed my
Brigade near the road until the Division could be found. From
this point we were soon shelled & I went off to join Doubleday.
We remained but a short time when Hooker, who was in
command, ordered all Troops under Arms & we were kept
in suspense—until near night, when we were ordered—the
whole Army—in 5 columns, to move forward; but in what
direction no one seemed to know. We crossed a new, & very
bad ford, in much haste, but there the Division was halted,
because no Orders had been given as to where we were to go.
The enemy's pickets were in the corn & popped at us before we
started, but eventually we moved forward, with Ricketts on
our right, but I suppose we did not get more than 2 or $2\frac{1}{2}$
miles, when Meade's Reserves engaged the enemy on our left,
just at dark & I was ordered forward, by ([Maj. Wm. A.]
Lawrence) Hooker, across a field, under heavy fire, to take &
hold a wood for the night—— Some of my men were wounded
in the operation, but we gained position & established our

pickets, connecting with Meade on the left, & along the Sharpsburg & Williamsport Road—— It was 10 o'clock before this was done, & Lieut. Col. [J. William] Hoffman, [Hofmann] Comdg. Doubleday's Brigade, came in, on my left afterwards, bringing up a Battery & placing it, in the night—— We lay on our arms, without supper & but for my rubbers I should have been badly off, for a light rain was falling a part of the night—— Every thing indicated an action with daylight next morning, & of course there could be little sleep under such circumstances.

Wednesday, 17' September, 1862—— Battle of Sharpsburg——

At daylight, as expected, the enemy—both sides—opened fire and the shelling was hot—— I had before light, counter-marched & held position, but about $5\frac{1}{2}$ o'clock was ordered forward, to follow Gibbon's Brigade, which was on the other side & to the rear of the open field—— Some of the men were wounded in crossing, without being able to return fire—— Passing thro' the wood, ploughed field, orchard & small meadow we reached the Cornfield where the remainder of the Division was & where we took positions in support of Gibbon. Remaining there from three to 5 minutes only, I recd. Orders to move my Whole Brigade across the Road to the Right, secure the wood on that side & hold it—— The 7' Wisconsin filed in front of us at the same time, having been preceded some 7 or 8 minutes by the 19' Indiana, which it joined in the wood, & behind which I filed in the 21' 23' & 35' Regts. in support, the 20' having been detached, after crossing the Road, to support [Capt. Joseph B.] Campbell's Battery [Battery B. 4th U.S.], where Gibbon himself was, with the 2' & 6' Wisconsin, on his left—— He, himself, was not

seen away from the Battery & straw stacks during the engagement—— We had been in the wood but a short time when a
body of the enemy was discovered moving to our right & rear,
which I reported to Gen. Hooker & was directed to watch &
check the movement with one of my Regts. Col. [Henry C.]
Hoffman, with the 23' was detached for this purpose & the
21' & 35' moved forward with the 2 Regts. in front, until the
troops in advance of us, on our left, were met by a Storm of
musketry that burst suddenly upon them from a corner of
the wood, before which they fell back & were rapidly driven
by the enemy, who poured out a heavy force from behind a
range of rocky hills & ravines pursuing our troops along the
edge of the woods, road & open field, toward the Battery——
It was a critical moment & I ordered the 2 Regts. of Gibbon,
as well as my own to throw themselves under the rocky ledge
parallel to the road & deliver flank, or crossfire upon the
advancing foe—— Just then Hoffman's 23' Regt. having been
relieved by one of Meade's, came in sight & at double quick
put themselves in the Same position—— Here we checked
the enemy & then drove, pursuing our advantage up to the
road, where my 21' & the 19' Indiana, forgetting everything
in the excitement, crossed the fence & before I could get them
back Lt. Col. Dyckman[18] of 19' was killed—— The enemy
soon rallied & finding that we were not re-inforced, came
down with their main body upon my Brigade & drove us back
to the ledge again—— Here we held on until one or more of
their Regts. coming upon us in our Rear & on the right flank,
attacked us; to repel which Col. [William F.] Rogers, on the
right requested the 6' (Wis.) & 19' (Ind.) to throw back their
Right, at right angles with our line—— They did throw back
their right & left too, & marched off the field, to which they
did not again return—— Our Cartridges being nearly spent

---

[18] Patrick was mistaken. It was Lt. Col. Alois O. Bachman of the 19th
Indiana Infantry who was killed at Antietam,

& our right turned, I withdrew the Brigade to a low spot opposite the Barn & in rear of some rocky knolls, where it remained, between our own & the enemy's Batteries long enough for the men to make Coffee, as they had not been able to get any breakfast—— Within about 40 minutes or 45— the lull that had followed our withdrawal from the ledge was broken by the arrival of re-inforcements. The 60' & 78' New York, commanded, as I understood, by Col. [William B.] Goodrich,[19] moved up & my Brigade followed in close support—— Knowing the Ground well, I directed Col. Goodrich to advance cautiously, following his skirmishers, until I could get re-inforcements to go in on his left & front in sufficient force to drive through the Corner where the enemy appeared to hold in masses—— Riding up on the hill, to find Gen. Doubleday, & through the Cornfield into the ploughed field beyond, I found that the enemy had been driven down the road, but not by that point of wood—— I begged Gen. Gibbon (whose Brigade had left the field & who was now riding over it) to ask that a strong force might be sent down to the wood, which I would direct towards that point—— Returning hastily to the wood I found Col. Goodrich dead & his troops with difficulty held in position, but assuming command I ordered the Regts. forward & the Skirmishers to the fence of the cornfield beyond—— While engaged in this 2 or 3 other large Regts. came over the brow of the hill, with rapid step under the belief that they were driving everything before them & taking such a direction that on passing the Corner of Wood where the enemy were so strongly posted, they would be taken in rear & flank—— In vain I endeavored to change their direction & advise caution—— No Comdg. Officer appeared to direct their movements & on they swept in front of the 78' & 60'—— The result was what might have been antici-

---

[19] The 60th and 78th were part of Goodrich's 3rd Brigade of the 2nd Division of the Twelfth Army Corps of Maj. Gen. Joseph K. F. Mansfield,

pated—the enemy, on a sudden, poured into their left & rear a most murderous fire which cut them up terribly, broke *their* lines, drove them back upon & put to rout the 78' & 60'—— Everything now was in the wildest disorder & throwing my Brigade once more under the ledge, we did our best to rally stragglers & hold our ground, until the Battle flags of the Rebels were within a very short distance of us, both in front & rear, of our right—— Every thing of ours having given way, I ordered my Brigade to retire by the right flank, which it did in perfect order, & under perfect command was marched along the road a few rods to a wood on the right, which it filed into & was thrown behind a fence perpendicular to the road, not only to hold against the enemy, if needed, but to catch stragglers & rally them—— This was about 1'clock P. M. & we remained there about $\frac{3}{4}$ of an hour, until order was restored in the fugitive Regts. & such as could be were rallied—— The Brigade was then moved back to the Hill, to which the Batteries had been withdrawn & placed in support, Gen. [Oliver O.] Howard giving me a few cartridges until I succeeded in getting some up from my own Train—— Gen. Hooker having recd. a ball through his foot left the Command of the Corps to Gen. [George G.] Meade, & Gen. [Edwin V.] Sumner assumed the direction of the whole affair—— By him I remained until reinforcements went forward, but the ground we had so hotly contested was not retaken by our Troops, & the carnage there was awful—— Night came down & all along our line, some 3 miles in extent, the firing ceased—— . . . The battle is one of the severest ever fought—— I rode over the grounds, just at dark, with Gen. Howard—— They are covered with dead & our men are being carried to hospitals—— My own loss is only about 257 & only one good Officer, Capt. [James R.] Barnett, of the 35', was killed[20]——

---

[20] The final and revised figures were 30 killed, 187 wounded, and 17 captured or missing for a total loss of 234,

Thursday[,] September 18' 1862—— Same Bivouack, by
    Battery.

We were not attacked last night, & this morning Sumner told
me that McClellan's orders were *'not* to attack' & if possible
have re-inforcements come up—— It seems to be fairly understood, that only Madcaps, of the Hooker stripe, would have
pushed our troops into action again without very strong
reinforcements—— We had all that we could do to hold our
ground yesterday & if we had attempted to push the enemy,
today, with the same troops, we should have been whipped——
Accordingly I have been perfectly willing to remain by our
Guns until we get help—— It is understood that some 20
thousand fresh troops have come in & we are to open the
battle at daylight tomorrow morning—— Our Troops have
rested all day & will be prepared for action, in Some degree,
tomorrow. [Col. W.] Henry Kingsbury[21] was killed, at the head
of his Regt. yesterday, at the Stone Bridge over Antietam——
The loss of no one has affected me so deeply—— He was a
noble fellow! His poor Mother will feel that life is now
valueless—— . . .

Friday Night, 19' September, 1862—— Camp near the
    Potomac——

Last night I slept very little, partly on account of constant
breaking in upon me & partly because I had great anxiety
about the Battle which the morning would bring with it——
I prayed much of the night—prayed for my country—prayed
for my children—prayed for myself— It was a night of
wrestling with God—— Did he hear? With the dawn of day
we were to engage the enemy & I had turned out my Troops

---

[21] Col. Kingsbury had commanded the 11th Connecticut in Isaac Rod-
man's 3rd Division of Burnside's Ninth Army Corps.

and had every thing packed to send off, when, lo, messengers to Sumner reported that the enemy had left in the night & crossed the river into Virginia—— Further than this—that Harper's Ferry had been re-occupied by our Troops—— We were soon after ordered to move & after hours of delay, *did* move to the front, only about 1½ miles, or perhaps 2 miles & this delayed by halts of some hours—— We finally moved into a piece of open woods & bivouacked for the night—— . . .

Saturday Night, 20' September, 1862—— Same Camp.

I had a good sleep last night. . . . Our troops have had their details of Regts. out yesterday & today, burying the dead—— The stench arising from the decomposition of the dead is almost intolerable——

Sunday Night— 21 September, 1862—— Same Camp,
    near the Potomac——

A quiet Sabbath, once more, for a novelty—— Rose rather late & after the usual duties of the morning, selected a place near by, in the woods, for worship. . . . After dinner & towards evening, I mounted my horse & took a ride, with Beckwith, to see the left of the Battle Ground, where Kingsbury fell, & Burnside was in command—— The enemy's position was *very* strong at that point & it was at the Stone Bridge over the Antietam, on the Harper's Ferry road, that he was killed—— Poor Fellow! I loved him! . . .

Tuesday Night, 23' September, 1862, Same camp on the
    Potomac——

. . . About 4 o'clock . . . I mounted & rode over to see [Gen. Ambrose E.] Burnside—— He says that Hooker's [First]

Corps has been detached from his Command, he does not know why, but he supposes that an entire re-organization of the Whole Army will soon be effected and if so, he will then help me all in his power, to change position. He advises me to see [Randolph B.] Marcy,[22] at once, & to tell him how I am placed. . . .

Wednesday Night, 24' September—— Oak Grove Bivouac—— Same Camp [.]

. . . I went over to Head Quarters this morning & had an interview with Marcy—— If Hooker or Gibbon do not interfere, I think there will soon be a division formed for me—— [Gen. James B.] Ricketts came over to see me & followed me to Head Quarters, to consult me in relation to his being placed under the Command of [Gen. George G.] Meade, who is his junior—— He has protested against it, but I advise him to obey Meade's Orders, especially as they are personal friends—— . . .

Thursday Night—— *25' September.* Oak Grove Bivouac, near Potomac.

. . . Was sent for to Head Quarters to assist in making notes for the Affair at South Mountain—— [Lt. Col. James A.] Hardie[23] says there is a great deal of Managing & Manoeuvering—— . . .

Friday Night, 26' September, Oak Grove Bivouac, between Antietam & Potomac——

. . . After Bkft. we had work that kept me until about 9 o'clock, when Court met & except from about 12'30″ to 3, we have

---

[22] Col. Marcy retained his post as McClellan's Chief of Staff.

[23] Col. Hardie was an Aide-de-Camp and Acting Assistant Adjutant General and one of the key figures on McClellan's staff.

been in session all day, or until about 5'30"—— Col. [John W.] Stiles ['] case[24] was concluded. . . .

Sunday Night [,] 28' September. Still in our old Bivouac, at Oak Grove——

. . . Throat feels badly today & I am gargling with Salt & Water—— . . . The Chaplains had been here, yesterday, to invite me to talk to the men but I felt so bad that I declined, & this morning I told Chaplain Robie that I could not speak to them; but they had all made up their minds that I was to speak & so I *did* speak—God gave me strength though I had a violent headache—— I talked some 20 or 25 minutes & was well rewarded by the attention they gave—— After Service some 2 or 3 Citizens came up to me to shake hands & introduce themselves—— One a Mr. Payne, whose 2 Sons are in the 23' & a Mr. Baldwin—father of Capt. [Ambrose N.] Baldwin. Mr. Payne's eyes were streaming & he wrung my hand—— 'I don't wonder, now, that my boys love Gen. Patrick'—— 'They all love Gen. Patrick.' These were words of comfort & strength to me—— I was repaid for all my labor. . . .

Tuesday Night [,] 30' September, 1862—— Camp Barnett, near the Potomac——

In the early part of last night I slept well, but there came along, after about Midnight, a wandering fellow from the 35' blathering & open mouthed, who bolted into camp & began a conversation with the sentinel—— It aroused me instantly & I asked who he was, & what he wanted—— He said he

---

[24] Col. Stiles, commander of the 83rd New York Infantry (9th Militia) was accused of "skedaddling."

was 'out looking for White Oak Bark'—— I had him hug a
white oak tree for the rest of the night & think he will stay
in Camp tonight—— I could not sleep again however. . . .
Ricketts went to see McClellan, who treated him most
courteously & knew of nothing against him—— He would
give him an answer tonight, as to whether he would relieve
him or not—— Ricketts feels very much better than he did
last night——

Wednesday Night, Tattoo, 1' October, Camp Barnett,
near the Potomac, Md.

. . . I rode over to McClellan's Head Quarters—— [Capt.
James P.] Kimball with me. All were off to Harper's Ferry to
meet the President etc. Saw only [Cols. George D.] Ruggles[25]
& Hardie—— Hardie told me that I am wanted as Provost
Marshal General. . . .

Thursday Night, Tattoo [,] *2' October*—— The same
Camp Barnett——

This has been rather a singular kind of a day. . . . I was
engaged in Office writing for some time, & . . . about one
o'clock, I recd. an Order to turn out my Brigade, as the
Division was to be reviewed by the President. We marched
from here before two o'clock to the grounds near Doubleday's,
where, not finding him, (& receiving a note from him that he
was unwell) I took command of Division, & soon found that
the whole [First] Corps—Meade's & Rickett's [sic] Divisions,
were also coming on. By 3 or $3\frac{1}{2}$ o'clock, all were in readiness.
We waited, & waited & waited. Reynolds & Meade went to
hunt up the President. He was on the Battle Field. He finally

---

[25]Col. Ruggles had been Gen. John Pope's Chief of Staff.

ran away, in an Ambulance, & drove to Sharpsburg, without putting off the Review, or saying a word to McClellan. Reynolds came up about 7 & dismissed us. . . .

Friday Night, Tattoo, 3' October—— Camp Barnett—— Maryland.

. . . After Breakfast I took hold of business for some time, but at 9½ turned out the Brigade, to march over to the Review Ground. Again the Corps was out & Again I found the President as little to be relied on as Yesterday. He was to have reviewed us at 11 o'clock, but 12, 1, 2, & 3 o'clock came before he arrived. We were burned up. disgusted & weary. At length he came, rode down in front of the line and turned off to see [John] Buford's Cavalry & then go up to see [Gen. William B.] Franklin. . . . I want one more good day, to allow the Brigade to wash themselves & their clothes—the latter in boiling water. The Officers & men are without Clothing, for Change, are ragged & filthy. Many of them have vermin upon them & cannot get rid of them except by a thorough boiling process. So I propose to use tomorrow for the purpose. . . . McClellan was with the President, in undress. I did not speak to him, not being near him. As the President came down the line he shook hands with Meade, Ricketts & myself, Division Commanders & asked us to join the Cortege, which we did, but I was with [John F.] Reynolds & [George W.] Morrell— the latter a Major General. I do not know for what he is made a Major General, really. There is a very important & extraordinary Order just issued, establishing a Corps of Provost Marshals in all the United States whose duties shall be to arrest deserters, spies & disloyal persons with Jim. Draper as Provost Marshal General for the War Department, at Washington! Look out, now, for Inquisition! I think trouble will grow out of the working of this Order.

Saturday Night, 4' October—— Camp Barnett—— Near
the Potomac [,] Maryland——

. . . Our men are poorly prepared for Storms. Their Shelter
Tents are worth very little for protection, & they (the men)
are getting very weak & unable to endure much exposure. . . .
I am sending everywhere for Tents, but do not get them. No
news of any kind is stirring today.

Sunday Night, 5' October, Camp Barnett, Near the Potomac, Maryland.

. . . I rode over to Head Quarters of the Corps & found there
Reynolds, Meade & [Gen. Truman] Seymour. Found some
Orders & information there that I needed & then rode over
to Gen. Ricketts ['] Camp. Found Mrs. Ricketts there & soon
after Gen. [Abram] Duryea came over. Mrs. R. read to me
her Report of the 2' Bull Run. She came on here to write it for
her husband. She says that from the time she was married, she
has always made out his Muster Rolls & Reports, until
now. . . .

Monday Night, Tattoo, 6' October, Camp Barnett, near
the Potomac [.]

. . . This Morning I found an alarm paper, to the effect that
Fitz John Porter had reported the enemy on the opposite side
of the River, that they had 2 Guns in position & the woods full
of Infantry. Reynold's [sic] Rifled Battery was prepared for
action before daylight, but we have no further news & the
belief is that the Sunday Visitors to the opposite Shore, where
they had picked up a great many muskets, were "the Infantry
in the Woods." . . . Recd. a note from Hardie asking if I would

accept the appointment of Prov. Mar. Gen. I replied,
"Yes." . . .

Chapter V

Provost Marshal General of the Army
of the Potomac

OCTOBER 7, 1862, THROUGH DECEMBER 14, 1862

McCLELLAN NEVER RECORDED what moved him to appoint
Marsena R. Patrick his Provost Marshal General Undoubtedly Patrick's reputation for absolute honesty and his
moral fervor as well as his experience as a military governor
in Fredericksburg made him a likely candidate for the post.
His oft-expressed concern for protecting persons and property
from the criminal element in the Army was probably another
factor. Not so flattering to Patrick is the plain fact that he
had not proved an outstanding combat commander and was
marked for a staff position. Whatever the reasons for the
choice, Patrick was apparently happy with his assignment and
went to work with a will.

Patrick had about a month to learn the size and shape of
his new job before the Army moved into Virginia in pursuit
of Lee. While McClellan rested, Confederate Cavalry under
J. E. B. Stuart made him look a bit silly by riding all the way
around the Army of the Potomac between October 9 and 12.

In Kentucky the Confederate two-pronged attack under
Braxton Bragg and E. Kirby Smith ran into trouble at Perry-
ville on October 8. On the 30th of the month McClellan
finally began his leisurely pursuit of Lee into Virginia. On
November 7 Lincoln lost his patience with McClellan's "slows"
and gave the Army of the Potomac to Ambrose E. Burnside.
The likeable and bewhiskered Burnside led the Army to
Fredericksburg and disaster cn the 13th of December.

159

Tuesday Night, Tattoo, 7' October——— Camp Barnett,
   near the Potomac, Md———

. . . While at Breakfast an Order came directing me to report
immediately at Head Quarters & appointing me Provost
Marshal General. . . . Met [Lt. Col. James A.] Hardie, first,
as he had desired & got a general idea of what was wanted———
[Gen. Andrew] Porter is at Harrisburg & Maj. [William H.]
Wood[1] is acting for him——— I saw Wood & several other of
the Officers, but without entering specially into details of my
duties, I agreed to go over tomorrow & take them up. . . .

Wednesday Night, 8' Oct——— Head Quarters [,] Army
   of the Potomac, near Knoxville [.]

. . . [Lt. William W.] Beckwith & I started at 9' or 9'30" from
our Camp. . . . We got on through the village of Sharpsburg &
went to where I had left Head Quarters Yesterday morning.
Nothing was there. The Camp had broken up at 9.00 &
removed, as we learned, some 12 or 14 miles towards Washington. We could only know the route by following the Train
—an enormous one! We took, as it proved, a longer road
than was necessary, coming down thro' what is known as
Pleasant Valley. . . . This road strikes the Rail Road at
Weaverton some 3 or 4 or 5 miles below Harpers Ferry. We
came on to Knoxville, below Weaverton, then perhaps, 2
miles lower down, on the Pike. . . . Here we found arrangements for Camp & after a while the Tents were raised. . . .
We spent our evening very pleasantly. Several of my Old
friends being on duty here. [Alfred] Sully, (Brig. Gen.) is also
here, to report for a Brigade.

---

[1] Gen. Andrew Porter had been Provost Marshal General of the Army
of the Potomac until the end of the Peninsula campaign, when illness
forced him to request relief. During the Second Manassas and Antietam
campaigns, Maj. Wood of the 17th U.S. Infantry had been acting
Provost Marshal General of the Army.

Thursday Night, 9' Oct.——Camp, Head Quarters, near
   Knoxville [.]

This morning I rose early. . . . I mounted & took in a survey
of the Camp—how it is laid out, etc. etc. then I looked at the
neighbors around us that we are to protect, & that involved
quite a ride. It was very uncomfortable riding as the day had
been intensely hot & the road as dusty as it well could be &
full of Waggons. . . . I am not able yet to say, that I know
any thing about duties, but am suspicious that I shall not
like the position, from the fact that I may be snubbed up
by almost any body. I am not supreme, as I used to
be in my own Camp, & there is nothing fixed, or established,
apparently. . . .

Friday Night, 10' October—— Head Quarters [,] Army
   of the Potomac, near Knoxville [.]

. . . It came on to rain & I sat down to work when Gen.
[Darius N.] Couch came in & staid nearly an hour. He relieves
[Edwin V.] Sumner in command of that [Second] Corps. . . .
[Randolph B.] Marcy & [Gen. G. B.] McClellan are not yet
back. . . . Mrs. Marcy & Mrs. McClellan are in the General's
Tent. I hear them talking.

Saturday Night, Tattoo, 11' October, '62, Head Quarters
   Potomac, near Knoxville.

. . . The morning was cold & cheerless, but I rose early &
went about my work, after my usual half hour to myself &
my God. As soon as Breakfast was out of the way, I mounted
& rode off towards Crampton's Gap some mile, or two, &
finding the genus Loafer Extant in that neighborhood, I

came back & sent out some Cavalry Patrols, who returned, this evening, with quite a large number of stragglers & marauders. . . .

Sunday Night, 12' October, '62. Hd. Qrs. Potomac, near Knoxville [.]

. . . I was up in the usual season & after breakfast put on Sword & Sash & Coat, for [a] Review of 93' [N. Y. Vol. Infy.] which came off at 9 o'clock. I then rode thro' their Camp and the Camp of the 8' [U. S.] Infy. then over to the Camp of the 2' [U. S.] Cavalry. . . . Service was . . . held at the A. G. Office by an Episcopalian. It was a very good Sermon, on the "Christian Profession." Mrs. Marcy & Mrs. McClellan were there. I did not pay my respects at all. . . .

Monday Night, 13' October, 1862—— Camp between Brownsville & Burnside [.]

. . . I do not sleep as well as usual in this Head Quarters Camp. . . . At 9½ o'clock this morning I rode over to [Maj. Charles J.] Whiting's [2nd U. S.] Cavalry Camp, after having packed up & loaded everything of our own, at Head Quarters, for a move up beyond Burnside's Camp. . . . The March was not one of great length, but it was near night before we got into our Tents. It is not a good Camp Ground, but is in the midst of a beautiful valley, known as "Pleasant Valley." . . .

Wednesday Night, 15' October, '62. Camp, Quarters, near Brownsville——

. . . This morning . . . Judge [Sen. Ira] Harris & his son William, called again . . . but I received an Order which made it necessary for me to go over [to] Harpers Ferry. . . . We went *over* the mountain, supposing the River to be directly on the other side of it, but we took a *very* round about way, riding twice as far as needful, but having the most delightful ride over these Mountain roads & the most glorious views imaginable. We reached Harpers Ferry, fording the River & taking Capt. [Duncan A.] Pell, Provost Marshal, along with us, went up Loudon Heights, where all the Stragglers are confined. . . . The view from Loudon Heights is magnificent. . . .

Thursday Night, 16' October—— Hd. Qrs. Army of Potomac—— near Brownsville [.]

Last night I sat quite late, talking with [C. C.] Trowbridge, then came to my own Tent & took up "Schalk's Art of War," which kept me till near 11. . . . I have been engaged in Office business all day. . . .

Friday Night, 17' October, '62—— Head Qrs. Army of Potomac, near Brownsville [.]

. . . After our Breakfast I went over . . . & arranged to go over to Sharpsburg, to see the Commanders of the 1' & 5' Army Corps—[John F.] Reynolds & [Fitz John] Porter, about appointing Provost Marshals etc. . . .

Saturday Night, 18' October, '62, Head Quarters, Army of Potomac, Near Brownsville——

. . . Came to Tent & worked until about 10 o'clock, then saw Williams, Marcy & McClellan; then started off for Maryland Heights, with Beckwith. . . . We wound up the Mountain side by a very good horse path & reached the Signal Station in safety. From that point, although the Atmosphere was too smoky to see in the *distance,* we had a most magnificent view. Pleasant Valley with its thousands upon thousands of snowy tents, its long black lines of soldiery on drill, its endless streams of Waggons & horses——The Valley of the Potomac below Sandy hook, covered more sparsely with Troops, more densely with little villages, & higher up the junction of the Shenandoah with the Potomac—the banks of each River & Bolivar Heights between covered with its masses of Infantry & Artillery, while on Loudon heights, & Maryland Heights (a little below us) Our Flags were flying & the Big Guns by their side to protect them. Far in the distance lay Charleston & Martinsburg & Shepherdstown, & other villages, indistinctly seen thro' the smoky atmosphere. It was a sight seldom seen by man, & one which we enjoyed, exceedingly. We had the use of the Glasses of the Signal Corps, & made the most of them. . . . All indications are, that Hooker is playing a game to overthrow McClellan. Mrs. [Nancy Hooker] Wood & Mrs. Brainerd are with him, "nursing" him, in Washington.[2] . . .

Sunday Night, October 19' 1862—— Head Quarters, Army of Potomac, near Brownsville [.]

. . . I slept until about 12'30" when I was aroused by boisterous language, etc. which I supposed belong to the Servants in rear & called out to them to be quiet. But after a little I found that it was a number of Officers 3 or 4 tents below here. Being in doubt as to my powers I did not go down to them, but after a while I found that it was a drinking bout & several Officers of Rank were concerned in it. The muss was kept up until about 4 o'clock this morning & no one in the neighbor-

---

[2] Gen. Joseph Hooker was wounded at Antietam on the 17th. Mrs. Nancy Hooker Wood was his elder sister. Mrs. Brainerd was a younger sister,

hood slept a wink. It was a most disgraceful operation. . . .
Well, I found that I must do something about these matters
& as I had to go to [Gen.] Seth Williams about other business,
I intended to broach this. . . . I am to take all this Authority
of keeping matters straight in Camp into mine own hands, &
there will be an Order to cover it. The Matter of Trade, also,
will come into my hand, as well as this matter of secret service.
I shall be able to get these matters into shape after a while &
establish a system, I trust, that will work Satisfactorily. . . .

Monday Night, 20' October, 1862, Head Quarters [,]
  Army of Potomac, near Brownsville——

Have had a consultation in relation to my duties with Hardie
& have drawn up a Memorandum, in regard to Trade etc. . . .

Wednesday Night, 22' October, '62—— Camp in
  Pleasant Valley—— Army Potomac [.]

. . . I have been engaged on Office duty all day—— Sent
[Lts.] Mehaffy & Beckwith over to Harpers Ferry, to parole
prisoners—— Have concluded to send forward to Baltimore
& Fortress Monroe a lot of about 60 prisoners & as [Capt.
James P.] Kimball is in a bad way about clothing, I will send
him with them, to Baltimore. . . .

Thursday Night [,] *23' October, '62*—— Ebbit [t]
  House, Washington [,] 10 o'clock P. M.

Rather an unexpected change of Quarters since 10 o'clock
this morning—— I was up at the usual hour & spent my
morning in the usual way, until about ten o'clock, when I

went over with certain papers to Gen. [Seth] Williams, relating to men in Convalescent Camp—or Hospitals—or absent—— Seth soon after came over, having seen the General [McClellan], who thought it best for me to go to Washington, if I could & rectify, if possible, these various difficulties & causes of complaint—— So I made my arrangements [,] got my papers together & wrote instructions for operations in my absence & by 12′30″ or 1′ P. M. I was riding down to Knoxville, in an Ambulance with Beckwith—— He returned & I took the train at 2′30″—— It was full so that I was unable to sit down, any of the way, until we reached the Relay House,[3] nearly 100 miles—— There I did get a seat & about 6′30″ to 7 o'clock, this evening reached Washington & I came directly, to this House. . . .

Friday Night, 24' Oct. Ebbit [t] House, Washington, 11 o'clock [.]

Up early this morning & went out before Breakfast—— Came back & took Breakfast with Paymaster [Thomas M.] Burt. . . . Went over to Wadsworth's & while there [Gen. Christopher C.] Augur came in, then [Gen. John H.] Martindale, who pressed me to do down & hear his defence [sic], which I did, meeting there [Gens. William S.] Harney, [Silas] Casey and others—— From there I went over to see Gen. [Nathaniel] Banks & agreed to go down to Alexandria & look over the Convalescent Camp—— Went over to [Gen. Daniel H.] Rucker's & got Ambulance to carry me. . . . On reaching Alexandria I called on Gen. [John P.] Slough, Military Governor, dined with him & then rode up to the Camp, where I found the establishment under charge of Col. [William W.]

---

[3] Just outside of Baltimore; it is the point where the Washington Branch of the Baltimore and Ohio Railroads connects with the main line.

Belknap——— Arranged with Gen. Slough as to the future &
returned to this House to Tea, then put on my coat & called at
Jno. [John] Potts, on my way to Heintzelman's,[4] where I
remained until after ten o'clock, talking over war matters etc.

Saturday Night, 25' October, 1862———Ebbit [t] House,
  Washington [.]

Up this morning at daylight & went over to the Clothing
Depot, to overhaul my big chest & get out such Articles as I
need for winter. . . . I met at the National [Hotel] Gen.
[Rufus] King, just starting for Fort Monroe, & his Father[5] &
Mrs. Ricketts just leaving for New York. . . . Went to see Gen.
Banks & arrange with him, finally, about convalescents———
Went thence to see Gen. [Lorenzo] Thomas [The Adjutant
General] about a great many things & from thence to see Col.
[Stephen H.] Long [Chief of Topographical Engineers] & get
a Map of the Country around Harpers Ferry, which I find
to be tolerably accurate. . . . Have spent the evening with
Major [Alexander E.] Shiras.[6]

---

[4] Some idea of Patrick's business in Washington can be gleaned from
a summary of the positions of the people he visited. Major T. M. Burt
was an Additional Paymaster for New York Volunteers. Wadsworth was
Military Governor of Washington, Heintzelman commanded the Defenses
of Washington South of the Potomac, and Augur was recuperating from
wounds received at the Battle of Cedar Mountain. Martindale had been
charged by Fitz John Porter with cowardice at the Battle of Malvern Hill,
but the inquiry exonerated Martindale. Harney was assigned to "special
duty" at the War Department. Casey commanded a small division posted
in Washington, while Banks commanded the Defenses of Washington.
Rucker was Depot Quartermaster for Washington. Slough commanded
the "Camp of Convalescents, Stragglers, and Recruits" in Alexandria,
while a future Secretary of War, William Worth Belknap, was in direct
charge of the camp. John Potts was the Chief Clerk of the War Department.

[5] Gen. Rufus King's father was President Charles King of Columbia
University.

[6] Major Shiras was an Assistant Commissary General of Subsistence.

Sunday Night, 26' October, Ebbit [t] House, Washington——

I went to bed last night with orders to call me at 5 so as to be off in the Train at 6—— I was called & went down to Willard's to take the Carriage but learned that there was no 6 o'clock Train on Sunday & that *no* train would run to Harpers Ferry today. . . . I had agreed with [Gen. Irvin] McDowell, the day-no, yesterday, to call & give him some opportunity to explain Bull Run—— I went & staid nearly 3 hours, the result of that interview has been quite a change in my mind as regards McDowell. . . .

Monday Night, 27' October, '62—— Camp—Head Quarters [,] Army Potomac [.]

. . . I *did* take the Cars at 6 o'clock, came on to Relay & got some Breakfast, thence to Knoxville. . . . Having telegraphed to [Lt.] Beckwith, yesterday, he met me at the Cars & brought me up to Camp—— On arriving up here in the Mountain Country I found that the rain storm, which was quiet enough in Washington, was accompanied here with a perfect Gale, blowing down the Tents of the Staff & playing very many pranks, to the great annoyance of the General & all the Officers. . . . The Head Quarters were to have moved today, but on account of the Storm it has been delayed—until tomorrow, at ten o'clock—— Then we move to Berlin, where a Ponton Bridge has been thrown across the Potomac & Burnside[7] has already crossed some of his Troops—— It is intended that his [Ninth] Corps, now commanded by [Gen. Orlando B.]

---

[7] Burnside had been placed in command of the Defenses of Harper's Ferry and the Second, Ninth, and Twelfth Corps——an interesting anticipation of his own division of the Army of the Potomac into "Grand Divisions" for the Fredericksburg campaign.

Wil[l]cox, & Hooker[']s [First] Corps under [John F.] Reynolds shall cross at that point soon—— The movement, as it seems, is to be on the East of the Mountains bordering the Shenandoah [the Blue Ridge]—— . . .

Wednesday Night [,] *10'30" P. M.* Camp near Berlin [,]...
Md [.]——Hd Qrs. Army Potomac [.]

. . . After Breakfast was engaged in Office business for some time then sent for to Marcy's Tent to see about arrest of correspondents etc. . . . The Troops are crossing, not rapidly, but cautiously, into the Ancient Dominion—— There has been a very great accident to us today, at Harper's Ferry— the burning of an immense amount of Forage stored there, by the Rail Road, & the loss of about 24 Freight Cars—— All, as Beckwith tells me, through the utter stupidity or folly, or knavery, of the Conductor, whose Car took fire, & might have been detached, but was run directly through the piles of Hay & Grain—— The Conductor & Engineer are in arrest. . . .

Thursday Night [,] *10 o'clock, Berlin, Oct. 30'* HdQrs. [,]
Army of Potomac——

Last night just as I was preparing for bed, a little before 11 o'clock, one of the Operatives (Secret Service) came down here, with some information that it seemed important for me to communicate to Marcy, at once—— It related to the movements of the Rebel Troops towards the Shenandoah— & was brought in by deserters, today—— It seems that the Rebels are hard pressed for clothing & supplies & the impression among the Troops is, that they will fall back to Staunton & Richmond to winter. . . . I rose early & we had an unusually early breakfast, enabling me to get to work nearly, or quite 2 hours earlier than Yesterday—— I needed this time very much, as I have been obliged to examine a number of Cases of Examination before our detectives & prepare to send off a lot of State prisoners to Baltimore, also a number of paroled prisoners, who do not wish to go South & will be sent North for liberation—— My Order in regard to the Convalescent Camp, stragglers etc. has been issued today & I have sent one copy of it to Gen. [N. P.] Banks and another to Gen. [John P.] Slough—— My Order Regulating trade goes out in my own name, directed to my Marshals in the different Army Corps. . . .

Friday Night, 31' October—— Head Quarters, Camp
    near Berlin, Md [.]——

I have had a laborious day. . . . These Counterfeiters have given me a great deal of uneasiness & trouble——I have turned one of them over, this evening, to the U. S. Marshal from Philadelphia—or Baltimore—I have forgotten which. . . .

Sunday Night, 2' November [,] *'62*—— Same Old
    Camp, near Berlin——

. . . As there was a great deal that wanted to be done here, today, in the way of business, I concluded to stay behind, sending all others along, but directing Beckwith to return, with his Waggons, for Forage etc. & remain here, with a part of them, until Kimball comes up with Stragglers. . . . There has been firing all day, between [Gen. Alfred] Pleasonton & the Rebs. at Snickersville, without much result——

Tuesday Night, 4' November—— Camp between Upperville, Waterford & Millville, Loudon Co [.]——

Yesterday morning, at about 8 o'clock, I got away from Berlin. . . . and after a disagreeable ride, as the dust was flying
badly, reached Wheatland where I found [Maj. William H.]
Wood & the Staff Officers of my Department, but the Head
Quarters had moved to Fillemount—— So we came on, thro'
Union & Fillemount where we found that Head Quarters had
moved further on—— So we rode on, some 3 miles further,
& found Head Quarters, but no Gen. McClellan there. He
had gone to the front, where there had been Cannonading all
day and Pleasonton, with some Infantry to help him, had been
driving [Gen. J. E. B.] Stuart thro' Snicker[s]ville Gap. . . .
Was up early this morning & breakfasted by about 7' o'clock
—or earlier, & moved by 8—— We came on to Bloomfield &
the General had moved to Upperville—— We rode on to
Upperville & remained there a short time, where Camp was
located, but soon after the location was changed, as it was
found that the Rebs. had retired from Snickers Gap & were
now holding Ashby's Gap. . . . We are now moving parallel
to the Mountains in a southerly direction with the Troops &
our Camp has been thrown back towards Millville, some 4
miles from Upperville, & cannonading is going on now, at
Ashby's Gap. . . .

Wednesday Night, 8 o'clock, 5' November—— Head
Quarters, Camp near Rector[s]town [,] Va [.]——

. . . We are here about 15 miles in front of Manassas Gap, &
close upon the Rail Road. . . . I am distressed to death with
the plundering & marauding of the Army—— I am sending
out detachments in all directions & hope to capture some of the
villians engaged in these operations. . . .

Thursday Night, 6' November, 1862——Camp near
Rector[s]town [,] Va. [.]——

. . . Was up early this morning & as soon as breakfast was over
I started out to put a stop to depredations—— I know not
how many men I have had arrested today. . . . I have got a
number of horse thieves in Custody & have handled some
marauders very severely—— . . .

Friday Night, 7' Nov. (9'30") [.] Camp near Rector[s]-
town, Va [.], Loudon County——

. . . My Office business . . . has been as large today as I could
manage. . . . The Brandy that Mr. [William] Kelly sent me,
last February, which I have kept so carefully, was stolen out
of my Tent Yesterday, just when I most needed it. . . . This
evening I went over to Gen. McClellan's Tent & found [Gen.
Herman] Haupt there, but could only stay some 20 minutes
as I had work to do & a Military Commission is now in progress, trying the case of a Soldier of the 8' for attempting a
rape on a colored girl. . . .

Saturday Night, 8' Nov. '62—— Camp near Warrenton,
Army of the Potomac [.]

. . . After Breakfast I made my Adieu to Camp & rode on with
a few Orderlies—only 8 or 10—— My object was to start up
something like a thousand men or 12, or 1500, who got in
last night, & could not be started. I used my whip freely before
I could start them; but got them to Salem & the Cars had
left—then pushed them to White Plains—5 miles further——
Set off those of [William B.] Franklin's [Sixth] Corps there,
& started the remainder on as far as Gainesville, it being the

only place where rations could be obtained—— I left them
there (White Plains) & returned to Franklin's where I took
my grub & found [Gens.] Baldy [Wm. F.] Smith, [W. T. H.]
Brooks & [John] Newton with him—[8]also Gen. [Calvin E.]
Pratt—— From there I came back. . . . Found Head Quarters
in a wood, but no trains for a long while & 9 o'clk before our
Tents were pitched—— All as cold as Charity & dark as
Egypt—— We have had supper & I am for bed at 10′30″ to
keep warm—— But this is not all—— At Midnight, or later,
an Order was recd. by McClellan to turn over to Burnside
the Command of the Army of the Potomac & report at Trenton [New Jersey]—— The Army is in mourning & this is a
blue day for us all.

Sunday Night, 10′ 30″, 9' Nov. Camp near Warrenton,
    HdQrs [.] Army of Potomac [.]

. . . Since 9 o'clock we have had quite a scene—— Gen.
McClellan has taken leave of the Officers of his Staff at these
Head Quarters—— I went over with them & presented
them—— There was a crowded house & a feeling as deep as I
have ever seen—— It is known that his removal was planned
& to be carried into the effect the moment the Elections were
over—— They did not dare to remove him before the Election—— Now that [Horatio] Seymour[9] is elected by Such an
immense majority over Wadsworth, their Anger is uncon-
trollable—— The Order relieving him is dated on the same
day that the news of the New York election reached Washington—— He is ordered to report, by Letter, at Trenton, where
his Wife is—— Tomorrow he leaves, but as the Troops have

---

[8] Generals Newton and Brooks were Brigade Commanders and Smith
commanded a Division in Franklin's Sixth Corps.
[9] Seymour, a War Democrat, was elected Governor of New York over
James S. Wadsworth who had campaigned as a Lincoln and antislavery
Republican.

demanded to see him, he has decided to see them, once more & commences with mine—— The Regulars are uproarious & demand that McClellan shall be removed, if at all, to the Command of the Army—— If the day is any how tolerable there will be a magnificent scene tomorrow, for the Troops love him with a devotion almost idolatry.

Tuesday Night, 11' November—— Head Quarters [,] Army of Potomac, Camp near Warrenton——

. . . Yesterday morning I rose very early & had breakfast at a little after 7 o'clock then turned out the Troops—— We found a place, near by, where they could be paraded for review, but without Marching, & there we drew up the 2' Cavalry, the McClellan Dragoons, the 8' Infy. the Sturgis Rifles & the 93' N. Y. Vol.—— They all *looked* pretty well & *did* pretty well—— The General & his Staff (an immense Staff of high Officers) came out & we received him—— I rode down the front with him & he wanted to turn off, but I would not let him, and as we passed around the right, the signal flag waved & the Troops cheered him, but it was irregular & just as he passed the front I gave Snowball the reins & swung my cap with a call for Once More & All Together. It was magical in its effect & the result was splendid—— It is much talked of—— Then we rode down thro' the Corps of Couch & Porter—— All drawn up in masses on each side of the road for miles—— Such waving of tattered banners & shouts of the Soldiery! He went on down to Franklin, then back to Reynolds & thence home. . . . We had a rough time last night, as Officers & men had been drinking, to drown grief & the Camp was noisy; but in their cups men spoke their minds. . . . I went into town after Breakfast . . . and as the train had arrived, I took leave of Gen. McClellan, whose eyes were wet, as he came out of the Hotel [.] It was some hours, however, after he went to the Cars before he could get away. Strangely enough, the train that was to take him away, brought up [Gen. James S.] Wadworth, who told me he had come up to see (& advise) Burnside—— Well! Perhaps it is all right, but I think the Administration adds insult to injury. . . . At 4' or 4'30" we turned out again & received him—[Burnside] handsomely—but not enthusiastically—— He was well pleased & all seemed gratified—— After dismissing the Troops the Officers were called to the Tent & presented to him in due form—— He appeared well—very well, but all seemed to think there was one they liked much better. . . .

Wednesday Night, 12' Nov. 9'30"—— Camp near Warrenton, Head Quarters——

. . . As soon as breakfast was over, went into town. . . . [Gen. Joseph] Hooker was there, having been ordered to take Fitz John Porter's [Fifth] Corps, while Porter goes to Washington to answer [Gen. John] Pope's[10] charges. . . . Halleck & Meigs & Haupt are here, in town, with Burnside, who has not yet been able to remove himself to Camp and will not until they get out of the way. . . .

Thursday Night, 13' November, 10'30"—— Camp near Warrenton [,] Va——

. . . Had Breakfast at 8—— From that time until about 2 o'clock I was busy in all sorts of work, but Murray & his

---

[10] Pope had charged Porter with refusal to obey orders while in the face of the enemy during the Battle of 2nd Manassas. A military commission was appointed on November 17th to investigate the charges. On November 25th a Court Martial was ordered. It met, almost daily, from November 27th to January 10th, 1863. Porter was found guilty and relieved of command. Hooker retained command of the Fifth Corps.

Brother, the Doctor came to see me. Murray lives about 6
miles from here, towards the Junction—— Has been in the
Rebel service as Lieut. Col. under [Maj. Gen. William] Extra
Billy Smith,[11] but got out some months ago. . . . They staid
until I was ready to go off & Murray rode with me, to guide
me & tell me of the whereabouts of the people, the roads etc.
etc. . . .

Friday Night, 14' Nov. 9 o'clock—— Camp near
Warrenton [,] Va [.], Hd. Quarters [,] Army of the
Potomac [.]

. . . After about 9 o'clock I was out about Camps etc. etc.
came then to the Convalescent etc. Squad—— Turned over
320 for the first Corps. . . . Returned just in time to be taken
[photographed] in a Group of Burnside & his Generals——
Burnside insisted upon my being taken as I was, with my
riding whip in my hand. . . . This evening some of the Sutlers
have been to me & I have helped some, others I have not
helped. . . . We are to move back, as I infer, towards Frederic[k]sburg & the Acquia Creek——

Saturday Night, 15' November [,] Camp near Warrenton, Head Quarters [,] Army of Potomac [.]

This has been a very busy day. . . . There has been a reorganization of the Army, to a Certain extent, by throwing 2 Army
Corps into one Grand Division, constituting an independent
corps, in most respects, having all the powers that have been
exercised, heretofore by the Commanders of an Army——

---

[11] "Extra Billy" Smith was a former governor of Virginia who commanded a "Virginia Brigade" in Ewell's command of the Confederate
forces.

[Edwin V.] Sumner commands the right, [William B.] Franklin the left & [Joseph] Hooker the centre—— This evening as we were at Dinner who should walk in but [Lt. John V.] Bouvier, looking as fresh & fine as silk—— His lung (left) is ruined but he looks well & says he feels pretty well. . . .

Sunday Night, 16' November, Camp near Warrenton——
    Catletts—— Cedar Run [.]

. . . Today's papers announced the arrest of [Col. A. V.] Colburn & [Capt. J. C.] Duane,[12] of McClellan's Staff & their order to Washington—— Why & wherefore is only surmised——

Tuesday Night, 9'30" [,] *18' Nov. '62* [.] Camp at Mrs. Carter's near Falmouth——

. . . After Breakfast we waited the arrival of somebody to indicate Orders for the day—— Dr. Cooke & Mr. [Herman] Briggs came over to see me & remained until Burnside arrived—— We finally decided that I would move on . . . to Falmouth to be in readiness for marching into Frederic[k]sburg with the first [troops], but that Head Quarters should stop at Hartwood for the night. . . . I did not stop at Hartwood, but came on this side & called, for a few minutes, on [Darius N.] Couch & [Edwin V.] Sumner, each at his respective Head Quarters—— I found Couch about $2\frac{1}{2}$ miles from here on the S. W. side of the road, & Gen. [Oliver O.] Howard with him—— Found that [Winfield Scott] Hancock's Division

---

[12] Colburn had been an Aide-de-Camp and Duane was the Chief Engineer officer of McClellan's staff. They had been among the handful of officers that McClellan had ordered to accompany him into exile at Trenton.

was here in Falmouth, having taken possession Yesterday, after
an Artillery duel with the Batteries on the other side of the
River, which they knocked to pieces & forced to retire, while,
it is said, the enemy retreated from the heights to the cellars
of the town——— It is not known how many Troops are there,
but not any large force, & I do not know what our plans will
be about taking possession of the town——— There are a great
many troops concentrating here & hereabouts——— All the
Grand Divisions of Sumner, Franklin (& as I understand)
Hooker—leaving only [Franz] Sigel behind——— The Corps
of [John F.] Reynolds moved down from Fayetteville to Hartwood today. . . . I had many recognitions from people along
the Road & Sumner says they don't inquire for any one but
me——— He has some great jokes at my expense. . . .

Wednesday Night, 19' November, 1862———Camp near
Falmouth, (Mrs. Carter's Farm) [.]

It was late when we got breakfast this morning & I went off,
soon afterwards——— I took a turn down town & secured Dr.
Rose's house, then across to the Phillips place, then to the Wallis
[Wallace] place, where I supposed Gen. Burnside would
establish his Head Quarters——— Sumner came there & [Gen.
Orlando B.] Wil[l]cox took possession of the Phillips House &
Gen. [William W.] Burns[13] of the Wallis [Wallace] House———
I came home & met Gen. Burnside with whom I returned to
the Lacy House, then took *his* Escort & came over to Camp,
where [Maj.] Haller had been pitching, or laying out Head
Quarters; but being directly in cannon range from the Hills on
the other side it was changed to the other side of the road. . . .
We are badly off for Forage & Subsistence——— The people
through here have nothing at all left to them.

---

[13] Gen. Willcox commanded Burnside's old Ninth Corps and Gen. Burns
commanded his 1st Division.

Thursday Night, 9 o'clock, 20' November, Camp near Mrs. Carter's [.]

Slept very well last night & rose early this morning, as I had a great deal of business to do—— Sent off Capt. [Henry C.] Welton to Alexandria for prisoners. . . . I have elaborated a system of Provost Duties & submitted for examination—— Also an attempt to correct horse stealing—— Have ordered the arrest of a Lieut. Reynolds for marauding & have made out a system of Rail Road passes on the Road between here & Acquia Creek—— Also a system of passes to & from Frederic[k]sburg—if we ever take it. . . .

Saturday Night, 9 o'clock, 22' Nov. Camp near Mrs. Carters, near Falmouth [,] Va [.]

. . . Got an early Breakfast & started off, for [Edwin V.] Sumner's Head Quarters, meeting him & Burnside by agreement—— A summons was drawn up for the town to surrender, by 5 P. M., failing which 16 hours would be given to remove women & children, preparatory to shelling—— This was addressed to "Mayor & Council"—— I went down & raised a white towel, waited a long time for some one to come & was finally recd. in a Ferry Boat, by Col. [William A.] Ball of the 9' Virginia Regt [.]—— I was not permitted to present my communication to the Mayor [Slaughter], except thro' the Military [.] Col. Ball despatched a Courier to the Commandant, but it was $3\frac{1}{2}$ hours before any one arrived—— Then came Maj. [G. Moxley] Sorrell [Sorrel], of Gen. Longstreet's Staff & took my communication returning after 2 hours & saying it was in the Mayor's hands—— At about 7'30" I recd. a reply from the Mayor, who handed it to me in person, accompanied by Hayes & Dr. [William S.] Scott——[14] It was

---

[14] Unknown to Patrick the surrender summons was being taken to Gen. Lee who had arrived on the scene. Other accounts say that Samuel S. Howison, not Mr. Hayes accompanied the Mayor and Dr. Scott during these negotiations.

very dark when I recrossed the River, Maj. Dorwell & the others taking me over & pleading for more time—— I rode to Sumner's & reported then to Burnside's. . . . Found that an agreement had been made that I should be at the Lacy house at 9 this morning, to receive the Mayor & authorities [.] Went down & soon after a deputation of Mayor etc. attended by two or three Officers arrived—— I declined receiving the Officers & they all returned—— Then negotiations were again renewed & I went to see about placing Batteries down the River with Gen. Wil[l]cox—— While there the trains with women & Children started out & a skunk of a fellow, against orders, fired at them, without effect—— He did not fire at the Second train—— The Mayor, Dr. [William S.] Scott & Mr. [William A.] Little, were accompanied [by] Gen. [Joseph B.] Kershaw & Col. [Elbert] Bland [7th S. C.]—— I recd. them at the Lacy House, by the Back way & kept them nearly an hour—— The agreement finally is that they have until 11 o'clock tomorrow to remove the rest of their people—— that the town will not be shelled until *she* fires etc. etc. When they left I went up to Sumner's where it was ratified by Sumner & Burnside—Hooker, Franklin & a host of Generals were there. . . . The probability is that we move camp in the morning, as the enemy are *now* on the other side, in large force under [Gen. James] Longstreet & we must have a fight—— Had our Ponton Train arrived, as it ought, we should have crossed the River before Longstreet arrived, on Thursday, as there was less than a Regt. in town——

Sunday Night [.] *8 o'clock, 23' Nov. '62.* Camp Rufus
    King, Hd. Qrs. Army of Potomac [.]

. . . It seems as though the Cavalry had determined to see how bad they could behave, in our rear and they are stealing, ravaging, burning, robbing & marauding on the road, in rear of us, to a most alarming extent—— . . .

Monday Night [,] *24' Nov. Camp Rufus King,* Hd. Qrs. [,] Army of Potomac—— 9 o'clock P. M.

. . . I have been engaged in office duty thro' the day—— Overhauling in regard to prisoners of war & of State, to get rid of them. . . .

Tuesday Night, 9'30" 25' Nov. '62—— Head Quarters [,] Army of Potomac [,] Camp Rufus King.

I slept well last night & after Breakfast this morning . . . mounted & rode down the River—— I found two guns well down, on the heights, opposite this end of the Pollock property—— There I found [Sid] Deming [of the Associated Press] & another man, who rode with me to Pollock's Mill—— From there I went to Mrs. [John Bowie] Gray's [of "Traveller's Rest"] where I found my men, well employed, having arrested some negroes & hunted out the position of a Battery nearly opposite—— I saw Mrs. Gray, her Sister, and several young men, her nephews, I presume—— From there I went to Mrs. [John] Seddon's where I had more men & was warmly received by Mrs. S. who had her Mother, Miss Grinneau & several other Ladies there—— I was very handsomely treated, but could only stay for a few minutes, after which I came to Mrs. Strothers—— Her husband got out of the way when the Army came up & will keep away, I suppose—— On my way down (or back) I examined the site of the Battery intended to knock our Gunboats in coming up. . . . Deming has been in & says Burnside feels very blue—— Lee & the whole Secesh Army are, or will be, in our front——

Wednesday Night, 9 o'clock, 26' November, 1862—— Same Camp—— Rufus King [.]

. . . Horses without number are stolen, all over the Country & Brigade, Division and Corps Commanders wink at it——

They get up false, or made up papers & think to quash pro-
ceedings in that way—— I am Sorry to say that Burnside has
not shown, thus far, enough back bone to enable me to stop
the robbery—— I have referred the matter to higher authority, this evening, & await the result. . . .

Thursday Night, 27' Nov. (Thanksgiving) [.] Camp
Rufus King, Army of Potomac [.]

. . . This morning I was up early & had my Coffee etc. before
any others were moving then started off, with my orderly, for
Acquia Creek. . . . After getting through there I started back
& came to the Brigade—— They were expecting me & I rode
to the 20' & 23' spending a little time to see the Officers, then
went up to the 21' where dinner was waiting & I sat down——
Meanwhile word was sent out for the Brigade to be formed
& by the time I had called on Gen. [Gabriel R.] Paul they
were ready for me—— First. A prayer by the Chaplain of
the 23' next a Thanksgiving Psalm was read by Chaplain
Robie—— Then I talked to them half an hour—Causes &
reasons for Thanksgiving—thanks that *their* homes have not
been invaded—compare their homes & State with the homes
made desolate in this State—— What are they to do when
they return home? Think of it *now* & prepare to resist the tide
of evil by establishing habits of self control, of sobriety, chas-
tity of speech etc. . . .

Friday Night [,] *28' Nov. 9'30"*—— Camp Rufus
King—— Head Quarters [,] Army of Potomac——

. . . I had occasion to see Burnside & he told me of his having
been to Belle Plain, last night, to meet the President; that he
goes up, tonight, to meet him in Washington—that Lincoln

tells him the country will wait until he (Burn-) is ready—that Halleck is not to be the authority, (who says Burnside must fight a battle *now*, even if he is to lose it) but that Burnside shall have 50,000 more men immediately. . . .

Saturday Night, 9 o'clock, 29' Nov. [,] *1862——* Camp Rufus King, Head Quarters [,] Army Potomac [.]

. . . The night is cold, but pleasant & there is a moon that will, I hope, enable me to catch some spies that have crossed the River, & which, I think, are Mrs. Gray's Proteges. . . .

Monday Night, 1' December, 1862, Camp Rufus King, Head Quarters [,] Army of Potomac [.]

Rose this morning early & intended to have gone out soon after Breakfast, my escort being in readiness for me soon after 8 o'clock, but business came on, with such a rush that I could not get off—— Rose & Briggs came in, saying that their country is overrun, completely with thieves, marauders & vagabonds of all classes—— They were followed by Dr. Michael Wallace & Miss (Dangerfield) Lewis, with similar complaints from the other way & while *they* were here, Mrs. Washington & Miss Grimes (the Old Maid) came in, filling up my Tent & keeping me tied, for two hours, to hear their detestable lingo—— Troops down here are behaving as badly as it is possible for them to behave—— I have been over to see [Gen. Edwin V.] Sumner, who sends out to [Gen. Alfred] Pleasonton[15] to scour that whole country & *shoot down* any one found committing these depredations—— I hope & trust that it may be productive of some good. . . .

---

[15] Gen. Pleasonton commanded a Cavalry Division attached to Sumner's Right Grand Division.

Wednesday Night, 9 o'clock, 3' December, '62, Camp
Rufus King, Head Quarters [,] Potomac [.]

. . . Attended to business until 9 o'clock, then mounted Snowball & with [Col. James A.] Hardie & [John] Buford, rode
over to [George] Stoneman's & from thence to [Joseph]
Hooker's where they were on a Court. . . . I staid there & saw
[Daniel] Butterfield & some others—arranged matters about
Provost Marshals of Grand Divisions etc. when Hooker was
summoned to appear at Head Quarters & we rode over together—— [William B.] Franklin & [Edwin V.] Sumner were
already here, & I went about my own business, of all kinds——
Kept at it until about 3 o'clock, then rode over to Sumner's &
endeavored to effect an arrangement about Corps & Grand
Division Marshals, but the proper Order had not gone over
from here, officially. . .

Thursday Night, 9'15" [,] 4' December, Camp Rufus
King, Head Quarters [,] Army Potomac——

. . . Sutlers & Traders without number have been here, News
Agents & news boys have been applying for passes etc.
etc [.]—— By direction of Gen. Burnside & in consequence
of the Raid into King George County, I ordered the withdrawal of Guards from all the houses down the River & have
had to pay pretty roundly for it—— The Ladies have written
me, some spicy & some pathetic letters, Dr. [Hugh] Mosson
[Morson], in person, presented himself, & I referred him to
Gen. Burnside—— The result was, that he sent [Lewis] Richmond [Assistant Adjutant General] to tell me to act as I
thought proper—— So I have ordered all the Guards back to
their places down the River—— The questions of Sutlers is
occupying a large share of public attention & [Quartermaster
General] Meigs has issued, his Pronunciamento, & had it pub-

lished, as I understand. It is a Letter to Gen. Burnside, which he received yesterday, or this morning & sent over to me, for examination—— I shall now, I think, serve all traders & Sutlers alike, sending them to Belle Plain, to unload on the Beach & haul up by Waggons. . . .

Saturday Night [,] 6' December, '62—— Camp Rufus King, Head Quarters [,] Potomac [.]

. . . I rose pretty early & have been at Office work all day, some of it of a very unpleasant kind. . . . A Mr. Taylor was sent up for being concerned in piloting the Rebels across the Rappahannock into King George & cutting off the Compy. of Capt. Wilson. . . . Another party was arrested for being disloyal & wealthy—for having been a Surgeon in the Confederate Service & for having aided in the arrest of the Clerk of Capt. McGraw of the Flotilla—— I did not wish to examine him until I could get some witnesses, but at his request I did so, sending for Gen. Parke—— Well, I found him to be the Son of Wm. Wirt, a most accomplished gentleman of fine literary attainments etc. etc. He has proven his innocence & I shall parole him tomorrow, allowing him to go home, to stay on his place——

Sunday Night, 7' December, Camp Rufus King, Head Quarters [,] Potomac[.]

Last night was very cold, the earth freezing to the depth, I should think of 2 inches & I am told that the River is frozen over at the U. S. Ford, above here [.] It has been cold & freezing thro' the day—— Tonight is still colder & by tomorrow morning Troops can cross the river, I presume, a few miles above. . . .

Monday Night, 8' December, 1862—— Camp Rufus
King, Head Quarters [,] Potomac [.]

. . . Gen. Butterfield & several others were in & my time was
used up. . . . [Col. Daniel] Van Horn has been up, too [,]
from Belle Plain & Gen. [Herman] Haupt from Acquia
Creek—— They say that the ice has prevented the Boats from
getting up to the wharves for a couple of days & we are short
of Forage & Subsistence on that account—— We are trying
to get up a System of Guard duty etc. etc. for the Rail Road—
but it is hard work, owing to the want of System at these
Head Quarters in making details & enforcing the carrying out
of their General Orders. . . .

Wednesday Night, 10' December, '62 [.] Camp Rufus
King, Head Quarters [,] Army of Potomac [.]

. . . Rose early & went to Bkft. a very little after 7, came back
& was engaged in business for about 2 or 3 hours, was then
with Burnside & afterwards went down to Depot, to attend to
various matters. Soon after 12 went up to Sumner's to meet
Burnside, Wil[l]cox, Couch, & others—— Stoneman & Dan.
Sickles, [Brig. Gen. Amiel W.] Whipple & another General
whom I did not remember—— Well! We discussed & talked
& discussed again the plan of Battle, which is to come off
tomorrow. We broke up, by Burnside's going over to Hooker's
& the others went down to the River, to overlook & reconnoitre. . . . We are under Orders to move (the Staff) with the
General at daylight tomorrow morning. . . . Citizen prisoners
are being taken up by the pickets throughout the country——
I have been overrun by that kind of business. . . .

Thursday Night, 11' December, '62—— Camp Rufus King, Head Quarters Potomac [.]

Well! Once more in my own Tent & all safe—— Went to bed at about 10½ o'clock & had a good nap, then I was roused at 2 o'clock by the noise of [Brig. Gen. Henry J.] Hunt[16] & his Staff, taking the field—— Then there was a lot of loafers in his Tent & that I had to go in & shut up—— I did not sleep after 2 o'clock & at Four Burnside came in, to talk about matters & arrange for the day—— It was a difficult business to get my own affairs all arranged & to get guides for the Corps from my Old Regts—— They came about 7 o'clock, which was the time I was ready to move with the Cavalry, & also with Gen. Burnside. The ground was frozen very hard, & as waggons had been running all the night, the ground was very smooth & the horses being smooth shod, could scarcely stand—— We have rather a change in the weather it being quite mild tonight, after a day that has been particularly soft & sticky, so far as the earth is concerned—— We were up, & breakfasted at 5—— The first guns were fired at 4'55", but about ½ past 5 it became continuous Artillery fire, from our side, as it was necessary to protect our Bridge Builders—— We all went over to the Phillips House which we made Head Quarters during the day, Burnside remaining there thro' the day—— The Engineer parties attempted to throw Bridges across, but were beaten back with heavy loss by the Sharp-shooters stationed in the houses—— This finally operated in such a way as to cause a suspension of firing for a considerable time—— The flames had burst forth & the Street of Commerce was pretty well used up—— I sat at the Lacy house & watched operations, having gone down to see what was meant by the White Hdkfs. from the windows [.] It proved to be colororde [sic] people, wanting, I suppose, that we should send for them—a thing utterly impossible—— Well! heavy fire was finally opened between 1 & 4 P. M. under cover of which the Ponton bridge was thrown over, without much loss-a Regt. going over in the Pontons & cleaning the fellows out of the houses—— Well! [Oliver O.] Howard's Division was crossed over, & perhaps more, just before dark, to hold the town—— [William B.] Franklin has crossed perhaps a Division below, & all are resting until an early hour tomorrow to cross & begin a terrible fight—— [Gen. T. J.] Jackson will then have returned from Port Royal & joined [Gen. James] Longstreet—— The whole will then be upon us & we must carry their position at whatever cost—— We returned to Camp to stay tonight & break at $5\frac{1}{2}$ tomorrow. . . .

Sunday Night, 14' Dec. '62, Camp Rufus King, Head
     Quarters [,] Army Potomac——

Two nights without entry in this Book!—— Two weary nights, & I so fatigued that the only thing I could do, after getting my hard work done, was to go to bed! After a night of little sleep, Burnside came to my Tent at 4 o'clock to talk over matters & when he left I got up—— Breakfasted so as to leave at $5\frac{1}{2}$, but it was 7 o'clock before *he* moved—— I moved at daylight & crossed the Bridge where I found Howard's skirmishers & sent them to close the gates of the Mill Race, from the paper Mill & also to open those at the Heston Mill—— Was in town until the time appointed by Burnside for me to meet him at the Phillips House—— There I returned, & after reporting, found that it was only a few questions & for me to keep in communication with him—— I was in the town & out of town, & on the bridges & all about, establishing Guards etc. having with me the Cavalry & 2 companies of the 8' Infy [.]—— When I went into the town a horrible sight presented itself—— All the buildings more or less battered with shells, roofs & walls all full of holes & the

---

[16] Gen. Hunt was now Chief of Artillery for the Army of the Potomac.

churches with their broken windows & shattered walls looking desolate enough—— But this was not the worst—— The Soldiery were sacking the town! Every house and Store was being gutted! Men with all sorts of utensils & furniture—all sorts of eatables & drinkables & wearables, were carried off & as I found one fellow loading up a horse with an enormous load of carpeting & bedding I ordered him to unload it, which failing to do, I gave him a cut or two with my riding whip that started him in a hurry & then put him with my prisoners—— I made some of the Officers ride up to Head Quarters with the Mantle Ornaments hanging at their saddles & turned them over to Hooker [.] In this kind of work the day was spent. . . . But little fighting was going on during the day, except to keep the town clear, which was taken possession of by the Corps of [Darius N.] Couch, [Orlando B.] Wil[l]cox & a division of [George] Stoneman's—— In going through the streets I was fired upon several times from the outskirts of the town & their pickets held their own firmly—— The next morning (Saturday 13') I was again roused by Burnside in my Tent—— After he left I was up, & saddled as soon as Breakfast was over—— Went into town & was about there till 12 at which time I had to meet Burnside & the Generals Comdg. Grand Divisions & Corps—— I found, in the town a most deplorable state of things—— Libraries, pictures, furniture every thing destroyed & the brutal Soldiery still carrying on the work—— The consequence was, that when they went into it (the fight) at about 12 a great many were left behind, in the houses they were plundering—& Couch sent over for me to clear the town—— This was impossible although I put in my Cavalry & 4 companies of Infy. that I had sent for to Potomac Creek—— The engagement has been terribly destructive—the batteries of the enemy all converging upon our Troops as they advanced to carry the centre & repulsed them——This was repeated with our best Troops, who could not do any more—— On the left Franklin's Strong position helped him & he took 500 prisoners by surprise—— The day closed sadly & I remained until late in town, coming in so sadly fatigued that I lay down as soon as I could get my dinner (7'30" P. M.) from sheer inability to sit up—— I slept well & rose at 6 this morning—— After Breakfast went to town myself & was there till about ten, when Burnside wanted me at the Phillips House—— There I remained for a long time, to see what he wanted—— It was, at first, to make a reconnaissance, but after learning the exact state of affairs & seeing the enemy's works revealed by the clear atmosphere of today, it was decided to make no work today & I went back to do what I could in town—— It was long after dark when I got home. . . . [Sid] Deming the Reporter for the Associated Press has just been in & says he has seen Franklin— that he has lost in killed and wounded & missing, about 4000, or 4500—— Sumner must have lost near 6000—— It is believed that our whole loss is equal to 12000—— More than the loss at Antietam—— This, too, without gaining anything & in reality inflicting no loss at all upon the enemy scarcely—— It is understood that Hooker's Corps is withdrawing, tonight, from the other side of the River—— A wise step in my opinion, if followed by the withdrawal of all the Troops from that side of the River, where the enemy may, at any moment, slaughter us by wholesale.

Chapter V I

Demoralization and Reorganization

DECEMBER 15, 1862, THROUGH MARCH 14, 1863

THE DEMORALIZATION OF THE ARMY OF THE POTOMAC after Burnside's "Mud March" of January 21 to 23, coming as it did on the heels of the disaster at Fredericksburg, is apparent in these pages. Things were not much better in the West.

Grant's setback when Nathan Bedford Forrest tore up his base of operations against Vicksburg at Holly Springs, Mississippi, on December 20 was followed by Sherman's failure to get onto dry ground at Chickasaw Bluffs just above Vicksburg on the 28th and 29th. William S. Rosecrans remained in control of the field when Braxton Bragg retreated after the indecisive fighting around Stone's River or Murfreesboro, Tennessee, which occurred from December 31 to January 3, 1863, but it was hardly a clear-cut victory. Even at sea the Federals seemed to be doing badly. As Patrick noted, the "Monitor" foundered off Cape Hatteras and Galveston Bay was reopened to the Confederates.

The surprise that greeted the elevation of Joseph Hooker to command of the Army of the Potomac quickly turned to approval as his talent for organization was recognized. Even Patrick's difficulties with the new Chief of Staff do not obscure his growing awareness of the vigor and hope that Hooker brought to the Army.

Monday Night, 15' November [December], '62[.] Camp
Rufus King, Head Quarters[,] etc.

. . . I was hardly thro' breakfast when Dr. [Hugh] Mosson
[Morson] presented himself, his safeguard having been set
aside, his house taken for a Hospital etc. etc. . . . I went
down the River as far as Mrs. [John A.] Seddon's [of
"Snowden"] finding Col. (now General [David McM.], Gregg
in Command—— He tells me that [Gen. William B.]
Franklin gave Orders to take the forage wherever they could
find it——' Accordingly it has been taken without stint——
Well! I saw that it was useless to attempt to save it, so I had
an Officer go up to Franklin & make the Statement of the
case to Franklin, who gave the Order, then, in writing—— I
had a time at Dr. Mosson's [sic]—— Mrs. Seddon & Mrs.
Gray were overjoyed at the sight of my old hat. They hung
to me as to a Father. . . .

Tuesday Night[,] 9'30"[,] 16' December—— Camp
Rufus King etc.

. . . The Troops have resumed their former positions——
The General sent over a flag today, & the result is, an agreement to exchange prisoners, bury dead etc. . . . There is a
feeling of deep and painful anxiety as to the future. No
confidence is felt in any one. [Gen. Ambrose E.] Burnside will
resign his position & [Quartermaster General M. C.] Meigs is
talked of as his successor—— He will be insufferable to the
Troops. . . .

---

[1] Gen. Franklin's Left Grand Division was spread out over most of
Falmouth Heights and the country to the southeast of Fredericksburg.

Wednesday Night, 17' Dec. 9'30"—— Camp Rufus King—— Hd. Qrs. [,] Potomac [.]

Another dismal sort of day. . . . Found it tolerably comfortable outside & rode over to the Depot & elsewhere about prisoners etc. taking me until ten or 10½ o'clock—— I then came up, after learning that their flag agreed to exchange prisoners at 12 m. today—— Well, I came up here & made full arrangements, then went back & got the Reb. prisoners to the River[,] 459 in number (215 having already gone to Fort Monroe)[.]

Thursday Night[,] 18' Dec. '62—— Camp Rufus King—— Hd. Qrs.[,] Potomac[.]

Up early this morning. . . . A certain Rev. Mr. [Alex.] Reed, of the Christian Commission, came to see me & I gave him a horse to ride & some advice to be guided by. . . . The winding up of the exchange of prisoners was going on all the Afternoon—— [Lt. William W.] Beckwith & [Lt. John V.] Bouvier were both over in the town & well pleased at their interview with Reb. Officers who say that their works were actually held by two Brigades against Sumner & Hooker,[2] their position being impregnable. . . . Burnside has gone down to Acquia, to meet [Gen. Henry W.] Halleck & talk over military matters—— The papers say that McClellan is to resume the command——

Friday Night, 19' Dec. '62, Camp Rufus King, Head. Quarters[,] Army of Potomac[.]

. . . The Committee on the Conduct of the War, "Ben Wade, Covode & Co," came down today, bringing with them the

---

[2] Gen. Sumner commanded the Right Grand Division and Gen. Hooker the Center Grand Division, and the implication was that two Confederate brigades were holding off four full Union Corps.

Sergt. at Arms of the Senate, who was so drunk he couldn't walk nor work——³ At the request of the Committee, through Gen. [Herman] Haupt—I took him in & let him lie on my bed till he could sleep off his intoxication, which continued until about 4 o'clock, when the whole party, I think, left. . . . There is a great deal of anxiety throughout the Army as to the course that will be adopted by the Administration—— The impression is that the Cabinet will be broken up & reconstructed—— that [Gen.-In-Chief] Halleck will be compelled to withdraw & that, very probably, McClellan will replace him—— These are only conjectures. . . .

Saturday Night, 20' December, 1862—— Camp Rufus King, Army of Potomac[.]

. . . One of the prisoners died last night from exposure to the cold and I am now trying to get them all off as soon as possible. . . . Mr. [William H.] Seward has resigned his place in the Cabinet & it is said that Halleck & [Edwin M.] Stanton follow, in quick succession, the President having asked all his Cabinet to resign——⁴ Burnside keeps quite close and I have not seen him, scarcely this week——

---

³ Senator Benjamin F. Wade of Ohio and Representative John Covode of Pennsylvania were the most zealous members of the Committee on the Conduct of the War and were particularly fond of holding hearings in the field immediately after a Union defeat. The Sergeant at Arms of the Senate in December of 1862 was George T. Brown.

⁴ Actually Secretary of State Seward, under pressure from Radical leadership in Congress, had tried to free Lincoln to reorganize his Administration by submitting his own resignation. Lincoln contrived to get the resignation of Secretary of Treasury Chase, a leader of the Radicals. Lincoln then rejected both resignations, thus keeping the leaders of both the Moderate and Radical Republican factions in his Cabinet. Neither General-in-Chief Halleck or Secretary of War Stanton contemplated resigning at this time.

Sunday Night, 10 o'clock, 21' Dec. Camp Rufus King,
   Army Potomac[.]

. . . Burnside went to Washington last night & it is rumored,
but not believed, that he has resigned the Command of this
Army—— The papers say, that the whole Cabinet resigns, in
consequence of the request of a Senatorial Caucus of the
Republicans—— The news is too good to be true & wants
confirmation—— May it be confirmed! . . .

Monday Night, 10'30" 22' Dec. Camp Rufus King,
   Army of Potomac[.]

. . . Gen. Burnside has not yet returned, tho' he may be
here in the night run—— Every thing remains unsettled about
our Affairs in the Army & no one knows what is to be done one
hour ahead. . . .

Tuesday Night, 23' Dec. 1862—— Camp Rufus King,
   Army of the Potomac[.]

. . . [This afternoon] Burnside . . . wanted me to arrange
for a flag of Truce. . . . So I had to go & see about a Boat
etc. and between 1 & 2 we went down. . . . We have
arranged so that citizens on both sides can return to their
homes. . . .

Wednesday Night, 10 o'clock[,] 24' Dec—'62. Camp
   Rufus King, Stafford Co.[,] Va[.]——

This has been a busy day. . . . Started off at about 9'30" &
called at Sumner's. . . . Came back to the Lacy house &

looked around, then down to the River Bank at 12, for sending over the flag of truce to receive the answer agreed to be delivered to-day from Gen. Lee—— I also had sent over to get some permits for persons to come to this side & go to that side. . . . L.[orenzo] Thomas[,] Adjt. General, arrived with Mrs. Thornton, sister of [Sen.] J.[ohn] J. Crittenden [of Kentucky],[5] from California, on her way to Richmond. . . .

Thursday Night, 25' December (Christmas)[.] Camp
    Rufus King, Falmouth[.]

Went to bed last night with a great deal of noise going on, it being Christmas Eve. . . . We have had an excellent Xmas dinner, the Band is playing & the evening very mild——

Saturday Night[,] *27' December, '62.* Camp Rufus
    King—— Army of Potomac[.]

. . . There have been a great many people here today to see me, of the Citizens, wanting help—— I know not what they will do for food. . . .

Monday Night, 29' December, Camp Rufus King, Hd.
    Qrs. Potomac[.]

. . . Read my chapter as usual & asked the Divine Favor for the day—then went to Breakft—— That over I saw Gen.

---

[5] John J. Crittenden, Senator and Representative from Kentucky, had fought hard and long for compromise. He had given his name to the major Senate effort at Compromise in the secession winter of 1860–61. He was now a Representative from Kentucky, having been elected on a Unionist Party ticket.

Burnside & the arrangement was made to move at 9 o'clock tomorrow morning. . . . Examined some of the Confederate prisoners & found that the Troops were falling back——

Tuesday Night, 30' December, '62. Camp Rufus King, HdQrs[.,] Army Potomac[.]

. . . At about 4½ o'clock Burnside came into my Tent & told me that there was work going on which required us to remain in position for 3 or 4 days & that we would not move—— I am greatly disgusted but there is no help I suppose. . . . [Gen. William W.] Averill [Averell] has started on an expedition that, I fear, will be disastrous—— He goes to cut Rail Roads at Louisa Court House and Suffolk—— The Army is once more to cross the River in two places—— one above & the other below, near Schinker's [Skinker's] Neck—probably not before Friday. . . .

Wednesday Night, 31' December 1862, Camp Rufus King, HdQrs.[,] Army of Potomac[.]

Last night I went to bed at about 9'45" after having taken a Brandy Toddy & in the course of 15 minutes was asleep, but was again roused by the Card players at [Gen. Henry J.] Hunt'[s] Tent—— I remained awake an hour, then wrote a note & sent it, a little after 12 o'clock, requesting the noise to be stopped—— My rest was broken up for the night, however. . . . Much solicitude is felt in regard to the Message of Governor [Horatio] Seymour [New York], tomorrow, as it is understood that he will strike the key note of the Opposition[.] I trust that he will act wisely, but firmly & meet the Administration fairly & squarely—— Say, "thus far mayest thou go, but no farther" to Abraham Lincoln—— If he is discreet[sic] & honest he can do much to stem the tide of corruption & radicalism that now are . . . ruining us—— Burnside went down, late last night, & took a Steamer for Washington, where he has been today—— I do not yet know what movements have been going on today, or will go on tomorrow. I cannot see that more than Franklin and Hooker can move, but it is said that Troops go down to Suffolk by water—— So ends the last day of 1862——

January 1'[,] *Thursday Night.* Camp Rufus King, Head
  Quarters Potomac[.]

. . . There has been a constant run of business, of all kinds keeping me very busy—— [Capt. James P.] Kimball & [Lt. John V.] Bouvier went over to the Brigade, as it was New Year[']s day & had a pleasant time from 12 till 5. . . . We are all feeling quite down the mouth—— The country is in a bad state & the Rebels have been getting the advantage of us in every direction. . . .

Friday Night, 2' Jany.—— Camp Rufus King, Head
  Quarters, Army of Potomac[.]

. . . I had a singular Call this P. M. A carriage drove up with a Gentleman & Lady—— They proved to be Henry Moncure & wife She a beautiful young wife, reduced to the necessity of coming to ask permission to go to Baltimore & dreadfully frightened at the tales she heard about me—— Almost in hysteria—— But after a little she got over it, took a cup of Tea & some cake & with an overflowing heart started away—— I gave Moncure $15.00 to pay his way from Washington to Baltimore——

Saturday Night, 10'30"[,] *3' Jany.* Camp Rufus King,
Head Quarters Potomac[.]

. . . Sent for all the prisoners who were at Acquia & paroled
them to return to their houses in Stafford Co. It has been a
sin to keep these men in such condition, but there was no
help for it. We have been hard at work with prisoners etc. all
day and I have been examining prisoners of all classes,
deserters, contrabands etc. Have gathered a great deal of information in regard to the other side and of the people down
below, on this side the River. . . .

Sunday Night, 9 o'clock[,] *4' Jany.* Camp Rufus
King—— Head Quarters Potomac[.]

. . . Was sent for to General Burnside's after Breakfast and
found him quite under the weather—— He is feeling
badly—— Had to arrest Gen. [W. T. H.] Brooks yesterday
for insubordination[6] & to do several other disagreeable
things—— The President will not let him make any movement & every thing hangs by the eyelids—— The reverses of
[Gen. William S.] Rosecrans have had a very chilling effect
upon all of us,[7] and the loss of the "Monitor" off Cape Hatteras,
where she foundered, seems to add to our calamities about as
much as we can bear. . . .

---

[6] In his order of January 23, 1863, in which he tried to have several
general officers dismissed from the service, Burnside charged Brig. Gen.
W. T. H. Brooks, commanding 1st Division, Sixth Army Corps, with
"complaining of the policy of the Government, and . . . using language
tending to demoralize his command."

[7] At the Battle of Stone's River or Murfreesboro, Tennessee, Rosecrans' pursuit of Braxton Bragg received a decided check. The action
stretched out from December 31 to January 3. The fight was a draw,
but when it was over Bragg withdrew southward to Tullahoma.

Monday Night, 5' Jany. '63—— Camp Rufus King, Head Quarters of Potomac[.]

I went to bed last night at about ten o'clock. . . . There was a great deal of noise & noise is on the increase at these Head Quarters. . . . Got off at about 8'30" for the new Camp—— After staying there until the Prisoners arrived & putting them at work I came home—— Found Henry Byrd Lewis here— re-arrested by the order of Gen. [Edwin V.] Sumner, who did not know that he was in my hands—— So I have sent down to his home Lieut. [Paul] Quirk, to keep him in custody—let him get his witnesses & then return him to me, for further confinement. . . .[8]

Wednesday Night, 7' January, '63—— Camp Rufus King, Head Quarters of Potomac[.]

This is a cold night. . . . It is rumored & *now* believed, that Hooker is to command this Army. [Gen. Benjamin F.] Butler, (according to rumor) is to be Secretary of War[9] & Fremont to be the Commander-in-Chief—— This is now an Abolition Government——

---

[8] It would take a book to untangle the story of Henry Byrd Lewis. The case grew out of a quarrel between Lewis and Dr. Rose, both of King George County, Virginia, and both of whom had been officers in the County Militia. It involved a threatened duel, an ambush in which Dr. Rose was killed, and a maze of legal technicalities involving the County Sheriff, Confederate authorities, and several different Union authorities. Lewis was popped in and out of jail, frequently at his own request, by both local and Union army officers. On January 8, 1863, Patrick dumped the whole mess in Judge Advocate Joseph Holt's lap.

[9] Actually, Gen. Butler, having been relieved by Gen. Banks of Command at New Orleans, was in the process of rejecting Lincoln's offer of a major command in the Mississippi Valley to the north of New Orleans. Butler later contended that he was offered Grant's command.

Friday Night, 10 o'clock, 9' Jany[.]—— Camp Rufus
   King, Hd. Qrs.[,] Army Potomac[.]

. . . Robbery of the worst kind is the Order of the day with
all our Cavalry Regts. & they are doing our cause a vast deal
of injury—— Governor [Horatio] Seymour's Message is
out—— It is an elaborate document & takes high ground for
the suppression of Rebellion, but denounces many acts of the
Administration as Unconstitutional——

Saturday Night, 10 o'clock[,] *10' January 1863*——
   Camp Rufus King——

. . . The day has been spent on Office duty. . . . [Gen.
Alfred] Pleasonton has been here & had a long talk about his
System of picketing & outpost duty, and his treatment of the
people—— He has more sense than [Gen William W.] Averill
[sic]——

Sunday Night, 9 o'clock, 11' Jany. [']*63*—— Camp
   Rufus King, Army of Potomac[.]

. . . The news we get is bad—that Vicksburg is again the
place of disaster & defeat to our Troops under [Gen. William
T.] Sherman—that there is some mishap at Galveston & that
Jno. [Gen. John Bankhead] Magruder has captured
Pensacola——[10] These items of intelligence are making bad

---

[10] Gen. Sherman's failure to find the key to the Vicksburg defenses at
Chickasaw Bluffs had come on December 28 and 29. Had he known,
Patrick might have been encouraged by Sherman's capture of Arkansas
Post on January 11, 1863. The news of the Gulf Coast was garbled.
John Magruder's Confederate forces had recaptured Galveston on Janu-
ary 1. Nothing of consequence had taken place at Pensacola.

work amongst our Troops, already dispirited by our reverses—— Should our Troops be paid off before the next action, I predict very large desertions & no possibility of staying them. . . . There is a probability, I think, that Burnside will not long remain in command—— The contest is between Franklin & Hooker for the succession.

Monday Night, 9 o'clock[,] *12' Jany. '63*—— Camp
   Rufus King——

. . . There is to be a movement this week—— So Burnside says. . . . The ground is muddy every morning from the effects of frost coming out of the ground—— I am tired of this kind of life. . . .

Tuesday Night[,] *10'30"*[,] *13' Jany.* Camp Rufus King,
   Army of Potomac[.]

. . . Was with Burnside some hours about Guides & that class of men, looking over maps & giving that kind of information. . . . Burnside is rather obtuse in his conceptions & very forgetful—— I have had a great deal of Office business today & much of it of no very pleasant character—— There is a growing idea on the part of the Cavalry, that I am in the way of their unlicensed robbery & they are trying their best to overthrow my authority—— Sumner is for backing them——

Wednesday Night, 14' Jany. [']*63*[,] *10 o'clock*[.] Camp
   Rufus King—— Head Quarters etc[.]

. . . Was with the General some time at two or three several times during the day—— We are trying to get information on all subjects connected with the road about the Fords & beyond, on the other side of the River——

Thursday Night[,] *15'–10'15"*—— Camp Rufus
    King—— Army of Potomac[.]

. . . Have a busy day, not accomplishing much, but getting guides, hauling up all my old Brigade & questioning all the Officers about the country between the River, Plank & Telegraph— —Have been with Burnside a great deal of the time, looking over the maps etc. Have had more work on hand, a part of the time, than I could carry. . . . I suppose that we shall cross above, with the right of our Army, under Hooker and be governed by circumstances as to crossing over the remainder—— If we cross above, the Gunboats will make a demonstration below probably in the neighborhood of Briscoe mines. . . .

Friday Night, 16' Jany[.]—— Head Quarters[,] Army of
    Potomac, Camp Rufus King——

. . . Have been gathering information for the move & have one or two men more who know all about the country between the Plank [Road] & River—— Eben. Magee is up here & I have also sent for Stratton—— Williams has been here & is now gone—— Harding has gone home for a few hours but is to return here tonight[.] Bouvier has been all day at Acquia Creek & only returned in the evening. . . .

Saturday Night, 17' Jany. '63[.] Camp Rufus King—
    Head Quarters Potomac[.]

An awful cold night & little sleep last night. . . . Have been trying to draw up something for Provost Marshals, in view

of the Desertions & of the forward movement—— [sic]
Deming says the men do not want to cross the River——
Bates—[Daniel] Sickles' Prov. Marshal has been here to say
the Excelsiors are determined to run if they can get a chance,
having been paid off today—— Last night 15 men from a
New York Regt. of Bartlett's Brigade deserted—— I believe
the men are unwilling again to fight, at this point, if they can
get clear of doing so. . . . There is a bad state of things all
around—— Deserters tell me that it is known on the other side
that we intend to give battle & they are preparing to meet
us—— They have had an extra supply of Ammunition issued
to them & notice to turn out at a moment's warning——
Their Artillery is, tonight, moving up to the right, to take
charge of the crossings at the fords—— So it is said——
Hooker says he can have command of this Army when he will
say the word—— He asks but 5 days to whip Lee & 15 is all
he will ask to take Richmond—— He must be drunk——

Sunday Night, 18' Jany.—10'30"[,] Camp Rufus King,
   Army of Potomac[.]

. . . I have given [Capt. J. W.] Forsyth orders to arrest all
persons on the Boats with the pass of [Col. Lafayette C.]
Baker—— Prov. Mar. War Dept." He is sending them down
(detectives) on board the Boat. . . .

Monday Night[,] *19' Jany*[.]—— *9 O'clock*[.] Camp
   Rufus King, Army of Potomac[.]

. . . The detectives are all in arrest at Acquia & I have
reported their confinement to the War Department—— It

---

¹¹ Col. Baker who thought of himself as head of the "Secret Service"
of the United States. This is the opening shot in a long and bitter
controversy between Patrick and Baker,

will, probably, raise a breeze——— In all probability I shall be called to Washington by the Secretary——— It was expected that we would move the Army today——— It is deferred, I think until Wednesday. . . .

Tuesday Night, 9 o'clock, 20' Jany[.]——— Camp Rufus King, Head Quarters[.]

. . . Up early & breakfasted, then Saw Burnside about the arrangement of Troops for Rail Road Defences, Depots & Landings. . . . The Troops moved at 12 o'clock, in readiness to go over the river at 2 or 3 points between Falmouth & Scotts Dam——— It has been a cold day, but the night will be terrible. . . . Senators [James W.] Nesmith [Oregon] & [Milton S.] Latham [California] are at [Brig. Gen. Rufus] Ingalls' where I have just left them. [Henry J.] Raymond ("Little Villain") is also here, to see tomorrow's fight[.][12]

Wednesday Night, 21' Jany[.]———Camp Rufus King, Head Quarters of Potomac[.]

Last night was one of the most disagreeable possible. . . . Gen. Burnside was to have moved at 5 but the storm & darkness prevented until after 8——— I took my 2 aids & a Cavalry escort of 25 men & started off so bundled up that no rain reached me ——— Burnside's Head Quarters were at Wroton's about 6 miles from here——— I went out there & to Banks Ford, back, & to Franklin's Head Quarters, this side of there, where I left Burnside & came home by 3 o'clock——— It has been an awful night & day, the 24 last hours & this night is the same———

---

[12] Gen. Ingalls was the quartermaster general of the Army of the Potomac and Raymond was the editor of the New York *Times*.

Our men are stretched along the River Bank for 6 or 7 miles above Falmouth, & are in the woods, except some of the Artillery, but horses & men are chilled & loaded with mud —— The Artillery & Ponton Train can scarcely move, off the road, & the ground has become saturated—— The movement is, necessarily postponed—— How long it is impossible to say, but the men are greatly demoralized[.] The Sick & Stragglers are very numerous—— At 11 o'clock last night the Secretary of War telegraphed for the arrest of [Sid] Deming of the Associated Press—— I sent him to [Gen. John H.] Martindale[13] this morning——

Thursday Night, 22' Jany. Camp Rufus King, Head Quarters Potomac[.]

Last night was again rainy, windy & uncomfortable, but the rain has finally ceased & there is very little wind tonight, but the mud is awful. Our Camp is flooded with liquid mud. . . .

Friday Night[,] 23' Jany. Camp Rufus King, Head Quarters of A. Potomac[.]

. . . Morning came—a dark one, but eventually the clouds lifted, so that about noon we had a look at the sun—— It was very much needed, from the fact that every body was in the dumps—— The Order was given today for the men—the Troops, to fall back again to their positions, occupied before the move on Monday[.] They have been passing all the day & their appearance is not very soldierlike, or encouraging—— It is said that a very bad feeling has sprung up in the Army

---

[13] Gen. Martindale had become the commander of the Department of Washington, and its troops which constituted the Twenty-Second Army Corps.

against Burnside, growing out of his Fredricksburg failure and this last sad attempt, which is, perhaps, more disastrous to him than the first—— The Officers at Head Quarters are much disgusted at a certain want of decision, even in Small Matters—— He has, today been having his Quarters put in condition, evidently with a view to permanency in spite of his repeated assurances that we would move, the moment *our* Army moved forward—— We are now without wood & without water—— We are all disgusted. . . .

Saturday Night, 24' Jany. Head Quarters[,] Army of
    Potomac, Camp Rufus King——

. . . Have not been very busy today, excepting to give, or sign furloughs—— The whole Army seems to be asking for them—— I believe that, at least, a dozen Officers, perhaps more, left here (Head Quarters) this morning—— I have been trying to work, but there is a very oppressive feeling in Camp, among both Officers & men, which prevents work from being done. . . .

Sunday Night, 25' Jany. Head Quarters[,] Army of
    Potomac, Camp Rufus King[.]

. . . The Secretary of War has ordered the release of the two or three detectives now in charge down at Acquia—— Gen. Burnside is said to have tendered his resignation——

Monday Night, 26' Jany[.]—— Camp Rufus King,
    Head Quarters[,] Army of Potomac[.]

. . . When I came out to breakfast I learned from Col. [Edwin R.] Goodrich that Gen. Burnside had been to see the

President & Secretary—that he had offered his resignation, which was not accepted—that he then demanded the removal of [Gen. Joseph] Hooker, or the acceptance of his resignation—— A paper was then handed him to the effect that, at his own request Gen. Burnside was relieved from the command of the Army of the Potomac & a leave of Thirty days granted him, with the Officers of his personal Staff—— Against this he protested, as he did not ask to be relieved, but it was of no use—— Gen. [Edwin V.] Sumner was relieved, in the same way & sent on 30 days leave—— Gen. [William B.] Franklin was ordered to turn over the Command of the Grand Division & report in Washington. Many persons think it is probable that Franklin will have a trial. Undoubtedly there is a great deal of disloyalty, according to Judge [Joseph] Holt's interpretation of that word, in Franklin's command—— Gen. Hooker was ordered to the command of the Army of the Potomac—— He came over early & at about 10′30″ we all met at Burnside's Tent & took leave of him. He made a few remarks, to which, as there seemed to be some feeling, I thought proper to reply, and prevented any thing unpleasant from taking place—— We paid our respects to Hooker, who assumed command & by 12. M. Burnside was on his way to Washington, followed by Hooker, who goes up there to organize & get ready for work—— He has desired me to go forward & do as I have done, using his name in the same manner that I have used Burnside's & McClellan's. . . .

Tuesday Night, 27' Jany[,]—— Head Quarters[,] Army
   of the Potomac[.]

. . . As soon as I am able I shall go to Washington & get such things as I need for the Prisoners—— They ought to work, but we have no Tools. . . .

Wednesday Night, 28' January—— Camp on the Hill
    Side—— Snow Storm[.]

One of the most disagreeable days——24 hours——that I
have ever experienced—— The rain turned into snow & it has
been raining & snowing all day. . . . Well! The Army of the
Potomac has stuck fast in the mud and the Head Quarters
have, not only been removed, but several of the Staff, with
Gen. Hooker, have returned to the old Camp. . . .

Friday Night, 30' Jany. '63[.] Camp on the Hill Side, in
    Snow & Mud——

. . . I was up early & at 8 o'clock was on my way to Head
Quarters—— Roads almost impassable, even on horseback—— arrived there & saw Hooker a half hour before he
had his Breakfast—then saw [Rufus B.] Ingalls & gave him
the Detective endorsement[,] then another interview with
Hooker & Pleasonton—the latter I shall have difficulty with.
. . . [Gen. Daniel] Butterfield now Chief of Staff, delights in
papers & Orders—— Hooker is determined to do a great
many things that are right & some probably, that are
wrong—— The President has the names of about 80 Officers,
who are to be dismissed the Service for having spoken dis-
respectfully of him in reference to the removal of McClellan
& the [Fitz John] Porter Court Martial. . . .

Saturday Night, 10 o'clock, 31' Jany[.]—— Camp on the
    Hill Side[.]

. . . The great business of the morning was, getting of
deserters, of whom about 344 were despatched to their Regts.
but a number more have since come in. . . .

Sunday Night, 1' Feby. Head Quarters of Potomac, Camp Rufus King——

. . . I have just come from Butterfield's tent and am very much disgusted with his manner and the view he takes of our affairs—his Ex Cathedra way of speaking, & the flippancy of the whole Head Quarter[s] establishment—— Hooker has gone to bed having just returned from Washington—— O I am sick, sick, sick!

Monday Night, 2' Feby. Camp Rufus King, Head Qrs.[,] Army of Potomac[.]

. . . My opinion of Butterfield & Co. has not improved by any thing that I have seen today—— If there is not more *weight*, we shall go into the upper regions, thro' the Agency of Gas! I find that many arrests have been made, without my knowledge, and it is not known by whose authority they were made—— I expect that the Grand Divisions will be broken up tomorrow, & the old System of Corps again resumed—— Of this thing I am glad, tho' it may be that something equally objectionable will be established. . . .

Wednesday Night[,] *4' Feby*. Camp Rufus King, Head Quarters etc[.]

. . . There is now a great deal of grab game going on among Sutlers & Quarter Masters—— The Sutlers bring their goods out of Belle Plain, perhaps a mile, then transfer to Government Waggons, go back & get other goods from Belle Plain, to be treated in like manner—— We have captured several Waggons & their contents are now in the Government—or in my hands. . . .

Thursday Night, 10'15"[,] *5' Feby.* Camp Rufus King,
Army of Potomac[,] HdQrs——

. . . Have just come from a talk with [Gen. James S.]
Wadsworth——[14] He has come to the conclusion that my
policy is correct, so far as the people here, citizens, are concerned—— I am trying to make up a System of Secret
Service, but find it hard to organize where there is so little
good Material—— It seems probable that I shall take a few
men into my employ at once—— Several have offered, but
as yet none have been employed—— I do not fancy the class
of men & think they do not fancy me——

Sunday Night, 8' Feby. '63, Camp Rufus King, HdQrs[.]
Potomac——

I was up very late last night—— Did not go to bed until 12'30"
or one A. M. Mr. [John F.] Seymour, the Brother of the
Governor, was here with me from about 11 o'clock——[15] We
talked over all sorts of matters about the public affairs of the
State of New York & of the United States. . . . Breakfast
8'30" & at work ever since—— I had first a call from Mrs.
J[ames] S. Green's Father ([John M.] Whittemore of New
York) then after they had had a long interview with Butterfield,
the wives of both the Greens came to see me—— Mrs. J. S.
is a very pretty woman & Mrs. Duff [Green][16] is much like
Mrs. Huntington of Rome. . . . This evening a Detective
named McKelvey from Washington has been here—— I will,
probably, engage him for my secret service Department——

---

[14] Gen. Wadsworth had come down from Washington to command a
Division in the First Corps.

[15] John F. Seymour acted as a private secretary to his brother.

[16] James S. Green had been a United States Senator from Missouri in
the 36th Congress and was a Buchanan Democrat. He was a cousin of
Duff Green.

I have a paper [from] the other side, from Mrs. Gray's friends, with the names of Lee, Longstreet & [Maj. Gen. Lafayette] McLaws—— So Longstreet is here——

Monday Night, 9' February—— Camp Rufus King, Army of Potomac.

. . . I took an opportunity to have a good talk with Hooker—— I have talked plainly & fairly with him about the state of things in the Army, about the Officers etc. He has read me the letter of Burnside—or rather Order No. 8, dismissing Gen[s]. Hooker, Brooks, Newton—several others—for insubordination, treason etc. I am very much surprised at the Order & Hooker swears that "Burnside shall eat it, or he will have his ears, as soon as the War is over." . . .

Tuesday Night, 10' February '63—— Camp Rufus, Army of Potomac[.]

. . . I have made some arrangements about secret service Department—— Have had a long conversation with Col. [George] Sharp[e] of the 120' N. Y. as to the organization of the Dept. with him, a Lawyer, for its Chief—— He appears well, & I think he would be a pleasant man to be Associated with. . . .

Wednesday Night[,] 11' February '63—— Camp Rufus King—— A. of P.

Had no sleep last night . . . a Dominie & a Woman—not his wife, had been put in [Edward] Martindale's[17] Tent by

---

[17] Edward Martindale was the son of Gen. John H. Martindale, Military Governor of Washington. He was currently serving on Patrick's staff.

[Capt.] Beckwith—— They jabbered away until a late hour—— Then Martindale came home & tried to get into his Tent, about 11 o'clock——

Thursday Night, 12' February, 1863. Camp Rufus King[,] Army of Potomac[.]

. . . Had a long talk this morning with Hooker, on business & learned that Pleasonton stands no higher in the opinion of Hooker than he does in mine. . . .

Friday Night[.] *13' Feby. 1863*—— Camp Rufus King, Army of the Potomac[.]

. . . Was turned out at daylight by a long tongued blather-skyte in the shape of an Orderly, who wanted a Pass! I sent him off with either a flea, or a flounder in his ear—— Was overrun with business all the morning, but got off at about 12 M. for Falmouth, where I closed up the Shops in a hurry, taking a Squadron of Cavalry—— Ordered out all the men & had a registration made of all having permits—— Gave Orders for all persons not registered to leave within 36 hours, or have their property confiscated. . . . Found that I was wanted at Gen. Hooker[']s—— Very Stringent Orders are being issued in regard to Passes, trade etc. A new Head Quarters Sutler is appointed—all other revoked—— One Newspaper Agent for the whole Army. . . .

Saturday Night, 14' Feby. 1863—— Camp Rufus King, Army of the Potomac[.]

. . . Dan the Magnificent [Butterfield] was in command today, & improved it by sending for the Staff as often the gas pressed strongly within him which, of course, was pretty often. . . . There has been quite a sad affair in our neighborhood today[.] The Phillips House was burned, & only the walls left standing tonight—— It is said that it took fire by some of Stoneman's Officers trying to get a Sibley Stove to work in the Attic—— Not a bucket of water could be had to quench the fire—wells all dry—— . . .

Monday Night, 16' Feby. 1863—— Camp Rufus King, Army of Potomac[.]

. . . Hooker is, today, reviewing Sigel's [Eleventh] Corps, at Stafford Court House—— There is a great rush of Sutlers etc. for extension of time—— We are sending off hosts of Sutlers, Traders etc[.] beyond our Lines. . . .

Wednesday Night[,] *18 Feby. 1863*—— Camp Rufus King, Army of Potomac[.]

. . . I have been telegraphed to, from Washington, to go up & Speak before the Young Men's Christian Association, in the House of Representatives, on Sunday Night, but I do not see how I can get away to do so—— It would be doing an act of Christian Duty, however, I think——

Friday Night, 20' Feby. 1863—— Camp Rufus King, Army of Potomac——

. . . [Rev. N. L. "Ninny"] Harris [a West Point friend] staid here last night & so did Gen. [John H.] Martindale—— The Latter telegraphed me that he would be down to see me on

Official business & I sent down to receive him—— He *did*
come & we sat & talked together until midnight, endeavoring
to digest a plan by which some of the difficulties of intercourse
between Washington & this Army may be obviated. . . .

Saturday Night[,] *21' Feby*[.]—— Camp Rufus King,
   Army of Potomac[.]

. . . I had an interview with Gen. Hooker on some indifferent
Subject which led to a long & very interesting conversation on
personal matters in which I told him a few things about his
Chief of Staff [Butterfield] that angered him very much. . . .
I have had no reason to find fault, so far, with Hooker. . . .

Sunday Night, 22' Feby. 1863—— Camp Rufus
   King——

. . . The National Salute was fired, today, by the Guns of
Each Corps, I think, and from the other side they were
responded to by the Rebels, probably at the Head Quarters
of their Army. . . .

Friday Night[,] *27' Feby*[.]—— Camp Rufus King——
   HdQrs.[,] Army of Potomac[.]

. . . I have been a busy man for the last three days—— On
Wednesday I went to Washington, after a hard day's work—
leaving here at 7 o'clock, or After & taking a boat immediately
on arriving at Acquia, which landed me at Washington, in
the rain, on 6 St. Wharf, at daylight—— I took my way to
Ebbitt House so as to breakfast, then to see [Maj. William B.]

Rochester, then [Sen. James W.] Nesmith—then to War
Office—[John] Potts, [Thomas M.] Vincent, [Geo. D.]
Ruggles, [William A.] Nichols, [Lorenzo] Thomas & [Edward
R. S.] Canby——— The Sec. War and the Asst. Sec. [Peter H.]
Watson. . . . Then to see [John H.] Martindale—then to
War Office—then to get my pay then to see Mrs. Canby———
Staid till near 6 & went then to dine with Jno. Potts; after-
wards went to Willards at 8 & saw Senator [Ira] Harris, Mr.
[Erastus B.] Corning, Mrs. Hayden & ladies in the room at
Willards——— We then went & had a Sit in [George B.]
McClellan's room for an hour, or more & I went up at 10, or
after, to see [Alexander S.] Shiras, staid until 11'15" & came to
Ebbitt House, then home—that is, to my Boat—by about
12. M.[18] . . . Reached home not far from two o'clock & went
to work——— Find a deal of work behind & have been hard at
it ever since——— It is a hard department to work in & I
cannot manage it under Butterfield——— He makes more work
than I am able to carry out & I am pretty much decided to
resign & go——— I think to give Hooker notice to get a Provost
Marshal as soon as convenient. . . .

Saturday Night, 28' February.

. . . Some very insolent endorsements, signed by [Gen. Seth]
Williams but written by Butterfield, caused me a deal of
writing and kept me under the Spur for some hours. . . .
Hooker was to be home this evening, but has not yet returned.

---

[18] Maj. Rochester was an Additional Paymaster; Senator Nesmith,
Oregon's senior Senator; John Potts, the Chief Clerk of the War Depart-
ment. Both Maj. Vincent and Lt. Col. Nichols were Assistant Adjutant
Generals in the office of Gen. Lorenzo Thomas, The Adjutant General
of the Army. Peter H. Watson was one of the Assistant Secretaries of
War, and both Generals Ruggles and Canby were on "Special Duty" in
the Secretary of War's Office. New York State was represented by Ira
Harris in the United States Senate and Mr. Corning in the House of
Representatives. Col. Shiras was the Assistant Commissary of Subsistence; and Mrs. Hayden was probably the wife of Maj. Julius Hayden.

. . . Just before night I received another ill bred & insolent endorsement on an Official paper, and that has settled the matter with me—— I have written to Gen. [Seth] Williams, requesting him to ask the Comdg. General, so soon as he returns, to relieve me from duty as Provost Marshal General, & have written to [Gen. E. R. S.] Canby asking him whether I had better ask for Western or Southern duty; or whether I might not as well go home——- I have not had time to say any thing of my visit to Washington—— My adventures there, were strange & somewhat amusing, as well as exciting—— I found, after a long conversation with [Asst. Secty.] Watson, that I had been suspected, for a long time, of dishonest practises—— That an emissary of [Col. Lafayette C.] Baker stated that [Capt.] Mansfield had sent Salt to Richmond in large quantities, on *my* printed permit, that the Salt was found with Such permit, in Richmond—— That vast amounts of plunder had been sent North, from the Sack of Frederic[k]s-burg, supposed to be by my permission & assistance—that I had arrested witnesses who were to testify in the Hall case to shut off investigation etc. etc. He told me that I was to have been dismissed 2 or 3 times, but circumstances prevented it—— I would have been dismissed now, within a few days past, but that such a Storm was raised about his ears that he became satisfied that he *must* be in error, but could not see how—— Baker swears hostility eternal against [Col. Rufus] Ingal[l]s [Chief Quartermaster of the Army of the Potomac] & myself—— Ingal[l]s is charged with a vast amount of peculations in Forage, which Baker is hunting out & from this cause arises the hostility of Ingal[l]s against Baker—— The reason why Burnside would not act against Baker was, that when he was here last Summer, he kept a woman whom Baker passed down here, to him & who was one of Baker's creatures—— Watson told me that he had heard Burnside ask Baker to come & see him—— So too, Hooker, is to some degree in his clutches——— He went up to Washington the other day, drew his pay in the middle of the month, went to a gambling house, staid all night, lost all his money, went to Morris Miller[19] next day & drew his commutation for fuel & quarters——— These be queer things, certainly——— Why Baker is so powerful may be accounted for from the fact made known to me by Wilkes of the "Spirit [of the Times]" that he is, really, in the employ of Seward—is his tool & monster—and is only nominally on duty in the War Department——— Seward uses him to dog political men—women are kept at the Hotels with false keys & every guest is under surveillance——— Well! I came to the conclusion, that where so much roguery exists, the Country is hardly worth saving——— Some of the hangers on of the Army were wanting to come down with me, on the Boat, & [John A.] Duff, [George] Wilkes, [Maj.] Charley Whiting & myself[20] came down in a carriage together—to the foot of 6' Street, at 12 o'clock——— Wilkes is very full of information & gave me some that really is valuable——— I called to see Old [Alexander] Shiras, staid with him a long while—till 11'15" and got a great deal of 'Shiras talk.' . . .

Monday Night, 2' March, '63. Camp Rufus King, Head
    Quarters Potomac[.]

. . . I have had the usual amount of Butterfield's fooleries to meet today, & at 5 o'clock had an Order from Butterfield "to tell all I know about the Northern Neck immediately"——— I commenced, but the Order has been very much modified & it seems, now, that only some *little* things are wanted, for the

---

[19] Maj. Morris Miller was a Quartermaster in the Office of the Quartermaster General in Washington.

[20] John A. Duff was a Purveyor for the Headquarters, Army of the Potomac. Wilkes was a correspondent of the New York *Tribune,* and the *Spirit of the Times.* Maj. Whiting commanded a detachment of the 2nd U.S. Cavalry.

information of those who are going on an expedition,
tomorrow, down the River—— We are, tonight, gathering
up the Guides etc. of the expedition. . . .

Tuesday Night, 3' March, '63. Camp Rufus King, Head
    Quarters Potomac[.]

. . . I have been trying, to some extent, to arrange my papers,
but can do little until my successor is named—— It will take
me some days before I can get my papers into such shape as to
enable me to leave as I could wish—— I expected to have
had my orders before this time, as Gen. Hooker said he would
relieve me as soon as he could. . . .

Thursday Night, 5' March '63—— Camp Rufus King,
    Army of Potomac[.]

. . . There has been another nice matter in connexion with
my Pass—— The Scouts sent out by Col. Sharpe were arrested
& sent back by [Gen. William W.] Averill [sic], notwithstanding they had my pass—— It was a great piece of arrogance
& stupidity combined, which caused 'Fighting Joe Hooker' to
swear very wickedly & send for Averill [sic] in a great
hurry—— What the said Averill [sic] caught is a question
yet undecided. . . .

Friday Night[,] 6' March '63——— Camp Rufus King,
    HdQrs.[,] Army of Potomac[.]

Another busy day has passed & I am again in my tent, quietly
at about 10 o'clock. . . . I get nothing as to my being relieved,

and tonight I have been at Head Quarters with Butterfield & Hooker but nothing said on that Subject. . . .

Saturday Night, 7' March, '63—— Camp Rufus King, Hd.Qrs.[,] Army of Potomac[.]

Another busy day & week—— I thought, last Saturday night, that my services with this Army were nearly closed, but I seem no nearer the end to be attained now, than then—— My work is increasing continually and no such efforts are made to release me as I was led to believe would be made—— I am sent for & discussions take place, frequently, in the Tent of the Comdg. General, Butterfield being present, but as yet, nothing comes of it. . . . A Mr. Stanley has been here also to see me from New York—— He is the detective of the Spirit of the Times—— He hopes to be used with the Army of the Potomac——

Monday Night, 9' March, '63—— Camp Rufus King, Hd. Qrs.[,] Army Potomac[.]

. . . I have had all sorts of interviews—— The most disgusting was with the representative of a *loyal* association to furnish the Army with the papers that are 'truly Loyal,' such as the Tribune, Evening Post & Chronicle—— They want an exclusive privilege & to furnish the paper at 5 cents—— This is the scheme. . . . I forgot to say, that in my interview with Butterfield this morning, he took great pains to show me that he had no knowledge of [John A.] Duff & [John T.] Tully, but that [George] Wilkes is the real man, & they are only his junior partners[.][21]

---

[21] Mr. John T. Tully and Mr. William C. Stewart were the general newspaper agents for the Army of the Potomac who brought the newspapers down from Washington and delivered them to eight local agents who distributed them through the Army. It was a lucrative business that inspired a great deal of competition. It also opened a door to favoritism by the exclusion of some newspapers from the Army.

Tuesday ĸ*ight, 10' March, 1863*—— Camp Rufus King,
   Head Quarters Potomac[.]

Rain, Rain, Rain! . . . I have been busy all this evening
with various matters. . . . Sharpe has gone to Washington,
to carry important despatches to Gen. Hooker, who went up
at about 1'45". . . . I have had hold of some very hard cases
today and have been obliged to cut short some very enter-
prising Sutlers. . . .

Wednesday Night, 11' March—— Camp Rufus King,
   Head Quarters Potomac[.]

. . . Hooker does not get back yet—— I have been annoyed
very much by Butterfield being in command[.] He thinks
himself very smart, but is in reality nearly a fool about some
things—— I am utterly disgusted with him—— He would
keep me doing nothing but answering his follies. . . . The
FitzHughs did not cross the river at all, as they had several
thousand dollars in specie and that Butterfield prohibited
from passing over. . . .

Thursday Night[,] *12' March* [']*63.* Camp Rufus King,
   Army of Potomac——

. . . There has been a wedding today & a Ball tonight at
Sickles' Head Quarters—— One of his Officers could not get
away to be married & the foolish girl came down to be married
here—— Had a nice visit from [Gen. Herman] Haupt this
afternoon, & Ned [Edmund] Schriver, now Inspector General,
has but just left here—— He is ordered here as Inspector
General U.S. Army[.]

Saturday Night, 10'30" 14' March, '63—— Head
Quarters[,] Army of Potomac——

Two busy days gone since I put my pen to paper in this book.
. . . Yesterday morning Haupt came down & breakfasted
with me—— Then went off with me & we examined some
torpedoes for blowing up bridges—very nice & ingenious—
and as experience proves very effective—to be carried in the
pocket by Scouts etc. Also the augers for boring the holes for
them[,] also the augers & socket for making the tenons for the
little floats—for crossing rivers—— Also the plans for suspension bridges of wood—[blank] inch boards, to be hung across
a stream of 100 feet span—or more—the latter I have his permission to use on the farm—— They should be covered with
pitch—— Also immense floats for making temporary bridges—
for rail road purposes & transportation of loaded cars on Rivers
& elsewhere. . . . This evening I am feeling tolerably well.
. . . Thus ends the last day of my 52' Year-—— Melancholy
thought——

Chapter VII

Chancellorsville

MARCH 15, 1863, THROUGH MAY 7, 1863

MARCH WAS A MONTH OF PREPARATION. Under Joseph Hooker's prodding the Army of the Potomac was visibly pulling itself together. Leaves and furloughs were sharply reduced, efforts to learn Lee's whereabouts and condition were stepped up. Some of the little luxuries brought to the Army by sutlers and traders became scarce; soon the sutlers and traders themselves were gone. Newspaper correspondents were curbed. The cumbersome Grand Division organizations of the Army under Burnside disappeared, although the habit of making a single commander responsible for two corps while in combat persisted. If Patrick's reaction is typical, the officers and men of the Army felt, and liked, the stronger hand on the reins.

Grant's fourth and fifth efforts to get at Vicksburg failed in March when Union forces at both Yazoo Pass and in Steele's Bayou could not find a way to reach dry ground to the north and east of Vicksburg. In April, however, Grant's final effort began when Porter's gunboats passed the Vicksburg batteries on the 16th and with the transports began ferrying Grant's army across the Mississippi on the 30th. From his new position below Vicksburg Grant was ready to cut loose from all supply and communication lines and fight his way into the rear of Vicksburg, laying siege to the fortress city if necessary.

The Chancellorsville campaign opened on April 27.

Sunday [,] *March 15' 1863*—— Head Quarters [,] Army
of the Potomac [.]

This is the beginning of a new 'Year with me'—— . . . Within
the last year there have been very many narrow escapes for
me & I have felt that there was a Special Providence—a
Guardian Angel watching over and protecting me—— In the
terrible fights of [2nd] Bull Run, South Mountain & Antietam,
the Lord God was to me both a Sun & a Shield! The night of
the 18' of September I shall never forget—that night of
wrestling with the Angel of the Covenant—— And how it was
answered—— This 52' Year of my life ought to bring me
nearer to God than any year of my previous life and yet I
sometimes feel that I am less spiritually minded & more con-
formed to the world than heretofore—— Especially has this
been the case since I have been at Head Quarters, from the
fact that I have almost no association with Christians, no
opportunities for privacy & retirement, no chance to talk with
& to the Troops—no way of gaining strength by exercise and
reflection—— My mind & my time wholly absorbed by public
duties, it becomes a question whether I am even prepared to
die. . . .

Monday Night, 16' March, 1863—— Head Quarters [,]
Army of Potomac, Camp R. K.

. . . Another poor correspondent—[Edwin F. Denyse] of the
[New York] Herald—was arrested this evening & [Gen.
Daniel] Butterfield's order to iron & throw him into the Guard
House was carried out only partially, as I have sent him to
Acquia but not in irons—— He & several others, are to be
tried on Wednesday. . . .

Tuesday Night, 17' March 1863—— S. [.] Patrick's day
in the evening, 10 o'clock [.]

. . . In accordance with a Special request (following an
Order) from Hooker, I agreed to go over & witness some of
the festivities at the Head Quarters of Meagher's Irish
Brigade—— [Gen Henry W.] Benham joined me, as I could
not go when Hooker left, & after going far out of our way
we brought up in the midst of a grand steeple chase, from
which the crowd soon adjourned to drink punch at [Gen.
Thomas F.] Meagher's Head Quarters—— Every body got
tight & I found it was no place for me—so I came home,
[Capt. James P.] Kimball & [Col. George H.] Sharpe
remained & came home at dusk, tight as bricks. . . . The day
has been pleasant overhead, but so muddy under foot as to
make the Hurdle & other races dangerous for Horses &
Riders——

Wednesday Night, 18' March, '63—— Head Quarters [,]
Army of Potomac—— In Camp [.]

. . . I have some infamous Letters from Washington, hatched
up by [Col. L. C.] Baker & [Assist. Sec. Peter H.] Watson, to
annoy me—— They will be referred to Gen. Hooker tomorrow. De Nyse [Denyse], correspondent of the Herald, has been
tried by a Military Commission,[1] at my Office this morning. . . .

---

[1] This is Edwin F. Denyse of the New York *Herald*. In a letter published in the *Herald* on March 14th, Denyse had written of "unmistake-
able preparations now being made for a speedy movement of the army"
and added that "no one in the army doubts" that it "will come at the
earliest possible moment." Hooker ordered Denyse's arrest and after
trial before this Commission he was sentenced to six months at hard
labor in the Quartermaster's Department, but Hooker subsequently
commuted the sentence to transportation outside the lines.

Thursday Night [,] *19' March, '63*—— Head Quarters [,]
Army of the Potomac [.]

Another busy day—— After a sound sleep I rose in good
season this morning & spent my time in the usual way until
Breakfast—— I then wrote to Hon. P.[eter] H. Stanton
[Watson], Asst. Sec. War, saying that So far as the Pillage of
Frederic[k]sburg was concerned, I had nothing further to say,
and that a Court of Inquiry would elicit the facts in the
case—— I am disgusted with these continued attempts to
implicate me in the pillage of Frederic[k]sburg & have sent a
copy of the Letters to Hooker. . . .

Friday Night, 20' March—— Head Quarters [,] Army
of the Potomac [.]

. . . I have been very much at work, as usual, today, and have
had some curious business transactions—— Gallagher [a
sutler] has been before me & I am closing up his matters——
He is a keen fellow. Charlotte? Nicholas, Col. [John] Morgan's colored woman was here to arrange about Supplies & I
have made arrangements for sending out to her tomorrow.[2] . . .

Saturday Night [,] *21' March, '63*—— Head Quarters [,]
Army of the Potomac [.]

. . . [Lt. John V.] Bouvier went to Washington yesterday
morning & was to be back tomorrow, but I have telegraphed
to him to remain tomorrow, in order to ascertain what frauds

---

[2] Col. Morgan of the Eagle Mine was a Union refugee living in New
York. His household, consisting of 10 Negro servants, was left destitute.
Patrick arranged to send supplies sufficient for a month to the house at
Eagle Mine, about three miles from Benson's Mill on the Warrenton
Road.

are being practised at the discharge Offices about Washington. . . . More newspaper arrests—— One a Dr. [L. B.] Hovey of Dansville [N.Y.] Somebody is sending me a great bundle of newspapers daily—more than I can get an opportunity to read, at any rate. . . .

Sunday Night [,] *22' March '63.* Head Quarters, Army of Potomac, (10'15" P. M.) [.]

. . . I had to do some business writing until the ten o'clock mail closed, . . . I then sat down & spent my time until 3 o'clock, rationally, in reading & thinking—— I had the Memoir of an excellent man—Deacon Daniel Safford—— A plain man, but a good man & full of the Holy Ghost! . . . Gen. [Edwin V.] Sumner died yesterday morning, in Washington [Syracuse, N. Y.], from congestion of the lungs—— He was just leaving for the West, to relieve Gen. Sam.[uel R.] Curtis—— He was a mere soldier—a man of the world & nothing but a man of the world. . . .

Monday Morning—Night—I should say at *9'30"* [,] *23' March '63*——

. . . There is some probability that the Rebs are preparing something for us, as the Tents are whitening hills where they have not before been seen and [Gen. D. N.] Couch sent over word that a thousand Rebel Cavalry had come down to the River this Afternoon. . . .

Wednesday Night [,] *25' March, '63.* Head Quarters, Army of the Potomac——

. . . Gov. [Andrew] Curtin [of Pennsylvania] has been here and I suppose is still here, with Hooker—— I had a Singular Letter placed in my hands today by Butterfield in relation to the charges made against Hooker, of being drunk—— A Pennsylvania Doctor says he fell from his horse when riding thro' their Camp. . . .

Friday Night, 27' March '63. Head Quarters [,] Army of Potomac, Camp Rufus King——

. . . This morning I concluded to go down to Acquia today, as I have had numberless appeals from there, requiring my personal attention—— So at 9'30" or 10' I went down & looked about Falmouth Station a while—then to Acquia with [W. T. H.] Brooks & wife, Gibbon, [Col.] Ingalls etc. Spent the day in looking over the Prison Ship, Hospitals, Sutlers ['] establishments etc. Then I Saw the 21' under arms—— They had a dress parade—— It was very well done & I had to say a few words to them. . . .

Saturday Night [,] *28' March '63. Head Quarters* [,] Army of the Potomac——

. . . A Lieut. & three Sergts. from the 8' Alabama, came in & gave themselves up today—— They are Northern men and were forced into the Service—— The Lieuts. say that the order is, if a man resigns his commission, he is conscripted at once, before being permitted to leave the Camp——

Sunday Night, 29' March, '63. Head Quarters, Camp Rufus King——

. . . I have a Letter from Mr. [William] Kelly, in reference to the two Years ' Regts. & think I will go up to Washington to see about it—— The Governor [Seymour] desires my services, if possible, in re-organizing these Troops & preparing them for service, once more, in the field. . . .

Thursday Night, 2' Apl. '63. Camp Rufus King, Head Quarters [,] Army of Potomac [.]

A hiatus of 2 nights in my Diary. . . . Hooker had come home & told me that the plan for the 2 Years' Troops to re-enlist etc. had been decided upon at Washington, entirely different from our agreement, or request of the State—— Well! I came to the conclusion that I would see if any thing could be done—— So I took the evening run & awoke at Washington, on the little Osceola—Breakfasted & went up to town—— Did a few errands got my pay & then to the War Office—— Saw Canby, Potts, Fry, Townsend & Ruggles & Vincent——[3] It is believed that I succeeded in getting off the issue of the Order for two or three days & that my views are approved by the parties with whom I have talked—— That was my main business & it kept me closely—— Young [Edward] Martindale went up with me having resigned in order to go into the cotton speculation at Baton Rouge—— I tried to see his Father but did not succeed, as he was at the Capitol, before the War Committee—— Mrs. Canby had gone to Kentucky but I dined with the General & there met Gen. W.[illiam] S. Ketchum whom I had not seen since—Florida! . . . Went then to [Gen. Samuel P.] Heintzelman's & took a walk with them to the President's House, but would not go in, and ran back over to John Potts' where I staid till 10 and then went over to Shiras ['] & staid till 11, then went to the Boat, where Col.

---

[3] Gen. Edward R. S. Canby was still on "special duty" in the Secretary of War's Office. John Potts was Chief Clerk of the War Department. Lt. Col. James B. Fry was the Provost Marshal General of the Army. Col. E. D. Townsend was an Assistant Adjutant General, as were Col. George D. Ruggles and Major Thomas M. Vincent, all working in the Adjutant General's Office.

[James E.] Mallon and [Lt. Edmund] Ned Kirby joined me—— We came down & arrived at the dock just in the nick of time & came up on a Car loaded with Oats, very comfortably—— Got here in time for breakfast & have been all day at work—— Gen. Hooker has been reviewing the 1' Corps today, by Divisions. . . .

> *Friday Night, 3 April '63*—— Head Quarters [,] Army
>   Potomac, Camp Rufus King [.]

Went early to bed last night and slept quite well, except that about 1'30" I was aroused by a Band (from a German Regt. as I understand) serenading Gen. Hooker—— It was about the sweetest music I ever heard—— They played four pieces & decamped. . . . This evening Orville Brainerd arrived—— Hooker had been reviewing the 6' Army Corps & was with [Daniel] Sickles and several others—said to be a little drunk—— Orville came here & dined—— I sent for Joe Wood[4] & then let them go—— I suppose they are now over at Hooker[']s Head Quarters.

> *Sunday Night, 5' April '63*. Head Quarters [,] Army of
>   Potomac [,] Camp Rufus King——

The Snow Storm of last night continued until late this morning—piling up the Snow in huge drifts. . . . The President & his party were expected last night, but the storm prevented—— I do not quite know *who* are here, but some of them have arrived & the Bands have been serenading them. . . . Orville Brainerd left this morning for home, perfectly disgusted. His uncle did not feel disposed to give him a Sutler's privilege, or

---

[4] Joseph Hooker Wood was the son of Hooker's older sister, Nancy Hooker Wood. Orville was the son of a younger sister.

any other exclusive right as Orville expected and so he cleared
out in a huff—— He appears to me to be drinking pretty
hard, as near as I can judge.

Monday Night [,] *6' April '63*. Head Quarters [,] Army
    of Potomac [,] Camp Rufus King——

. . . It was about 8½ o'clock when I recd. orders to go over to
call on the President at 10—— So we went over—all at Head
Quarters & called on him—— I crawled out the Back Way
as soon as presented—— Came home and remained until
about 12'20" then rode over to see the Cavalry Review. [Brig.
Gen. George] Stoneman's [Cavalry] Corps was out, all who
could be spared—On Thrashleigh [Sthreshley][5] Farm. . . . The
President reviewed, Hooker & Stoneman played the Hosts——
I staid & saw it all over—a muddy time they had, indeed.
Came back here, unharnessed & went to work. . . . The enemy
have had us in plain Sight all day & if they had desired, could
have dropped a Shell amongst us——

Wednesday Night [,] *8' April '63*—— *Head Quarters* [,]
    Army of Potomac——

Slept well, rose early, found myself with a bad cold. . . . I
went out to the Review of the 6' Corps & the Reserve Artillery
at Sickles ['] Head Quarters, taking possession of the ground
with the Cavalry (3 Squadrons) & about 80 Lancers, which
had been ordered to report to me—— The President & Cortege were in full feather. . . . The ground was bad, but
the Troops behaved admirably—— They made a very fine

---

[5] The name of this farm is pronounced the way Patrick spells it, but
it is correctly spelled Sthreshley and it adjoins the Wallace "Little Whim"
property on the North.

appearance but the great curse of our country is, that every body wants to do just as he pleases—— The crowd is enormouse at these shows. . . .

Thursday, 9' April, ['] *63*——Head Quarters [,] Army of Potomac [.]

. . . I had to go over to Court at Gen. Sickles' Head Quarters & lost an hour, in consequence of the non arrival of members of the Court and it was finally postponed, until next Saturday, to enable the Officers to attend the Review of the 1' Corps today and of the 11' Corps tomorrow [.] I hope the President will soon get off so that we can once more get to work. . . . The roads are fast drying up & every thing indicates a speedy movement of our Troops. . . .

Head Quarters [,] Army of Potomac, *Friday* [,] *10' April 1863, 4' P. M.*

. . . The President & Gen. Hooker are out reviewing the 11' (& 12' ?) Corps, which will wind up, I suppose, his (the President's) tour of Inspection & Review. . . .

Monday Night, 13'—— Camp Rufus King, Head Quarters [,] A. of P.

. . . Tomorrow *we* devote to packing and the next day, Wednesday—we are to March—— The men are to have 8 days ['] Rations with them, 5 in their Knapsacks & three in their Haversacks. . . . Getting rid of all our prisoners today. Have been *"Taken"* today, with my staff as there is quite a call for the Provost Department—— Yesterday some of the papers—

Leslie [*Frank Leslie's Illustrated Newspaper*], I think, brought
a wood cut of me that every body seems to recognize. . . .

Tuesday Night, 10 o'clock—— 14' Apl.

. . . Met Maj. Gen. Fogliardi, of the Swiss Army, who is here,
as a Guest to study war—— A thorough Frenchman & fine
Soldier. . . . I have had the Pollocks up here in arrest &
a Dr. Wynkoops for giving information—sent them all
home——[6] A Butterfield display——

Wednesday, 2'30" P. M. 15' April. Head Quarters [,]
    A. of P.

One of the very worst Storms of the Season! It was as
pleasant last night as any night we have had in a long while,
but rain came on soon after Midnight and has continued
ever since, though I think it is now abating its *fury* somewhat—— There has been quite a high wind some of the time,
as well as heavy rain—— Its consequences will be very grave
to us, I fear, and may defeat the movement of our Troops——
However, it is about as bad for their Troops as it is for
ours. . . .

Friday Evening, 17' April, '63 [.] Head Quarters, Camp
    Rufus King [.]

. . . Today I was hard at work until 5 o'clock then mounted &
rode down to the Batteries this Side of Pollock's, to look

---

[6] Surgeon Alfred Wynkoops was charged with informing Mr. Pollock
that the Federal Cavalry had been withdrawn from the flank of the
Army. Patrick replied, on April 21, after investigation, that pickets on
both sides of the river readily exchanged information, along with
tobacco and newspapers, and anyway, the removal of the Cavalry had
been observed by several Confederate Officers from the opposite side of
the River.

across the River with my glass—— The Rebs[.] were enjoy-
ing themselves at their games. Ball playing was going on in the
Old Camp of the 20' near Mrs. Fournahoye's & it was sad
to see our men all looking on, knowing that but a few hours
longer of any thing like truce will be permitted & these men
will be shedding each other's blood. . . . There is nothing from
the Cavalry, save that it has been halted at Rappahannock
Station by the rise in the river from the last heavy rain. . . .

Saturday Night, 18' April—— Camp Rufus King, Head
    Quarters [,] etc. [.]

. . . The Cavalry news is rather discouraging—— At 12
o'clock last night they had not crossed the River and the
whole movement is known to the enemy. . . . Senator [Henry
W.] Wilson's remark, when here last time (2 or 3 days ago)
are not yet fully believed—— He Said that "Ten days of
good weather will wipe out this Rebellion"—Perhaps it will!
Things do not look like it now, however. . . .

Sunday Morning, 9'30" [,] *19' April,* Camp Rufus
    King—— A. of P.

. . . The news of the morning is not such as to make one feel
very agreeable—— We hear nothing from the Cavalry that is
at all Satisfactory—indeed the last news was that Stoneman
was about to fall back—— It is not yet *known* that Suffolk
is in the hands of the enemy but it is generally believed that
such is the case, especially as it is known that after our
despatch was sent forward to the Secretary of War, it is
announced that the President comes down here this morning
to confer with Genl. Hooker—— I very much fear the result,
if Suffolk has fallen, as it precipitates upon us 25 to 30

thousand victorious Troops under Longstreet to dispute our crossing below here—— All this makes me feel very sad—— I hope the President may bring us better news. . . .

Monday [,] *3 o'clock P. M.* Camp Rufus King [,] Army
   of Potomac [.]

. . . Hooker now says that Suffolk and Washington (N. C.) are not only safe but that the Troops at both those points will move forward in concert with us. . . . I have not heard how Stoneman is getting on, or what he is doing.

Wednesday Night, 10 o'clock [,] *22' April*—— Head
   Quarters [,] A. of P.

. . . Had a long talk with Hooker about Army matters and our movements, which are looking better. I am Sorry to say, a rain has set in within the last hour & is now falling steadily, as though for a rainy night——

Thursday Night, 9'30" P. M. [,] *23' April*——

. . . Had a call from a Mr. [William W.] Harding, Editor of the "Philadelphia Inquirer," who must have staid here an hour & a half or two hours, talking up all about newspapers & newspaper arrangements. He is to arrange with Wales of the Baltimore American to send down a reliable man, as the Agent for both papers and have them play against the [John W.] Forney [–] [Samuel] Wilkeson clique——[7] I have also

---

[7] Forney owned the Philadelphia *Press* and the Washington *Chronicle,* but spent most of his time with his job as Secretary of the Senate. Samuel Wilkeson was head of the New York *Tribune*'s Washington office.

had Lyford the embalmer here, and gave him an overhauling for assuming to be a "Government" Embalmer etc [.] etc. . . .

Saturday, 2.30 P. M. [,] *25' April——*

. . . Caught some parties [of] Soldiers with Whiskey in the road & secured them. . . . Have had a couple of women up for examination they having come from Richmond—— Have sent them down to the Lacy House to be examined— Searched—by these ladies—Mrs. Harris & Mrs. Beck. . . . I have had the Sutlers of Head Quarters up today for selling Liquor. . . . The whole crew—[George] Wilkes [New York Tribune], Stanley, Gallagher & Compy. are as rotten as can well be—— Hooker is mixed in and linked with as big a set of Scoundrels as can be found on this Continent.

Monday Night, 9 o'clock [,] *27' April——* Head Quarters [,] Army Potomac [.]

. . . Every thing looks forward, now, to immediate action, the 11' & 12' Corps moved this morning, at daylight and the 5' followed today—— Hooker goes up tomorrow, himself, to Morrisville—— Will Cross at various of the points above— Germania [Germana] & Elyes [Ely's] Ford, to clear them out on the left & turn their Batteries—— Sedgwick [Sixth Corps] & Reynolds [First Corps] will come near where they did before & attack, so as to employ all these troops in our front, until Hooker can get in their rear—— He sent for me & gave me a long talk about matters, confidentially. There have been a number of Officers in arrest today, sent over to me and tonight I have Robt. Wallace & Arthur Bernard here, prisoners, for Signalling the enemy last night—— It will be Strange if this should be proven on them.

Tuesday Night, 28' April—— Camp Rufus King [,] A. of P.

This morning I was up & at work pretty early—— Sent off those prisoners to Acquia—— Was at Head Quarters and all about—— Hooker left, I should think, about 9 o'clock. . . . I mounted at about 3 o'clock & went down through all the 6' & 1' Corps—— They were massing in the Valley in rear of the Hills, between here & the Fitzhugh place—— Saw them all & gave any instructions, as far as possible—— [Gen. John F.] Reynolds [First Corps] is to cross at Pollock's Mill— [John] Sedgwick [Sixth Corps] above Pollock's House. The 3' Corps [Sickles] supports both—— So far, I think the rebels have not the slightest idea what we are about today—— Even the Pickets know nothing about it. . . .

Tuesday Night, 28' April—— Still at Camp Rufus King——

. . . I have . . . a long and interesting Letter from Mr. [William] Kelly—— He . . . gives me his views upon the War policy—the views of the Democracy of New York—— To conquer a peace, but be ready to negotiate whenever the South manifests a disposition so to do. . . . There is a curious state of things now in this Army. Confidence enough is felt in Hooker, I think, but not a great deal in some of his Corps Commanders. Reynolds, who will command on the extreme left has the perfect confidence of his Troops & of the Army, but [John] Newton, who commands the 6' (while Sedgwick commands the two Corps) does not, I think, amount to very much. [John] Sedgwick, *I fear,* is not enough of a General for that position—— He is a good honest fellow & that is all. I do not think his officers have very much confidence in him—— [Daniel] Sickles & the most of his crew, are poor— very poor concerns, in my opinion—— Hooker will, probably, be in the way of *controlling* the whole, after the first success is gained, but not till then. . . .

Wednesday [,] *5 o'clock P. M.* [,] *29'* [*April.*] Camp Rufus King [.]

Went to bed at 11 o'clock last night, but was soon routed up—Say a little after 12 o'clock, by a call for me—— About 100 men of the 26' New York had laid down their Arms & refused to March, on the ground that their time had expired—— I am ordering them to be turned over to Col. [William F.] Rogers, for work in the redoubts—think we will put them to burying dead horses if we hold on a little longer. The morning came & pretty sharp work with Reynolds & Sedgwick—— This between 4 & 5 o'clock A. M. They crossed the River, at each place, with a Division, & sent me up about 80 prisoners, taken in the Rifle Pits—— All from [Gen. Jubal A.] Early's Division [Stonewall Jackson's Corps]—— We are getting from them a deal of information, but they all want to be exchanged—— Gen. Hooker came down from the Corps above before noon and reports all well—— They are rapidly moving into position & tonight they will, probably, cross in force—— They have been taken napping, undoubtedly—that is to say they must be in the dark as to our plans, I think, certain. Unless they are a great deal stronger than I think they are, they *must* be driven if Hooker gets across & in their rear, by their left Flank—& I think he will. All things have been working admirably today, but a heavy rain has just set in & I am afraid of the Consequences, somewhat—— All has been quiet on the left & Sedgwick & Reynolds are simply to hold their own until the roar of battle is heard on the right—— Then there will be a push for the Rail Road—— The Stillness today, & quiet, has been painful—— Troops massing & all done so quietly. . . .

Thursday Night [,] *30' April, Camp Rufus King, Va*[.]

This has been a most extraordinary 24 hours, last past! When I rose from making my last entry, I was sure that the Ball would be well opened before this time, but, save a little cannonading in front of Sedgwick & Reynolds, I have heard nothing at all—— The 3 Corps (5'[,] 11' (12') are in position near Chancellorsville without a fight, and the 6' Corps—no, the 3' has moved from its former position up to the Right & crosses at the United States Ford, now in our possession, as I learn, before morning. In that Case, Hooker, who left here at about 5 P. M., today, will have near 60,000 men at Chancellorsville by daylight. So far as we can see, or judge, they still believe that we are making all our arrangements for a ground attack in front of Sedgwick & Reynolds—— The body of their Troops are there apparently and unless they are playing us a deep game, we shall cut them sadly to pieces— being on their flank & rear—— We cannot understand *how* they are so blinded and that is all that makes us afraid some deep plan is laid for us—— However, my belief is, that they must skedaddle tonight, or get a terrible licking hereafter. We have been quietly awaiting developments today, and so have done little—— Had a long talk with Joe [Hooker] this morning & with Butterfield tonight—— All seems to go well. . . . [Lt.] Tattnall Paulding has reported to me, this evening with 150 Cavalry, for driving the Woods towards Banks Ford, U.S. Ford etc. All Stragglers to be driven over to their Corps—— I shall start him off at daylight unless I hear something further.

. . . I have Stopped all newspapers coming from Washington today & shall do so, probably, tomorrow. . . All looks hopeful this evening.

Wednesday Evening [,] *6' May.*

It has been some time since I had the pleasure of making memoranda in this Book. On Friday Morning the 1' Inst. [Capt. William W.] Beckwith [,] [Lt. John V.] Bouvier & I breakfasted early & started for Banks' Ford, where I had orders just as I was leaving, to cross with my Cavalry & go to the front—— I had before given orders for Lieut. [Tatnall] Paulding to scour the Country for Stragglers as far as United States Ford & Lieut. Nichols, with the remainder, to scour in rear of 1' & 6' Corps. . . . When we arrived at Banks Ford we found the pontons not laid & the enemy holding on the other side—— Left word for the Cavalry to follow and come to U. S. Ford—— We reached the Fords & crossed. . . . The Cavalry finally arrived & part were sent to the Front & part kept for duty at the Bridges—— I sent Col. Crane to the front & left Beckwith & Bouvier at the Bridges & Telegraph Station, returning home myself, at 6 o'clock, riding pretty fast—— It is a three hours ['] ride being about 15 miles to the Fords, by the shortest route & 5 from there to Chancellor[s]ville where all our Troops are congregated except 1' & 6' Corps. On *Saturday Morning (2'),* early, I was off, after having been kept very late the previous night at Butterfield's to talk over every thing—— Prisoners taken by Sedgwick all say that no re-inforcements had arrived for the Confederates. I reached the Telegraph Station where [Capt. James P.] Kimball had been over night, left Snowball for Tom [Chambers] to take back, mounted & rode to the front—— Found Hooker, [George] Sharpe & Crane—— Had a talk with Hooker about his plans—— All were working admirably and I believed the game was all in our hands—— An hour or two after the troops arrived, the Shells flew[,] the Divisions went in with a rush, to the Wood & the musketry was terrific—— The Enemy had massed their Troops on a certain point, then let Sickles drive them until that point was reached, when the whole mass opened and the 11' Corps ran away to "fight mit Sigel" in the rear. *Saturday*[.] The Troops of other Corps were then put in and checked the Stampede—— We fought for some time & then came a halt[.] [Brig. Genl. David B.] Birney's Division [1st of Sickles' Third Corps] brought in a good part of the 23' Georgia, & as there was no arrangement made for them I started back to the Bridges & got them over the Bridge soon after dark—— There was nothing going on during the Night—— I lay down under a bush, but was so frequently run over that about 12 o'clock I went into the Telegraph room & stretched out—— *Sunday Morning, 3'*[.] I washed my eyes open got some bread & meat out of my Haversack, break-fasted & went to work. The crossing of Troops, Supplies, Strag-glers[,] prisoners, sick & wounded, the care of roads, depots, communications & Telegraphs, with an occasional visit to the front & establishing of Provost Lines kept me busy all day—— Nothing was done in front—— Reynolds had come up from the left & the bridges were thrown over at Banks' Ford—— All were expecting a fight, as there had been a severe attack in the morning, early, resulting in the death of Maj. Gen. [Hiram G.] Berry [Comdg. 2nd Div. Sickles' Third Corps]. On our left it was known that a severe fight had put Gen. Sedgwick in possession of Frederic[k]sburg & Col. Crane was ordered over there to do duty as Marshal—— All was silent after the Morning's fight in our front & the whole thing seemed very strange—— At night I laid myself down in com-fort, under a *fly* with Beckwith & Nichols & Slept—— On *Monday Morning, 4'*[.] We were turned out early by a Shelling of our Waggon Camp from about Banks Ford, which did little harm before it was silenced but it started all the

Stragglers for the trenches & I put in the Cavalry behind them & caught, perhaps, a thousand. I was engaged in much the same way as Yesterday, but the Silence in front was ominous & I could not account for it. Our Troops were ready for a fight and we did nothing but remain in position—— A rumor came to us that Jackson was crossing the River to come down in rear & burn Acquia, So I got on my horse & came down home, to arrange with Colonel Rogers in case of an attack—— Found things in a Strange State—— Jackson instead of crossing above had passed around to his own left & rear, come in behind Sedgwick & driven him 4 miles out of town—— I saw a part of the fight as I was coming home, in the darkness. . . . *Tuesday Morning*[,] *5' May,* I was about starting off with my 2 extra horses, when I recd [.] a telegram to hurry to the front[.] I did so, leaving Tom [Chambers] to come up with the horses—— I rode directly through to Head Quarters & found "no battle," but evident preparations for a retreat—— This was most extraordinary, as there was not the slightest cause for it, the Troops being in the best of Spirits & double the enemy in number[.] I went back to the bridges, after a cup of tea with [Gen. Henry J.] Hunt, & there staid—— . . . I recd. orders about 3 o'clock P. M. to "Stake out the Ford" & did so, it being up to the belly of a horse, but before it was completed a tremendous thunder storm came on, the torrents poured down the steep banks and the River commenced rising almost immediately—— The Order was given for the movement to begin at 7'30" & Hooker crossed over, himself, at about 7'—— Soon the crossing was impossible, the bridges having been deranged by the flood so that the upper one had to be taken up to lengthen out the others—— Instead of 7'30" it was after 11 before the first bridge could be crossed —the Artillery, Packs, Ambulances, Servants, Orderlies & detached commands, with Stragglers of all kinds, began to pour in & overpower the Guard of the 12' Corps—— From 7'30" until daylight I was at the Bridge & thereabouts, whip in hand, using it freely & directing the movement successfully, until every wheel & hoof had crossed the bridges, & a Regt. of Infy. had helped the Artillery up the hills, just as day had made its appearance. Then came the Troops & the pontons were taken up, without molestations, the fact being that the enemy had commenced their retreat 12 hours before *we* retreated. On *Wednesday Morning, May 6'.* After bringing over my Cavalry & Starting off the last of the prisoners, we took a cup of coffee & I went to see Hooker—— He was just about starting for home—— Sedgwick had already recrossed at Banks Ford the previous night & the Army returned to their old Camps, (or on their way there.) I rode a part of the way with Reynolds—— Have seen Hunt and Sykes & many other Generals, all of whom are perfectly astonished at the retrograde movement—— No Confidence is felt in Hooker—— A Movement of the 1' Corps is ordered, secretly, for tomorrow night, to cross the River & Capture Frederic[k]sburg—— I suppose to wipe out the disgrace! There is a feeling of universal disgust & indignation. I am in doubt as to what will be the result to Hooker. As I remarked above, I came home most of the way with Gen. Reynolds & arrived here wet, cold & shivering—weary, hungry & disgusted. . . . I feel perfectly disheartened & cannot see the close of this War—— It is now in the hands of Gamblers.

Thursday Night [,] *7' May*—— Camp Rufus King [,] Hd.Qrs. A. of P.

. . . Attended to business until 10 o'clock, then sent down—went down to Acquia [Aquia], taking [Capt.] Beckwith and Col. Crane with me, to see the 21' and 23' before leaving—— Col. Rogers had telegraphed up to know at what hour I would be there that the Officers might meet me—— They were there, with many of the 35' and 20'. . . . Spoke of our associ-

ation together, of the regard they had for me etc. etc. and in
testimony of their love the Officers & men of the Command
had called me down to present as a token of their regard what
I would see by turning my eyes to the rear—— And there I
saw, and must say the tears started—the most splendid service
of silver—— Massive, rich, elaborate & in excellent taste. Of
course I was taken completely by surprise, for I had no warning that any thing of this kind was in progress—— I made the
best reply to it that I could and our eyes all moistened, I
believe—— That over I shook hands with the Officers as they
passed out and the ceremony was over, but after going to the
Prison Ship I dined with them in their Mess Room and had
a very pleasant time. . . . The President & Gen. Halleck have
been here today and I understand that the whole thing has
been represented by Hooker as a grand Success and Abraham
has gone back well pleased with every thing—— The movement of this evening, by the 1' Corps, across the river has
been suspended—— It is not known when it will come off. . . .

Chapter VIII

Gettysburg

MAY 8, 1863, THROUGH AUGUST 10, 1863

IT WAS BECOMING increasingly apparent that even the mauling that Lee gave the Army of the Potomac at Chancellorsville could not destroy its morale. An Army that could fight as this Army did at Gettysburg, scarcely two months after it had been so thoroughly beaten, was made of pretty stern stuff. Patrick's record of the internal friction, the gossip, and headquarters politics that beset the Federal Army must, therefore, be taken with a grain of salt.

Patrick's view of the Battle of Gettysburg is novel. His business was with those who, in one way or another, were avoiding the fight. He was looking after stragglers, prisoners, and the dead, and as a consequence he saw little of the glory and heroism that is usually remembered.

In the West Grant moved eastward from the Mississippi. By May 14, he had captured the state capital at Jackson, scattered Joseph E. Johnston's small force, and turned back westward to face John C. Pemberton. In battles at Champion's Hill and at the Big Black River on May 16 and 17, he forced Pemberton to give way. By the 18th of May Grant was ready to tie down the siege of Vicksburg. When assaults on May 19 and 20 developed the strength of the Vicksburg defenses, Grant began regular siege operations. In six weeks it was over and Vicksburg surrendered on July 4, 1863.

In the Middle South William S. Rosecrans, in a series of brilliant maneuvers between June 23 and July 7, forced Braxton Bragg out of Middle Tennessee without a fight. Bragg retreated into Chattanooga and the mountains south of the Tennessee River and the stage was set for the battle of Chickamauga.

Friday Night[,] *8' May '63*. Camp Rufus King[,] Army
of Potomac[.]

Today I have been engaged in Office duty entirely. . . . [Gen.
Joseph] Hooker sent for me this evening and we have had a
talk—— He says that [Gen. John A.] Dix has an intercepted
dispatch from Lee, setting down the Rebel loss at 18000
men——[1] I don't believe it at all. [George] Stoneman has
reached Kelly's Ford in Safety and has cut the Rail Road &
Bridges & Canals & Telegraphs, and has taken prisoners to
within 3 or 4 miles of Richmond without loss. His movements
have been a complete success as it now seems.

Saturday Night[,] *9' May, '63*. Camp Rufus King——

Up & breakfasted at the usual hour, worked until ten o'clock
and then Started for Acquia. . . . I came up at 3'—
4'45"—— Found a letter from [Packer] Prentice & he says
they are feeling very keenly, in New York, the loss of confidence
in Hooker, as it is now beginning to be understood that he has
made an unmitigated failure—— Every body is feeling badly
& Hooker & [Daniel] Butterfield are attempting to punish the
newspapers for telling the truth—— . . .

Sunday Night, May 10'—— Camp Rufus King, Head
Quarters[,] A. of P.

. . . I have had telegraphic dispatches of all Sorts during the
day and *one* requiring all [New York] Heralds brought to the
Army to be burned, on account of abusive Editorials of Gen.
Hooker & Gen. Butterfield—— Butterfield ordered them

---

[1] Gen. Dix commanded at Fortress Monroe at this time.

burned. . . . There is a feeling of universal disgust among the Officers as to the management of Gen. Hooker and the Herald nominates Gen. [Daniel] Sickles for the command of the Army, insisting that Hooker should be removed at once. . . .

Monday Night[,] *11' May '63*. Head Quarters[,] Army of Potomac[.]

. . . We have done nothing but the usual Office business today—— Things are in a singular state.

Monday Night——

The newspapers are quiet & respectful, for the most part, but some are outspoken & call for a change. The Commanders, as a general rule, I think, have but one single opinion—— Mr. [Wm. W.] Harding, Editor of the Philadelphia Inquirer, called to see me this Afternoon & staid to dinner. He is down here with Gov. [Andrew] Curtin of Pennsylvania to inquire into matters. . . .

Tuesday Night, 12' May, '63. Head Quarters[,] Army of Potomac[.]

. . . Captain George D. W. Clinton, of the 21' was arrested in Washington, the moment he landed, by [Col. Lafayette C.] Baker's detectives—— [Capt. John A.] Haddock came down today, and he says, the Charge made against Clinton, is, that he has been selling Commissary Stores—— I am inclined to think it is true, but do not fancy this sort of interference——

It is said that Baker sent a Dutch Baker down, with Marked
Money, to buy Flour of Clinton, at Acquia. I shall not interfere, in any way, in these operations of Baker. . . .

> *Thursday Night*[,] *14' May*—— Head Quarters[,] Army
> of Potomac——

. . . I have just been looking over letters from the other Side,
sent in by "flag of truce" and get some news—— Jeb Stuart
was in command of Infy. during the late battle—— I got a
letter, by *mistake* from Jeff. Davis to a Mississippi Colonel &
gave it to Butterfield[.] . . . Col. [George] Sharpe and
[Lt.] Bouvier are at U. S. Ford attending to the crossing over
of our wounded, amounting to some 1200 or 1500 men.

> *Friday Night*[,] *15' May '63.* Head Quarters[,] Army of
> Potomac——

. . . I rode over this Afternoon, to Falmouth, to see Duff
Green about the Factory & the Cotton etc. etc. with reference
to the Whittemore claim etc. etc.[2] . . . This evening I have
been over to see a splendid Sword presented to Col. [Henry F.]
Clarke,[3] by the Subsistence Officers of the Army of the
Potomac—— [Senators] Ben. Wade [Ohio] & [Zachariah]
Chandler of Mich. were there——[4] Mrs. Graham leaning on
the Arm of the latter.

---

[2] Duff Green and his cousin, James S. Green had been arrested on
suspicion of aiding the Confederates. They had been released and sent
North. They had gone to New York to stay with John M. Whittemore,
James Green's father-in-law. Whittemore had then made application to
have some baled cotton owned by the Greens shipped to him in New
York.

[3] Col. Clarke was the Chief Commissary of Subsistence of the Army
of the Potomac at this time.

[4] The arrival of Wade and Chandler marks the usual post-defeat
appearance of the Committee on the Conduct of the War upon the
scene of a recent battle.

Sunday Night, 17' May '63[.] Head Quarters[,] Army
  of Potomac[.]

. . . This evening I have been out to the site selected for our
new Camp, as it seems we are to move Head Quarters in the
course of a day or two. . . .

Monday Night[,] *18' May '63*—— Head Quarters[,]
  Army of Potomac——

. . . There is nothing new today. [Capt. James P.] Kimball
returned, this morning, from Washington—— Says that
Hooker Stock, in Washington, is rather low at present. Every
thing seems to indicate a quiet time for a few days. . . .

Tuesday Night, 19' May, '63—— Camp Rufus King—
  near Falmouth[.]

. . . Went up to the new Camp Ground & was gone two or
three hours, I suppose—— The Order was given to break
camp before I returned, but I had so much to do that *we*
concluded not to go until tomorrow—— Gen. Hooker & most
of the Staff are already gone——

Thursday Night, 21' May, '63—— Head Quarters, New
  Camp——

. . . Have had all sorts of people about me during the day——
Mrs. Stuart kept me, not unprofitably, over an hour. I obtained
from her several facts—— She is a Cousin of Mrs. Robert
Lee and the General's daughter, Mary—— (Mary Lee, 24

Years of Age, next younger than Custis) has been living with her since last Summer—— J. E. B. Stuart has sent Officers for her, but she does not choose to go. I learned many other things in relation to Lee & others. . . .

Friday Night, 22' May, 1863—— Head Quarters[,] New Camp——

. . . There is nothing new today except that Hooker is doing some of the business that has been heretofore done by Butter-field, the latter having gone to Washington & New York on leave—probably to account for this "Telegram to the Broker's Wife" when the Army fell back. . . .

Saturday Night[,] *23' May, 1863,* Head Quarters, New Camp——

. . . Worked until near 12 and then went over to Hooker & had a talk of half or three Quarters of an hour with him, resulting in my getting a great deal of work off my hands, or rather, prepared for action—— He leaves very much to me—— I am satisfied with *his* operations when Butterfield is away—— Pleasonton is busy & has captured some 3300 dollars in Confederate Money, turned it over to me, & I am turning it over to [Col. George] Sharpe for use on the other side. . . . Mrs. Stuart came up to see me, ostensibly for the purpose of following mules—in reality, for the purpose of taking my advice for Mary Lee as to her returning South—— I gave my advice and shall endeavor to find some way of getting her over before long. . . .

Monday Night[,] *25' May, '63*—— Head Quarters[,] Army of Potomac[.]

. . . Lieut [George H.] Watson is taking the place of Capt. [Lafayette] Lytle, but is not the man I would like to have here,

on duty with me. He has not much, if any refinement, or culti-
vation. . . . Have got into my hands, from Gen. Hooker,
considerable discretionary power, in the absence of Butterfield,
whose absence has been productive of excellent Results——
I hope to get some of the prisoners off from Prison Ship [at
Aquia] soon. . . .

> *Tuesday Night, 26' May*—— Head Quarters, New
> Camp[.]

. . . Gen. Hooker left last night for Washington & Butterfield
has come back, bringing some half a dozen ladies with him, his
wife, as I understand, being one of them—— George H. Stuart
of Philadelphia, Agent [Chairman] of Christian Commission
called, with Mr. [Charles] Demond of Boston and Mr.
Read——We had a pleasant time for a half hour & they
left—— I have written a severe Letter to [Assist. Sec. of War
Peter H.] Watson, relative to the taking up of [James S.]
Green's Pass & Parole papers by [Col.] L. C. Baker. . . .

> *Wednesday Night, 27' May '63,* Head Quarters[,] Army
> of Potomac[.]

. . . Had a Mrs. Brosman—a Female Woman [and private
trader] after me, who was a regular Doll Tear Sheet & I had
to threaten her with a file of the Guard if she was not
quiet. . . .

> *Thursday Night*[,] *28' May.* Head Quarters[,] Army of
> Potomac——

. . . I have had many citizens here from King George, about
their horses & property, taken by the 8' Illinois Cavalry &

have sent some home with their animals, including Mrs. Ashton. It has been a *hard* day for me, some way. Have had a great many females & some Ladies to deal with. . . .

Friday Night, 29' May—— Head Quarters[,] Army of Potomac——

. . . Hooker has sent for me & Butterfield has sent for me in relation to the [George] Wilkes['] Sutlership at Head Quarters—— Hooker claims that he did not know anything of this Wilkes having an interest in it & wants me to manage some way, to break up the nest. . . .

Monday Night, 1' June, '63—— Head Quarters[,] Army of Potomac[.]

. . . Dr. [Abram] Hooe came up, bringing Letters from his family and bunches of roses and flowers, Asparagus, Bacon and no one knows what. . . . Then came Letters from Mrs. [John] Seddon & Mrs[.] Stuart, with calls for help, but an Order of Napoleon [Butterfield] has knocked all help in the head. . . .

Tuesday Night[,] 2' June—— Head Quarters[,] Army of Potomac——

. . . Col. Sharp[e] returned this morning & brought his Wife with him, as well as several other Ladies but I have not seen them—— They are over at Head Quarters and the Band is playing for them.—— It is all a farce this business of not allowing ladies to come to the Army when every one that has a friend at Head Quarters can get permission without applying to me for a pass. . . .

Saturday Night[,] *6' June*—— Head Quarters[,] Army of
   Potomac[.]

. . . Having made my arrangements to go to Washington, at
night, was not to be thrown out by any fooleries of Butterfield—— So I got off in the evening run, at 7'45" and on
arriving at Acquia, found a nice little Boat the Matamora, to
take me up—— . . . Was up early & walked up to my Hotel,
where I breakfasted at 6 o'clock and then went down to the
Street to Work . . . at [Gen. Samuel P.] Heintzelman's
Office, [Gen. John H.] Martindale's, [Gen. E. R. S.] Canby's,
[John] Potts['], [Col. Ed. D.] Townsend's, [Gen. M. C.]
Meigs['] & some others. After a late dinner I called to see Mrs.
Canby & staid an hour, or more, then went to Heintzelman's
house. . . . Staid till 10'30" and went home—— Slept pretty
well & very late. Next morning, after Breakfast, went down to
6' St. Wharf. Staid some time with [Augustus G.] Robinson
& [Calvin D.] Mehaffy, then came up & arranged with Dunn,
of Adams Express Co. (with R & M) about Transportation to
the Army of Potomac—— That done I left R. & M. and went
up to see Martindale about all sorts of business, then to Col.
[Joseph S.] Conrad's, to Gen. [Daniel H.] Rucker's, Elisha
Camp's, to Col. Wm. Hoffman's, to the War Office etc. etc.[5]
Agreed to dine with Jno. Potts at 5 o'clock, went home &
found a Telegram recalling me to the Army—— Went down

---

[5] Gen. Heintzelman was commanding the Defenses of Washington
south of the Potomac. Gen. Martindale still commanded both the
Department of Washington and the Twenty-Second Corps. Gen. Canby
continued on "Special Duty" in the Secretary of War's Office. John
Potts was the Chief Clerk of the War Department; Col. Townsend was
an Assistant Adjutant General; and Gen. Meigs was still the Quartermaster General of the Army. Robinson and Mehaffy handled details
of transportation to the Army of the Potomac; and Col. Conrad was in
charge of the Discharge Department of the Army of the Potomac. Gen.
Rucker was Depot Quartermaster for Washington, while Elisha Camp
was an Assistant Quartermaster. Col. Hoffman was the Commissary
General of Prisoners.

& dined, went to the 6' St. Wharf & took a Tug and started by 6'15" for Acquia—— Turned in & slept from 7'30" until 10'30" when we reached Acquia, took a Special train & came up to Falmouth, where I had to wait some time for my horse—— Got to my Tent at about one o'clock & went to bed. . . . I had heard, at 6' St. Wharf, that our Troops were in possession of Frederic[k]sburg, that the Rebels had moved up towards the right & that our Army was also moving in the same direction to head them off——

Saturday Night[,] *6' June,* Head Quarters[,] Army of
  Potomac——

On turning out this morning I find the real state of things to be this—— The Rebels, Yesterday morning, had changed Camp & the impression was that they had cleared—— Only a few pickets were seen & the pontoons were thrown over, at Franklin's Crossing—— Not much resistance was made at first, but we finally had a sharp little fight & in clearing the Rifle pits captured, without much loss to ourselves about 92 prisoners —— The Division has been lying across there all day, but this Afternoon the enemy are massing about Howisson's [Howison's] and preparing for Action—— We do not seem to be doing any thing to sustain our position, if attacked, and our Troops are scattered all the way from here to Bealton—— We understand that they are re-organizing—that Longstreet's & Jackson's Old Corps are divided into 3, Ewell taking Jackson's and A. P. Hill having enough added to his Division to make up a Brigade—A Corps I should say. . . .

Monday Night, 8' June—— Head Quarters[,] Army of
  Potomac——

. . . Today I have been engaged in all sorts of business, Amongst other things I have seized upon & now hold, large amounts of

Bogus Jewelry, Watches etc. all from the same houses that
furnish the vilest of Obscene Books, of which I have made a
great haul lately. This evening [Alfred] Pleasonton is preparing to dash on [J. E. B.] Stuart——

Tuesday Night, 9' June—— Head Quarters[,] Army of
    Potomac——

. . . The weather has been quite pleasant, but not as cool as
Yesterday. [John] Sedgwick's [Sixth] Corps remain in about
the same position as heretofore—— Some Artillery practice
towards right, but nothing more—— Pleasonton has been
engaged up the River, in a severe fight, which has cost the life
of our best Cavalry Officer—Col. [Benjamin F.] Davis—— We
had a bad report, in the Afternoon, but, towards night,
learned that [John] Buford was driving the Enemy. . . .[6]

Wednesday Night[,] 10' June—— Head Quarters[,]
    Army of Potomac[.]

. . . Col. Sharp[e] & Lieut. Bouvier have gone to Alexandria,
today, to Examine and parole some (it is said) 400 prisoners,
captured by Pleasonton—— I doubt there being that number
—— Pleasonton thinks he has broken up Jeb Stuart's Maryland Raid, which was to start this morning. . . . I have had a
talk with Hooker today, about various matters, which talk has
been very satisfactory—— It came to personal matters finally
and we had a talk about Sickles and some others, that has
relieved my mind very much—— He also directed the Sutler
Book to be brought & read the orders given to [Gen. Oliver O.]

---

[6] This was a fight at Beverly Ford and Brandy Station. Col. Davis had
commanded the 2nd Brigade of the 1st Division of the Cavalry Corps.

Howard & [Gen. Henry W.] Slocum at 9'30" on Saturday
May 2'[.] This puts the *onus* on those Generals, for the giving
way on the right[.] There has been a bonfire in rear of my
Tent, burning up a large quantity of Obscene books, taken
from the Mails.

Thursday Night[,] *11' June*—— Head Quarters[,] Army
    of Potomac——

. . . I had the pleasure, this morning, of a call from my old
friend [Gen. Herman] Haupt, who brought his Wife and Son
to Gen. Ingalls['] Tent and came for me to call on her. I
found her very like Nellie Clarke, only a little older, but
wonderfully young for the Mother of so many children. . . .

Friday Night, 12' June, '63[.] Head Quarters[,] Army
    of Potomac[.]

. . . I have had a great deal to do today, and have had, in
addition to my usual duties, to get rid of this businees of opening bids for the Sutling at these Head Quarters and for the
furnishing of Newspapers & Periodicals to the Army at 5 cents
each—— I had a Council of three officers present at the opening, so that they could protect me in any attacks that the
defeated Competitors might make upon me for unfairness, or
any thing of that kind, hereafter. We have not declared the
successful bidders, but I suppose that [John M.] Lamb has the
Newspapers & [William J.] Babcock the Sutling, as they are
the highest bidders, and in conversation since, appear to be
fully acquainted with the terms & ready to meet them. . . .

Saturday Night, 13' June—— Head Quarters, Army of
    Potomac——

Our last night in this Camp—— We move at 3 A. M. tomorrow, for Dumfries, on the road to Manassas—— All the Corps
are on the move—— Sedgwick crosses tonight, to this side &
moves on Dumfries—— There will be nothing but Cavalry
between ourselves & A. P. Hill after midnight, I suppose——
We are likely to be outgeneralled & for ought I know, whipped
out again by Lee, at Manassas—— The day has been a very
busy one—— It was not until Afternoon that we decided to
move so soon, I believe & the result has been a very hurried
State of Affairs. . . . I think & know, that Hooker feels very
bad—— He is prohibited from crossing to Whip Hill and,
like McDowell, is shut up to the defence of Washington[.] . . .

Sunday Night, 14' June—— Head Quarters[,] Army of
    Potomac[,] *Dumfries*[.]

The usual state of affairs on a badly managed march. . . . We
were to have had our start at 3 o'clock, but did not get off
until 5, or 5'30″—— The 8' & 93' got off, but the Train had
a bad time in getting under way—— I found the road blocked
with all sorts of obstacles—— Miserable Officers in charge of
Artillery, Siege Guns & Train. This made very great delays and
I had to turn in several times to get Waggons out of the way
—— We halted for Waggons at Stafford and again at
Dumfries, before coming into Camp, just off the Quantico. . . .
We have come about 25 miles—— I sent [Lt. George H.]
Watson to Acquia, to get rid of prisoners by putting them on
shore and let them free as soon as proper, on evacuating the
place—— . . . The Wallkill is towed up to Alexandria &

remaining there.[7] It is almost certain that Lee makes another Northern Campaign.

Tuesday, 16' June, Camp one Mile N. W. of *Fairfax Station,* Fairfax C. H.

Yesterday morning no one seemed to know what was to be done & every body lay in bed as long as possible, having had very little sleep—— . . . It was not decided that we should move until about 8 o'clock and the sun was then out *very* hot—— Our first stretch was to the Occoquan, where we found a single Ponton Bridge, and a very bad hill—— Mountain, almost, to ascend—— Another bridge was eventually thrown across 2 miles below that relieved us a little & by which *some* of the Teams & Siege Guns were sent to Alexandria—— There we halted a long time, as Gen. Hooker was there. . . . It was about 5 o'clock when we started on our last 9 miles stretch—— It was almost dark when *we* reached here, passing the R. R. Station about one mile. . . . Orders have been given to hold Acquia, until further Orders—— The great body of Lee's Troops arrived at Winchester two days ago—— They have driven [Maj. Gen. Robert H.] Milroy from Martinsburg to Harpers Ferry & have invested that place it is reported. The Cavalry have crossed at Williamsport, it is said, seized upon Hagerstown & marched to Chambersburg without molestation. We are preparing for a rapid march and are sending to the rear every thing superfluous. . . . Yesterday & today the weather has been intensely hot—— It is killing for men to march this weather. . . .

[7] The Wallkill was the prison barge that Patrick kept anchored off Aquia Creek.

Wednesday, 17' June—— 9 hours & 30 minutes A. M. [,]
Same Camp——

When I closed this Book yesterday, it was with the expectation
that we should be on our way to Maryland long before this——
The Orders were all given for the Corps Commanders to move
by different roads, to Leesburg—— Head Quarters were to
move at 7 and afterwards at 8, this morning, in the same
direction—— By direction I ordered forward Col. Root & his
Command to Noland's Ferry, North Side of the Potomac——
Also sent to all Provost Marshals at Alexandria and Washington to send forward all Officers & men of this Army in same
way—— This morning, just as we were striking Tents & preparing to load, we were directed to "hold on" and not move
until further Orders—— There seems to be doubt as to Lee's
Movements and it is understood that A. P. Hill remains near
Frederic[k]sburg, Ewell's Position undertermined, & Longstreet investing Harpers Ferry. I suppose we are waiting for a
more definite understanding of the true state of affairs. . . .

Later—— Evening——

A *very* hot day—— We have accomplished very little today
—— Stragglers, very many of them not yet up and the
different Corps in position, tonight, along the neighborhood of
the Leesburg & Alexandria Rail Road-nearly to Leesburg
—— [Alfred] Pleasonton has had another fight, with Fitzlee's
[Fitzhugh Lee] Brigade I think, & drove them, though with
very heavy loss on *our* side. . . . I find that the understanding
now is that [Henry W.] Halleck is running the Marching and
Hooker has the role of a Subordinate—— He acts like a man
without a plan and is entirely at a loss what to do, or how to
match the enemy, or counteract his movements—— What-

ever he does is the result of impulse, now, after having failed,
so signally, at Chancellorsville——. . . . He has treated our
"Secret Service Department" [headed by Col. Sharpe] which
has furnished him with the most astonishingly correct information with indifference at first, & now with insult——

Friday Night [,] *19' June*—— Camp Head Quarters near
    Fairfax C. H.

Yesterday I was not in a condition to write. . . The day was
the hottest of the Season, I lay panting for breath & weak as a
cat. At 3 o'clock orders [came] to move Head Quarters to
Fairfax C. H. . . . I had got off but little way when a violent
thunder storm came up. . . . The Military state of affairs is
unchanged since yesterday, mainly—— There are constant
Cavalry skirmishes, & heavy fights in the vicinity of Aldie &
Middleburgh. We get a number of prisoners, but our losses are
heavy. We get accurate information, but Hooker will not use
it and insults all who differ from him in opinion—— He has
declared that the enemy are over 100,000 strong—it is his only
salvation to make it appear that the enemy's forces are larger
than his own, which is all false & he knows it—— He knows
that Lee is his master & is afraid to meet him in fair battle.

Saturday Night[,] *20' June,* Head Quarters, Fairfax Court
    House——

Last night we had a pretty heavy rain. . . . The day has been
lowery & showery—— I sent off a Letter to Mrs. Patrick, by
today's mail—— This evening I took a ride on the Germantown & Vienna Roads coming in near our old Rifle Pits. . . ,

Sunday Night[,] *21' June*—— Same Camp, near Fairfax
   C. H.

. . . Was up at the usual hour this morning & spent my time in
the usual way. . . . This evening I rode out by Flint Hill, to see
something about the roads. . . . Came back to dinner & then to
see Gen. Hooker—— He feels better—— Pleasonton has had a
heavy fight today, all his Cavalry being engaged. . . . From the
sound of the guns, Pleasonton must have driven them——

Tuesday[,] *12 o'clock M.*[,] *23' June*—— Camp near
   Fairfax Station—no—C.H.

. . . Nothing was going on during the day, in the way of
hostilities, except that some Waggons of [Col. John] Moseby's
[Mosby] Amm—no—Pleasonton's Ammunition Train were
attacked & burned by Moseby's [sic] Guerilla Band, somewhere near Chantilly. . . . I had sent in by [Capt. J. P.]
Kimball to see Dr. [John] Van Ingen in Washington & have
him write to [Gov.] Seymour that I would make up a Division
of New York Troops, for the War, if permitted to do so, and
would join him (S) as soon as this campaign should be over—
in a very few days. I then went to see Hooker, presuming that
he would not object to such arrangements, after the next battle
should be fought—— He is, however, decidedly opposed to
my leaving my present position, Says he can get Division Commanders & Corps Commanders-Adjt. Genls.[,] Inspector Genls.
& other Staff Officers, without any difficulty, but at present,
there is no man in the Army whose duties are so important as
mine, so far as discipline & interior economy is concerned——
He was very much troubled about it—— Said he would give
me any command I desired in this Army, but there was no one
in which I could, possibly, be more useful than in this—— To

some remark of mine, that I did not seem to be doing any
thing his reply was 'Well, if *you* are not, I would like to know
who is doing any thing'—— "I am not only satisfied with the
way you do your duty & manage your Department, but more
than satisfied"—with much more of the same sort, winding up
by saying "there is no body in the Army to replace you & you
must write to Gov. Seymour why I cannot be willing to let you
leave me"—— Soon after a Letter arrived from Albany, from
Dr. Van Ingen and then Dr. Van Ingen himself, with words
from [Gen.] MacClellan [sic] to me of Strong affection, & an
urgent appeal to remain, for the present where I am—— He
& Seymour both think the same, but the Division will be
organized! Dr. Van Ingen found McClellan with the
Governor & spent a day with them—— The feeling is strong,
that McClellan must resume his position with the Army. . . .
Genl. Hooker went to Washington this morning, with [Gen.
Rufus] Ingalls[.]

——*10 o'clock P. M.*——

The day has closed without any thing very extraordinary. . . .
Gen. Hooker went off, this morning, with Gen. Ingalls, I think
for Washington and has not yet returned—— It seems to be
the idea that we are to go off somewhere, to remove the Head
Quarters Camp tomorrow or next day—— The movements of
Gen. Lee are not at all understood, apparently. . . .

Thursday[,] *25*['] *June '63*—— 9 A. M.[,] Camp near
Fairfax C. H.

. . . The 1'[,] 3['] & 5', I think . . . 3 corps any way—will cross
the River tonight at Edwards' Ferry & then seize upon Cramp-

ton's & South Mountain passes, if not already held by the enemy. Genl. Hooker intends that *all* shall be over the River by tomorrow night—— The probabilities are that the enemy wishes to fight near his old ground, at Antietam & South Mountain. . . .

Thursday Night, 25' June—— Camp near Fairfax Station[.]

This has been a day of anxiety & helplessness—— We have done nothing, Scarcely, except to pick up the Stragglers of other commands & got off some 50 or 60 loads of Stuff to Fairfax Station, left by Troops of Gen. Stahel's command. . . . I believe we are about ready for operations and the Order is out for us to move tomorrow morning at 3 o'clock, for Poolesville—— To be there tomorrow night—— The knowledge of the enemy's whereabouts is not great and I am fearing that we shall catch a blow in the wrong place, if we all cross the River again. . . .

Friday Night[,] *26' June,* Head Quarters[,] Poolesville[,] Maryland[.]

At 2'30″ this morning we had breakfast, & at 4'30″ started off, in a drizzling rain, which has continued most of the day making the roads extremely bad, choked as it is with Trains constantly[.] It was about 24 miles to Edwards' Ferry, where are 2 pontoon bridges, and where I found a deal of trouble —— Capt. Allen & Lt. Austin are there & I put them to work, clearing the Roads & Bridges with a detail from the 20' Regt. now lying there. . . . I staid to dinner with the 20' & then came on to Poolesville, about 5 or 6 miles, where Head Quarters had been ordered to halt—— It is a most disgusting hole. . . . I am fatigued [and] feel very much disgusted and satisfied that there is great want of a Commander.

Sunday Night[,] *28' June*—— Camp near Frederic City, Maryland——[8]

Yesterday morning at 8 o'clock the order was to March, for this place. We started & came on 6 or 8 miles before being overtaken by Head Quarters. I never ride with Head Quarters longer than I am obliged to and held back—— After a ride of 22 miles thro' a lovely country, we reached here. . . . Woke earlier than I wished this morning and after breakfast went over to Head Quarters, to find a change—— Gen. Hooker had been relieved from Command and [Maj.] Gen. [George Gordon] Meade placed over the Army of the Potomac. Of course this has caused great commotion, but as yet I have heard no regret. . . . All Corps are moving toward Harrisburg, or Baltimore, or Washington today, the Rebels being at Harrisburg, probably, ere this—— Our Mail for Washington was obliged to turn back today & that *from* Washington was, probably, captured together with 150 Teams, near Rockville, by FitzHugh Lee's Cavalry [of Stuart's command], which crossed the River below here & near the Mouth of Seneca Creek. We are cut off from Washington, but Pleasonton has been sent out to reopen communication & catch FitzHugh Lee—— What Meade will do is a question, but he has taken hold of work with a will—— Hooker had the Officers together to say Good Bye at 6 this evening—— He is ordered to Baltimore, & there to report to the Adjt, General—— He says, that finding he could not control the Army without interference from Washington, he

[8] In Patrick's day Frederick, Maryland, was spelled both with and without the final "k."

sent in his request to be relieved from Command. He leaves few friends behind him, altho' personally, he is the most agreeable commander I have yet served under. . . .

> *Tuesday Night*[,] *30' June*—— Camp near Taneytown,
> Md.[,] Hd Qrs. [,] A. of P.

Yesterday morning we were ordered to move at 8 o'clock. . . . I went in town, expecting a Regt. to report to me for Provost duty. I had no one to help me, and spent an hour or two in clearing streets, only to be filled up again. . . . It was drizzling & raining until night—— I reached Middleburg & selected Camp. . . . The Troops did not get in until a very late hour, altho' it was but a 20 mile March—— The Roads were completely blocked with Trains & Troops—— At a late hour I was called into town and sent for two Squadrons of Cavalry to go back to Frederic & clean out that town, which was reported full of drunken men & Stragglers. . . . An order was expected for us to be off early, but it was put off until 10—— It was only some 5 miles or 6 and I sent the Staff forward, while I remained behind and went back to Middleburg and all around, gathering up Stragglers. . . . The Enemy are concentrating in the direction of Gettysburg, or perhaps York. . . . They have broken up our Rail Road Communications with Washington & Baltimore, but the Telegraph wires are said to be up again —— I intend to have Parker try the Mail again tomorrow. He has attempted it twice & was obliged to return. The day has been drizzling, but no heavy rains—— Meade has issued two excellent business Orders for battle.

> *Monday Night, July 6' 1863*. Barn Near White Church,
> Baltimore Road, Gettysburg, Pa.

Spent *Wednesday, the 1' Inst.* in & about Camp near Taneytown, overhauling trains & examining prisoners etc. sent down from Reynolds & Cavalry. . . . Just at night, about 9'30" came orders to be ready to move at 10—to send every thing to Westminster & leave the 8' & 93' with Head Quarters—— Meade left at 12'30" but as we had to examine a great many prisoners, I did not leave until about 2—— The news of a repulse in front & that Reynolds had been killed, was confirmed & his dead body passed me in town—— A Sad beginning truly. . . . It was only 12 or 13 miles & we reached the Head Quarters of Gen. Meade at a little before 6, after having established a depot for prisoners & placed Col. [R. Butler] Price with his Cavalry in charge. This day, *Thursday*[,] *2'*, the Troops were drawn up in the form of a Horse Shoe, but the 5' & 6' Corps did not arrive until near night, or afternoon. The fight was very heavy & we were obliged to leave the place we had selected under the furious shelling & musketry—— Gen. Meade had to abandon his own Head Quarters for a time & I had my hands full, with the Prov. Guards to keep the Troops from breaking——It was hot work & I had several lines formed, so that very few succeeded in getting entirely through—— Just [at] night Beckwith found a place where we could keep a few prisoners. . . .The Troops were in good spirits & fought gallantly—— The 5' & 6' Corps came up towards night & took position for the morrow—— Our losses were heavy, but the enemy's greater—— Meade handled his Troops well. . . . Next Morning[,] *Friday*[,] *3' July*—we went early to the front & took position, but we had, at different times terribly hot fires —— I never saw such artillery fire as came upon us at one time —— It was terrific & I had my hands full with those who broke to the rear, but we succeeded in checking the disorder & organized a guard of Stragglers to keep nearly 2000 Prisoners all safe—— The battle was in our favor & though we lost heavily we gained largely. . . . It became evident that the enemy had been worsted before the close of the day & a new place selected, at White Church, for our depot, I sent off the prisoners after night, to Westminster & lay down, under half a shelter tent, in the rain, for the night. . . . *Saturday Morning*[,] *4' July*——— I went down to the front again & re-established our depot——— Gen. Meade had been obliged to move into the woods, near his former Head Quarters on account of their condition & the Score of dead horses piled around them———, Every body was without any thing to eat & waiting for subsistence——— Busy gathering men from their places of retreat & straggling Enemy opened two or three times, but not heavily & the picket firing was in the same way——— I went into the edge of town, but was fired at by the Sharp shooters & just missed their fire. At night, as we had been drenched in a most terrific rain, we concluded to take shelter in a large barn, the only one in the whole country not occupied for a Hospital. . . . It was evident, by night, that the great Struggle was over, but our Army was too weak to follow up the advantage gained——— *Sunday Morning*[,] *5' July*———- Slept well, under Shelter from the rain & after Breakfast went to Head Quarters, now established on the Baltimore Pike——— Found that the enemy had withdrawn tho' but for a short distance from town——— I was soon ordered by Gen. Meade to go into the town & make arrangements with responsible parties for the burial of the dead & Securing of the property on the battle field——— Beckwith & I rode in——— Had a great deal of difficulty in getting hold of Some respectable parties to do any thing with, the people being nearly all Copperheads——— I took a cup of Coffee at the house of a Mr. Wills, whose wife is a cousin of [Capt. Charles] McClure——— I called together the leading citizens (Union) at his Office, made the necessary arrangement & Set a man at work——— Came back to Head Quarters, thoroughly disgusted with the whole Copperhead fraternity of Gettysburg & the country about, as they came in Swarms to Sweep & plunder the battle grounds. . . . A Copperhead Editor, confined for pointing out the refuge of Union Soldiers to Rebel Officers, was

brought before me & Affidavits substantiating the fact presented, to accompany him to the Baltimore Prisons—— So
much for the work of a Sunday after the battle of Gettysburg.
Monday Morning[,] *6' July*—— I turned out early & had my
Breakfast—— I then rode down to Head Quarters & after a
while went into town, leaving two of my horses to be shod as
their feet were badly torn on the rocks during the engagements
——The Corps having moved out of town I put Allen in
charge, with the Cavalry of Col. [R. Butler] Price, starting
the Cavalry on all the roads & over the Battle field, to pick up
Stragglers & prisoners, wounded, from the Rebels. . . . I had
hardly seated myself when I was sent for to go & see Maj. Gen.
[Isacc R.] Trimble, out some 3 or 4 miles beyond Gettysburg.
He was wounded & left behind—— His leg had been
amputated below the knee & he had sent a Message to Gen.
Meade, to whom he was known, to have some arrangement
made by which he could be brought into town & his family
sent for to Baltimore—— I made the arrangement for himself,
his Staff Officer & a wounded Lieut. Had a pleasant interview of nearly half an hour, & then returned to town to make
final arrangements for leaving in the morning. . . . The battle
has been more disasterous for them than was supposed——
Their losses will not be less than from 25 to 30,000—— The
field, however, presented an awful appearance, many of the 1'
Corps men being yet unburied & their bodies presenting a most
hideous spectacle. . . .*Tuesday Morning*[,] *7' July*. Rose early.
. . . It was 6 o'clock when I left and a half rainy day, making
it necessary to wear our Gum clothes all the time. It was a very
hard march of 30 miles & I had a rough time in driving up
Stragglers, Officers & Men. . . . *Wednesday Morning* was so
very rainy that no fires would burn in the open air. . . . I . . .
came on to Middletown, where Gen. Meade had halted & in
which neighborhood all the Corps had assembled—— I had a
busy time until dark, keeping the trains, for miles, from getting

blocked & moving them on. . . . *Thursday Morning*[,] *9' July*
—— . . . Gen. [Andrew A.] Humphreys was announced as
Chief of Staff, to the surprise of all, as it has been understood
that Gen. Warren would have that position—— Butterfield
was struck by a spent piece of shell, in the back, at Gettysburg,
fortunately for him & to the joy of all, has gone home. I was
very busy until about 4 o'clock, moving Trains etc. then followed Head Quarters thro' the Pass, to a Camp near the
Mountain House. . . . We lay under the mountain where we
fought on the 14' of Sept. last & pursue the same road as we
did on the 15' to Antietam Creek. . . .

Friday, 10' July, 1863 [Camp near Antietam Bridge]——

. . . It was decided to leave all the trains here at Mountain Pass,
to move forward ourselves to a point near Antietam Bridge, on
the Williamsport Road, with only such a supply as might be
necessary for a bivouac & to keep us 3 or 4 days. . . . The Line
of Battle of our Troops is about $2\frac{1}{2}$ miles, or about 2 miles,
perhaps, on an average, in our front & on the right—— We
are only about 3 miles from the old Antietam Battle ground.
. . . Probably we shall make no attack until the enemy's plans
are developed, as he holds a very strong position & is intrenching——

Head Quarters[,] Army of Potomac, Camp near Antietam
    Bridge. *Saturday*[,] *11' July*[.]

. . . As there has been little going on, save slight movements
of Troops—I have been about Head Quarters & out to Jones'
X Roads, along the lines, during the day—— Gen. Meade does
not intend to attack until he is in better condition & the enemy

are still more straitened—— We are not in a condition to do
much until the Army is reorganized. *Sunday*[,] *12 July*—— A
most painful day—— Nothing going on—not any movements
of Troops—— Our Troops simply watching the enemy. . . .
The day was intensely hot until 2 or 3 o'clock, when a very
heavy rain came up & the ground was soaked. . . . *Monday
Night*[,] *13' July*—— . . . The day has been rainy & save that
we have had a great deal to do with prisoners & all that kind of
work, there has been noting going on—— The Country is full
of the employees of the Press, Christian Commission & curiosity
hunters. I have had a great deal of trouble with them. . . . The
Rebels, it is now certain, have a Bridge across the Potomac at
Falling Waters & seven Rafts——- They are short of supplies
of all kinds & admit a loss of some 40,000 men, but they are so
strongly intrenched that we cannot attack them, with success.
I should not be surpised if they cross the River tonight——

Headquarters[,] Army of Potomac, near Antietam Bridge,
 July 14'[.] *Tuesday Night.*

. . . On getting out, I found from prisoners, or run-away
negroes, first, that the Rebels had commenced crossing the
River immediately after dark last night & that all, or nearly
all, were over this morning—— We have been following up
today and the Cavalry have harassed their rear, taking it is
said, some 1500 prisoners in all—— Their lines were strongly
intrenched—too strongly to be forced by us—— *We* are
satisfied with what has been accomplished and believe, as
we did at Antietam, ten months ago, that it is a mercy to us
that the Rebs left as they did—— We could not attack them
safely—— Gen. Halleck telegraphed to Gen. Meade, that
"the President was mortified & surprised that Lee should be
allowed to escape, & that unless Meade's future operations

should atone for past tardiness etc. etc." or words to that effect—— Meade was justly indignant & replied, "I desire immediately & unconditionally, to be relieved from the Command of the Army of the Potomac"—— I have just learned, 8'30" P. M. that Halleck has apologized, saying that "it was not intended to censure but to Stimulate him"—— The Order is out to move the Head Quarters to Berlin tomorrow & for the Corps, all, to rendezvous there & in Pleasant Valley. . . . The day has been intensely hot & the night is equally so—sultry! There were riots in New York yesterday, of a very serious & fatal, character growing out of the Conscription. . . . The whole Country is in an uproar & it would take little to upset the Administration, which is known to be so corrupt, by all.

Head Quarters[,] Army of Potomac, Camp near Berlin,
   Md[.]—— *Wednesday Night, 15' July*[,] *'63*——

. . . I left camp at 6 o'clock and came on to Boonsboro. . . . Got all prisoners turned over to Escorts and started for Middletown, where I found the Staff (my own) and we started. . . . Gen. [Daniel] Tyler rode with me as far as Jefferson, where we struck the Frederic & Harpers Ferry Pike—— This we followed to Petersville & there turned off to occupy our old grounds here. . . . The 8' In. arrived about 6 o'clock & within half an hour they were under orders to proceed, with all possible dispatch, to New York—— (They got out of Camp about 2 o'clock this morning)—— The last statements from New York show the whole city to be in the hands of the rioters & a great destruction of life & property. . . .

Thursday Night, 16' July, '63—— Camp Head Quarters[,]
   Army Potomac[.]

. . . We are to remain here but one or two days. . . . Gen.

Meade showed me his correspondence with Halleck—— That Officer ought to be removed from the position he disgraces.

Friday Night[,] *17' July*—— '63. Berlin, Head
    Quarters[,] A. of P.

. . . There has been almost nothing going on today, though the Pontoon Bridge is down & troops can cross. . . .

Sunday Morning, 19' July, 9'30"—— Camp near
    Lovatsville, Va.——

. . . The first order was to move at 8, then at 11, but it was about 3, or 4, when we did move, I expect, as we had only 4 miles to come—— We followed the Reserve Artillery, which I regard as the worst managed Concern on a March, that we have. . . . I have ordered Col. Price to remain at Berlin until Tomorrow when *all,* I think, will be over the River, or ought to be. . . . The morning is Scalding hot, almost & already frying.

Monday Night[,] *20' July,* Camp near Union, Hd. Qrs.[,]
    A. of P.

This has been a very hot day & I feel much fatigued & weary though we have only marched 12 or 15 miles today and I was not over 3, or $3\frac{1}{2}$ hours on the road. . . . Since arriving here I have been out to pick blackberries, which are very plenty & nice. . . .

Tuesday, 5 o'clock P. M.[,] *21' July*—— Same
    Camp——

Contrary to expectation, we have remained in our Camp all day, having been pretty well assured that Lee is holding himself in the valley, & waiting for [Gen. Braxton] Bragg, or [Gen. P. G. T.] Beauregard, or both, to reinforce him which will enable him, either to re-cross the River, or to threaten Washington. Our Army is in no condition to fight another battle—— The discipline is horrible. There is no responsibility any where, & Commanders of every rank, cover up the rascality of their Troops—— There is a vast deal of Stealing of Horses, & depradations [sic] of all kinds. . . .

Markham Station, Manassas Gap, *Thursday Night, 23' July, 1863*——

Two busy days since I made a note—— Late on Tuesday evening I found that it would be necessary to go out myself in the morning, as the Troops were marauding greatly—— So I had Breakfast at about 6 & started off. . . . Went to see [Gen. George] Sykes but missed him & got back to Head Quarters at 12′30″ to find every thing packed, in order to move at 1 o'clock, to Upperville. . . . I went early to bed. . . . & rose to Breakfast at 6′30″ as we were to move at 7—— It was to be a general Movement & I had to send out to call in all detachments etc. Head Quarters was ordered to Piedmont 6 miles—— We reached there, & Meade went to the front leaving me to care for the movement—— At 12 orders came to establish Head Quarters 2 miles ahead—— It was done & tents pitched—then came an order to move 5 miles further— to this point——Here we are, in a beautiful mountain Country, very near the enemy and within 10 or 12 miles of the Shenandoah—— Whether we are to fight a battle *here,* or they slip between us & Warrenton, remains to be seen—— It is not understood what Meade's plans are, but unless he does something to keep better discipline in his command, there will be few troops to put into action—— Officers & men are turned

thieves & robbers—— The whole country is full of Stragglers
& the Officers all permit it and say nothing——

Salem—Loudon or Fauquier Co. Va[.], *Friday Night,*
24' July[,] 1863——

. . . Breakfasted as usual & I went about business, intending
to go to the front, as Gen. Meade had remained there all night
& we had an occasional discharge of Artillery. . . . I did get
off between 9 & 10 o'clock, to the front, and rode up nearly to
the point where Gen. Meade was stationed, when I met a
couple of Staff Officers, returning from Gen. Meade, with an
order to break up Camp & march with all despatch to Salem.
. . . The Whole Valley was alive with Troops, pouring down
through, to get on the lines to White Plains, Warrenton etc.
where they can get something to eat. Some of them have not a
cracker left—— We had a rough march to Salem, 12 miles.
. . . We leave early tomorrow morning for Warrenton, where
nearly all the Troops are ordered to rendezvous as soon as
possible. . . .

Monday, 27' July '63—— Hd. Qrs. Camp near
Warrenton, Fauquier Co.[,] Va.
Once more at my table, making memoranda, very briefly.
. . . We reached here about 9'15" & found the old Head
Quarter Camp Ground unfit to re-occupy, as was the intention,
but after a little while other ground was selected on the
Sulphur Springs Road. . . . I put the town under Martial
Law & went to work—— Gen. Meade came up at 11 & from
that time until 3½ or 4, or 5 o'clock, I was passing the Army
& its Trains through town—— Had a very hard time & had
to use my riding whip more than I wished. . . . An Officer

belonging to the Cavalry of my Command with the Cattle Herd, was shot dead at the door of Mrs. Campbell's house, by half a dozen of Mosby's men, dressed in the federal Uniform—— His body was brought in this Camp to be shipped today for home—— The Country seems to be swarming with them & we have lost a number of our Officers & men in that way. . . . I have had much to vex me, not the least of which is the *Cheek* with [which] these murderous Wretches apply for protection & Subsistence—— I have had a talk with Meade and have asked him to relieve me, but he will not do it at present—— Says I must not think of it etc. etc.—the same old Story—— I have agreed to hold on until our next halt, where we must reorganize—— Have had a severe & Scorching Letter from Mr. Secretary Stanton, also from Major Gen. Halleck, charging very great delinquencies & misconduct etc. etc[.] upon the Provost Marshal General of the Army of the Potomac—— Meade refers it to me & in the morning I will probably answer it. . . .

Wednesday Night[,] *29' July '63.* Head Quarters[,]
    A. of P. Warren-[ton,] Va.

. . . This morning I was with Gen. Meade & [Seth] Williams in relation to trade & passes etc. for Sutlers—— Fat Andy [Andrew M. Hepburn] has been over the coals again and it is now evident that Ingalls intends to uphold him in all his operations giving him such facilities as no other man has & transportation over the road at all times ,free of cost. . . .

Thursday Evening[,] *30' July.* Camp near Warrenton[,]
    H. Q.[,] A. P.

. . . This Morning I took a look around town to see that all was right and again closed up Fat Andy's establishment——

Ingalls wrote me directly after—— Few believe they are not in partnership—— Then I had a delicate duty to perform in withdrawing a permit I had given to a Niece of Judge Blair & a Cousin of Mr. A. Linkin, to look for horses in Camp, well satisfied that She & her "Friend Miss Bailey" are spies for Moseby [Mosby]. There is very little, or no do[u]bt of it. . . .

Friday Night[,] *31' July '63*—— Camp near
  Warrenton[,] Va.——

. . . This evening I have been out to see Mrs. Robt. Lee, the Widowed Sister of Robt. E. Scott & guardian of his Children. She is very Ladylike & the only Union Lady, of the real Old Virginia Families that I have met with—— She has long been stripped of almost every thing by our Troops. . . .

Saturday Night, 1' Augt. Head Quarters[,] Army of
  Potomac, Germantown[.]

Last night . . . Mr. [John A.] Cole of Christian Commission came to consult—— Waggons belonging to Sutlers, quite a Train, have been Captured including one belonging to the Christian Commission—a $1200 fit out ! . . . This morning we prepared to move 8 or 10 miles & packed up our kit by 7'30"—— I left Camp for Gen. Meade's & then to town, where I was, preparing for the 6' Corps, to turn over the town to them. . . . There is a very good feeling existing in regard to our Troops in *town,* where they have been kept close, tho' their outrages in the *Country* have been perfectly infamous.. . . .

Monday Night[,] *3' Augt.* Camp near Germantown——

. . . I was in the Saddle an hour this morning & 2 hours this evening—— The country is very sparsely settled, nearly all fences & landmarks having been destroyed—— The Soldiery are overrunning the whole Country, especially the Cavalry. . . .

Tuesday Night, 4' Augt[.]—— Camp near Germantown,
    Fauquier Co.

Last night I slept tolerably well, but was roused by the return of my Scouting party about 2 o'clock—— They succeeded in capturing ten men of the 6' Cavy. out on a robbing expedition & representing themselves as belonging to a patrol from me. . . .

Thursday Night, 6' August—— Head Quarters[,] A. of
    P.[,] Germantown——

Slept as well as usual last night and rose at the usual hour in the morning—— My habit is to rise at such hour that I may read a Chapter in the Bible, and the "Words of Jesus" for the day of the month, then present my petitions in behalf of my Family, myself, my Country—— Then comes breakfast, after which, Office work until I either go, or am sent for, to Head Quarters—— The day has passed much in the usual way—— I was at Head Quarters twice & am, now, pretty well satisfied that this Army will be ordered to remain here for the present, making such demonstrations as will *hold* the enemy here, if possible, & prevent *them* from re-enforcing Charleston, to which point *we* are detaching whatever can be spared from other Armies & some from this——

Friday Night[,] *7' August.* Head Quarters[,] Army of Potomac, Germantown[.]

. . . A large lot of prisoners brought in from the neighborhood of Hartwood, including Mr. Irwin, on as stated, an Order from the Secretary of War to arrest all Male Citizens who decline to take the oath of Allegiance. . . .

Monday Evening, 10' Augt. Camp near Germantown, Va[.]——

. . . Today I have had as much business to attend to as I could manage & have had a long talk with Meade—in fact, have talked some hour & a half, perhaps, at two Sittings—— On the Score of public utility, we are both agreed, that, as the War Department has determined to quarrel with me all the way through, it is advisable that I leave this Department, although it is a matter of great doubt as to who is to be my Successor—— There seems to be the trouble—— I have asked to be allowed to go home & shall put in an application for 15 days['] leave of absence tomorrow. . . .

Chapter IX

The Bristoe Station Campaign

AUGUST 14, 1863, THROUGH NOVEMBER 17, 1863

GETTYSBURG left Meade's victorious Army of the Potomac as exhausted as was Lee's Army of Northern Virginia and no serious pursuit was attempted. By the end of July Lee had retreated to a position in the Iron Triangle between the Rappahannock and the Rapidan centering on Culpeper Court House. Meade followed at a safe distance and only the cavalry of the two forces saw much of each other.

In September the Confederates detached Longstreet and sent him west to stiffen Braxton Bragg's resistance to the Federal advance under William S. Rosecrans. On the 19th and 20th Bragg turned on Rosecrans at Chickamauga Creek and, with the help of Longstreet, sent the Federal Army reeling back into Chattanooga in spite of the heroic stand of George H. Thomas. Hooker was then sent west with the entire Eleventh and Twelfth Corps, leaving Meade and Lee, each substantially reduced in strength, glaring at each other. In October came the Bristoe Campaign during which Lee attempted to turn Meade's right flank but Meade moved quickly and after a rear-guard action at Bristoe Station both armies returned to their previous positions along the Rapidan and the Rappahannock.

Patrick shared in the general let-down after Gettysburg. He took a short leave home, but returned to an office filled with sutlers, newspaper contractors, and court martial cases. He immediately tried to resign.

Geneva, [N.Y.] *Friday, 14' August——* In my own
house, or boarding house.

Quite a change of locality since my last writing. . . . On Tuesday Morning, I rose at daylight, packed my Trunk, . . . came
off about One o'clock, or 1'30" in my spring Carriage, arriving
at Warrenton Junction before 2 P. M. I telegraphed to [Col.
John H.] Devereux [U. S. Military Railroad] at Alexandria to
have a Locomotive ready to take me up to Washington but
the Trains were delayed so that I did not get off until after 3
o'clock, . . . Devereux sent a Car up to the Capitol Gate with
me & there I took a Hack for the Ebbitt House . . . at 9 o'clock
went to see [Gen. Samuel P.] Heintzelman—— His family are
all away & he is growling—— He is terribly enraged at [Gov.]
Seymour, [Gen.] McClellan & all Copperheads. . . . Had little
sleep & at 5'30" was turned out, and at 6'30" was in the
Baltimore Cars—— At Baltimore I got some breakfast & at 9'
10" was off for Harrisburg. Thence to Elmira, where we
arrived at 10'30" P. M. Wednesday. . . . Took the Cars at 5'
for Jefferson, where I found Capt. Tuthill & his Steamer Amos
—— Went on board & found a good breakfast—— On arriving at Geneva, Renie was awaiting me at the Wharf in the
faint hope of my being on board—— The family were all in
the back yard and there was a general breaking down of all,
Wife Children and all—— They had received my Letter two
hours before, saying that I was to have a leave, but could not
say *when.* . . .

Saturday Night—— 15' August— '63[.] Geneva[.]

. . . We took a walk, (Wife & I) to the upper part of town to
call on Mrs. Webster. . . . From Mrs. Webster we had a tale
of Suffering so far as her Mother is concerned that is perfectly

Shocking—— She has been removed beyond the lines & her house taken for the use of the Officers—— Gen. [David] Hunter is the author of a great many very strange vagaries & oppressive Orders. . . .

Monday Morning[,] *17' August*——

We rose rather earlier than usual, as I was to be off for Rochester—— Mary wanted to go with me & I had, already concluded to take Buck [Brayton Patrick]. . . . I had taken Buck up to get some clothes for him, but I was obliged to order a coat for him, not being able to fit [him]. . . .

Wednesday Morning[,] *19' August*

We made an early turn out, breakfasted, had prayers & were getting into the carriage by 7 o'clock, for Ovid. . . . We spent our day most delightfully, the whole family being along & full of merriment until we got home, thoroughly tired & ready to go to bed early. . . .

Friday Night[,] *21' August*—— At my Home in Geneva
——

I packed my Trunk soon after I had my breakfast. . . . Then I arranged all about my money matters at the Bank—— Then I went out & made some calls. . . . This evening I have been out to see Mrs. Webster & take letters for her to send by Flag of Truce. . . . We are begining to feel badly in view of a Separation now so near at hand——

Saturday Morning, 22' August.

We rose early, breakfasted & had our prayers—— Then went
out for our Good Bye. It was a Sorrowful parting! The girls &
boys followed to the Cars before the Adieu! It is sad to leave
those we love, perhaps never again to meet on earth. . . . The
journey [was] pleasant to. . . . Rhinebeck where Mr. [William]
Kelly gave me a warm greeting, at the Cars. . . . We rode up to
Ellerslie where all the ladies . . . gave me a most hearty reception. . . .

Tuesday[,] 25' August,

Was a little Showery in the morning but I was out & took a
two hours['] ramble before breakfast. . . . After a sad leave
taking Mr. Kelly took me to the Cars but we . . . arrived in
New York at 4'15" instead of 2'15" leaving me but little time
for any business. . . .

Wednesday[,] 26' Augt.

Found us in bad humor, delayed on the way, so that we did
not get away from Baltimore until late in the afternoon &
reached Washington at 5'30". . . .

Thursday Morning[,] 27' Augt.

I was called in time for the cars leaving at 4 o'clock—— Got
into the Bread Car & sat down on my Trunk, got out my
Blanket & as it was cold, wrapped myself up & snoozed it until
we arrived at the Junction 7'15" A. M. where I found an
Ambulance & Orderly awaiting me—— I was soon in Camp,

where I found all well. . . . On reporting to Gen. Meade we had quite a talk, of an hour nearly, on matters connected with the War—— He thinks that the South, except their Leaders, will be willing to give up the Territory[,] all Territories, as free Soil[,] & to make Emancipation a settled policy, gradual, but certain & effectual in all States—— He believes that he & Lee, or any other 2 candid and honest men, can settle this matter without any more fighting. . . .

Friday Night, 28' Augt[.]—— Head Quarters[,] Army of
    Potomac—— Germantown[.]

. . . All the early part of the day I was engaged in matters requiring the personal acquaintance of the General & had to be with him. . . . All my Staff . . . went over to Rappahannock Station, this P. M. to witness the presentation of a Sword to Gen. Meade by his Old Division[,] the Pennsylvania Reserves. . . . Of course there will be a drinking frolic after the Gen. leaves.

Monday Night[,] *31' Augt*[.]—— Head Quarters, Ger-
    mantown——

. . . This evening it is decidedly uncomfortable on account of the cold—— I have spent the day in hard office work—— Have made out the discharges of the 200 Dutchmen who leave tomorrow for New York. . . . The new Orders in relation to Sutlers has given me an increase of labor & confinement. . . . [Chester W.] Sternberg (Lieut. Col. of the 21') is here tonight and took dinner with us—— He says he failed in examination before the Board, for the Colonelcy of a Negro Regiment. . . .

Tuesday Night, 1' September—— Camp near Germantown——

. . . The 20' Vols. (Dutchmen) came down and gave me a
serenade—— They sang their songs very sweetly, and being
educated men, in many instances there was great ability, and
much taste, too, displayed by them. This morning I got them
off. . . . They took a very affectionate leave of me, & some of
these poor fellows actually shed tears—— Poor honest
Germans. . . .

Saturday Night, 5' September, Camp near Germantown[.]

This has been a very pleasant day, neither too warm nor too
cold. . . . Feel glad that Saturday night has come, to give us a
little respite from labor—— We have work all the time and
plenty of it. . . .

Monday Night, 7' Sept. Camp near Germantown,
  Fauquier Co.

. . . There was a Review, today, of the 3' Corps, near Beverly
Ford, but I was not able to go to it, although I wished to do so,
as I am now on the lookout for a Command. . . .

Tuesday Night, 8' September, '63. Camp near Germantown.

. . . After my morning work I had to go over to Head Quarters
and was more than an hour, almost two, over there, talking
with Humphreys about matters especially connected with my
Department and the treatment of Citizens. . . .

Wednesday Night, 9' Sept. '63. Camp near Germantown

. . . These Sutler's papers are a very great nuisance—— They keep me tied up a large portion of the time & prevent me from doing any thing else. . . .

Friday Night, 10' Sept—— *'63*—— Camp near Germantown, Fauquier Co.

. . . Was over with Meade about newspaper matters—— I am to give them an overhauling. . . . These loud mouthed people are Some of them with the Christian Commission & make so much noise I must overhaul them. . . .

Saturday Night, 12' Sept, '63—— Camp near Germantown[.]

. . . Our scouts have returned from the other side of the river and bring report that Longstreet's Corps (and perhaps other Troops) are moving South—— . . . The Cavalry have been gathering at Rappahannock, today, to cross, in force, for a reconnaissance & Pleasonton has gone up this evening. . . .

Sunday Night, 13' Sept. '63—— Camp near Germantown, Va[.]

. . . I was sent for about 9'30″ to Gen. Meade's and as he was alone, staid till 1'30″—— Had all sorts of a talk with him and learned a great many things that I knew nothing about before; or rather, that I [k]new very little about. It was interesting to know about many of these plots. . . .

Tuesday Night, 15'—— Head Quarters[,] A. of P. near
Germantown[.]

Was busy last night and did not make any entry in this book.
. . . I had . . . to go over to Gen. Meade, to see about a recom-
mendation for [Col. William H.] Penrose, for the appointment
of Brigadier General—— Had a talk about being relieved
myself, and pushed it as far as I could, with any propriety. The
trouble is about a Successor—— Meade thinks that [Gen.
Alexander S.] Webb would do better than any one he can
think of, but is rather afraid to try him——[1] I have written to
John Sedgwick, to ask what his dispositions are in relation to
the Divisions of his Corps. . . . Prisoners have been coming in
yesterday & today, until we have about 150, and some
deserters. . . .

Thursday Evening[,] 17' Sept. '63—— Camp near
Culpepper C. H., Va.

. . . I went to bed on Tuesday night, not much dreaming of a
move, but early in the morng. was turned out by an Order to
move, at 9 o'clock to Culpepper. . . . We took the Bealeton
road, crossing very near the same spot that we did about 13
months ago, when on Pope's Retreat. . . . It had been decided
to have Genl. Meade take Mr. Wallack's [W. D. Wallach]
House (Editor Washington Star) as Wallack [sic] was getting
his family out of the way. So we came to the house, and after
Meade came up, and it was decided to take that spot. . . . Was
in town & saw Gen. Webb, who was commanding in town,
came back and waited for the Waggons—— The distance they
had to come is 19 miles. . . . and at the River Crossing, Gen.

[1] Gen. Webb was then commanding the 2nd Division of Gouverneur K.
Warren's Second Corps.

[Seth] Williams['] Waggon upset turning into the Stream the desks etc. of the Adjt. Genls. Office. . . . Rebs. are holding the line of the Rapidan, apparently in force, and we must move very cautiously. . . .

Friday Night, 18' September, Camp Hd[.] Qrs[.] Army
of Potomac, Culpeper.

Went to bed at a little after ten o'clock, last night. Did not sleep very Soundly. . . . At present the Locomotives are running the greater part of the night and do a great deal of Screaming. . . . Judge Davies of New York, with his Son [Henry E., Jr.], now Colonel of the Harris Light Cavalry, called to see me—— He is down laying pipe for the promotion of his Son——[2]

Saturday Night, 19' September, Camp near Culpepper,
Va.

. . . Went up to see Genl. [Seth] Williams in the morning and took up my application to be relieved from the duties of this Department as soon as practicable—— I have been out to see Gen. [John] Sedgwick this Afternoon, 4 miles beyond town and had a talk with him—— He recommends Gen. [Henry D.] Terry for the appointment of Provost Marshal General—— Since coming home I have sent up this suggestion to Gen. Williams—— I hope it may be acted on. . . . Mr. [Charles A.] Page, Correspondent of the New York Tribune, comes here in place of [Thomas M.] Newbold [Newbould]—— He is only

---

[2] The Judge's mission was either unnecessary or very successful for the promotion to Brigadier General of Henry E. Davies, Jr., is dated September 16, 1863, and he commanded a Brigade in the Bristoe Campaign in the following month.

just from Charleston & gives a most interesting description of [Gen. Quincy A.] Gillmore's operations in that quarter——

Sunday Night, 20' Sept[.]—— Head Quarters[,] A. of
    P.[,] near Culpepper.

. . . There is an Article in today's Chronicle that shadows forth the policy of the Administration—to class with Rebels & Rebel Sympathizers all who shall vote the Democratic Ticket this Fall——

Monday Night[,] *21' Sept*[.]—— Same Camp——

. . . Generals [O. O.] Howard, [J. H. Hobart] Ward and [Gershom] Mott were here to see me in the early part of the day, and General [Horatio G.] Wright this evening—— Wright is very desirous of having me get into the 6' Corps with him —— He is helping me in the matter—— Meade is slow and does not want to relieve me—— I am struck by some statements of Mr. [John Minor] Botts to me, in regard to McClellan—— One, to the effect, that Kirby Smith told him, that McClellan's heart was with the South, and that, alone, prevented him from taking Richmond in '62—— Botts believes McClellan to be a thoroughgoing Traitor——

Tuesday Night, 22 September, Camp at Culpepper, Hd.
    Qrs. Army Potomac[.]

A very beautiful day, and very comfortable—— A Capital day for Campaigning, but we have been lying Still and doing just nothing. . . . Rumor has it (not the papers) that [William S]

Ros[e]crans has been defeated, by the failure of Burnside to effect a junction with him. . . .[3]

Thursday Night, 24' Sept. Same Camp——

. . . There is a movement of the Army—in retreat—— The 11' & 12' Corps [Under Joseph Hooker] are to go West, it is said. . . .

Friday Night[,] 25' September '63—— Camp near
    Culpepper, Head Quarters[.]

. . . We have been expecting a movement today, but the orders are not yet out, although the Cavalry has gone mostly to the rear—— I suppose this Army of the Potomac will now be broken up, or greatly reduced, so that it will become merely a defensive Army—— I have *some* hope that I shall be allowed to go to Florida, but that hope, I confess is not very strong——

Saturday Night, 26' September '63—— Head Quarter[s]
    Camp, A. of P.[,] Culpepper.

. . . Recd. a Letter, this morning, from [Gen.] Frank Wheaton, earnestly hoping that I will take the Division and saying that Terry will be glad to accept the position and will make a good Provost Marshal General—I hope he will. This evening Col. [Edmund] Schriver has been sitting with me, until about 9'30" when I had to go out and see about an arrival of Deserters, from Washington, 400 in number, & to see about Guards for

---

[3] This is the way the Chickamauga disaster looked to the Army of the Potomac. Burnside was at Knoxville, Tennessee, while Rosecrans was being routed at Chickamauga Creek.

them—— This business of deserting I should think, would soon be dried up, seeing that so many have been shot of late. . . .

Sunday Night, 27' Sept. '63—— Head Quarters[,] A. of
     P.[,] Culpepper, Va.

. . . An invitation today from Hon. Jno. Minor Botts to dine with him, with [Gens. George G.] Meade, [Alfred] Pleasonton & [William H.] French—— of course I did not go and would not, under any ordinary circumstances. . . .

Monday Night, 28' September. Camp at Culpepper——
     Va[.]——

. . . The day has been lovely—— A beautiful September, October day. I was at Head Quarters for a while this morning, found but little prospect of a move, although it is evident that Meade does not know what he is to do. . . . I sent my Cavalry to join Pleasonton's, but that was all. . . .

Tuesday Night, 29' Sept. Head Quarters[,] A. of P.[,]
     Culpepper

. . . This evening I have written to Julia [Patrick], detailing the Action of the Administration in regard to the McClellan testimonial culminating in the order relieving Inspector Davies and ordering him to Santa Fe because he assisted in getting out the Subscription papers for the McClellan Testimonial. He has been here this evening and shown me the Order. . . . The idea now seems to be that this Army will be broken up, that it is so thoroughly McClellan as to be dangerous. . . .

Thursday Night, 1' October—— Camp near Culpepper
   C. H.

. . . There does not now, seem to be so much of an opportunity to get out of this Department as there was yesterday
and I apprehend that it will not be very soon that I leave.
Col. Davis has just been in here to say Good Bye—— He leaves
tomorrow morning for New Mexico—Santa Fe—— We have
had a talk, and so we had before, when [Theodore] Barnard
of the Associated Press was here—— He says that the people of
Maryland are very much exasperated against the Administration—— I know it. . . .

Saturday[,] 5 *o'clock P. M. 3' October.* Camp near
   Culpepper——

Last night was so very uncomfortable, with rain and wind.
. . . The bridge (RR) over the Rappahannock was carried off,
as I understand & no Mail has yet come in—— Yesterday
Gen. Terry was ordered with his Division, across the River, to
guard the R. R. from Rap. Station to Manassas. . . . This
sets at rest any change for me at present. . . . Meade told
me, yesterday, that he did not intend to stay here & that he did
not intend to re-cross the River—nor yet to attack Lee in
front——

Monday Night[,] 5' *October, '63——* Same Camp——

. . . Col. Sharpe is not the man to place much reliance on,
so far as business in a *business* way is concerned—— He is
quite too fond of a nice time, loves fun and is very irregular
in all his ways—— Things in town do not work at all to suit
me and they clash with each other—I mean the Regimental
Commanders. . . .

General Patrick and his staff. Photographed at Head-quarters, Army of the Potomac, near Culpeper, Virginia, on October 6, 1863, by Timothy H. O'Sullivan. (From the Prints and Photograph Division of the Library of Congress.)

Tuesday Night, 6' October, 1863—— HdQrs.. Camp Camp near Culpepper.

. . . After Breakfast, as [Lt. John V.] Bouvier was to go away at 10'30" [T. H. O'] Sullivan came down and gave us a sitting & a standing—— He took two pictures of the Staff— (Six of us) & made one Stereoscopic picture of us sitting. He thinks they will all be good—very good and from appearance I judge so myself—— We said Good Bye to Bouvier and sent him off at 10'30". . . .

Wednesday Night, 7' October, 1863—— HdQrs[.],
near Culpepper.

. . . I have been sending the prisoners, for a night or two past,
into town to stay & sleep, as there are no tents to protect them
here. I have been reading the Newspapers, including the
Herald's "Report of Genl. Lee" of his Maryland Campaign—— A good sensible report, and in the main, correct,
I have no doubt, although I do not believe they took as many
prisoners as stated, any more than I believe the reports of our
own Generals as to the numbers of prisoners taken by our
Troops. . . .

Thursday Night[,] 8' October, 1863—— Head Quarters
near Culpepper

. . . We had a good thing today in the way of a joke. . . . A
couple of men caught with a sweat cloth, gambling, were set
to work in the rain, in a public place, near my Office, playing
with beans instead of dice & having a placard on their backs
"Gamblers"—— They were at it from early morning until
dark with nothing to eat. . . .

Friday Night[,] 9' October 1863—— Camp near
Culpepper C. H.

. . . This morning, after Breakfast, I directed the arrest of
three of the leading citizens of Culpepper, Judge Shackleford,
Mr. Stollard and Col. Freeman. They were sent to Washington,
to be held for Exchange against other Citizen prisoners. . . .
There was to be an Execution in the 2' Corps this Afternoon
and I sent a Photographer over to take a view. . . . There

Sketch, with caption, by the famous Civil War artist, Alfred R. Waud, of the incident mentioned by Gen. Patrick in his Diary for October 8, 1863. (From the Prints and Photograph Division of the Library of Congress.)

is something going on upon the other side—— They are either making a feint, preparatory to an evacuation of our front, or they are preparing to give us our annual Bull Run Flogging and it is not yet known which——

Saturday Night, 10' Oct. '63[.] Camp HdQrs. Army of Potomac[,] Culpepper, Va.

. . . There has been a great deal going on with the Troops. . . . Every thing has been ordered to the rear today, and it is probable that we shall break camp ourselves, early tomorrow. I have given all the necessary orders therefore and only wait for the word—— My Letters—for the Rebs—I have left where they will reach them, probably—— Every thing is ready now, I think for moving. The impression is that [A. P.] Hill is flanking us, on our own right, today.

Sunday Night, 11' October, '63 Head Quarters near Rapp.[ahannock] Station.

Went to bed at 10'15" last night. . . . At 3'45" had some breakfast—— By 5 o'clk. every thing of mine was packed. . . . I sent off the Staff & went to town myself to get every body out and all the Stores etc. etc. Staid until about 9 & returned, supposing that Meade had gone—— Not so—— He was in a great Stew fearing the Corps. would get tied up in town and that his right was being turned by Lee's whole army. He blew up generally—— He left at about ten o'clock for this place (Bowen House) Pope's Old Head Quarters. . . . [John] Buford is having or has had, quite a Cavalry skirmish near Stevensburg. This night will develop the plans of Lee, without doubt.

Monday Night, 12' October, Head Quarters near Rappahannock Station[.]

Went to bed last night with every thing prepared for a speedy removal—— Ingalls ordered the teams to be in readiness to move before daylight (and I think the most of them have been in harness ever since). . . . A Mr. Bradford had been overhauled by [Gen. Alfred] Pleasonton, yesterday, and sent to me today—— I went to see Meade about it, but he decided to send him to Washington, to return home via Fort Monroe—— It was a difficult and delicate task, to Send him away, when I am Satisfied that he intended no harm—— I got on my horse and rode down to see Gen. [Horatio G.] Wright, in relation to it as he is Bradford's Brother-in-law. Wright can do nothing, of course, except to write to Halleck. . . . About 3 o'clock [Capts.] Lytle & Beckwith accompanied me to the front—— We halted at the Earthworks thrown up, on the heights across the River, and with our glasses, for some time, watched the movement—— It was a splendid sight to look out on the broad plain & see a front of say 4 miles, covered with Troops. The 5' & 6' Corps were supported by the 2' under [Gen. G. K.] Warren. They have all moved forward as far as Brandy Station & hold there tonight. . . . Buford has done the fighting driving the enemy through the woods beyond Mr. Botts & towards Culpepper. . . . Now I want to say a little about the affairs of this Army generally. . . . For several days past it has been evident that Lee is planning some sort of a move, to work us out of our position in the neighborhood of Culpepper—— Whether it be his object to blind us by making a feint of turning our right & attacking us in flank or rear, or that it is a real move of his Army, en masse, to strike a blow of this kind, with his whole force, getting in our rear, is a problem to be solved by time, and I fear, by time only. There are few indications that there is any force in front, save Cavalry and, perhaps 1000 Infy—— All the rest have disappeared to the right, being traced no farther than somewhere about Orange Court House, excepting perhaps a Division, which took the Sperryville Road a day or two since—— Now this movement indicates—or *may* indicate, that Lee is sending of [Gen. Richard S.] Ewell's Corps to re-inforce [Gen. Braxton] Bragg & to prevent us from ascertaining the fact, or pushing on to Richmond after the fact being known, he threatens our communications with a portion, or perhaps, the whole of [Gen. A. P.] Hill's Corps—— The fact that we are only getting prisoners, or deserters, from the One Corps, causes the almost universal belief that One Corps is being sent to Bragg and that Lee is playing us with a Single Corps, or even less than a Corps. Gen. Meade, however, adopts the other theory, which may be the true one; that both Corps are passing to our right & rear, to get between us & the heights of Centreville, to give us battle on our own ground—— I mean the old Bull Run ground, where we have been twice shamefully defeated. One theory of Meade's, however, seems to be utterly destitute of any foundation—that the enemy have received large reinforcements. There are no troops to re-inforce Lee's Army, beyond the calling in of such men as have been absent, and the partial filling up with conscripts of some of the Regiments. If Meade acts upon his own theory & falls back without giving battle, it will ruin him, should it be proven that Lee has not both Corps with him & following us up. Meade's head is tolerably clear, generally, but when he gets "Lee on the Brain" he errs thro' timidity, based on obstinacy. . . .

Tuesday Night, 13' October—— Head Quarters[,] A. of
     P. near Catlett's, Va.

When I went to bed last night it was with the expectation that we should move today, to the Rapidan—— At daylight I was surprised to find that all our Troops had been withdrawn in the night, from the other side of the River & were taking up position in line of Battle, near Warrenton Junction, expecting enemy from Warrenton way. . . . There has been a very strange state of things today—— No one knows where the enemy is, save [Gen. David McM.] Gregg, who reports that he fought a large force last night, on one of the fords above Rapp. Station—— We stopped some hours at the junction & then took up a new line from Bristoe, via Catlett's to Auburn & Greenwich etc. Here we are for the night & I have the 20' Regt. picketing in our front to guard against 2 Squadrons of Rebel Cavalry, said to be in the woods ⅓ of a mile from us, towards Auburn.

Thursday Night[,] 15' October, Camp near Centreville[,]
    Va[.]——

Yesterday morning, very early we were turned out & our teams,
all except Ambulances, ordered to Fairfax Station—— The
whole Army was ordered to fall back to the Centreville
heights—— We staid on the ground until nearly all had passed
& then I came on to Broad Run, to hurry up the trains etc. It
was well that I did so, for after leaving there [Gen. Harry]
Heth's Division of Hill's Corps pitched into the 2' Corps &
caught a Tartar, for Warren thrust his men right under the
cover of that Rail Road Embankment & mowed the enemy
down, without any considerable loss himself. . . . This
morning we have sent off some 430 prisoners, not including
wounded—— *They* lost a great many in killed. We have done
nothing today except to make every thing ready for action &
secure our flanks. . . . Whether there is to be a general
engagement remains to be seen tomorrow. Lee can have the
opportunity if he wishes. Meade will go down & meet him on
the plains of Manassas, or where ever there may be a chance
for a fair stand up fight.

Friday Night, 10 o'clock[,] 16' October, Camp near
    Centreville, Va[.]——

. . . Today we have done little more than make preparations
in the way of Subsistence etc. . . . The General is holding
on here, preparing, still, to meet the Rebs. . . .

Saturday Night, 17' October, '63. Camp near
    Centreville——

. . . This has been a day of *hanging on,* like one or two that
have preceded it, and I see little prospect that any thing will

be done by Meade, although he knows that the Rebs are lying at Bristoe & thence to Catlett's—— It does seem to me, that holding these heights, as we now do, and having our rear thoroughly protected, as it is, and all our communications perfect, that we *might* give them battle, with every prospect of Success—— I fear that it will be too late, unless we pitch *in* at once, for *they* cannot remain long in this position, so far from their base and line of Supplies—— I shall not be surprised at their falling back, any time. . . .

Saturday Night, Warrenton Female Seminary,
     24' October 1863[.]

[On] *Monday Morning (19')* the Army moved to the front, Head Quarters breaking at 7—— Moved to the field west of Groveton & south of the pike, where we encamped for the night. . . . *Tuesday Morning,* we moved to Gainesville, past our fighting grounds & halted several hours in great discomfort, Gen. Meade having made up his mind that the enemy would offer battle at Buckland's Mills, New Baltimore & Warrenton—— Although *we* were pretty sure the enemy re-crossed the Rappahannock, in force, on Monday morning—— After many hours, it was decided to encamp at Gainesville. . . . *Wednesday Morning (21')* We moved forward to Warrenton. . . . *Thursday Morning, (22')* I did not rise until about 11 o'clock, as it was a raw atmosphere. . . . *Friday Morning (23').* . . . Meade had gone to Washington, on call yesterday, but the Secretary being absent he returned this Afternoon (Friday). . . . *This Morning, Saturday,* opened a rainy, disagreeable day & that caused me to remain here [Warrenton Female Seminary]. . . .

Sunday Evening[,] 25' October—— Camp near Fisher's, Warrenton[.]

. . . There is a great deal of curiosity felt in regard to the causes of the removal of Rosecrans from the Army of the Cumberland. It is now said that a main cause was his complicity with the operations of Truesdelle [sic].

Monday Night, 26' October, '63. Camp near Warrenton (in) Va[.]

. . . I spent most of the day in the Office. . . . I should record the birth of a Son to Florry Prentice[,] 17' Oct.[ober]. Pretty rapid generation since the Wedding Night.

Tuesday Night[,] 27' October, 1863, Camp near Auburn, Va[.]——

. . . We were ordered to move at 8 o'clock, & establish Head Quarters at Auburn, some 7 miles or less, in the direction of Catlett's. . . .

Wednesday Night, 28' October—— Camp[,] Head Quarters, Auburn——

. . . I have been with Meade twice today—— He acts Strangely, keeping up no continuous picket line towards the enemy, who are, as guerillas all around us, stampeding our horses & running them off every night. Lee's Army is, a large portion of it, on this side the Rappahannock, throwing up Rifle pits & making himself very strong, generally—— Meade is doing nothing & appears indifferent—— If he would attack Lee now he could nearly Annihilate his Army. . . .

Friday Night, 30' Oct. '63—— Head Quarters Camp, Rocky Hill——

. . . Up at the usual hour & breakfasted—— Just as I came from table recd. Orders to move to this point, near the Murrays. . . . We have rather a pleasant Camp, between Murray's & the Rail Road, which is just now in running condition to this point, having been entirely relaid to this point from where the Rebs. destroyed it, beyond Bristoe. This has been a triumph in railroading. Meade does not seem to have any settled policy, but it is understood that he thinks of fighting Lee, who is snugly posted, behind his earthworks, at the River and on this side of it, not 2 hours['] march from us——

Saturday Night, 9 o'clock, Head Quarters Camp[,] Rock Hill, Va[.]——

. . . Business does not go very slowly—smoothly I mean, the exactions of the Officers for their Agents, & the gross rascalities of the latter, making me a deal of trouble—— I hate to take hold of these things but I suppose I must, or I shall catch it from [Sec.] Stanton. A part of the fault is Gen. Meade's, as he has never been in command of men, immediately, knows nothing of the wants of an Army so far as the rank and file are concerned & does not seem to care much about them if he can avoid trouble. The matter of tobacco alone is causing much disaffection as the men are without it, and Sutlers not being allowed to come up. Officers are putting in enormous supplies for themselves, ostensibly, but in reality, for their men—— The people, too, all about here, are stripped of supplies, and *they* ask for permission to purchase from the Commissary, a few articles, which can only be given on oath of allegiance. . . .

Monday Night[,] *2' November*—— Camp in Mrs. Col.
Murray's Yard.

. . . After Breakfast I went to work writing a lot of business
Letters, closing up business papers etc. etc. In this work I
have been engaged almost the entire day, excepting to attend
to an unusual number of calls from women, who come here
for help, and I am unable to help them. . . .

Tuesday Night, 3' November—— Camp at Col. Ed.
Murray's place.

. . . I have succeeded in getting a permit through, for Tobacco
for the men—— Meade does not seem to comprehend the
wants of an Army so far as its men are concerned. . . .

Wednesday Night[,] *4' November, '63,* Camp in Col.
Murray's yard[.]

. . . It is now the Indian Summer and the weather is perfectly
beautiful. . . .

Thursday Night, 5' November, '63—— Head Quarters,
at Col. Murray's[.]

. . . [Gen.] Seth Williams came over just at sunset, to tell me
that we were to move tomorrow; but I have been over this
evening and find that the movement is postponed. . . . We were
to have gone to the neighborhood of Kelly's Ford I think——
It is said that we are likely to go to Falmouth & Frederic[k]s-
burg again—— If so, it is a great oversight that we have

delayed the movement so long, as [Gen. Wade] Hampton's
Cavalry, 600 strong, crossed over, on Monday or Tuesday,
and commenced tearing up the Rail Road from Acquia. . . .
What ever we do, as it seems to me, we shall have to fight
unnecessarily to secure position on the other side of the River;
a something that we might have secured with great ease, if we
had only acted vigorously and got the start of the enemy, as we
might have done so easily. . . .

Friday Night, 6' Nov. '63. Last night at Col. E. Murray's
place——

. . . A move has been ordered for tomorrow morning, including
our whole force, to the Rappahannock, Head Quarters going
to the front of Beal[e]ton, towards Kelly's Ford—— We are to
cross the River, without doubt, but whether to go towards
Culpepper, or Frederic[k]s burg is more than I can tell——
There are indications that look like Frederic[k]sburg——

Sunday Night, 8' Nov. '63—— Camp near Rappahannock Station (Bowen's)[.]

Yesterday morning, at 7, breakfasted & packed up—at 9
started, via the Junction & Germantown, for Carter's, 2½ miles
from Kelly's Ford. . . . Orders were to be ready to start at daylight this morning . . . We went to Kelly's Ford & remained
until 2 o'clock on the Hill, . . . At 2 it was decided that we
would come to this, our Old Camp of the 11' & 12' Ult. . . .
The Troops are as far out as Brandy Station and it is the
impression that the Rebs. are falling back to the Rapidan. . . .

Monday Night, 9' Nov. Camp near *some* Church, Culpepper Co[.]——

I think every body in this Army, or at these Head Quarters, perhaps, is disgusted tonight. . . . After Meade was moving I went over—say at 10 o'clock, and found that we were not to move Head Quarters today; so I went about heavy work until about 1'15" when an Order came to move at 2' P. M. It was hurrying times, but we got our Teams off in due season and about 3 P. M. followed Meade, to near Brandy Station, where we had a long halt—the second of the day, for the Site of Camp to be selected. . . .

Wednesday Night, 11' Nov. Head Quarters Camp, near Brandy Station[.]

. . . I have had here, this evening, Capt. Brisbane [James S. Bresbin] of the 6' Cavalry, Maj. [Julius] Hayden & Col. [Samuel B.] Hayman—— Hayden has resigned his place on the Third Corps Staff & goes to his Regt. at Fort LaFayette —— He had become very much disgusted with Meade, who refused to extend a ten days['] leave, to have an operation performed on his Wife for Cancer in the breast—— I am sorry he leaves this Army, for he is one of our best Inspectors——

Thursday Night, 12' Nov. '63—— Head Quarters Camp, near Culpepper——

Last night, at 10 o'clock, I had a kettle of warm water to take off the chill from the tub of water, then took upon myself the pleasure of a thorough scrubbing, before my fire; a thing I have not before done since I was sick—— It has made me feel all the better today. . . . John M. Botts came to see me and bring his long winded articles to read to me. . . . It seems that Jeb. Stuart arrested him, took him to Culpepper, kept him a few hours & set him free, making no charges against him—— Botts was desirous of being martyrized by being taken to Richmond, but it is probable that Lee prevented it, fearing the consequences—— He says that the Confederate Army has nearly ruined him, having carried off 3000 bushels of Corn, 17 Stacks of Wheat & all the Corn they could lay their hands on —— He makes very heavy complaints. . . .

Friday Night, 13' Nov. Camp Head Quarters near Brandy
 Station——

. . . There is a strong feeling rising up against Meade because he does nothing to keep up his Army or provide for its wants, outside of Ordance, Subsistence, Quarter Master's Stores—— I am trying to get him to act for the Supply of Sutlers' Goods, but thus far without Success. . . .

Saturday Night, 14' November, Camp near Brandy
 Station——

. . . Gen. Meade went to Washington this morning leaving [Gen. John] Sedgwick in Command—— From deserters, refugees & contrabands we learn that Lee's main body has withdrawn from the opposite Side of the Rapidan, last night & this morning, leaving only such Cavalry as might be necessary to hold the line temporarily and cover their retreat. . . .

Sunday Night, 15' November, Head Quarters[,] A. of P.[,] Culpepper Co.

. . . In consequence of the intelligence brought in last night, [John] Buford, or some of the Cavalry, were directed, this morning, to make a reconnaissance in the direction of the fords & wake up the enemy. . . . The impression, from all the information that has reached us, is, that Lee's forces are divided—that A. P. Hill has sent, (or gone with), two of his Divisions, to Richmond, or Bragg; and that Ewell's Corps has gone down to the vicinity of Frederic[k]sburg; some to Spotsylvania Court House and thereabouts, within supporting distance of Fred'sburg. . . .

Monday Night, 16' Nov. '63——Head Quarters near
    Brandy Station——

. . . Was up to see Gen. [Andrew A.] Humphreys & spent an hour talking over business matters with him—— He & Meade are profoundly ignorant of the wants & necessities of the Army —— And I think they will never learn—— Some half a dozen British Officers from the Scots Fusiliers, stationed in Montreal, are here, and [William H.] French turned out his [Third] Corps for them. . . . Gen. Meade reached here again this evening—— Gen. [Seth] Williams was here a few minutes ago, having been with Meade in Washington, but does not know what instructions Meade has brought home with him—— [Eben] Magee & [Dan] Plen [Plew] are home and say that the Rebs. have not fallen back any distance from the River, but are fortifying, (the people say they are secretly placing Torpedoes etc. within the works, expecting them to be taken by the Yankees, who will then get blown up) between Rapidan & Orange Court House. . . . There is a determination among many of the Troops, not to serve after the Expiration of their 3 Years['] enlistment——— At Frederic[k]sburg, yesterday, there were only about 80 Cavalry, but they were building watch fires enough for a Division——— There are no other Troops below Ely's Ford——— A. Clay Rowe & King, of Frederic[k]sburg, are turning their Confederate Bonds etc. into Tobacco, in the expectation that our Troop will yet be there, this Winter, as they say that Lee cannot get any re-inforcements & must fall back. . . .

> *Tuesday Night, 17' November, '63*——— Camp near Brandy Station, Va[.]

. . . Just at this moment comes in something in the shape of an application again for "Fat Andy" [Hepburn]———⁴ I wish he was hanged, or out of my way. . . . Meade does not yet move and I don't know much of his plans, but he seems to know little about his Army. He disgusts by his Apathy and indifference as regards his Troops. . . .

---

⁴ The Headquarters Sutler, said to be under the wing of Quartermaster General Rufus Ingalls.

Chapter X

Mine Run Campaign

NOVEMBER 18, 1863, THROUGH MARCH 9, 1864

THE MOVEMENT OF MEADE between November 26 and December 1, described here by Patrick, soon acquired the name of Mine Run Campaign. Meade had attempted to cross the Rapidan to the east of Lee and turn his right flank, but he soon discovered that Lee, who had reacted quickly and taken a strong position behind little Mine Run, was nicely covered. Meade then retreated to the north side of the Rapidan on the night of December 1. Good campaigning weather was at an end and both armies began to prepare winter quarters. Patrick's Diary faithfully records the drop in Army morale with the failure of the Mine Run Campaign. The growing dissatisfaction with Meade failed to come to a head because no one could suggest a suitable successor.

Winter weather aggravated the effects of the war and many families neared starvation. Succor for destitute families, trade with the Army, and with those lucky Virginians who still had something to exchange became a major concern to Patrick and Washington authorities in the winter of 1863–1864.

On November 25 Grant led the Union armies to victory at Lookout Mountain and broke the Confederate siege of Chattanooga. Coupled with his victory at Vicksburg, Chattanooga assured Grant his third star and command of the Armies of the United States, which he assumed on March 9, 1864.

Wednesday Night, 18' November, '63—— Same
    Camp——

. . . Last night, for the first time in many months, I read some
2 hours, in McClellan's "Armies of Europe," including his very
able criticism upon the operations around Sebastapol——[1]
What a mistake that he was relieved from the Command of
this Army. . . .

Thursday Night [,] *19' Nov. '63.* Head Quarters near
    Brandy Station, Va [.]——

. . . [Meade] says we will strike out very soon and he rather
thinks we will cut loose from this line, entirely—— I cannot
make out his plans, because he cannot make them out himself—— He does not want to move until he knows every
thing—— Without a shadow of proof he insists that Lee has
80,000 Troops, when, even in Richmond, Lee's force is not
put beyond 40,000 and we have every reason to believe *that*
to be, 5,000, 10,000 or even 15,000 too large an estimate.[2] . . .

Friday Night, 20' Nov. '63—— Head Quarters, near
    Brandy Station [.]

. . . I have been unusually overrun lately with calls for assistance in making Brigadier Generals & Colonels and I know not
what—— It seems to be of little use to Say, I am without

[1] This was McClellan's portion of the report of the 1857 Military
Commission to Europe headed by Capt. Richard Delafield. Both the
Commission and McClellan devoted a great deal of attention to the
Crimean War and the Siege of Sevastopol.
[2] The Abstract of the field return of the Army of Northern Virginia
for November 20, 1863, shows Lee reported 48,586 officers and men
present for duty.

influence, for my name is in demand—— Col. [Benjamin F.]
Baker has been here on that errand. . . .

Saturday Night, 21' Nov. '63. Same Camp—— Rainy
   Night!

. . . This evening comes news that [Gen. James] Longstreet has
driven [Gen. Ambrose E.] Burnside back to Knoxville——
We may look for any disaster from Burnside. He is unfit to be
in any separate command. . . . I have been reading, carefully
the address of Edward Everett at Gettysburg. Good, but not
quite correct——[3]

Sunday Night, 22' Nov[.] '63. Camp near Brandy Station.

. . . The Storm cleared up in the latter part of last night, and
this has been a glorious day for drying up the roads & hardening them. Nothing is yet known, so as to decide our personal
arrangements, of the intended movement, though, I suppose
we are about ready to start. . . .

Monday Night, 23' Nov. '63—— Camp, Head Quarters
   near Brandy Station[.]

. . . We have packed all surplus baggage, Official & personal
and sent back to Alexandria, by Order—— We expect the
different Corps to move at 2 o'clock tomorrow morning,
though the order has not yet been issued (7 o'clock.) . . . Parker
(Mail Agent) tells me, that growing out of complaints in regard
to my stopping packages, made to the P. M. General [Mont-
gomery Blair], an investigation took place & was continued

[3] Lincoln's "few words" obviously made no impression on Gen. Patrick.

for some time, resulting in an Order of the Post Master
General, to all Post Masters to seize these packages of obscene
books & burn them wherever found——

7'30" P. M.——

The Order of movement is out—— Troops move tomorrow at
daylight, force the crossings at two points below the Rail Road
& strike off towards Robertson's Tavern, on the road from
Orange, to Spotsylvania Court House—— Head Quarters
move at 7 in the morning & go to the neighborhood of Germania [Germanna] Mills—— The Order is well planned. . . .

> *Tuesday, 12½ o'clock P. M.*[,] *24' Nov.* Same Camp, near
> Brandy Station[.]

Well! Here we are, still tied up in Camp, after having made
all arrangements for a move at 7 this morning. . . . We breakfasted soon after 5 o'clock and while at breakfast the order
came over for suspending the movement on account of the
weather—— We have had rain all the morning & the ground
is very soft—— It is not now raining, but the weather is not
at all settled, I very much fear that notice of our movement
may reach Gen. Lee; that he will get all the details & be
prepared to meet us at the weak Points. . . .

> *Wednesday Night*[,] *9'30" P. M.* Camp near Brandy
> Station [.]

This has been rather a dull day. . . . Went up & had a long talk
with Meade & Humphreys this morning, then examined a
deserter by the name Mollere, a Louisiana man, who may be

a Spy—— At all events, he is one of the very shrewdest of men & I have sent him to Washington this evening. He got in from [Gen. George A.] Custer's Command[4] at midnight and says that Jeff Davis reviewed Ewell's Corps Yesterday, & would review A. P. Hill's today—— Says that Ewell is absent and Early is in Command of the Corps. . . . At 9 o'clock, precisely, orders came that "Head Quarters will move at 7 o'clock tomorrow morning["]—— I fear that we shall have trouble in moving our Trains in mud.

Notes from my Pocket Memoranda, in the Field

Thursday Morning, 26' Nov. (Thanksgiving Day) [.]

The whole Army of the Potomac was in motion at Daylight, or should have been—— *We* were up early & ready to move at 7, but I suppose it was 8 o'clock when Head Quarters Trains moved out, & Meade himself started for Germania [Germanna] Via Brandy Station & Stevensburg—— I followed, with my Cavalry, more slowly & independently. . . . On reaching Germania about noon, I found the 2' Corps [Warren] there, awaiting the arrival of French at Jacob[']s Ford, before laying the Pontons—— Meade was very angry (& justly) at this terrible delay & carelessness about roads on the part of the 3' Corps—— After waiting a long time, Warren was ordered to throw over a Brigade & put down the Bridges—— He did so & crossed over his Corps. . . . The Army was ordered to keep on the move all night, in order to get the position it *would* have had but for the *balk* of the 3' Corps, which (Meade said at the moment) would cost us a delay of 48 hours, & full notice of our movements to Lee. . . .

---

[4] Gen. Custer, of the golden ringlets, commanded the 2nd Brigade of Judson Kilpatrick's Division in Pleasonton's Cavalry Corps.

[On] *Friday Morning*[,] *27' November,* After a very cold night, & very little sleep, we turned out before day & got every thing in readiness for a move, but Head Quarters did not move until near 9 o'clock—— It was very hard work getting up the hills, after crossing the Bridge, the ascent being very steep[.] Gen. Meade went on, but I remained for some time, clearing the bridge & roads of Teams, Troops etc. . . . I went on, with the Cavalry, to within about a mile of Robertson's Tavern where Head Quarters had halted—— The road from the [Orange] Plank [Road] to the turnpike, some 3 miles, or more, was very bad, as was the Plank in certain spots—crossing runs & the like—— Otherwise the roads were good, all the way from Brandy—— The Pike, after we struck it, was very good. . . . The 1' and 5' Corps [Newton & Sykes], crossing at Culpepper Ford, came in on the plank & took their position. The 2' Corps, crossed at Germania [Germanna] & came into position via the pike; but the 3' Corps, after fooling away Thursday on the North Side of the River, finally crossed at Jacob's Ferry & again got lost in trying to reach Robertson's Tavern—— [Gen. John] Sedgwick followed the 3' Corps across the Jacob[']s Ford & came into position on the right—— [Gen. William H.] French after floundering about all day, (notwithstanding McGee [Eben Magee] was sent to guide him) got into an engagement with the divisions of Early & Rhodes [Rodes], his men, of his own Old Division gave way & he would have been flogged but for assistance given him by Sedgwick's [Sixth Corps] Troops who were near by him—— He wrote to Meade that he had repulsed the enemy & taken about 900 prisoners—— He delayed the whole Army all day Friday, and did not get his position at all that day—— He lost in killed, wounded & missing near 1000 men & his 900 prisoners dwindled down to 40! Of course there was a good deal of surprise & dissatisfaction felt by all, at this want of cooperation on the part of French but Meade became very greatly out of temper about it. . . . At night we found Mrs.

Fogg & Mrs. Mayhew, with Mrs. Stiles, attached to our Train & tonight (Friday) I hear of their being actually engaged in plundering a house the Troops broke into—— The Guerrillas attacked our Trains at Brandy just after we left & carried off the mules of over 20 Teams & burnt the Waggon[s.] On *Saturday Morning* [,] *28' November*—— Slept pretty well, considering; rose at 5'30", breakfasted at 6' packed up & sent our Teams to the rear at 7, expecting an assault upon the enemy's lines, as [Gen. G. K.] Warren had asked permission the night before to assault—— I also sent the prisoners back 1½ miles, with Supply trains & 20' Militia—— Meade rode to the front at Robertson's, soon afterwards & I followed with my Cavalry, establishing a depot & waiting for French's 900—— By the time we reached Robertson's it began to rain, but we had a cover (sheds) for our horses & Orderlies, while the Genl. & Staff got into the house which had been deserted & where not even a chair remained—— There we sat on the floor, or lay down & lounged about until 3 P. M. The enemy had fallen back from this point, along the pike, to the western banks & heights beyond "Mine Run," where they had been engaged all night in fortifying a very strong natural position—— At 3 we rode about a mile to the front & within 300 yards of our Batteries, where we remained, lounging, the rain having ceased & permitted us to build fires—— Meade was engaged nearly all day in massing his Troops on the Pike for the purpose of assaulting the Centre; but the rain made the roads so heavy that it was too late for attack that night—— Our Teams were ordered up and we encamped after dark, in a miserably wet hole, in the woods. . . . Every thing seems to go wrong with us, as might be expected at this late Season. . . . When I turned out for breakfast, at day break, the 5' Corps [Sykes] was moving up from Robertson's Tavern to the relief of the 2' [Corps] which went over to the extreme left, on the plank, near Good Hope Church—— We breakfasted & packed up all our Tents, expecting to send everything to the rear, as an attack would be made—— We waited, however, & waited & lounged about all day—— It was *Sunday the 29' November*—— The wind & cold had done a deal in drying up the mud—— The Siege Guns (8) were planted on the left of the pike, the enemy's Batteries being at too great distance for the effective range of Napoleons[.] Their batteries were about 1700 or 1800 yards distant from ours—— I went out & examined the line. It is, naturally, very strong, on a high ridge sloping down to Mine Run, which divided the two Armies—— These heights have been fortified, strongly, and besides their regular lines of breastworks, & multitudes of Rifle Pits, they had planted long lines of Abattis, in their front—— All sorts of obstructions were placed in our path & in making an assault our men would be under the most murderous fire for full half a mile, before making the crest—— All were agreed that the enemy's line *must* be turned, or we should not be Successful—— The Stream itself is a serious obstacle, the banks, in most places being very difficult, either steep, or marshy—— The Rebs. were still at work & had been, ever since we crossed the River—— Gen. Warren, as it was understood at dark, on this (Sunday) evening, had been strengthened by 2 Divisions of French's Corps & perhaps some others, making from 25[,]000 to 30,000 men, with reference to an attack early in the morning, (Monday.) Perhaps it was well, as it was Sunday, that no attack was made—— The Teams were ordered up again to be unloaded. . . . The ground was so muddy that I had to throw in pine boughs to keep from Sinking. . . . Our horses suffer, being on about half rations, of Oats, & *no* Hay—— Our men suffer on picket. . . . It is reported that some of the wounded (of whom there are 400 in the Ambulances of the 3' Corps) died of cold. . . . *Monday Morning* [,] *30' November* rose clear & bitter cold—— It is said that more were frozen last night—— We were all up early & breakfasted & struck our tents by 7 o'clock, sending every thing to the rear, the Order having been given for a general attack all along the lines at 8 o'clock, the main attack to be made on the left, by Warren; the Secondary by Sedgwick on the Right, & the Centre follow up. All was anxiety & expectation—— It wanted but 10 minutes of 8 o'clk. the time for the signal to assault, when Meade recd. a despatch from [G. K.] Warren, saying that the enemy were in stronger position than he had supposed, & that, as the attack had been ordered on *his* report of the previous evening, (that he could easily carry the left) he had taken the responsibility of suspending the assault—— This was a terrible shock to all, and Meade instantly ordered the whole movement to be suspended, sending off his Aids as fast as horses could carry them—— He, himself rode over Warren's & did not return until near 2 o'clock—— It is said that there was a very stormy time & I presume it is true; for Meade has a fearful temper & Warren has been so puffed & elated & swelled up, that his arrogance & insolence are intolerable—— While Meade was on the Left, Sedgwick was at Head Quarters and all was quiet save that one division of the 3' Corps (as I understood) advanced to the first line of Rifle pits, unmolested, but lost a few men when falling back. . . . Towards night I was up at Head Quarters & Saw [Gen. John] Newton—— Think he was very drunk when talking to Meade—— Think [Gen. W. H.] French, too, has been tight a good part of the time during this movement—— The plans being given up for the day, we again sent for our Waggons & got our Tents up just at dark. . . . Our pickets suffered intensely and the wounded suffered still more—— The ground—rather the roads, had frozen hard & winter seemed to have set in—— A general feeling of disappointment & despondency had, on Monday Night, taken possession of the whole Army—— I have never seen the Troops in as good Spirits as they had been up to about Sunday—— The fact that French and other Generals, had reported that it was impossible to assault in front with any prospect of Success, became generally known & was fully believed, although every one, so far as I knew, had

expected to make the assault, regarding their chances of life
as very nearly worthless, yet determined to do their utmost——
[On] *Tuesday Morning* [,] *1' December,* rose early again &
breakfasted not knowing what would be the order of the
day—— We did not strike Tents, nor load Waggons much,
but held on to await the final development of affairs——
There seemed to be so strong a feeling of the hopelessness of
an Attack, that Colonel Sharpe, on behalf of others, came to
me to ask that I would go & talk with Meade, to dissuade
him from further attempts to attack—— He stated what was
true, that Meade had become so much exasperated at the
failure of his plans, or of his Corps Commanders, that he was
like a Bear with a sore head & no one was willing to approach
him——that as I was one of his Class Mates, and one to
whom he had never spoken unkindly I ought to use my
influence to carry this point—— It was so strongly urged that
I concluded to go up & see what was the condition of
affairs—— On meeting [Seth] Williams, [Rufus] Ingalls &
[Alfred] Pleasonton, I found that a Council had just broken
up & that it had been decided to withdraw our Army to its
former position—— The Trains were accordingly set in
motion to recross the River and in the course of an hour the
whole thing was settled—— It was said that 5 men of the 5'
Corps had been taken out of the trenches, frozen stiff—— The
men could not handle their pieces to load & it was useless to
try further. . . . *Wednesday Morning* [,] *2' Dec.* found us,
rising rather later than usual after our night march. . . . As
the Order had designated Brandy Station and our old grounds
as the position to be taken on Wednesday night, I concluded
to come on, without waiting for Gen. Meade, as I wished to
get here before the Troops. . . . I travelled moderately, with
my remaining Cavalry, passing all the Troops & reaching here
about one, or half past one—*might* be 2 o'clock. . . . Col.
[George] Sharpe rode up & Said that Gen. Meade had halted
at Stevensburg and established Head Quarters for the night,

greatly to the disgust of all his Staff—— He said that Meade
had been so snappish and cross that no one dared to speak to
him during the whole day—— I accordingly made my dispositions for guarding the Camp by the Cavalry & had just
got through, when Meade rode into my Camp & dismounted,
Saying that he had come to Stay with me until his Trains were
in & Tents up, he having given up remaining at Stevensburg—— He did stay until after 9 o'clock, dining with us,
and giving me a history of the whole movement—— I cannot
now go into it, but it was very interesting.[5] . . .

> *Thursday Night, 3' Dec.* Head Quarters, near Brandy
>   Station [.]

. . . [Lt.] Col. [Jacob B.] Hardenburg [Hardenberg] sent up
a lot of refuse lumber from Brandy Station, a small window
sash & a pair of andirons. As there was nothing else to do,
we set to work and laid a good floor in my big Tent, which is,
now, *very* comfortable although the night is cold, following
a very pleasant day. . . .

> *Saturday Night, 5' Dec. '63* [.] Camp near Brandy
>   Station [.]

. . . We are "Stampeded" occasionally, since our return, by
the movements of the enemy—— Two days ago, the Troops
were put under Arms, and expected a general attack; but it
proved to be only Ewell's Corps moving back to the positions
they had occupied previous to our movement across the
River—— Today we were again Stampeded in a Similar

---

[5] In his testimony before the Committee on the Conduct of the War,
given on February 1, 1865, Patrick described this visit and testified that
Meade had "come to my tent very much depressed, and said that he was
conscious that his head was off."

manner & orders given for every thing to be sent to the other side of the Rappahannock—— Troops were to be held ready etc. etc. It proved to be the attempt of the enemy to hold the same Fords (Raccoon & below) they did before the movement, which alarmed the Cavalry and they reported the Rebs. crossing in force in 3 Columns—— I think it is the intention of the General to remain here for some time—— He & his Staff are getting floors in their Tents & preparing to make themselves comfortable for the winter. . . .

Sunday Night, 6' [December,] 9 o'clock, Camp near Brandy Station [.]

. . . Was sent for by Gen. Meade, who was much exasperated at the lying statements of [Thomas M.] Cook, the Herald correspondent who stays with [Gen. W. H.] French, over at the 3d Corps—— He and [Gen. Andrew A.] Humphreys were just reading it and had concluded to have him arrested for trial by a Military Commission—— I sent over to French's Head Quarters, but Mr. Cook had gone to Washington—— So the matter rests for the present—— It seems to be the idea, that this fellow is employed by French & his Clique, to forestall public opinion & set up French, before 'Official' papers are made public—— There is quite an exciting discussion going on, among the newspapers, about Gen. Meade's Successor, the radical papers taking it for granted that Meade is to be removed—[John] Sedgwick, [Joseph] Hooker, [George H.] Thomas & even [Alfred] Pleasonton, have been named. . . . I am sending off 11 prisoners of State, who were arrested for prudential reasons, on the other Side of the River, & brought here, when we returned. . . . We have very important information, in relation to affairs in Richmond, from our Agent there, which, if acted upon, would ensure the release of our Richmond prisoners & the Capture of Davis. . . .

Monday Night, 7' December, '63—— Camp near Brandy
Station, Va [.]——

. . . [John A.] Cole, of the Christian Commission, has been
here, to arrange about a Chapel for Head Quarters——
Parker, too, has been here about the Mails, which there is
some disposition to interfere with. . . . I do not feel right
towards Meade, for his entire want of management, as to the
interior discipline & economy of his Army—— He makes no
arrangements to meet their wants in a reasonable and business
like manner, and the consequence is, a bad state of affairs
generally—— I am greatly disgusted at it—— The Press is
very severe on Meade, and the general impression is, that he
will be relieved, but his Successor cannot be named so
easily. . . .

Tuesday [,] *8' Dec*—— *'63*—— Camp near Brandy
Station, Culpepper Co. [,] Va [.]

. . . My first work . . . was to listen to the Statements of Mr.
Stringfellow & his daughter, relative to the operations of the
Troops—especially of the 3' Corps, in the way of marauding,
foraging and burning—— They have robbed every citizen of
his forage and Subsistence, have torn down good houses for
the lumber and bricks, and where they could do nothing in
the way of carrying these things off, they have burned houses,
barns, outhouses & meat Houses—— They have burned down
2 or 3 good houses nearby, and have pulled down the
Church, near Pleasonton's Head Quarters, for the bricks
alone—— I have requested Stringfellow to give me names and
dates, so that I may lay the matter before Genl. Meade. . . .
I was sent for by Gen. Humphreys, to talk this matter over
with him—not *this* particular case, but the general relaxation
of discipline, the disposition to plunder, burn & commit all

sorts of depredations & vandalism, by our Troops—— I told him what were the causes of this terrible conduct—that Gen. Meade had taken no steps to check this conduct until the evil had become too great to be borne. . . .

Wednesday[,] *9' December '63, 10'30" P. M.* Camp near Brandy, Va.

. . . Dr. Van Ingen was here at Breakfast—— He brought us news, that there was talk of Gen. Pleasonton's being ordered to Supersede Gen. Meade and Col. [William F.] Rogers tells us the same tale. . . . Meade does not seem ready to act——

Thursday Night [,] *9 o'clock, 10' December, 1863*—— Camp near Brandy, Va[.]

. . . The President's Message is in—— Don't think very highly of it—— This morning I went to see Gen. Meade & we agreed upon a plan for the Sutlers & Gen. Williams is to issue the Order forthwith—— Another Order, still more Stringent than any thing we have ever had, will be issued in relation to the destruction of private property—— The General is determined to make examples of all offenders. . . .

Saturday Night, 9'30" [,] *12' December '63*—— Camp near Brandy Station [,] Va[.]——

. . . Spent the morning as usual. . . . [Capt. Philip] Schuyler received his order here. . . . Will, probably, be here tomorrow night, or Monday. . . . It rained quite steadily from about 9 until some 3 o'clock. . . .

Wednesday Night, 16' December, 1863—— Head Quarters [,] Army Potomac [.]

. . . I have been overrun with applications, of a personal & special character—both yesterday and today—— Applications for Bakeries, for Agencies, for Eating Houses, for any & every thing in fact, even to holding my horse, if I pay, roundly. . . . I have had a number of persons here with letters from influential personages to back them, in order to get positions—— It is absolutely frightful, the number that come to the Army for this purpose. . . . [Col. Sharpe] tells me that [Daniel] Sickles openly announces his intention to fight the battle with [Henry W.] Halleck, who has made more serious & damaging charges against him than Meade did—— He will ask for, either a court of Inquiry, or a Committee of Investigation in Congress—— It is probable that he will succeed in flooring both—— He is all powerful at the White House & is the Gallant of Mrs. Lincoln, going there at all times. Although the President is Sick—too ill to see persons on business, he (Sickles) is said to call on him at any time. . . .

Thursday Night, 17' Dec. '63—— Head Quarters [,] Army of Potomac (Brandy) [.]

. . . I have been trying to make up Rules & Regulations for the Washington Office, but Beckwith will have to go down & Start it, on Saturday, with Capt. [Jacob L.] Snyder & his Clerks—— [Gen.] John Buford died yesterday of Typhoid Fever, at [Gen. George] Stoneman's House in Washington—— President Lincoln, on being told that he *must* die, made him a Major General, for Gettysburg! . . .

Saturday Night [,] *19' Dec. '63*—— Camp near Brandy Station [.]

. . . We hear nothing of any move of the Army—— People

here are preparing for as much comfort as they can take in our present location. . . .

Sunday Night, 20' Dec. '63. Camp near Brandy Station [,]
   Va[.]—*8'30"* !

The Band (I suppose, of 6' Cavy.) has just burst forth, at Gen. Meade's Head Quarters. . . . We hope to get our Head Quarters['] Chapel Tent up by next Sunday, even if we remain *here*—— There is much dissatisfaction at the "put-off" policy of Gen. Meade, who never does any thing about Troops unless he is obliged to —— If any accident to our line of communications should happen, we would be in a pretty fix. . . .

Wednesday Night, 23' Dec. '63—— Camp near Brandy
   Station, Va [.]——

. . . I have been exceedingly busy all day, with matters connected with the trade of the Army—— I have had the Oyster business in hand it having been referred back to me by Gen. Meade—— I have, this evening, sent down an Advertisement, to appear in the Chronicle, & it has been telegraphed to the Associated Press. The bids are to be opened on Saturday the 2' of Jany—'64. . . .

Friday Night, 25' Dec. (Christmas) 1863, Camp near
   Brandy Station [.]

Christmas day has once more come and is almost gone. It was quite comfortable when I got up this morning, the Stove being in very good working order & making the tent very comfortable—— We were not in a hurry about getting up & it was 9 o'clock when we came out from breakfast—— Although it was not intended to do much business today, I have been busy myself the whole day. . . . We had a big Turkey for dinner & I can feel it *very* slightly in my Shoulder, as my Children would say——

Sunday Night, 27' December '63 [.] Camp at Brandy Station [.]

Last night I was engaged until a late hour & made no entry. . . . Yesterday Meade sent down for me & we had a two hours ['] talk—— He knows little of his Army, excepting so far as the fighting material is concerned & it is difficult to do business with him—— He tells me that there is no doubt that [Winfield S.] Hancock has been offered the Command of this Army & will take it as soon as he is able to take the field—— I think he is correct. . . .[6]

Tuesday Night, 29' December '63—— Brandy Camp——

. . . Yesterday the 93' Regt. was preparing to leave, and this morning 3/4 of the Regt. having re-enlisted, got off, on a 35 days['] leave—— It took all my time, nearly, to attend to them and get them ready to Ship North. . . .

Wednesday Night, 30' Dec. '63. Brandy Station——

. . . I have been working at my own affairs, all day—getting off the business of my office and drawing up various Rules etc.

---

[6] Gen. Hancock had been recuperating from a severe wound received at Gettysburg. He returned on December 29, 1863, to resume command of the Second Army Corps, not to take command of the Army of the Potomac.

about Sutlers & Traders, and followers of the Army—— I
have also before me the matter of Trade, under Treasury &
War Regulations—— [John H.] Skinker, and his Associate,
[J. H.] Hudson, both came down here yesterday evening and
I have put the papers before [Andrew A.] Humphreys, Gen.
Meade having gone up to Washington last night, to be absent
some two or three days. . . .

*The 114th Pennsylvania Volunteer Infantry, a Zouave out-
fit, assumed the duties of Camp Guard for the Headquarters
Camp of the Army of the Potomac during the winter of 1863–
64 while the Army occupied winter quarters near Brandy
Station, Virginia. Under General Patrick's general command,
the immediate commander of the 114th was Charles H. T.
Collis. (From the Prints and Photograph Division of the
Library of Congress.)*

Thursday Night, 31' December, 1863—— The last of
  1863!

This has been a very rainy, dismal day. . . . There is nothing
going on, today, in the way of Army news. . . . And so ends
the year 1863—— Thanks be to God for His Mercies!

New Year[']s Day! 1864! Near Brandy, Va [.]——

This, I hope, is the last New Year[']s Day that I shall spend
away from my family—Either on Earth or in Heaven! . . .
There is a great rush, now, among the Ladies, wives of
Officers, about coming to the Army, and permits for them
to come & stay 20 days, on approval of Corps Commanders
& pass from this Office—— This, as it strikes me, is very
unwise, but I suppose it cannot well be avoided. . . .

Saturday Night, 2' Jany. Head Quarters [,] Army
  Potomac——

. . . This evening I have opened the bids for Oysters and have
written to the house of Maltby & Co. [,] Baltimore, to send on
their man Tyson, as best bid—— It has been a work of some
care & trouble, but I think it will be a satisfactory arrangement. . . .

Sunday Night, 3' January '64—— Same Camp——

. . . After reading a while in the Morning and attending to a
few calls of business, I mounted my Mare and rode over to
[Gen. Winfield Scott] Hancock's [Second] Corps, where, to
my great disappointment, I found empty Quarters—— The
General had gone out to visit his Divisions and to look along
the front. . . ,

Monday Night, 4' Jany. '64. Camp near Brandy Station.

. . . Sedgwick's [Sixth] Corps is to move tonight for an expedition to the Valley, to cut off [Jubal] Early, if he can. . . .

Tuesday Night, 5' January—— Same Camp——

. . . I got the first rush of business off this morning and then went off to see Meade and got this Trade Supply District business at work. . . . Col. [Henry F.] Clark [e] is no longer Chief Commissary of this Army, but Capt. [Thomas] Wilson is——[7] Clarke goes down tonight with Gen. Humphreys, in a Special Car. . . .

Saturday Night, 9' Jany [.]—— Camp near Brandy
        Station——

Once more at home after an absence of almost four days. . . . I went up to the War Office and found [Gen. Edward R. S.] Canby—— Had a talk of half an hour, or So, with him and then went down to see [Sen.] Judge [Ira] Harris, where I had a nice time, all the family being there—— [Gen. Ambrose E.] Burnside came in, too, and sat for a little while and we were all very jolly—— Talked with the Judge about Florida & Texas etc. etc. I found there, & wherever else I mentioned it, to Canby and others, an indisposition to hear one word about my leaving the Army of the Potomac. . . . Next Morning (Thursday) I was up in good Season and breakfasted about 8. . . . Then I . . . went to the War Department, where I spent the day, until 5 o'clock, with Canby, [Inspector General Col. James A.] Hardie, [Chief Clerk John] Potts, [Adjutant

---

[7] Captain Thomas Wilson replaced Col. Clarke as Commissary General of Subsistence of the Army of the Potomac.

General Ethan A.] Hitchcock [special advisor to Lincoln and Stanton] and those with whom I had business to do—— Then I went down & got my dinner, staid until say 6 o'clock and went up to Canby's[,] Corner of 22' Street & Penn. Avenue, having declined their invitation to dine—but I found them just sitting down to dinner & had to try it on again. . . . Then I went to [Gen. Samuel P.] Heintzelman's, but all were out & passed on to see Mrs. Potts. . . . Slept pretty well, and rose early next morning (Friday) breakfasted by 8 o'clock & went to the Office—— It had Snowed in the night so as to make sleighing in a Small way—— Staid at the Office until 9'30″ recd. my Sunday Letter from my wife & answered it; then went to the Treasy. Department to see Mr. [Hanson A.] Risley [a "special supervising agent"] & talk about Trade etc. . . . The arrangement with him was very satisfactory & he then desired me to step across the way to see Mr. Chase. . . . Then I went to the War Office—to Col. [William] Hoffman [Com. Gen. of Prisoners] about the Prisoners, to the Military Rail Road Office about the Deposits[,] and to Gen. [Daniel L.] Rucker [Depot Quartermaster] about various things; also to see General [Christopher C.] Augur [Milit. Gov. of Washington] about all sorts of business—— Saw [Col. Edward D.] Townsend and [Maj. Thomas M.] Vincent and then made arrangements with Canby about the commutation of these Officers etc. . . . Wrote to Col. Thomas & then went to see [Assist. Sec. of War, Peter H.] Watson, with whom I had a talk about the [Gen. Rufus] Ingal[l]s, ["Fat Andy"] Hepburn Matters etc. etc. Watson is greatly impressed with my manner! At 5 o'clock dined with Potts & there I staid till about 6'30″ thence to see Heintzelman & Wife, thence to see Gen. [Horatio] Wright & Wife & daughter, after that to see all at Joe [H.] Taylor's [Augur's Chief of Staff] & went home at 10'30″—— Went to bed at 11 & rose early. . . . Got home safely at 3—— Meade & Humphreys are both Absent & Uncle

John [Sedgwick] is in command—— The weather continues cold. . . .

Monday Night [,] 11' Jany –'64—— Same Camp——

. . . There has been a great deal of Office work on hand and some rather disagreeable. . . . I have got the Trade business for the Citizens at work & hope it will Succeed well—— Genl. Meade does not return yet and Seth Williams thinks he may not get back before the last of this week—— Seth has presented me with one of the "Smoking Caps". . . . We are losing all the Old Officers from Head Quarters, surely—— Col. [Edmund] Schriver goes tomorrow morning to Nash-ville—very probably, not to return—— It is rumored, & there are strong reasons for believing it true, that [Gen. William F.] Baldy Smith is to replace Meade in Command of this Army, backed by Grant—— This is producing much uneasiness in the minds of all who have the good of this Army at heart. . . .

Wednesday Night, 13' Jany [.]—— Same Camp.

This has been a very mild and pleasant day. . . . I have been as hard at work as usual and find that I have as little spare time as ever. . . . Had a call from a Mr. Latham, formerly of Washington, who brought me a nice mess of quails, or as they are called in this country, partridges. . . .

Saturday Night, 16' January—— Same Camp——

This has been a very busy day—— I rose at the usual hour this morng. & have been all day on the jump. . . . John M. Botts has been over today & has bored me some and pleased me Some—— I would like very well to see him, at any time when I have 3 hours to Spare. . . . [Capt.] Schuyler is home tonight & brings us a great deal of not particularly agreeable news, in regard to the manner of doing duty along the Rail Road. . . .

Tuesday Night [,] *19' Jany. '64* [.] Same Camp——

. . . The Express Office Sent its Agent (Mr. Dunn) down to confer with me, and we arranged all about matters, so as to prevent many of the evils that now pervade the receipt & delivery of goods—— Then I was at Head Quarters and saw Dr. [Thomas A.] MacParlin, the new Medical Director—— Had a talk with him about Vera Cruz & medical matters & Nurses generally. . . .

Thursday Night, (10'30") 21' Jany [.]—— Camp near
    Brandy Station [.]

. . . We hear from Philadelphia that Meade is very Sick, though better than on Friday & Saturday of last week—— He was in bed on Sunday, but thought he would be able to sit up by the next day—— Sedgwick does not run the Army with much vim! Why Should he? Ingal[l]s is trying on. . . . a game in which I think he will be foiled, if he is not very careful—— His endorsements are very foolish. There is an operation going on in the 3' Corps—a Grand Ball! Howard & others have been at it for a long time and applied to me for a kind of Carte Blanche to bring whatever they choose to the Army—— I referred it & got instructions to let down the rules a little [.] So I have done it. . . .

Friday Night, 22' Jany— '64. Camp near Brandy Station,
    Culpepper, Va.

. . . I have letters tonight from Geo. H. Stuart [Chm. U. S. Christian Commission], notifying me that I have been selected as one of the Speakers for the meeting of the Christian Commission, at the Hall of Representatives, in Washington, on the

5' February next. [John A.] Cole was here to see me last night
on the Same Subject. To him I gave the Same reply that I
give in all such cases—that while I stand as I do with War
Department, it is not prudent for me to attract public attention
towards myself—lest my means of doing good be cut short by
[Sec.] E.[dwin] M. Stanton. He would be down upon me, I
suppose, if he thought he could trouble me—— I shall therefore decline the honor of addressing them, while holding my
present position of P. M. G. . . . Have had a deal of disagreeable business—— Mrs. Payne has been on the Carpet & is
likely to have her business interfered with—— We have captured her letters & a box—— She is a hard case & yet our
Officers *will* go there & tell her & her daughters every thing. . . .

Saturday Night, 23' Jany. '64. Camp near Brandy
    Station——

. . . This evening I have received two despatches from [J. H.]
Skinker, to the effect that he is likely to be arrested, being in
trouble about this Trade Agency—— He asks me to go up
to Washington, but I cannot go—— I have telegraphed . . .
to [Assist.] Sec. Watson to send for him & give him a hearing
himself——

Sunday Night, 24' Jany. '64. Camp near Brandy station [.]

. . . I have had a letter, this evening, from [Capt. Charles E.]
Scoville, in regard to Skinker's matters—— It seems that
Skinker got a little corned on Friday & met Peleg Clarke,
Rollow & some body else. He talked to them very foolishly
about this fellow [L. C.] Baker & the Trade Agency etc.
Clarke went off & told Baker & there was a rowe [sic] about
the matter. . . .

Tuesday Night, 10'30", 26' Jany. '64——— Same
   Camp———

. . . I went to work & kept at it till 3, when General [George
W.] Getty came in & we had to talk of all matters down in
[Gen. Benjamin F.] Beast Butler's domain——— He seems to
be a *perfect* beast——— Both [Gen. James] Barnes & Getty
are perfectly disgusted with him. . . .

Friday Night, 29' Jany—[']64[.] Head Quarters, Army
   of Potomac[.]

. . . Had to blow up a Citizen for coming to the Army & going
into business without my Authority, without reporting to me,
as ordered——— Have telegraphed to Col. [James A.] Hardie
to see Maj. [Louis H.] Pelouze & stop his sending to me so
many prisoners—no—persons, on business passes——— It is an
old dodge to get down here & get into business. . . .

Monday Night, 1' February, 1864——— Camp near
   Brandy[.]

. . . I have . . . written, to P. H. Watson, Asst. Sec. of War,
sending him certain papers from [J. L.] McPhail[8] relative to
trade & Smuggling down on the Northern Neck[.] It has been
a gloomy & fretful kind of a day. . . .

Wednesday Night [,] *3' February 1864.* Camp near
   Brandy Station———

. . . I have had a long talk with [Gen.] Humphreys today, he
having sent for me——— He seems to think Gen. Meade will

---

[8] McPhail was the Provost Marshal General at Baltimore and a frequent
source of information about southern trade.

not be willing to have me leave him and that I had better make up my mind to have a re-organization of the Department as soon as may be convenient—— He and [Seth] Williams both think there will be no trouble about getting such Officers as I need for the Department to help me—— I recd[.] a very pretty note, this evening, from Mrs. McClellan, asking for my Photograph & Autograph—— I shall send it. . . .

Thusrday Night, 4' February, 1864, Camp near
  Brandy——

. . . I have just written a note to [Col. James A.] Hardie, Confidential, in regard to the view the Secretary may take in regard to my remaining in this Department. . . .[9]

Friday Night, 5' Feby—'64—— Camp near Brandy
  Station——

. . . Had several business letters that took me up to Head Quarters—— One from Gen—no—from Mrs. Lee [,] Sister of Robert Scott, Saying that her buildings and wood & every thing else is going & wanting to send her valuables to town—— I found [John] Sedgwick up there & he sent an Order to [Gen.] Gregg, to send a guard there. . . .

Saturday Night, 10 o'clock [,] 6' Feby—'64 [.] Same
  Camp.

. . . There is a movement on foot today—— [Gen. Benj. F.] Butler is making a demonstration on Richmond & [Gen. Judson] Kilpatrick was ordered to cross here, this morning while 2 corps would support him, in order to keep Lee from re-

---

[9] Col. Hardie, now an Inspector General, was becoming a channel for direct communication with Secretary Stanton. Hardie contended, however, that he was nothing more than a clerk.

inforcing [Gen. George E.] Pickett——[10] There has been more
or less firing all day—— The result I do not yet know. . . .

Sunday Night, 7' February '64—— Camp near Brandy
  Station [.]

. . . There was no firing after we went to bed, and at eleven
or twelve o'clock, in the night, the Troops were extricated
from their false position on the other side, one or two Divisions
having gone over to bring them off—— I understand that the
Cavalry are also back in position again tonight—— The
Medical Director tells me that we have lost 200 men—— This
is all I know—we have taken, in all (31) prisoners. . . .

Tuesday Night, 9' February, 1864—— Camp near
  Brandy——

. . . After Breakfast went to work and have been at it, pretty
busily all day. . . . Mr. Smith came to see me in regard to the
Trade Agency and Skinker—— [Col L. C.] Baker is after him,
and Skinker is too foolish with his tongue, when the wine is in,
to keep from committing himself. Smith writes to Baker by
tonight's mail, & has telegraphed him to do no more until he
gets the Letter. . . .

Wednesday Night [,] *10' February, 1864*—— Brandy
  Station——

. . . The day has been pleasant but rather cool, and tonight is
really cold—— I have been run down with business calls—
Rixey, of Rixeyville has been here about his negroes—— He
kept me a full hour—— Then came Dr. MacParlin & he
staid a full hour. . . . Col. [Theodore B.] Gates has been up,
preparing for the furloughs of his Regt. [. 20' N. Y. Mil.]——
He hopes to be able to get off by Friday——

---

[10] Lee had sent Gen. Pickett to attempt the recapture of New Berne,
North Carolina.

Friday Night, 12' Feby—'64—— Camp near Brandy
   Station——

Yesterday [Joel Tyler] Headley was with me & I could not
get up any thing to send him out of the way, so that I could
write, last night. . . . He is to write up Sedgwick's life and I
went up with him to see the General. . . . My work is . . .
behind, and I have been busy today in getting it up. . . .
[I went] down to see Gen. Henry J. Hunt, who has just
returned—— He has been to see Gen. McClellan & spent
a day with him, having a glorious good time—— The
feeling against him is changing since the publication of his
Report—— There is a strong feeling in his favor, all through
the Country. . . .

Saturday Night, 9 o'clock, 13' Feby[.]——Head Quarters[,] A. of P.

. . . The day has been pleasant & the forenoon quite sunny. . . .
We have been expecting to see Genl. Meade here today——
He still remains in Washington—probably to arrange matters
& plans for the future—— Thus far we seem to be doing
very little in the way of preparing for the Spring Campaign,
while all on the other side is charged with activity. . . .

Monday Night, 15' Feby—'64—— Camp near Brandy
   Station [.]

. . . We have a Report from one Richmond Emissary fully
corroborative of our own report made up on the 10'
Feby[.]—— Genl. Meade came home this Afternoon & I
went up to see him this evening for a few minutes—— Came
home & have looked over the "Peninsular Campaign in Vir-

ginia" by Rev. J. J. Marks DD." a self laudatory work, with
an eye to the Tiller, & popular favor by a stab at McClellan—— I did not read it long, but took up McClellan[']s
Report & read several pages in it. . . .

Tuesday Night, 16' Feby—'64. Camp near Brandy
   Station [.]

. . . I have been busy today, in all sorts of things. . . . Have had
a call from a Col. [Russell A.] Alger [,][11] 5' Mich. Cavy [.]—
who is detailed to spread the "Proclamation" in Rebeldom—— He found I was at it already, but left me 20,000
copies of Smaller print than those of mine. . . .

Wednesday Night, 17' Feby—'64—— Same Camp——

Last night was the coldest of the season & at 8 o'clock the
Thermometer stood at only 12 above 0. . . . [Maj. J. C.]
Duane has been down here & staid a whole hour & a half,
talking over matters in the Army——[12] He does not think
highly of Genl. Meade's administrative ability. . . . Col. Alger
has been here & gone to Washington. . . .

Friday Night, 19' Feby—'64—— Head Quarters [,]
   Army of Potomac [.]

. . . I learn that Genl. Meade went down to Washington this
morning——Why , I do not know. . . . This evening some 28

---

[11] Col. Alger was destined to wrestle with the military problems of the
Spanish-American War as McKinley's Secretary of War.

[12] Maj. Duane had been McClellan's Chief engineer officer after the
Peninsula campaign. He now served with the Engineers at the Headquarters of the Army of the Potomac,

of Moseby's [Mosby] men were brought in as prisoners, captured by the Cavalry near Paris, in bed—— They are a pretty tough set. . . .

Sunday Night, 21' Feby. 1864. Head Quarters [,] A. of P.

. . . *This* has been a pleasant day and I have enjoyed it. . . . I understand that Meade is back this afternoon & that Sharpe will not be down before Tuesday—— This matter of the Provost Marshal Generalship is about to be settled I presume this week—— I hope to go to Washington this week on this business——

Monday Night, 22' Feby. Camp at Head Quarters [.]

. . . The day has been very busy—— It began with signing orders for Skinker,—then about the usual work—then a tour with Hunt about Artillery Reserve Sutlers & how to regulate them—then a turn with Humphreys about matters connected with the Rixey business in particular & the Negro question in general—— [Lt.] Col. [Thomas W.] Hyde has been here on the same business. . . .

Saturday Night, 27' Feby—1864—— Camp at Head
    Quarters——

The last few days have been very busy & tonight I have not time to do more than note some *Mem.* for reference hereafter—— On Tuesday morning I went up to see Meade about various matters & had scarcely returned then I recd. a Call from the Sec. of War to go to Washington—— At 6 o'clock P. M. went up on Special train. . . . On Wednesday saw

Secretary, & arranged our matters by referring to Canby, also
saw [Charles A.] Dana[,] Asst. Sec. War. On Thursday did
various other work and went up to dine at Canby's—— Was
at [Montgomery] Blair's reception in the evening—— On
Friday Canby was sick & did not come to the Office. . . . This
morning [Saturday] I was up early and prepared to come
home, as I knew that Troops were moving. Reached here all
safe & spent an hour with Genl. Meade. . . . A little more
detailed account of my visit to Washington may be well for
reference hereafter. The call for me was based on a request
to have me sent up to talk over matters about my own Department—— A Special Train would go up at 6' P. M. to take
distinguished persons from the Review. I found on board
Senators [Morton S.] Wilkinson [Minnesota], [Senator-elect
William] Sprague [Rhode Island], V.[ice] P.[resident Han-
nibal] Hamlin & several others, including Mrs. [Kate Chase[
Sprague. . . . On *Wednesday morng.* breakfasted in my room
& then to Willards & War Office—— I saw Watson & was
referred by him to Dana, with whom I had a pretty frank
conversation about the Trade Agency Protest that I had just
recd. He had just recd. orders however, to start for Boston
and when I went to the Secretary of War, he talked a few
minutes and I suggested that the whole matter should be
referred to Genl. Canby, which was agreed to and the evening
was set apart for the business. So I went to see Genl. [Joseph
R.] Taylor, Old [Col. Alexander] Shiras, [Lt. Col. M. D. L.]
Simpson & [Gen. C. C.] Augur[.] Had pretty good understanding about business and then went down to the Kirkwood
for dinner, stopping at Willards for a few minutes—— Then
I called at Judge [Associate Justice Robert C.] Grier's [of the
Supreme Court] & saw Mrs. Beck[.] Went to my room &
thence to Willard's, where I found Judge [Supreme Court
Associate Justice Samuel Nelson] & Mrs. Nelson & Anna——
Staid only a little while & went to the War Office—— Found
Canby & his Wife—— Got a good hearty Smack and went

to work—— Kept at it until ten o'clk. Canby was fully posted on all these matters and coincided most heartily, in all my views—— He was to present them to the Secretary of War next day, for his Action. . . . *Thursday Morning,* after writing some letters (one to my wife) I went up to [Alexander] Gardner's for another Imperial[13] Photograph. He thinks it is a very fine one—— Then had an interview with Postmaster [Sayles J.] Bowen and afterwards with Postmaster General [Montgomery] Blair—— He talked very freely & invited me to his house. Went then to the War Department and had interviews with Judge [Maj. Levi C.] Turner (Judge Advocate)[,] [Col.] Hardie, [Majors] Vincent & [Samuel] Breck—— I had before seen Genl. [E. A.] Hitchcock & Genl. [Joseph G.] Totten, very pleasantly[.] On account of Cabinet business Canby was unable to see the Secretary & I went up to dine and spend two or three hours after dinner with Canby & Wife—— *He* was quite unwell from a very severe cold, but I had a very, *very* pleasant visit—— Then I came down—at $9\frac{1}{4}$ o'clock, and went into Judge [Montgomery] Blair's—— It was reception night and I there met several old friends—— I staid till about $10\frac{1}{2}$ and went home—— *Friday Morning* I was up early and at work—— After writing some time I went to the War Dept, and saw Hardie, [Maj. Louis H.] Pelouze and others, with whom I had business—— Then I saw Judge Turner, Wife and daughter, all at his Office—— Canby was too ill to be at the Office and so my day was lost, so far as the main business was concerned. . . . I went to dine with John Potts & after night I went to see Archie Campbell,[14] where I found his Wife and Mrs. [William L.] Marcy, (Gov. Marcy's Widow)[.] Had a nice time there and went over to see [Gen. Horatio G.] Wright, who lives close by—— He had an Order calling him to the Army & I smelled a Mice—— Staid there a

---

[13] The Imperial was a nearly life-size photograph that enjoyed a tremendous vogue in Washington during the Civil War.

[14] A West Point classmate.

while & went down to Willard's, where I found Mrs. [Col. George] Sharpe with a letter from her husband, telling of the Cavalry raid contemplated etc. etc. I staid there with her & Mrs. Steele, and their party—then with Generals [Abner] Doubleday & [John C.] Starkweather etc. etc. until nearly 12 o'clock when I went home—— On Friday Morning [Saturday] I decided to come down home—— I regretted leaving unfinished business but could not remain—— So I came off, with Wright, [J. C.] Duane & his Wife & a crowd of others. . . . I think my visit to Washington has been & will be productive of great good to the Service, by establishing harmony with War Office.

Sunday Night [,] *28' Feby '64.* Head Quarters [,] A. of P.

. . . [Gen. John] Sedgwick was at James City last night—— I do not know where he is tonight—— [Judson] Kilpatrick has started with about 5000 men for Richmond & crosses tonight at 10 o'clock at Ely's Ford[.] [Col. Ulric] Dahlgreen [Dahlgren] has 300 men with him.—— [Capt. John] McEntee is with them——

Monday Night, 29' Feby. 1864—— Head Quarters [,] A. of P.

. . . We have recd. news from the Raiders, up to 2 o'clock last night, at Spottsylvania Court House & Chancellorsville—— They captured 15 or 16 of the pickets, including a Captain & Lieut. Sedgwick is at Madison Court House, but thus far has not done much—— He is merely to *Steady* Lee and hold him in position. . . .

Tuesday Night, 1' March '64—— Head Quarters [,]
   Army of Potomac [.]

This has been a very disagreeable day—in fact, the last 24
hours have been very disagreeable—— We have had rain,
hail, sleet and a little Snow. . . . There is no news, as yet of
the Expedition—— The weather is affecting the Troops un-
favorably, who are on the expedition, I presume—— It has
been very . . . uncomfortable for those of us on duty in
quarters, even—— I have drawn up my reply to the charges
in regard to the Trade Agency, or rather, I have requested
that the whole matter be referred to Genl. Canby, for Such
action as he may think proper. . . .

Wednesday Night [,] *2' March, '64.* Head Quarters [,]
   A. of P.

Last night I worked rather late, as I had a matter on hand
evincing some rascality on the part of Herald Reporters etc.
I have Sent [John C.] Babcock to Baltimore this P. M. to hunt
it out. . . . The 6' Corps, and Custer's Regulars (Cavy.) are
back in their old position tonight, having accomplished their
object, to wit, the destruction of a park of Artillery below
Gordonsville and the withdrawal of all Troops this side
of Frederic[k]sburg, towards Madison Court House and
Stewardsville—thus leaving open the way, entirely, for the
Cavalry—— They have had a Start, as nearly as we can
judge, of 12 to 18 hours ahead of their pursuers—— The
Scouts are in and everything looks favorable for some success
in Dixie. . . .

Thursday 9' P. M. [,] *3 March* [,] *'64.* Camp at Head
   Quarters [.]

. . . We had our breakfast earlier than usual and then for the
work of the day—— It has been of all kinds and Sorts—— I

was at work drawing up matters for the regulations of Mails. . . . There is some bad news about Kill Patrick's [sic] raid—that he fell in with [Col.] Bradley [T.] Johnson's troops at Hanover Junction & had a fight, which was equivalent to notifying the Richmond Authorities that he was coming—— I am afraid he will accomplish nothing. . . .

Friday Night, 4' March, '64. Camp at Head Quarters [,] A. of P.

. . . Killpatrick [sic] has been heard from at Yorktown. He has done nothing but drive in the pickets to Richmond—— Probably gave notice of his proximity to the Capitol by his fight at Hanover Junction, which should have been avoided—— We have had a Singular operation going on today—— There has been an organized gang of Robbers in the Bull Ring[15] & every man who went in was thoroughly cleaned out— Every man has been overhauled today and the Rascals are in irons—over 100 have been examined and a dozen or 15 are in Irons. . . .

Sunday Night [,] *6' March, '64*——Camp at Head Quarters [,] A. of P.——

Did not sleep the latter part of the night, at all, and was up in very good Season—— Spent my morning in reading—— Read mostly the Summing up of the history and laws of the Hebrews, by Moses, in Deuteronomy. . . .

Tuesday Night [,] *8' March '64* [.] Same Camp——

Another busy day has passed away—— I was up in very good Season and after Breakfast went about my work—— Have

---

[15] Patrick's "Bull Ring" provided temporary quarters for prisoners of the Provost Marshal whose cases were pending.

written several Letters, attended to all Sorts of business, of all kinds & complexions—— Have been looking into the habits & associations of the people within and about our Lines— making lists of those who ought to be arrested etc. etc. . . .

Wednesday Night, 9' March, '64—— Head Quarters [,] A. of P.

. . . Genl. Humphreys was down here an hour or more, about all Sorts of matters, including the Head Quarters arrangements about Troops, Guard House etc. etc. It seems that the Richmond papers have an article about our "Bull Ring" that is mortifying our people at Head Quarters greatly—— Meade has had his hands full in this fight with [Daniel] Sickles and has given the War Committee fits—— [Daniel] Butterfield has been sent for, and I fear that the faction has too much power for Meade to withstand——[16] I have just been at Meade's Head Quarters and he has been Scoring [Alfred] Pleasonton—— [Rufus] Ingal[l]s caught a few also. . . .

---

[16] Patrick is referring to the major battle that was taking place before the Committee on the Conduct of the War. The ins and outs of the Affair would require a volume. Simply put, Meade was under attack for failure to destroy Lee's Army after Gettysburg and because he was a political moderate. Hooker and his Radical friends were trying to destroy Meade's military reputation. The testimony was being taken by the Committee in Washington. Daniel Sickles testified on February 25 and 26; Meade appeared on March 5, 11, April 4, and May 16; and Daniel Butterfield testified on March 25 and by the end of April virtually every major staff officer in Meade's command, all his corps commanders, and some of his divisional commanders, had been called to testify.

Chapter XI

Grand Plans and Preparations

MARCH 10, 1864, THROUGH MAY 3, 1864

ON MARCH 10 Lt. Gen. Ulysses S. Grant went down to the
Army of the Potomac to have a look around. In the weeks that
followed his influence began to be felt in a variety of ways.
Wagons and baggage for the Army were pared down. Troops
were stripped from Washington defences and sent down to the
Army. Familiar faces disappeared and men such as Phil
Sheridan, "a very quiet determined little man," took their
places. Grant planned to have all the Union armies move for-
ward simultaneously on May 1. Meade was to seek out Lee,
Franz Sigel was to move up the Shenandoah Valley, and
Benjamin Butler was to move up the James.

In the West William T. Sherman was given added responsi-
bilities. His Department of Mississippi embraced three armies.
He would have with him John B. McPherson and the Army of
the Tennessee, George H. Thomas and the Army of the
Cumberland, and John M. Schofield and the Army of the
Ohio. As Sherman later put it, his assignment was to "get after
Johnston" who had replaced Bragg in Georgia.

Things were not so tidy beyond the Mississippi. The Administration had long been committed to a Texas expedition of
some sort. Pressure from cotton- and land-hungry businessmen
and politicians had become irresistible. In spite of Grant's
misgivings Nathaniel P. Banks took off for Texas via the Red
River on March 12. After a fine beginning everything went
wrong—the weather, the river, and the Confederates under

345

Dick Taylor combined to defeat Banks. By mid-April the Red River Expedition was over.

Meade moved across the Rappahannock on May 4, only three days behind Grant's original schedule, a new record for the Army of the Potomac.

Thursday Night[,] *10' March, '64*—— Head Quarters[,]
A. of P.

... Genl. Grant arrived here today about 3 o'clock and in the
midst of a heavy rain——[1] He soon after sent for me and I
went up to see him, staid but a few minutes and then came off,
as I did not wish to stay to dinner—— He looks well, says he
is in good health and has changed but very little since I saw
him, except by 10 added years—— He was very cordial &
seemed to be much as I expected——

Friday Night, 11' March '64[.] Head Quarters[,] A. of P.

Had pretty fair sleep last night and a pretty rainy time today.
... I went about my work this morning in due season and have
kept at it very closely thro' the day, tho' I Spent an hour with
[Gen. Andrew A.] Humphreys about noon. ... General Grant
left this morning for Washington & Meade with him—— He
told me that he should return here after a few days—— I
suppose Meade has gone up on consultation. ...

Saturday Night, 12' March, '64—— Head Quarters[,] A.
of P.

... I was about my business in the morning, in the usual way,
when McEntee came in—— He has the same opinion of Kill
patrick [sic] that I have and says he managed just as all
cowards do—— He further says, that he thinks the papers are
correct that were found upon Dahlgren, as they correspond

---

[1] Ulysses S. Grant received his commission as Lieutenant General on
March 9, 1864.

with what D. told *him*. . . .[2] It seems that [Gov. Edwin D.] Morgan is arranging with Thurlow Weed to have *his* name brought forward in the Republican Convention as a Candidate for President——[3] What a Man! . . .

Sunday Night[,] *13' March '64*—— Head Quarters[,] A. of P.

. . . I have a letter from Mr. [William] Kelly—— It is rather desponding—— He is looking for a collapse of our money system—— A grand smash up, and I don't know that I have a reason to doubt the truth of his apprehensions——

Monday Night, 14' March, '64—— Head Quarters[,] Army of Potomac[.]

. . .Went about my work in good Season and kept at it very steadily. . . . Meade sent for me this evening. He has just got back from Washington and feels pretty well—— He thinks that Sickels [sic] has gone up. Butterfield will be arrested, in all probability—— I have good hope that he will be taken care of finally. . . .

Tuesday Night, 15' March '64—— Head Quarters Camp

. . . I have been with Meade and Humphreys, talking over 5' Corps Matters etc. etc. . . . This is the Commencement of my Fifty fourth Year—and a very Strong commencement it has been, in more Senses than one—— I have spent the day, & late into the night, in hard work, of a disagreeable character

---

[2] The papers included an address to his troops by the young Col. Ulric Dahlgren in which he urged his troops to burn Richmond and shoot President Davis and his Cabinet. The authenticity of the documents are still in doubt but the evidence of their genuineness is accumulating.

[3] Thurlow Weed, a power in both New York and National Republican circles, was a close associate of Secretary of State Seward. Ex-governor Morgan was Chairman of the Republican National Committee.

and am not yet through with it. . . . Last Birthday was Sunday
and I had a little more time for reflection—— I had passed
through a Year of extraordinary trials and hardships, thro'
battles & the chances of War. This year last past has been
much less eventful than that, and I have been far less exposed,
being under fire at Chancellorsville and Gettysburg only. . . .
On all Sides we are threatened and a deadly blow is being
aimed at us on the right & on the left—— If we are not
speedily re-enforced along our extended lines, I fear that Lee
will be pitching into our Rail Road. They will soon be getting
at active work, no doubt——

Wednesday Night, 16' March '64—— Head Quarters[,]
    A. of P.

. . . I slept pretty well last night and have been as busy as usual
today—— I got all the Brosman papers before Genl. Meade
this morning;[4] closed up all matters for the War Department,
including a Statement in regard to "Trade Agencies" and
intercourse with Citizens within our Lines—which I addressed
to General. [E. R. S.] Canby unofficially—— I have also made
up, with Col.[Geo.] Sharpe, Memoranda, for Canby, on which
to arrange our Bureau of Information for the coming Campaign. I have been at Meade's for Some time, both this afternoon & evening, on business and he has been reading to me
several of his papers I think he has *got* Danl. Sickles, decidedly.
He stands better now than he has ever done, before the
Country—— We have news from Richmond tonight by Some
of our own men, who went out with Kilpatrick and by another
who was captured at Mine Run, but bribed his Guard at the
Pemberton Prison for $50. in Greenbacks, to let him go——

---

[4] Mrs. Brosman was an unauthorized trader who had been ejected from
the Army on several occasions. In ways that Patrick never understood
she always managed to get a pass to return to the Army.

They have brought in a man named Lohman who has been employed on the Fredric[k]sburg Rail Road and brings information from Union Men to our War Department——
They send word that there is to be a strong attack made upon Norfolk, that 3 new Iron clads are to be in readiness, in about 3 weeks; that Longstreet's Corps is to come up & he is to lead in the attack—— The effort will be a very Strong one, both by land & water—— Jeb Stuart is at Hamilton's Crossing preparing for a Raid upon the Orange & Alexandria Rail Road, as soon as the River falls sufficiently for him to cross at or above Frederic[k]sburg—— We are not in a conditon to meet him, now that Kilpatrick's raid has used up all our horses & Cavalry —— However, we ought to be able to break up this raid with our Infantry, by occupying certain points immediately—— He ought not to be allowed to escape——

Thursday Night, 17' March '64, Camp at Head Quarters.

. . . The day has been cold and uncomfortable, somewhat, tho' pleasant overhead. The Ladies have been on the move & I have been introduced to several of them as I have met them in various places. . . . There have been many disagreeble things going on, including a collision, I suppose it may be called, with Ingal[l]s—— I shall put him through—— I have also had some trouble with [Lt. Col. Cyrus B.] Comstock, the Staff Officer [Sr. Aide-de-Camp] of Genl. Grant, on account of his being too large for his breeches. . . .

Friday Night, 18' March '64. Camp at Head Quarters

. . . I went up this evening to see Col. [Edmund] Schriver, who has just returned from the West—— He tells me that there is

a curious State of things in the Western Armies—— Not any
thing like discipline and every thing at very loose ends. . . .
We are looking for a raid by [J. E. B.] Stuart upon our Rail
Road, near Fairfax. . . .

Saturday Night, 19' March '64[.] Camp Head Quarters[,]
   A. of P.

. . . The Christian Commission man came up here to consult
about matters and things relative to a forward movement and
the time for them to be getting out of the Army. . . . I have
been up to see Meade about establishing a Prison at Alexandria
for my own people, that I do not wish to keep with me here,
nor send to the Capitol. . . .

Monday Night, 21' March, Head Quarters[,] A. of P.

The week of toil began this morning by my sending off Capt.
Lyttle [Lytle], to Alexandria, to secure Prison Room and a
Guard House & a Store House for Special purposes—— Then
I began a new era in the Sutlers' arrangements by having my
Stamped Autograph used instead of writing my name on
Sutlers' Orders. . . .

Wednesday Night[,] *23' March, '64*[.] Head Quarters[,]
   A. of P.

. . . The orders tonight, are, that *my* Troops shall be in readiness to be inspected tomorrow by Genl. Grant, who is expected
to be here tomorrow. So ends the day—— I have, tonight,
been reading McClellan's Report. . . .

Thursday Night, 24' March, '64—— Camp at Head
    Quarters[.]

This morning I slept very soundly and did not get up until I
was called—— Had the command in readiness to turn out, at
a few minutes notice, for Genl. Grant, but he went on to
Culpepper, without calling here, and Meade went with him—
I presume we shall soon know that he is here by his acts. . . .

Friday Night, 25' March '64—— Camp at Head
    Quarters——

I have had a not very profitable day, today. . . . Was at Head
Quarters to see about Marshal in the 5' Corps, I want a Field
Officer. . . . [Alfred] Pleasonton is relieved & ordered to report
to [Gen.] Sam[uel Ryan] Curtis——[5] I have an Order to send
off all ladies from the Army, including the Nurses, Agents etc.
of the various Societies. . . . Gen. Meade has been absent all
day, I suppose, with Grant. . . .

Sunday Night[,] 27' March, 1864—— Head Quarters[,]
    A. of P.

. . . We had our Sabbath Service, Bishop Whipple[6] officiating,
at 11'30" A. M. to a full house—— His Subject was "Easter
Sabbath" and after sermon the Sacrament was administered
—— Genls. Meade, Williams, & myself, Schriver, [Maj. William M.] Biddle, [Capts.] Beckwith & Schuyler, with many
others were communicants—— Some that I did not expect to

---

[5] Gen. Curtis commanded the Department of Missouri.

[6] Bishop Henry B. Whipple was the Protestant Episcopal Bishop for
Minnesota.

see and whose lives are at variance, somewhat, with their professions. . . .

Monday Night, 28' March, '64[.] Camp at Head Quarters[.]

. . . This evening I received a peremptory order from C. A. Dana[,] Asst. Secretary of War, prohibiting me from any further action in regard to Prisoners at Alexandria & ordering me to send up to him a Copy of Genl. Meade's Order for work —— I have sent the whole to Genl. Meade. . . .

Tuesday Night, 29' March '64[.] Camp at Head Quarters[.]

. . . I spent an hour, or more, with Humphreys this morning talking over Army matters—— He is a very queer fellow. Meade sent down for me tonight, and I have had a talk about [Capt.] Lyttle's [Lytle] resignation, which the General had disapproved, but I have renewed the application and I think it will be Successful. . . .

Thursday Night, 31' March, '64—— Head Quarters[,] A. of P.

. . . Meade has gone down to Washington, with Grant today, & I went over to See John Sedgwick this morning but lost him. . . . The resignation of Capt. Lyttle [Lytle] has been accepted and he leaves in the morning—— I am very, very Sorry to have him go. . . .

Friday Night[,] *1' April '64*—— Camp at Head Quarters
——

. . . I went down to Brandy Station this morning, on business with Christian Commission—— Came back and went over to Cavalry Corps Head Quarters—— [Gen. Philip H.] Sheridan has not yet arrived. . . .

Saturday Night[,] *2' April '64*—— Camp at Head Quarters——

I went to bed last night, in the rain, which finally ceased, but towards morning was followed by a "Sugar Snow" which has been falling, alternating with rain all day—— It has been very disagreebale. . . . [Gen.] Seth Williams came down, just before dark and took me up to his house, where I found Rev. Dr. Hall, who is to preach to us tomorrow, and Genl. [John] Gibbon, who has just come down here to take his command [2nd Division, Second Corps]——I find the [Col. L. C.] Baker crew [of detectives] down here again, and suppose I shall have trouble. . . .

Sunday Night, 3' April, 1864—— Camp at Head Quarters——

. . . I have been engaged, when not in church, in writing for Mary [Patrick], a 3 full paper Sheets, of counsel, advice and warning, in answer to her letters just received—— I have given her a history of my own early struggles for light, the various hindrances & trials attending it, as a guide, in some degree, for her—— I hope & pray it may be the means of leading her to the truth. . . .

Monday Night, 4' April, 1864. Camp at Head Quarters
———

. . . I was engaged about my business in the early part of the day as usual, and went up to be weighed again—I now come to 180 ! I don[']t know where it will land me, at this rate of growing. . . .

Wednesday Night, 6' April, '64. Camp at Head Quarters
———

. . . This morning, after some morning work, I took . . . the Ambulance & drove to the Station, as I wanted to see [Gen.] Sedgwick, who was going down to Washington—— I arranged with him to trade off the 93' Regt. for a Regt. of his Corps, commanded by Capt. [Col. Edwin C.] Mason, of the 7' Maine, now in [Thomas H.] Neill[']s Brigade. . . . Gregg met me and proposed that we should go over to his Head Quarters where Maj. Genl. Sheridan had arrived and taken command—— Gen. [Alfred T. A.] Torbert had joined us and we called on Sheridan, an old 'mate['] of theirs—— He is, apparently, a very quiet determined little man. . . . I have had [John A.] Cole up here tonight, talking up Sanitary & Christian Commission etc. . . .

Thursday Night, 7' April '64. Camp at Head
Quarters——

. . . After Breakfast this morning . . . I went to work—— Arranged matters with Meade about shutting down on Sutlers, Traders etc. A talk about correspondents, Grant and various other matters, then came home—— Have been fitting up for [John] McEntee to go the Harpers Ferry tomorrow, and for the Scouts to be off on their India Rubber Boats across the

river etc. etc. . . . . The Staff have all been (and are still) out
to witness an entertainment in . . . the Engineer Camp——
The Horse Artillery Theatricals——

Friday Night, 8' April, '64—— Camp at Head
        Quarters——

This morning, after Breakfast, finding that it would be a fair
day, I started for Culpepper, on horseback, having first seen
General Meade, who promised to join me at Genl. Grant[']s[.]
I went via Brandy, to Culpepper, halted at Col. [Edward B.]
Fowler's talked a while with him & examined the prisons,
then to see Sanitary & Trade Agents, and direct them to close
up. . . . From thence to see Genl. Warren [Fifth Corps],
with whom I talked a long while and got things into pretty
good shape—— Then I went over to the quarters of Genl.
Grant, but he had gone to the front—— He was expected
back very soon & I remained talked with [Lt.] Col. [Adam]
Badeau & Genl. [Henry] Prince some 15 minutes perhaps. . . .[7] Tonight the Christian Commission, consisting of
Rev. Dr. [E. N.] Kirk, Russel[l] Sturgis[,] Mr. Demond &
several others, under the charge of [Chm.] Geo. H. Stuart,
came here & staid nearly an hour, discussing matters—— The
interview closed with a prayer by the Rev. Dr. Kirk—— We
talked up Sanitary Matters——

Saturday Night, 9' April, '64. Camp at Head
        Quarters——

. . . In the night it came on to rain & is raining still, quite
heavily. . . . Meade has been in trouble about his order pre-

---

[7] Col. Badeau was an additional Aide-de-Camp and private secretary
to General Grant. Gen. Prince had assumed command of the 3rd Division
of the Sixth Corps.

paring for movements, lest it should be published. [Gen.] Halleck telegraphed down to Genl. Grant that Genl. Patrick had ordered it to be published & the Secretary of War had prohibited the publication——— It is an utter falsehood. . . .

Sunday Night[,] 10' April '64——— Camp at Head
    Quarters———

Last night was one of the most Stormy nights that I have any knowledge of since we came here and the bridges between here and Washington are impassable so that no Trains have been running today. . . . It was my intention to go to Washington tomorrow, but as the running of the Train is so doubtful, I may not go quite so early——— We have some news from Lee's Army, to the effect that Longstreet is about Lynchburg and is to come up and join Lee——— Only 2000 conscripts joined———

Monday Night, 11' April, '64——— Camp at Head
    Quarters———

. . . Was at Head Quarters with Genl. Meade some time came down and went to work——— Have been about as busy as usual today and have begun to pack and repack my kit, with reference to falling, or sending it back to the rear, very Soon. . . .

Tuesday Night, 12' April '64[.] 305 Penn. Avenue,
    Washington[.]

Was up in tolerably good Season, packed & prepared for travelling[.] After Breakfast I rode down with [Col. C.] Ross Smith [Sheridan's Chief of Staff] to the Station and there found the Chris.[tian] Comm.[ission] Delegates ready for a ride. . . . We reached Washington and separated—they to go to a meeting of their own, and I to see [Gen. E. R. S.] Canby. . . . Canby was sick & had not been down for two or three days—— I went over to see John Potts and Wife, and then up to see Canby, where I remained until about 10'30"—& then went home. . . . Canby meets me at War Office at 12 M. tomorrow. He is not *very hard* Sick, but broken down with hard work.

Wednesday Night[,] *13' April 1864.* 305 Penn. Avenue, Washington——

. . . Went to War Department—— Saw & talked with Gen. [Joseph] Taylor, [Alexander] Shiras and Genl. [Horatio] Wright—also the whole Engineer Board—— Canby came down and went to see the Secretary about my matters, but had to give up & go home—— I saw [Charles A.] Dana, with a house full of Senators etc. including [Ira] Harris & [Henry] Wilson—the latter very attentive to me—— Was in all the Offices & got pretty well along with all the *regular* business, but could not get the matter of the prisoners through, without Canby. I went up and dined with him at 5. . . .

Thursday Night[,] *14' April, '64.* 305 Penn. Avenue[,] Wash.

. . . I went to see [Gen. Christopher C.] Augur and arrange matters with him, after which I went to the War Department and finished up my business there. . . . Went down & called on Judge Harris, who went with me to see Mrs. Grant—— From there, after a half hour with Mrs. Grant & Mrs. [Laura L.] Wallen, I went to see [Associate Justice] Judge [Samuel] Nelson & Anna—— Mrs. Nelson had gone to New York. . . .

Friday Night, 15' April '64[.] Camp Head Quarters[,]
A. of P.

Rose early this morning and went . . . to the Office, where
I attended to such matters as presented themselves until time
for the Cars to start, when Canby came down & we took the
Cars—— Genl. Grant joined us and we came over to Alexandria, where [M. J.] McCrickett joined us & came as far as
where the trains meet, to talk about Road Matters—— We
reached Brandy & had our Officers['] Waggon down to meet
us—— Came home and went up to see Genl. Meade—— He
was out but we Saw Humphreys, Williams and Hunt——-
Came to Dinner & then to our room, where we talked until
about 10 then Canby went to sleep in [Capt. Charles E.]
Scoville's Tent. Scoville having gone down to Washington
with Some prisoners. . . .

Saturday Night[,] *16' April '64.* Camp at Head
Quarters[,] A. of P.

. . . It has rained so that Canby has not been out at all——
I have been with Genl. Meade, talking up various things
connected with our Affairs—— Have got them tolerably
understood. We have, (Canby & I,) done a great deal of
talking and I think he understands the department pretty
well—— The fall of Fort Pillow (Tennessee) is confirmed——[8]
Gen. Grant seems inclined to relieve [Col. Benjamin H.]
Grierson for letting [Nathan Bedford] Forrest through . . .

Monday Night, 18' April, 1864—— Head Quarters
Camp——

. . . After Breakfast I was about my work for a while & then
went up to Meade's, taking Canby to call on him—— Then

[8] It had fallen on April 12, 1864.

I came back and worked until 11 o'clock, when Genl. Canby, Capts. Schuyler & Beckwith, went with Meade to review the 6' Corps. . . . Canby rode Seth Williams' fine horse and looked right well—— They tell me that Genl. Grant rides the finest horse in the Army "Cincinnatti" [sic]—the Gift of a number of his Ohio admirers. . . .

Tuesday Night, 19' April, '64—— Head Quarters
    Camp——

. . . There was a trouble about my Spring Waggon this morning and I came very near not getting Canby off in time[.] In fact I had to Telegraph to halt the Train for him. . . . I have had Col. [Henry S.] Burton & his crew here on duty, [and] Col. [William R.] Rowley & his inquiries about the Department, from General Grant——[9] There is a world of work just as we are preparing to move—— Transportation is being cut down—— I fear we shall be in want for prisoners, if we are so fortunate as to take any. . . .

Wednesday Night, 20' April '64. Head Quarters Camp.

. . . I have . . . in most respects, prepared for the march that must soon come, I think—— The Orders given are of the most stringent character, so far as regards transportation and I am in doubt how we shall feel about it when we get started. . . .

Friday Night[,] 22' April, '64—— Head Quarters Camp,
    Brandy Station[.]

. . . I went up, on call, to Genl. Meade's, after 9 o'clock when he told me that the Review of the 2' Corps would come off

---

[9] Col. Burton commanded the Artillery Reserve under General Hunt. Col. Rowley was a secretary on Grant's staff.

today instead of tomorrow. . . . It was magnificent review, the best I ever saw, I think—— The 3' Division of Cavalry, under [Gen. James H.] Wilson, was also out—— Then we rode over & took a Lunch at Hancock's. . . .

Sunday Night, 24' April—— Head Quarters Camp, Brandy——

. . . Meade is in a great fever—— We have had all sorts of a flare-up with the War Department—— The Secretary has telegraphed Meade, and he has telegraphed me, in relation to Passes—— He has halted *every* body, in Washington and Alexandria, allowing no one to come down, either Officer or Soldier, or Civilian—— It takes all power out of the hands of our Officers in this Army—— Both yesterday and today I was annoyed by this strange work. . . .

Tuesday Night, 26' April '64—— Head Quarters[,] Camp A. P.

. . . In the morning of Yesterday I sent [Capt.] Beckwith down to Washington, to see what was meant by the War Department, in sending down Such Orders to us. . . . He has returned, tonight, and says it is impossible to account for the Order on any known principles, except that the Honorable Secretary got his back up about something & wreaked his fury on the Army of Potomac, as usual—— As it is, we are all tied up, and shut up, and none are allowed to come down, who are now in Washington. . . .

Wednesday Night[,] 27' April '64—— Camp at Head Quarters[.]

. . . This evening we have news of the fall of Plymouth [N. C.] and the surrender of Genl. [Henry W.] Wessells—— It is a Sad business & it Seems as if Somebody should be held responsible for it, as Genls. Wessels & [John J.] Peck both reported the expedition of [Gen. Robert F.] Hoke in time to have had re-enforcements—— Genl. [Ambrose E.] Burnside is at Alexandria with, as is said[,] 42,000 Troops—— It is believed that [P. G. T.] Beauregard is joining Lee with a large force from Charleston—— There is a Storm of wind raging now. . . .

Thursday Night, 28' April '64—— Head Quarters[,] Army Potomac[.]

. . . [Col. Edward D.] Townsend was down today, and has brought down an Order in relation to Spring Waggons, which takes them all from us, but it has made such an outcry that it will hardly be carried out—— At 11 o'clock or a little After, I went down to see the Artillery Reserve reviewed by Genl. Hunt. . . .

Friday Night, 29' April '64—— Head Quarters[,] Army of Potomac——

. . . I was about my usual business until towards 11 o'clock, when I had my Troops out for a Review. Col. [Charles H. T.] Collis made all the arrangements—— The 3' Penn. Cavy.[,] 2' Mass. Cavy.[,] 68' & 114' Pa. Vols. were out and the 7 Companies of the 20' N. Y. The latter appeared very well, tho' nearly all were recruits—— I gave the Officers warning as to their own Conduct & that of their men, on the march. . . .

Saturday Night, 30' April '64—— Head Quarters[,] A. of P.

. . . After a 7 o'clock breakfast, I mounted "Ginia" and taking a couple of Orderlies, rode to . . . Mitchill's Station. . . .

Arrived there, the Judge Advocate informed me that . . . he
would not require my testimony—— So I called to see [Maj.]
George Drew, a few minutes, then rode over to Genl.
Wadsworth's. Staid 30 minutes, perhaps, and then rode into
town, where I spent about the Same time with Grant. . . .
The Old 5' Corps are moving over to this Side of the
River. . . .

Monday Night, 2' May '64—— Camp at Head
    Quarters[,] A. P.

. . . I have been about many things today, making up lists
etc.[.] Major [William] Cutting of Burnside's Staff, came up
to see me on business. . . . From . . . [him] I learn that
Burnside comes forward, with his Command [Ninth Corps]
on Wednesday—— Of course *we* must move by that
time. . . .

Tuesday Night, 3' May, 1864—— Head Quarters near
    Brandy Station[.]

Our last night in this Camp—— Orders came down about
ten o'clock putting the Army in motion, at Midnight & from
that until daylight tomorrow morning—— *We* move at 5
o'clock in the morning. . . . We are going down to the left,
Hancock crossing at Ely's Ford & going over to Chancellorsville, while Warren crosses at Germania [Germanna], goes
on to Parker's Store, where he halts, and is followed by
Sedgwick, who crosses at Germania [Germanna] & bivouacks
on the hills—— *Our* Head Quarters will be between the 5'
& 6' Corps tomorrow night—— Burnside will follow us very
closely—— I have written to Mr. [William] Kelly tonight,

enclosing him a copy of Meade's battle Order—a very good one. . . . I am ordering up all my men Scattered from here to Washington. . . . Every thing seems to be ready for a movement, either on Richmond, or, to give Lee Battle on the South Side of the Rapidan[.] I think the intention is, to move down towards the Frederickshall Station, crossing the R. R. in that neighborhood & coming down on the North & West of Richmond, so as to cross the James River on the west of the City & unite with Butler, who is to advance up the River & attack Richmond via Petersburg—— The Cavalry under Sheridan will make a raid to Richmond & thereabouts, to destroy Rail Roads, communicate with Butler & perform such destructive work as they may be able—— It is all important that the Rail Roads be cut in rear of Lee & the bridges across the North & South Anna destroyed to prevent the mischief from being easily repaired—— The Roads are in very respectable condition, considering the amount of Rain that has fallen lately—— It is understood that Burnside's Corps, instead of remaining on this line, will follow us, immediately & although not a part of this Army will, nevertheless, act in concert with it—— Our Mails for some time to come, will be very much deranged & our supplies very very uncertain—— We start out with 15 days['] supplies and just as little baggage as we can get along with & be comfortable——

Chapter XII

Rappahannock to the James

MAY 4, 1864, THROUGH AUGUST 2, 1864

IN ORDER TO FREE HIMSELF from the inevitable political pressures of Washington, Grant chose to establish his headquarters with the Army of the Potomac in the field. There he could keep a sharp eye on the operations and personnel of the one Army to which he was a stranger. Meade remained in active command of the Army, freeing Grant from burdensome detail. Patrick continued to be primarily concerned with the internal operations of the Army. Grant's strategy called for a simultaneous forward movement of all Union armies on May 1. The Army of the Potomac got off on May 4 and immediately ran into Lee in the Wilderness south of the Rapidan. The fight that followed, May 5 through 7, set the pattern for the long bloody summer campaign of '64. Grant with about 120,000 men struck at Lee with about 65,000; Grant soon found that he could not successfully assault Lee's lines and moved to the southward around Lee's right flank. Lee promptly moved to interpose between Grant and Richmond. Grant tried Lee in the new position, and when his assaults failed, he again slid around Lee's right flank. At Spotsylvania, May 8 to 21, at the crossings of the North Anna River on May 23, at Cold Harbor on June 1 to June 3, the Wilderness pattern was repeated. Grant's losses in the entire campaign just about equaled Lee's entire Army, yet when Grant moved to the south side of the James on June 14 his Army was about the same size as when he had crossed the Rapidan. July brought the Confederate raid on Washington under Jubal

Early and the beginning of the siege of Petersburg. It was on the 30th of July that the Federals exploded their huge mine under a portion of the Confederate line, precipitating the disastrous "Battle of the Crater."

Wednesday [,] *4' May*——(From Pocket Memor-
and a——)

We started out early, had every thing packed & ready for a
move in good season. . . . Orders had been given, of the most
stringent character, in relation to the burning of Camps, etc.
the first breach of which was by the burning of the Camp of
the Scouts, for which I gave Dan. Plew a hiding on the Spot,
in front of the mounted Guides & made him march on foot,
all day under Guard—— Rode with my Cavalry on different
road from Genl. Meade, striking off to the left from Brandy
Station & coming to the plank only at Germania [Germanna]
——This is much the shortest road——The 5' Corps crossed
here & the 2' Corps at Ely's Ford without resistance——The
roads up the Hill, here, are horrible & I had a long time of
helping up Artillery etc. Warren [Fifth Corps] is at the front
& the enemy in *his* front—how strong, is not yet known. . . .
Meade & Grant are encamped close by and in fine spirits——
The Rebs. were taken by surprise, I judge, as one of their
despatches was read by our Signal Officers at Ten o'clock this
Morning to the effect—"The Yankees are moving, in force,
in the direction of Germania [Germanna] Ford."

Thursday[,] *5' May*——

Rose & breakfasted early & took the saddle, but remained
behind, myself, pushing up laggards, for sometime—— Eventually reached the Mine & Mill, on the Edge of the Wilderness,
from which we moved to the top of the Hill, overlooking the
Country for a distance, in all directions, from the intersection
of the Germania [Germanna] Plank & Old Turnpike Roads.
. . . Warren soon became engaged, the 6' Corps [Sedgwick]
went in on the right & the battle raged—— *Our* Troops (Collis
[114' Penn. Infy.] & the 68' [Penn. Infy.]) were sent over to

Warren & *we* were busy as usual in rear of the lines——
Towards evening [Charles] Griffin, [Romeyn B.] Ayres, or
both, pushed forward too far & lost one Section of [George
B.] Winslow's Battery, were driven back & the Regulars cut
up badly. . . .[1]

Friday[,] 6' May——

Up & breakfast soon after daybreak—— Meade resumed his
place on the hill, with Grant, & I took my Cavalry there
again—— Put detachments in rear of the lines—— Sedgwick
[Sixth Corps] on the Right, Warren [Fifth Corps] Centre &
Hancock [Second Corps] left—— Burnside [Ninth Corps][2] in
& coming in, with Warren—— I made the tour of the lines in
the forenoon, saw Burnside & agreed to help him; also his
Staff—— The Old 1' Corps was coming out as I went up, very
much broken & [Lysander] Cutler confused—— I found, soon
after, that they had been driven, that [James S.] Wadsworth
had been killed (or Mortally wounded)[,] [James C.] Rice
killed & [William W.] Robinson wounded——[3] Hancock was
then fighting furiously on the left & hundreds and thousands
of Stragglers were pouring out of the woods in rear of his
Corps—— I put in my Cavalry & rode down & drove back &
sent to Corps multitudes of these fellows, handling them very
roughly, as an Example—they being in full view of most of
the army. . . . The day was intensely hot & the dust like

---

[1] Ayres commanded the 1st Brigade in Griffin's 1st Division of Warren's Fifth Corps.

[2] Ambrose E. Burnside's Ninth Army Corps, just under 20,000 men,
was for the moment independent of Meade's Army of the Potomac of
just under 100,000 men. It was under the direct orders of Lt. Gen. Grant
until May 24, when it came under the command of Meade.

[3] This segment of the old First Corps was now fighting as the 4th
Division of Warren's Fifth Corps. It was under the command of Gen.
Wadsworth. Gen. Rice commanded the 2nd Brigade and Gen. Cutler the
1st Brigade. Col. Robinson led the 7th Wisconsin in Cutler's Brigade.

Ashes—— The enemy fought Hancock & finally set fire to the woods in front of him, that he could not follow—— I sent the prisoners under the 68' & 20' to the Train. . . . We had just got some dinner (or rather Supper), when a furious attack was made upon Sedgwick [Sixth Corps] and the enemy broke through, creating quite a Stampede—— My own Command was turned out & for 2 hours it was supposed that Sedgwick & [Horatio] Wright were captured, but [Truman] Seymour and [Alexander] Shaler were Captured, instead——[4] Reenforcements were put in, My Cavalry was put upon the plank [road] & the lines were again established along the 6' Corps. . . . I do not see that Grant does anything but Sit quietly about, whittle, Smoke, and let Genl. [John A.] Rawlins talk Big——[5]

Saturday[,] *7' May*—— No sleep during the night & breakfast found me unrefreshed—— The fighting was resumed along the Lines and the whole Army seemed to be put in, yet no considerable advantage was gained at any time, our troops fighting manfully and losing heavily—— My own Troops were following in rear of the lines & in the Afternoon the 22' New York Cavalry (Col. [Samuel J.] Crooks) was ordered to report to me—— It had been frightened nearly to death at first fire and skedaddled—— I set to work to gather it up & put it under Maj. [James W.] Walsh's [3rd Penn. Cav.] Special Charge—— One of its men was so paralyzed by fear that he did not even know his name, nor Regt. The fortunes of the day did not seem to be in our favor, though the Rebs. could not drive us—— Meade was thoroughly uncomfortable & seemed disposed, about 3 o'clock, to find another Camp—— We all started out, Staff, Escort, my Cavalry [1st Mass. & 3rd Penn.] etc. etc. made a Swoop of 3 or 3½ miles on the left & front, found no place apparently, came back & a general

---

[4] Gen. Wright commanded the 1st Division of Sedgwick's Sixth Corps while Gens. Shaler and Seymour were Brigade commanders in the 1st and 3rd Divisions of the Corps.

[5] Rawlins commanded Grant's field staff.

movement was ordered, of the whole Army, to the left——
My Cavalry & 22' New York were ordered out to accompany
Meade & Grant—— We started at 8 o'clock, the night being
dark & the roads crowded with Troops for 3 or 4 miles——
The Generals rode fast, they lost the road, cut their own lines,
ran beyond our pickets, after having put my Cavalry in front,
& deserting them, countermarched, & after one of the most
fatiguing & disgraceful rides I ever took, we arrived, some 2 or
3 o'clock, at Todd's Tavern, the intersection of the Brock and
Catharpin Roads—— Here were Cavalry, I believe under
Sheridan, & the ground all taken up. We found a very poor
place to Stretch ourselves out, without any thing for ourselves
or horses since morning and snoozed it, interruptedly until
daylight[.] *Sunday*[,] *8' May*—— At a little after daylight we
started again, taking a road to the left of that leading to the
Church (Piney Branch) & about 8 o'clock, or 9 o'clock, halted,
and got up our Fly. . . . but soon had orders to move——
Meade, after circling & swooping about as usual, until night,
directed [Col. Edmund] Schriver to get a Camp a mile in rear
of our position, which he did, in a ploughed field & I took
another, for our prisoners, adjoining. . . . We were on the
Piney Branch Road & Spotsylvania C. H. Road——
Monday[,] *9' May*—— Last night there was fighting going on
all night, the Rebels having followed us from the Lacy house
Battle Grounds, at a very rapid pace, & appearing to be but
2 hours behind us, at most—— We find them posted in a very
strong position in our front, from which we cannot drive
them—— Our own position, also, is very strong, & we have
been intrenching both yesterday & today, south of the Brock
& Spotsylvania Roads—— There was no sleep last night and
I rose this morning early to send the prisoners off to the Train,
where they will be able to get something to eat & where I will
keep the 20' [New York Mil.] & 68' as a prison Guard—— The
Train is about 3 or 4 miles away, on an Alsop Mill property,

between here & the plank—— I started them off intending to follow myself very soon, having given them a guide who had just come from the Train to me with a light Waggon—— I started after them, but Met Col. [Theodore] Gates, in a great fright, having been halted by Genl. Meade & "blown up" generally, with orders to countermarch his column. I went a little farther myself & met Meade, who was in a terrible stew & declared that I was on the wrong road & going directly into the enemy's lines—— I soon cooled him off however & in a huff was told to 'Go my own way,' which I did, keeping the prisoners on the road they started, all right. . . . Saw Burnside and Staff—& arranged about Provost duty, [for] the 8' Infy. . . . I have to record the sad fate of John Sedgwick [Sixth Corps] who was killed dead this morning by a Sharpshooter—— It has caused universal grief and sadness—— *Tuesday*[,] *10' May*—— . . . The morning was intensely hot but I got my valise up, had a wash & a change of clothes, . . . Gen. Grant recd. despatches announcing successes by Sherman [at Tunnel Hill and Dalton, Ga.], & the news was published in a circular thro' the Army—— The Troops shouted, the Bands played, etc. Butler had also been successful at Petersburg etc. etc. *May* be all true! After noon I went to the front, where the fighting was going on & directed the Cavalry—— There was to have been a ground Assault & I remained with Hancock & Warren—5 o'clock was the hour for the Signal, but some mistake of Warren's caused a *part* of his Troops to attack before the others were ready—a quarter of an hour before the time—and of course, all fizzled out. . . . I should also say, that the 6' Corps avenged the loss of their Leader by a desperate assault upon the enemy, capturing 913 men & 37 Officers[.] *Wednesday*[,] *11' May*—— Miserable Camp! Wet, stinking, disgusting[!] Rain, too, much of the time—— I was up early & moving about—— We have been fighting, without results, all day, both armies being strongly entrenched. . . .

Schriver has gone to Frederic[k]sburg and [John J.] Abercrombie, it is said, is at Belle Plain——[6] I have been trying to
get the Prisoners off to Washington, but unsuccessfully——
They have moved to the Tabernacle Church—— I have been
talking with Grant & [Assist. Sec. Charles A.] Dana on the
Subject, as I can get nothing from Meade—— He is cross as a
Bear, at which I do not wonder, with such a man as Grant
over him. . . . *Thursday*[,] *12' May*—— . . . Ordered to
move this morning at 4 to the *Hicks House,* some 4 or 5 miles—
perhaps not more than 3, towards the Court House, on a By
Road. . . . We had got started, in an uncomfortable sort of
a fog, which turned into rain by 8 o'clock & showers continued
thro' the day—— Just before we reached our halting place,
we crossed the route of a large number of Prisoners, which
I had to take charge of—— They were Captured by Hancock.
. . . Other Detachments kept coming in, until we had some
3000, in all—— They were, nearly all of [George H.] Steuart's
Brigade, with portions of others in the same Division——
Maj. Genl. [Edward] Johnson & Brig. Genl. [George H.]
Steuart (Md.) were prisoners—— Johnson was, apparently,
very glad to see me, but Steuart I had never known—— He
behaved very uncourteously to Hancock & I was glad that I
did not offer him any special act of courtesy, as I did to
Johnson, whom I sent forward in an Ambulance. They were
very much disgusted when they found that I knew their
organization & called out their Regts. as readily as I would
our own & formed them, to march off, by Brigade, under their
own officers. . . . *Friday*[,] *13' May*—— Same Camp——
. . . Heavy rain set in & we have had a rainy day, tying us
up. . . . An order of congratulation has been issued today
& an order of movement tomorrow. We are to assault (if the

---

[6] Col. Schriver was being sent to command the city of Fredericksburg,
while Gen. Abercrombie was to command all the troops in the Belle Plain
and Fredericksburg area.

5' & 6' Corps can get into position) at 4 o'clock A. M. Tomorrow—— (The rain will prevent).

Saturday[,] *14' May*—— Camp not far from Beverly house near the Ny [River]——

Last night we had heavy rains, rose at 2′30″ this morning, saddled & ready to start at 3—— Move out & wait until daylight—— Every thing in confusion on account of the mud, which was as deep as I ever Saw it in Virginia—— The 5' & 6' Corps & all Artillery, Ambulance & Head Quarters Trains were stalled, & all the roads blocked up—— After a while we succeeded in getting by the Columns, thro' the woods with my Cavalry & reached one of the Beverly Houses, on the North of the Ny, from the windows of which Spotsylvania Court House is seen 1½ miles distant[.] The Rebs. are there encamped, very strongly intrenched, getting the start of us badly—— We were lying around the House in mud & rain, with the Staff, until towards 3 o'clock. . . . The 5' & 6' Corps finally arrived & took position—— [Col. Emory] Upton took a house on the left & Meade was there, when the Rebs. made an Assault & came very near being captured—— The position however, was retaken in the evening by an assault from the 6' Corps—— Raining, and no rations tonight for our prisoners, escort, Guard etc. *Sunday*[,] *15' May*—— Same Camp—— The rain continued most of the night, & more or less thro' the day—— Since Morning there has been very little firing, the enemy being more strongly intrenched than ever, especially on the left. . . . *Monday*[,] *16' May*—— Same Camp—— Still another very quiet day—— I send out my Cavalry, but keep quiet & nurse myself a little—— But little firing during the day, which has been showery. . . . [David] Hunter is here, today, with Grant—— He is to relieve [Franz] Sigel, probably[.]

Tuesday[,] *17' May*—— Camp near Anderson House[,]

. . . Was preparing for the usual business of the day when
we were ordered to move a mile or two, near the Anderson
House. . . . We are receiving hundreds of Stragglers, now,
gathered from the rear. . . . The Heavy Artillery Regts. that
have been around Washington heretofore, are now coming
up—— They straggle badly—— There has been but little
firing going on—no heavy attacks, today, on either Side——
. . . We are ordered to move at 4 A. M. tomorrow, about
2 Miles to our right—— *Wednesday*[,] *18' May*—— Same
Camp—— Slept none—— Rose & took a slight Breakfast at
a little after 3—then moved to the point where Hancock made
his grand charge on the 12', and where 40,000 Troops were
massed for a grand assault this morning—— But the works
were found to be too strong—— After lying there some hours
& getting a large number of men killed & wounded, it was
decided not to attack, and the Troops were retired—— I had
my Cavalry busy in driving up the new Troops. . . . I should
have said, that Hancock drove through the first and second
lines of the enemy, but the third line seemed impregnable, &
it was decided by Meade & Grant not to make the attack. . . .
The weather is still uncertain. . . . *Thursday*[,] *19' May*——
Same Camp—— Slept well on my cot and quite late, as we
have not intended to attack here, and have done no fighting
save to repel an attack made upon [Robert O.] Tyler's Heavies[7]
on Frederic[k]sburg road, under the supposition that we were
leaving & that they could strike our Trains—— They were
repulsed and driven back handsomely, with heavy loss to
themselves—— We are preparing for a move. . . . Our next
march will be a long one. . . . *Friday*[,] *20' May*—— Same
Camp—— . . . I was up early and at work—— The
prisoners from the fight of yesterday have been coming in a

---

[7] Gen. Tyler's Division of Heavy Artillery joined the Army of the
Potomac on May 18 and 19,

good part of the day—— They were, many of them, taken this morning, having fallen asleep after the fight, near our lines. . . . Hancock has moved forward to seize upon Bowling Green & Milford. Our Supply Trains are ordered to Guinea's & thence to Milford.

Saturday[,] *21' May*—— Camp at Motley's House, near Guinea [Guiney's] Station[.]

I was routed out at 12'30" last night & got no more sleep—— At 5'15" we breakfasted . . . but Meade did not start until 10 o'clock—— I followed soon after with the Cavalry & we came up then to the party at Massaponnax Church. . . . After Meade left we followed on, some miles, crossing the Rail Road, until we came to the Motley House, near Guinea's [Guiney's] Station, where we found quite an alarm, the 9' Virginia Cavalry having taken possession of the Bridge in front—— I had to send down the 114' & the 3' Penn. Cavy. to drive them out, which they did after a slight skirmish. . . . We got into a snug Camp before dark, after a fine March—— Hancock is at Bowling Green, 15 miles from Port Royal, which is our new base. . . .

Sunday Night[,] *22' May*—— Camp near New Bethel Church——

Had a nice sleep—breakfast at 6 and Orders to move at 12 M. to this place, in the direction of the Fords of the North Anna—— We had a time, before Starting, in overhauling marauders & house plunderers, some of whom I caught—— Many complaints came to me & as I had a Culprit, I went to Meade, who told me that he really was unable to help me, that Grant had expressed himself strongly against protecting these people at all, and I learned that his Staff, were, themselves, engaged in sheep stealing, fowl stealing and the like, for I caught the men at it whom they sent. . . . I had quite a time capturing a party of Sheep Stealers, including those of Genl. Rawlins[,] Chief of Staff. . . . I am *very* tired—& feel very despondent about Grant's notions of discipline——

Monday Night[,] *23' May*—Not far from Carmel Church——

. . . We march at 7, following the 9' Corps Train—— And such a Train. . . . There is any quantity of straggling on these marches, from 9' Corps—which is in very bad discipline & its Staff Departments worthless. . . .

Tuesday[,] *24' May*—— South Bank of North Anna, opposite Jericho[.]

. . . Up at 3, to see about a move ordered at 5—— Bkft. at 4'30''—— Meade moved about 7, a few miles only, to Carmel Church where we lounged & waited for the movement of Troops—— Hancock [Second Corps] is in possession of Chesterfield Ford—— Warren [Fifth] has repulsed Longstreet at Jericho Bridge & crossed, the 6' [Wright] following & supporting him. Burnside [Ninth], at Ox Ford, between the other Fords, is held at bay by the enemy—— Warren sent in, at the Church, as the result of the operations at Jericho, some 600 prisoners. . . . I arranged, while at the Church, to send the prisoners to Port Royal. The day has been intensely hot & I came on, alone. . . .

Wednesday[,] *25' May*—— North Bank of North
Anna—— Quarles Mill——

. . . Looked about with reference to a new Camp, when
orders came to move over here at 2' P. M. We crossed opposite
here on a short Ponton Bridge & have a very comfortable
Camp. . . .

Thursday[,] *26' May*—— Same Camp, at Quarles'
Mill——

This has been a hot day, with occasional Thunder
Showers—— I have been in Camp all day, and have
been engaged in making up & preparing all things for
a Movement by the left flank, across the Pamunkey——
It is certain that we cannot move to the front, as we
have the enemy posted in front of Burnside with their
flanks on Swamps & Rivers so that we cannot dislodge them,
and it is now certain that we *must* come back to McClellan's
Base. Meade was opposed to our crossing the North Anna, but
Grant ordered it, over his head—— We move at 4 o'clock
tomorrow morning, for Hanover *Town* (not C. H.) & New
Castle. Our base changes to White House—— I have prepared my maps & am all ready. . . .

Friday[,] *27' May*. . . . Mangohick Church——

. . . At 4'30" Train moved—— I kept a Squadron with me,
in rear & moved myself at 5'15", half an hour after Meade.
We took the road via Carmel Church & Chesterfield to
Mangohick Church, 16 miles, which we reached in good time.

. . . The March has been an easy one, the roads good &
slight showers have lain the dust—— We got into Camp by
5 o'clock & I have been reading Dickens—— The Old Church
is a Curiosity, built in old times, when Virginia was a loyal
Colony of the British Crown & brought bricks from England
to build here loyal churches—— This Church seems to have
passed thro' various hands & is now out of order, the Rebels
having used it for a Forage Depot since the War.

Saturday[,] *28' May*—— Camp near Newton's &
    Taliaferro's, Hanover Town——

. . . Breakfast at 7—— Train hauls out at 8' & Meade leaves
at 8'30"—— I sent the Staff with him & kept behind, myself,
with a Squadron of Cavalry, until 12' M. then started off——
The men of Heavy Artillery have been plundering & destroying
every thing in houses & I gave one of them a good hiding,
whom I found in the act. It will do good, as it was in presence
of the Brigade of the 9' Corps to which he belongs—— Also
of the 5' Corps Trains. . . . We reached the River in a March
of 12 miles, perhaps & after some delay, got into our Camp,
some two miles from the pontoon Bridge. . . . *Sunday*[,] *29,
May*—— Same Camp—— . . . The Rebs. seem to have
fallen back from our front[.] [Assist. Sec. Charles A.] Dana
was over to see me for an hour & I sent off despatches for him
to Washington. . . . I sent out this morning, partly at
Meade's Suggestion, 100 Cavy. under Maj. [James W.] Walsh,
& Capt. Schuyler, to return as far as Mangohick, & drive up.
I Sent to the rear today 119 Prisoners of War & some hundreds
of Contrabands, who have been following us some days——
The weather is very hot during the days, but very cool at
night——

Monday[,] *30' May*—— Camp near Hawes['] Store, or
Shop—— 5 o'clock P. M.

. . . Camp broke at 7'30" & I left at 9'—— Rode by Dr.
Pollards['] etc[.] to Hawes['] house, where I found a wounded
Reb. halted there until Meade & Grant moved, then came
on a mile to our new Camp. . . . *Tuesday*[,] *31' May*——
Same Camp—— No sleep last night and an awful hot day——
The assault of yesterday on Burnside nearly destroyed [John]
Pegram[']s Rebel Brigade—— In the Morning I will send off
say 400 prisoners & over 600 negroes of all ages—— They go,
with the Train, to White House, our present depot—— We
have done nothing today but burn powder to little purpose. . . .

Wednesday[,] *1' June*—— Camp near the Vias House,
by the Roadside——

Slept finely last night, & breakfasted at 6' with orders to move
at 7—— Fifth & Sixth Corps ordered to Coal [Cold] Harbor,
& the 18' Corps, Baldy Smith, is to be up & join us on the
left——[8] I left directly after breakfast, for the Train or rather,
for the River, & to see the 20' about getting the prisoners
off—— The Sick, too, were to have been off, with the prisoners
at daylight, but it was 11 o'clock before the escorts reported.
. . . I got into Camp about 4 o'clock nearly roasted—— Sent
for [William] Swinton of the Times about Jno. H. S. Seymour's
plan for registration of the killed & wounded Soldiers from the
State of New York. . . .

Thursday[,] *2 June*—— Camp near Leary's—One mile
from Coal [Cold] Harbor[.]

No sleep, altho' troops were passing Camp all night—the 2'
Camp—and they *did* march like horses. . . . An Order to

---

[8] Gen. William F. Smith's 18th Corps was being transferred from
Butler's effort on the south side of the James.

move at 7', to near Coal [Cold]Harbor—— We came on, to
the Head Quarters of Gen. Wright, (passing the 18' Corps) &
there remained, till, say 4 o'clock, when this Camp was selected
& we came over here—— . . . There has been a heavy rain
this evening—— Have just received a Rebel Signal Officer—
Deserted yesterday[.] *Friday*[,] *3' June*—— Same Camp, near
Coal [Cold] Harbor—— No sleep last night, as there was a
constant running about—— Ordered to accompany the
General at 4—— Breakfasted at 3'30" & at Coal [Cold]
Harbor at 5—— There was a tremendous assault along the
lines (to judge from the noise) & [Gen. Francis C.] Barlow's
Division of Hancock's Corps carried the Works, but there
[were] no reserves, as usual, and the whole failed with a loss
(Meade told me) of 8000 men on our side, we taking but 300
prisoners—— In the evening the Rebs. assaulted our lines, but
were repulsed by the 2' Corps, without loss to ourselves. The
Morning was quite rainy, but the day has been cool & comfortable—— There is much feeling in regard to this murderous
& foolish system of assaulting, without supports, reserves, or
any adequate force to hold the works that may be
carried. *Saturday*[,] *4' June*—— Same Camp, Coal [Cold]
Harbor—— Another sleepless night, & a call to mount at
4'30" this morning. I rode over to Meade's and watched for
him to mount, but found that he had issued the order last
night, to annoy his Staff——After talking with Meade I set off
for the 2' Corps—— Hancock was in bed, but I sat with him
for a while. . . . The Sharpshooters were very busy & I had to
dismount before reaching the lines & leave my escort behind. I
came back to Gen. Wright's Head Quarters & arranged with
him in regard to the Christian Commission Waggons. . . .
But little firing has been going on & I have remained in Camp
attending to deserters. . . . *Sunday*[,] *5' June*—— Same
Camp—— . . . This evening a most extraordinary & terrific
fire of musketry opened suddenly followed by Artillery, & it

was kept up some 20 minutes or half an hour—— It was a perfect stampede and nobody was hurt! . . . *Monday*[,] *6' June*—— . . . Same Camp—— . . . [Charles S.] Wainwright[9] has been here, greatly disgusted, as is every one else, with Warren—a very loathesome, profane ungentlemanly & disgusting puppy in power—— It seems as if he & Meade were trying to see how much their Officers will bear in the way of injustice and insult—— *Tuesday*[,] *7' June, '64*—— Still near Coal [Cold] Harbor, Same Camp—— Ten o'clock. . . . Was up at Head Quarters about a Man named [Edward] Crapsey, of the Phil.[delphia] Inquirer, who is to be sent off on account of a Libel on Meade—— I have had rather an unusual amount of Office business on hand today—— [Gen. John J.] Abercrombie's Staff Officers, & [Capt. Nicholas] Hoysradt made bad work & are constantly quarreling, their papers being referred to me. . . .[10] *Wednesday*[,] *8' June,* [']*64*—— Ten o'clock P. M.[,] Same Camp—— . . . The Order of Genl. Meade relative to Crapsey was carried out this morning—— He was placed on a horse, with breast & back boards Marked "Libeller, of the Press"—& marched in rear of my flag, thro' the Army, after which he was sent to White House & thence North—— He was completely cut down—— It will be a warning to his Tribe. . . . *Thursday*[,] *9' June, '64*—— 9 o'clock P. M.[,] Same Camp—— This has been a very hot day, & this evening I have been trying to cool off—without much Success. . . . Have been at the general Office business of the day, troubled somewhat with this Court, as it was, today, trying a negro for a Rape on a White Girl, Colonel [George H.] Sharpe being assigned, by the Court, to defend the prisoner. . . . I was an hour with Grant & Dana, this

---

[9] Col. Wainwright commanded the Artillery Brigade in Warren's Fifth Corps.

[10] Capt. Hoysradt was Patrick's Provost Marshal at White House Landing. He was in a hassle with Gen. J. J. Abercrombie over the issue of passes for travel between the Army and Washington.

morning, about our prisoners & this evening Dana has been over here to talk over the same matter, about the holding of Rebel prisoners—— *Friday Night, 10' June*—— Same Camp, near Coal [Cold] Harbor—— I have been expecting an Order to move, but it is now late & the Order has not come—— We shall, probably, cross the Chickahominy & push for the James—— The day has been pleasant and not so hot as yesterday—— The evening is cool & I hope to sleep tonight. . . . *Saturday, 11' June*—— Same Camp—— near Coal [Cold] Harbor—— Another very quiet day has passed away. There has been little firing during the day, except in the front of the 18' where there is some shelling. . . . *We* shall not, perhaps, move before Monday. . . . Our Trains are ordered to Tunstall's, en route for James River——

Sunday Night[,] *12' June*—— Near Moody's, 2 miles from Despatch——

Up early this morning & prepared for an Inspection of Cavalry I had ordered at 8 o'clock. Found a Circular from Meade, requesting his Staff to meet at his Tent at 8, to be photographed in a group by [Mathew] Brady—— So after Breakfast I went up, but we did not get a sitting until about 9—I doubt if it prove a very good picture—— That done I inspected the Cavalry & went to my Tent—— We were ordered to move at 3. P. M. to Despatch Station. . . . I took with me Lieut. Carter, 3d Pa. Cavy. who was born in this vicinity & knows the roads. . . .

Monday Night[,] *13' June*—— Camp near Christian's, Charles city C. H.

Up at 4 o'clock this morning, bkft. at 4'30" and pack off our Train, I did not move, at first, with Meade, but took another

road, passing Emmans & St. James' Churches (halting an hour
at the last, a very neat Structure,) and Baltimore Cross Roads
to Long Bridge, where we found Hancock's [Second] Corps
crossing & crossed ourselves, with Meade. During the
remainder of the day we kept along near him, stopping a
number of times & furnishing Cavalry at his Call, until we
reached a point near Charles City Court House, or between
it & Westover's & Wilcox Landing. . . . We have passed some
splendid estates, in this neighborhood & found abundance of
Clover, with some Corn—— My Cavalry are out tonight,
picketing, in the neighborhood of Harrison's Landing. . . .
Tuesday Night, 14' June—— Same Camp—— Last night
was cold & so is this evening—— The day has been hot——
I was up at 5'30″ Bkft. at 7, and Office work until 11, when
I mounted & made the rounds of 5' & 6' Corps—— The trains
are crossing the Chickahominy at Cole's Ferry, on which road
I went some miles, then went down to the southern point of
the Douthard Estates, where [Gen. Godfrey] Weitzel & others
are engaged in laying Pontons—the 2' Corps crossing from
Wilcox Wharf to Windmill Point in Steamers, of which the
River is full—— I found the 6' Corps ravaging the whole
Country & killing Cattle Sheep etc. with perfect abandon,
while the houses are burning with the 5' Corps Head Quarters
in hailing distance——

Wednesday Night, 15' June—Camp in Douthard's Door
    Yard——

. . . This morning at 8' I was off for the landing, placing
Guards along the way & trying to get Stragglers up to their
Corps—— Went down to the Bridges & found Troops crossing.
Overhauled [Gen. Henry W.] Benham's Sutler & went back
a mile, where I found Meade had selected *his* Camp & [Capt.

Philip] Schuyler had Selected *mine* near by, in the Yard of the
Mansion, directly on the bank of the River which is alive with
vessels & full of bathers. This evening I have had an unpleasant
time, overhauling parties on account of plundering the
Douthards. . . . The 18' Corps passed up to Bermuda
Hundreds [Hundred] in Steamers today—— Gen. Meade has
sent me an Extraordinary paper relative to House Burning[.]

> *Thursday Night, 16' June*—— Camp 3½ Miles from
> Petersburg, near Bryan's[.]

Slept gloriously last night & were quietly breakfasting this
morning when we found (accidentally) that Camp was breaking up & we had to hurry—— We crossed the River (I left
a detachment behind) following Meade & *kept* following, over
a terribly dusty road, full of trains & troops with houses burning, on either side, attesting the march of the 9' Corps——
The day has been the most oppressive of the Season, so far.
Meade went up to City Point by Steam, allowing [Seth]
Williams to manage Head Quarters March. Arrived within
4 miles of town we found that the 18' Corps had, last night,
before the enemy were aware of their arrival, pitched in &
driven them from their outer & strong works Capturing some
300 or 400 prisoners, 12 or 14 Guns & holding the Strong
works on the west & Southwest of town—— This was done
mainly by the negro troops of Genl. [Edward W.] Hincks'
[Hinks] Command who are said to have behaved well, though
opposed by Citizen & Militia Troops—— We found Hancock
in position, in rear of these Captured works, which are of the
very Strongest character. We encamped about a mile from
Hancock just at dark—— An Assault was ordered at 6, but
did not amount to much. The enemy were re-inforced from
Richmond today—— Butler is *said* to hold a portion of R. R.
between Richmond & Petersburg[.]

Friday Night, 17' June, Same Camp, near Bryans (?) (Bailey's)—Petersburg——

. . . The General has again taken all my Cavalry and placed [it] at Warren's disposal, who, for some reason, failed to attack—— Last night, after 9 o'clock, I was ordered to send a Squadron clear back to the Mills, to drive up a Brigade almost of 9' Corps[.] The day has been very hot & our troops are suffering greatly——

Saturday Night[,] *18' June*—— Same Camp——

& a very hot day, finally Slept pretty well & felt so much better that I took the Saddle early. . . . Was under the lines of the 5'[,] 9' & 2' Corps, which were ordered to assault, repeatedly, but *did not,* to any purpose. Meade has been in a great stew about prisoners, sent [Capt. Francis M.] Bache down before I was up, gave [Col. George] Sharpe a blowing up, found he was wrong & then found that Burnside was the Scape Goat—— [Thomas] Wilson has been down to see me, having been superseded, so to speak, as Chief Commissary [Army of the Potomac], by Butler's Man, Col. Morgan—— He is asking to be relieved, as Meade does not sustain any one——

Sunday Night, 19' June—— Same Camp—— Another hot, *dry,* day[.]

Slept well and up early—— Made my Sunday toilet & then gave the necessary orders for hanging Johnson, the negro, for Rape, tomorrow morning at 9. . . . Senator Bell of Dexter [New York], on a[n] electioneering tour, [came to see me] under the guise of looking to the wants of our Troops—— He wanted to do various things, which I told him plainly, I would not allow, if I could prevent them & he left—— They are trying to get my Cavalry away from me and Meade is showing himself up as he really is, a very *mean* man—— There is a great deal of dissatisfaction in the Army about him——

Monday Night, 20' June—— Same Camp and a hot day——

. . . There was heavy firing last night until 10 or 11 o'clock, but I do not know what results followed, if any—— It is now known that A. P. Hill's & Longstreet's Corps, have both joined Beauregard, but Ewell is somewhere, with his Corps, on detached Service—— Said to have gone up to the valley—— He has been absent some days—— The Execution came off this morning[.] I went out, early, & examined the Gallows. . . . then went back for the troops & prisoner—— They arrived, just after a Shelling commenced, upon the very place where the Gallows was erected So that I had to form the troops below the crest & leave as few exposed as possible—— The Chaplain prayed with him; he acknowledged that he was a deserter, that he had changed his name & committed the crime charged upon him—— The rope was adjusted[,] the bandages placed over his eyes & the drop fell—— He never knew any thing after. A shell killed the Sergt. Major of a Mass. Regt. just at the time. [Rufus] Ingal[l]s has been ordered to Grant's Head Quarters,[11] & Meade has been at City Point all day—— Lieut. Parker has been here this evening about Mail operations—— The [Col. L. C.] Baker & [A. H.] Markland crew are very busy to get a foot hold in my Department——[12]

---

[11] Gen. Ingalls became, with this move, Chief Quartermaster of the Armies Operating Against Richmond.

[12] Col. Baker is Patrick's old "Secret Service" adversary and A. H. Markland was a special agent of the Post Office Department in Washington.

Tuesday Night, 21' June——— Same Camp———

. . . After Breakfast went up to see Meade but he was not up. I started for City Point. . . . Saw Ingal[l]s & had an arrangement with him etc. etc. I then went to see Genl. Grant, & was, soon after, joined by our old friend Dr. McCormick——— We had a pleasant time until Senator Bell came & asked to see Dana & myself together, about New York matters which finally took us to Dana's Tent, & resulted in agreement to send Dr. [John] Van Ingen down, as State Agent——— Old Abe arrived just then & broke up the Sitting. . . . Grant directed me to assume control, as usual, at City Point & Gates is now in command. . . .

Wednesday Night, 22' June——— Camp near 2' Corps Hospital———

Last night, just as I was going to bed, Meade sent for me, and had a discussion, in bad humor, about [William J.] Babcock, as Purveyor here & altho' satisfied that he was in error, still shows his meanness by saying that as Babcock is obnoxious to the Secretary [Stanton], I must send him away——— He then wanted me, as a personal favor to him, to take his nep[h]ew, Capt. [Alexander J.] Dallas, upon my Staff——— I am thoroughly disgusted with the fellow. . . .

Thursday Night, 23' June——— Camp half mile from Jones House[.]

. . . The whole country is now a bed of fine dust, without water any where near us, & all water very filthy. The men are suffering terribly from heat & dust & thirst & diarrhea. We have been tolerably quiet today. . . . I am feeling very uncomfortable, both physically & mentally (or morally.) The despicable Selfishness & indifference of Meade, causing him to set aside all the *rights* of his Troops, both Officers & men insulting almost all who approach him, makes me very sick at heart—— The men are refusing to assault any more, and the Officers cannot or will not expose *themselves* as heretofore——

> *Friday Night, 24' June*—— Same Camp, near Jones House, off Plank [Road].

. . . I sent off an expedition to Surry C. H. to gather stragglers reported by Genl. Butler, in that neighborhood. . . . Capt. Dallas has been hanging around all day, learning that at Meade's request, I have applied for him—— I wish he would go somewhere else—— There has been a disposition to rest in Camp, today, on the part of Genl. Meade, and to do as little work as might be. . . .

> *Saturday Night, 9'30", 25' June, '64*—— Camp near Jones'—— Jerusalem Road.

. . . The day has been perfectly melting, but I have had a little Screening of bushes put up, that saves me a little. . . . I have had a Mrs. Stiles here, who identified a man named Gordon, of the 72' New York, as the man who had committed the outrage upon her person last Saturday—— He will be tried tomorrow. . . .

> *Sunday Night*[,] *26' June*—— Same Camp and as hot as need be[.]

Today has been terrible hot and no let up. . . . A Court Martial has been in Session all day, trying the Rape Case on the person of Mrs. Stiles—— Tonight we have caught the other culprit & he will be tried tomorrow. . . .

Monday Night, Tattoo—— Same Camp——
27' June——

Have been busy since ever I got up this morning. . . . The Court Martial has finished the trial of the Rapers this evening, I believe. . . .

Tuesday, 28' June. Same Camp—— Ten o'clock A. M.

. . . We had on Sunday & yesterday a Court Martial in Session at my Office Tent, for the trial of two men who had committed a crime upon the body of a Mrs. Stiles living near Prince George's Court House. There seemed to be no clew to the perpetrators, at first, but the leader could not keep away from the Spot, after the crime, & was the *first* to speak of it as an outrage, before *any* other person knew of it—— He was arrested & to make his own Story good, he had to tell of his comrade—— They were identified by the woman & her cousin & both have been tried; with what results is not yet known—— The woman feels terribly and has been here to see me. . . . Military affairs are standing rather Still, outwardly, but in front of Burnside's [Ninth] Corps a gallery was started for the purpose of getting under a heavy Battery & Strong work of the Rebs, which would require about 4 or 5 days for completion. A detachment of Penn. Miners were hard at it on Sunday under the Special direction of Col. [Henry S.] Burton, to whom the whole work was committed—— On coming into Camp last night, he found an Order from Genl. Grant, directing him to report to [W. F.] Baldy Smith, as

Chief of Artillery—— This has stopped the works in front of Burnside, which is believed to be the very object of Smith—— He hopes to prevent Burnside from getting the start of *him*, by withdrawing Burton, and at the Same time to get the benefit of Burton's Services to forward his own Schemes—— Mede [sic], however, is making a strong protest against this Order, & the probability is, that it will be recalled—— Burton came over yesterday to say Good Bye, and went off disgusted—— The Troops, although not fighting as they have been, are constantly being picked off by Sharp Shooters & Rebel Shells——no place being Secure against them when within range. The Cavalry of [James H.] Wilson has gone out to cut the Roads on the West, but we have not Since heard from them—— Swarms of contrabands are coming in & are forwarded to City Point for the purpose of being used as Teamsters & Laundresses, down *there*——

Evening, Tattoo——

. . . . [Philip] Sheridan has crossed the River, near Wilcox's or Douthard's, and is expected up early tomorrow—— Fears are entertained in regard to Wilson's Cavy. as the enemy are extending their right and he will find it difficult to rejoin us. . . .

Wednesday Night[,] *29' June,* Camp near the Jones House.

. . . Our Troops are moving to the left, this Afternoon, Wilson's Cavalry being in danger, as he has sent in for help—— A large Rebel force has got between him & us—— Meade has called for all my force and I have Sent everything that is at my disposal[.] Every thing betokens a contest on the left. . . . Heavy Guns have been booming, much of the day, on our Right.

Thursday Night, 30' June, [']64—— Same Camp, near Jones House——

. . . The news of the morning was, that Wilson's entire Division of Cavalry had been destroyed by the enemy, while attempting to rejoin us on the left—— Subsequently we heard that Gen. [August V.] Kuntz [Kautz], with a part of his command had got in—— Others are coming in, it is said and I hope we shall not lose so heavily as was at first supposed. . . . It is believed that the Divisions of Fitzlee [Fitzhugh Lee] & Rooney Lee (& perhaps Hampton), with a Division of Infy. surrounded him——

Friday Night, 1' July—— Same Camp, Plank Road—— "Jerusalem Road"——

This has been the hottest day of the season and if we are to have it much hotter, I cannot see what is to become of us. . . . Wilson has succeeded in getting over to the Prince George C. H. Road with the loss of his Train, Guns etc. also about 2000 men and still more horses—— The number of men lost may be reduced as they are scattered every where and I am now engaged in gathering them up. . . .

Saturday Night[,] *2' July*[.] Same Camp, Jones Plantation, Jerusalem Road——

This has been about as disagreeable and uncomfortable a day as heart could desire, even for an enemy. . . . [Gen. James

H.] Wilson is back & the impression is, now, that his loss will not exceed a thousand men. . . . Sheridan is back, on the Prince George Road, somewhere, his horses, as well as Wilson's, completely used up—— It is said that *Wilson's* March has been one continuous scene of plunder & burning, and I am afraid, too, that Sheridan's has been no better—— I recd. a note from [Andrew A.] Humphreys, this afternoon, to the effect, that, at the Douthard's, our old encamping place before crossing the James, the Ladies had been violated by some of Sheridan's Cavalry—— I sent Col. Sharpe down to City Point, to take a Tug, run down & ascertain the facts in the case as soon as possible. . . .

[Sunday July 3] Evening 8'30" A. M.

The day has been oppressive but not so hot as yesterday. . . . Col. Sharp[e] telegraphs that he has been to Douthard's & the Stories are not true. . . .

Monday Night, 4' July—— Same Camp—— Near Jones
    House——

. . . The news from the front gives us much uneasiness—— [Richard S.] Ewell's Corps (under the command of [Jubal] Early), is believed to be on its way either to Washington or to Maryland & Pennsylvania—— [David] Hunter is so far West that he can do nothing to prevent the raid & there are no Troops up there able to meet Ewell's Corps——

Wednesday Night, 6' July—— Same Camp near Jones'
    (Jerusalem Road)[.]

Yesterday morning, after the usual morning routine, I recd. an Order from Genl. Grant, directing Brig. Gen. Patrick Prov.

Mar. Genl. A. of P. to assume the duties of P. M. G. of the "Armies operating against Richmond," and "including their lines of Communication with Washington & Baltimore"—— I started just about ten, rode down to see Grant & talked with him & [Rufus] Ingal[l]s about duty—— The Object is, to have a Central power to regulate [Gen. Benj.] Butler & others, but, as Grant expressly says, not to take me from the Army of Potomac—— I returned at night & saw Meade—— He became very angry not—as he *said*—with me, or with Grant, but with every body & thing—— He has learned that his Staff would, all, gladly, leave him, on account of his temper, and he has become desperately cross—— He told me, however, that he would get a Successor for me—— that he would not have any partnership with Grant etc. etc. This morning I again rode down to City Point, had an interview with Genl. Rawlins, saw Ingal[l]s again & agreed to *remove* to City Point again, tomorrow morning. [Capt.] Beckwith went with me, this morning & remains—— [Capt. J. R.] Leslie & the Mess, go tomorrow——[Capt.] Schuyler, [Col.] Collis & [Pvt. S. W.] Townsend remain here—— The Scouts, Guides, etc. with [Col.] Sharpe & [Capt. John C.] Babcock, remain here, until the questions now at issue between Meade & Grant are settled—— Meade said to me, only a few days ago, that the whole Bureau of Information was good for nothing—that it furnished no information not already received thro' the Cavalry—that it ought to be broken up & that Genl. Grant thought so, too—— I disagreed with him entirely and told him that he had refused to let us do what was desired & which we knew to be for the best interests of the Service—— I therefore told him, that I proposed to transfer that Bureau to Genl. Grant's Head Quarters & there give it a trial, when, if it still proved worthless, it should be disbanded—— This made him intensely angry, because he could not deny his own words, but said he would not permit the transfer, but that he *would* allow it to be broken up——— This shows the Animus——— He takes the ground that he *owns* the Army of the Potomac, that the Heads of Staff Departments are simply his *personal* Staff Officers & control their Departments & Exercise their functions *thro'* him, not *under* him as Subordinates governed by the laws & usages of their own Departments——— He treats his Staff Officers as his private, or individual Servants——— He, evidently, thinks them such———

City Point, *Thursday Night, 7' July.* Hd. Qrs. Genl. Grant———

This has been a busy day and I feel very tired this evening. . . . I took an Orderly or two with me & sent the Escort, with the Waggons, & led horses. . . . We rode past the Second Corps, and the Fifth Corps, then came to the 9' Corps[.] There I halted to see Burnside & found him, with no one to disturb our conversation, the others not being up yet——— I staid about an hour & took a cup of Tea with him. . . . I have not seen Genl. Grant today, nor any of his Staff——— I have, however, decided as to the course I shall pursue— viz, to leave Meade to take Such Steps as he may deem proper, but compel him to take the initiative. My object in seeing Burnside was to confer with him & as he has once been in Command of the Army of Potomac, & knows all about it, he seemed the proper man to advise me; & this he does, unhesitatingly. *First.* On no consideration whatever allow myself to send in my resignation of P. M. G.[,] A. of P. to Meade, unless Grant proposes it— because I am *not* Meade's Appointment & he in his Anger, would *Say,* that Patrick having got on Grant's Staff had *cut* him, Meade——— *Second*—Continue to run the machine for A. of P. to the best of my ability, taking such members of my Staff & of my Organization, as are

necessary to carry out the orders of Genl. Grant, & let Meade
do what he thinks his dignity demands.

City Point, *Friday Night, 8' July*—— Head Quarters of
    Genl. Grant——

. . . I have been all day writing & making notes etc. . . .
This evening, since Sunset, I have recd. an insulting message
from Meade, to know when I return to his Head Quarters——
I went over to see Rawlins & told him what reply I proposed to
send—that it was my intention to remain here several days, if
the Army remained in its present position, visiting the Army of
Potomac frequently, and at any time on call—— Rawlins
said he would talk with Genl. Grant about the matter & that
he would advise the sending of such reply as above. . . .

Head Quarters[,] Army of Potomac, *Saturday Night,*
    9' July[,] *1864.*

. . . I had drawn out various plans for carrying on business
in the Provost Department, without reference to the question
whether it is Meade's or Butler's or Grant's jurisdiction. At
eleven o'clock, or thereabouts, I received a very cutting Order
from Meade, to the effect that my departure was unauthorized
& that I would immediately return to these Head Quarters——
I immediately had my *own* baggage, Tent etc. packed, loaded
& with the Spare horses & Tom [Chambers], started to the
front, leaving all else behind, and telegraphed Genl. Williams
that I should be up this evening, to Head Quarters Army of
Potomac—— [J. H.] Winfield made Copies of such papers
as related to my coming to City Point, and was to send them
over, this evening to Genl. Rawlins—— I came out, on the

Cars, at 4 o'clock to the Forage Station—— There took my horse & came in—— Found my Tent up & dinner ready, with Col. Sharpe—— Went over & reported to Genls. [Seth] Williams & [A. A.] Humphreys—— Meade was engaged——

Head Quarters[,] Army of Potomac, near Jones House,
    Sunday[,] 10 July, 1864[.]

. . . I have sent out a Cavalry force to examine the Trains for Women & Sutlers' establishments—— I have also sent out an Order restoring Safe Guards to families within the lines— they having been called in by an Order of Genl. Meade, three days ago, though he now disowns the *intention* to give any such Order. . . . The Sixth Corps [Wright] is all off, after Ewell, up in Pennsylvania. [James B.] Ricket[t]s [3rd Division] left on Wednesday, & the other two Divisions have today, having marched to City Point in the night—— Little is known of Ewell's (or Early's) force, Save that [it is] his own Corps & [John C.] Breckinridge's Division (15000 Infy. in all)[,] [John] McCausland's Mounted Infy. (1000 strong) & 500 Cavy. with very little Artillery. It is probable however, that [John D.] Imboden, the Sam.[uel B.] Jones' Command, [Maj. Elijah "Lige"] White & Mosby have joined Early, swelling his numbers to, perhaps 25,000.[13] Up to this hour, I have recd. no Order from Meade (2 o'clock P. M.). . . .

    8 o'clock P. M. I have just taken a despatch over to Gen. Meade, from Col. Sharpe, asking to go to Baltimore[.] I have telegraphed him to go—— Meade says he has just received a despatch from Grant, saying that the Rebels have driven [Gen. Lew] Wallace across the Monocacy & are pushing for Baltimore & Washington—— The 6' Corps will, probably,

---

[13] This is Early's famous raid on Washington. Patrick's information was not very accurate. Early's command numbered about 14,000. The Jones troops were those of William E. Jones, not those of Samuel Jones.

get there to meet them—— [Gen. David] Hunter was at Cumberland [Md.]. . . .

Monday Night, 11' July—— Head Quarters[,] A. of P.[,]
Jones House——

. . . [Capt. W. W.] Beckwith has been up here today and we have prepared an Order, permitting Sutlers to return to the Army. . . . Have been preparing our Tents so as to be more comfortable, resulting in the usual way—an Order to move Camp tomorrow, of which I am very glad, as it brings us nearer to the Rail Road and City Point. . . .

Tuesday Night, 12' July—— New Camp, West of
Birchett's House——

. . . Came on between 9 & 10 to this point about 1½ miles (perhaps *two*) South of our Camp after crossing the James River. . . . Have had a deal of trouble about our Scouts, two of whom have been drunk & were Sent in, from the 5' Corps, in arrest—— The Rebs. are raising *hob* generally, in & about the neighborhood of Washington & Baltimore. . . .

Wednesday Night, 13' July—— New Camp[,] 1 mile
West of Birchett's[.]

. . . The day has been hot and dusty so that I did not go, as I thought of doing, to see Mrs. Stiles & read to her the Sentence of the Court, that Gordon & Geary be hanged on Friday. There is some feeling expressed by some of the Troops in regard to the Sentence. . . .

Thursday Night[,] *14' July——* Same Camp, near Birchett's[.]

Slept well & rose in tolerably good season—— Breakfast late—— That over & morning matters disposed of, I took Chaplain Rammell with me & started off over to see Mrs. Stiles & the Robertson family—— I read the Order to her & Rammell had quite a long conversation with her—— At their request we had prayers & then left—— The Chaplain came back, perfectly satisfied of the truth of her Statement—— He & a Catholic priest, have both been very anxious & diligent in behalf of their two patients—— Arrangements have been made for their execution near the Waggon Camp, as being a public place and also near the Teamsters, who, to a large extent, are the persons committing these outrages. . . . There is no mail tonight from the North—— The Rebels have torn up the Roads & cut the Telegraph wires, though there seems now to be no fear in regard to their expulsion. . . .

Friday[,] *15' July, 9 P. M.* Same Camp, near Birchett's House——

Up in good season & found work enough to be done until it was about time to move to the place of Execution—— Was there by 9 o'clock & the Cavalry holding the ground—— The 68' [N. Y.] & 114' [Penn.] soon came into position & then the Guard, with the condemned in a Waggon, with their Ministers—— They mounted the Scaffold & there I read the Order of the Court & Sentence—— The Clergy talked with them a few moments & at their request, Rammel Said for them, that they died hoping for mercy thro' Jesus Christ & acknowledging the justice of the Sentence about to be executed—— Rammell made a short prayer & both Clergymen

took leave of the condemned & left the Scaffold—— The feet
were tied, the eyes bandaged, the ropes adjusted, the tap upon
the drum & the drop fell! Scarcely a convulsion, both being
killed instantly—— They hung, perhaps, 5 minutes, when I
remounted the Scaffold & said such words of warning, of
reproof & of correction as seemed proper in the presence of
Such a Mass of life as stood before & around me, with the
dead hanging beneath my feet—— My words will not soon
be forgotten by those who stood before me—— Leaving the
Scaffold I turned over the whole to Col. [Charles H. T.] Collis,
who afterwards had them cut down, put in their boxes & sent
down to me, to City Point, where I had ridden from the place
of execution, with Col. [T. B.] Gates—— Arrangements were
made, by me, to have them embalmed tonight & sent off with
the Brother, Geary, by the morning Boat. . . . Had a talk
with Genl. Grant about Butler's matters & read to him the
Order which I proposed sending to Butler—— He approved
& I sent it off—— So Mr. Butler will probably know that I
have some power—— Grant says he will order me a Regt. of
Hundred day men, from Butler—— I staid to dine with him,
had a good talk & came off. . . .

Sunday Night, 17' July—— Same Camp, near
Birchett's[.]

. . . I had to go over & see [Gen. Henry J.] Hunt & he
returned here with me, to see about some positions, of Shafts,
of counter Mines, in front of Burnside. There have been some
deserters in today, who have given us considerable information
& among other things, that Longstreet's Corps were preparing
to attack us tonight—— I have just returned from Humphreys,
who thinks they will be ready. . . .

Monday Night, 18' July—— Same Camp, near
Birchett's[.]

Last night it seemed probable that there would be an attack,
by Longstreet[']s Division, & we went to bed expecting it; but
this morning we find that the Order was suspended because
so many of the 64' Georgia had deserted to us yesterday, &
had given us all information. . . . I have been engaged in
the usual business today, of the Office & making investigations
in about—a great many things, showing the greatest want of
discipline, on the part of both Grant & Meade—— This army
is nearly demoralized & the Cavalry is no better than a band
of robbers—— Burnside was over here this P. M. & staid an
hour—— He tells me that his mine was to be completed at
noon, today, tho' it will not, probably, be exploded for some
two or three days yet. . . .

Wednesday Night, 20' July, 1864—— Same Camp, near
Birchett's[.]

Last night I slept little, as the pickets kept up a continual
popping, almost equal to a Skirmish, interspersed with cannonading. . . . Genl. Butler has been up here today, to see
Meade—— He has been offered the Chicago Nomination &
is playing every one, to get some power over each individual—— Matters are in a very bad state in the political
world. . . .

Thursday Night[,] *21' July*—— Same Camp, near
Birchett's[.]

This has been rather a pleasant and comfortable day——
Slept tolerably well, breakfasted late, looked into matters with

Col. Sharpe in the early part of the day, got his matters all ready, so that he could act understandingly and sent him down to City Point, to arrange matters there, and at Bermuda Hundred with Butler, about sending off Scouts etc[.] in the direction of Orange Court House, to watch Early and get into Richmond. . . .

Friday Night, 22' July—— Same Camp, near Birchett's[.]

. . . I had a long talk this morning with Meade, of an old fashioned, friendly character, which he drew on, himself, feeling, as it seemed, that he had been foolish in his conduct toward me—— He gave me a great deal of information about matters past and present, relating to Grant, Butler, [W. F.] Baldy Smith & Co. Schuyler came up tonight & tells me that it is certain, now, that Butler leaves the command in the field— nolens volens—— Sharpe does not return yet, having duty to perform down there, but sends me word that he has organized a system of information to Richmond, also to Orange Court House, via Frederic[k]sburg. He is certain that Butler will be relieved, very Soon—— Meade does not believe it, because Butler has triumphed over Baldy Smith, who has been relieved & ordered to New York, probably, to be mustered out of Service—— It seems that Grant had a very high opinion of him when in the West & especially for his reconnaissance at Chattanooga, which it has been discovered *recently* was made by young West, an Officer of his Staff, who has left him because he, Baldy, appropriated it as his own, ignoring West and not giving him any credit for the service—— Grant, believing him all right, had Baldy made a Major General & assigned to a Corps—— Baldy's intrigues, however, for the command of Meade, first, his intense Selfishness &, finally, his intrigues against Butler & Gilmer [Gen. Quincy A. Gillmore?] disgusted

Grant, who ordered him to report to Meade, at Coal [Cold]
Harbor—— Since then he has quarreled with Meade & every
one else, ending in an attempt to thrash Grant over Meade's
Shoulders, for which Grant shut him up—— The discovery
that he has been plotting against Grant himself, within the
last 20 days, has brought matters to a head—— It is now the
intention to have [E. O. C.] Ord Command the 18'[,] Birney
the   10'[,] [Joseph J.] Reynolds (probably) the 19'[,] and
[W. B.] Franklin (or [C. C.] Augur) command the 3['] Corps,
the same as Meade Commands A. of P. [——]

Sunday, 24' July, 1864—— Same Camp, near
Birchett's[.]

. . . . Colonel Sharpe has returned from the Point & says that
the Butler removal is hanging again by the ears, in consequence
of complications at Washington—— Grant wants Augur, but
cannot get him, for good reasons, as I think—— If Augur
leaves, Washington will be without any competent commander, and a door will be open for the admission of [Daniel]
Sickles to that place. . . . Butler is determined not to send his
prisoners to City Point, and has paid no attention to the Orders
sent him—— I wish Grant would order him home——

Tuesday Night[,] 26' July, 1864—— Camp near
Birchett's[.]

. . . At City Point I did many things—— Had a long talk
with Grant about all sorts of things & in a very quiet and
friendly way—— It resulted in his saying that he would, himself, order all Butler's prisoners to be forwarded to me——
Butler had just been there before me—— He is certainly a

very troublesome man, and I wish he was out of the way. . . . .
Dr. [John] Van Ingen came down to see me last night. . . .
Van Ingen is to be in the employ of the State, as its Agent in
the Field & to have the entire control of all its agents down
here. . . .

Wednesday Night, 27' July, '64[.] Same Camp, near
Birchett's[.]

. . . Meade sent for me last night merely to have a *general*
talk of our affairs——— I could give him Some information and
he could give me a great deal——— 1' The feeling at the North
& East, that Grant has failed in this Campaign, is now fully
recognized by Grant & all his Generals, as well as the Administration, & the necessity of selecting a Scape Goat felt——— 2'
Sam. Wilkeson [of the New York *Tribune*] has been down
here to try the Soldiery, to see *who* can be most safely de-
capitated, commencing by an assault & all sorts of lies upon
Meade which M. referred to Grant, who denounced them
all——— 3' The plan to set Meade aside & replace him by
Hancock having failed, a Scheme for accomplishing the object
in another way, was set on foot—to consolidate the Departments North of the Potomac under one head, to repel Raids,
secure Washington & watch Grant's rear——— Genl. Meade to
have command of these Departments,[———] 4' That Grant,
who knows the dangerous chara[c]ter of Butler, having failed
to get rid of him, is now falling under his influence & is,
insensibly swayed by him——— 5' That the utter impossibility
of taking any active offensive measures is perfectly understood
by Genl. Grant, who admits that, at the least, he requires
50,000 men in reinforcements, before he can assume the
Offensive, but, unfortunately told the President when here,
that he did not need another man———& this double view of

Affairs by Grant is now quoted against him by Stanton & Halleck, who are leagued to overthrow him. 5' [6'] That the dead lock of [W. T.] Sherman & [John B.] Hood at Atlanta, after so much was said of the certainty of Sherman's immediate success, joined to the fact that [Gen. E.] Kirby Smith is now threatening Sherman's communications, causes a very disagreeable State of feeling on the part of Grant—— 6' [7'] The jealousy on the part of Corps Commanders against each other and against Meade—especially the bad blood that exists between Meade & Burnside—prevents any unanimity of counsels, or concert of action, even among the Troops belonging to the Army of Potomac—— 7' [8'] The Same Spirit attended in (No. 6) so hostile to Burnside, will prevent Meade, probably, from taking hold, with any vim, to carry out Burnside's idea of an assault following the explosion of his mine; which if a successful 'Blow Up,' as it seems to me, can be followed up by an assault, which will carry everything before it that the Rebs. have left here—— The Rebels have sent much of their force to the left, to oppose encroachments from our right & thus weakened their front——so much as to invite assault.

Friday Night[,] *29' July.* Same Camp, Near Birchett's[.]

Slept very little, as there was a constant bumming kept up all night, by Burnside, which will, I trust, be terminated tomorrow, as the order is out, to night, for us to take the Saddle at 3 o'clock tomorrow morning. Burnside will explode, then put in his Corps, supported by Ord with the 18'—the Cavalry to be put in South of the Town. We ought to be able to walk in, for only [Gen. Richard H.] Anderson's Division[14] (of Hill's Corps,) Bush. [rod R.] Johnson's & [Robert F.] Hoke's of

---

[14] Anderson's old division was now led by Gen. William Mahone.

Beauregard's are in front of Petersburg; the other Troops having been sent North of the Appomattox, to look out for their left wing—which was, in reality, turned by the Cavalry & 2' Corps today, but not held. . . .

Saturday Night[,] *30' July*—— Same Camp, Near Birchett's[.]

Last night I went to bed at about ten o'clock, but was obliged to get up—— Then about 12 o'clock came [Capts.] Beckwith & [Charles E.] Scoville, to See the Mortar firing in the night & also the Mine Explosion of this morning—— Between the cannonading, Musketry firing & running about, I got no sleep, as it was necessary to turn out at 2'30'' & take Saddle at 3—— Meade did not move, on account of the darkness, until nearly 4—— I went over to the Ninth Corps & remained until daylight, waiting for the Commencement, Supposing, of course, that Meade would go to the Front at the time—— As he did not come, I went to him & just then at about 5 o'clock the Mines exploded & a terrific cannonade opened, under cover of which the 9' Corps went forward over the Crater, Carried the first line of works & went into the Second, with little loss, for there were but few to oppose them—— There they halted—instead of rushing on & sweeping all before them—— The 18 Corps, instead of following up, remained so long before moving up, that the 9' Corps men got frightened, stampeded, and in a most extraordinary manner, without cause, broke to the rear, carrying every thing before them—— Every thing was in our favor, but nothing was carried out well—— We fell back to the first line & by 10 o'clock, the day was lost—— I withdrew my Cavalry & came home by 11—— We got a lunch (for we had no breakfast,) and soon after another cannonading caused me to send [Capt.] McEntee & [Maj.] Walsh to the front——— They returned, Saying that the Rebels had attacked & driven us back to the lines from which we started this morning——— We have lost heavily in killed & wounded— lost about [left blank by Patrick] prisoners——— All the prisoners we took were those blown up by the mine, of Evans['] Brigade, Bush. Johnson's Division——— They are all of South Carolina Regts.——— The 22' S. C. was nearly all blown up & either buried alive, or hauled out as prisoners——— We took (236) and perhaps (14) wounded & sent to Hospital——— Of one whole Compy—all but (4) were buried alive & none have been extricated[.]

Sunday Night, 31' July, Same Camp near Birchett's[.]

. . . There is much sadness & deep feeling in relation to the affair of yesterday——— From [Lysander] Cutler, [Charles] Wainwright[15] & others I learn that their Troops were all massed & impatient to rush in—in fact that it was difficult to restrain them——— There is not a doubt in their minds that we should have gone right in, had either the 2' or 5' Corps been permitted to go forward——— I recd. an Order to arrest Burnside's Telegraph operators (2) & sent [Capt. Philip] Schuyler over to make the arrest——— He brings back word that the Ninth Corps now exists but in name—that they have lost (   ) [left blank by Patrick] men; that the 18' Corps refused to move beyond the point first taken by the 9' Corps; that Burnside reported the fact to Meade in the presence of Ord, and that Ord admitted the fact frankly——— There was a row, after we came off, between Burnside & [Cyrus B.] Comstock, Burn. sending Comstock back to Grant, with a request that G. would never again send the fellow to him———[16]

---

[15] Gen. Cutler commanded the 4th Division and Col. Wainwright the Artillery Brigade of Warren's Fifth Corps.
[16] Lt. Col. Comstock was Grant's senior Aide-de-Camp.

Grant has, this morning, run down to Fort Monroe, to meet the President, and the impression is, that more of our Troops are being sent to Washington—also that the 9' Corps will be broken up & Burnside relieved—— If the matter be investigated nothing but Grant's presence will save Meade——

Monday Night, 1' August—— Same Camp, near Birchett's[.]

. . . After my morning work I was over at the Hospital of the 4' (Colored) Division, of 9' Corps—— There had come in between 600 & 700 wounded—— They bore their wounds & pain very patiently—— Their Officers being killed, they stampeded[.] I sent out a Mrs. Moore & her daughter, professing to belong to the Christian Commission—— There is a muss about it. . . .

Tuesday Night, 2' August[,] *'64*[.] Same Camp near Birchett's[.]

Slept pretty well last night & was up in pretty good season this morning. . . . Found my Mrs. Moore here, with Dr. Prince—— She had been to Genl. Grant and got an overwhelming pass—— She brings all sorts of accusations against Cutler—— I went over to Genl. Meade about the matter, and he is so perfectly disgusted that he wants to rescind his order banishing Ladies, but finally asked me to talk to Grant about it—— They are to stay as long [as] they think proper—— She is a Screamer. . . . I find the papers detailing our Victory of Saturday[.]

Chapter XIII

Beginning the Siege of Petersburg

AUGUST 4, 1864, THROUGH NOVEMBER 8, 1864

THE FALL OF 1864 BROUGHT AN END TO the war of movement for the Army of the Potomac. Lee's skill, the defensive capabilities of the single-shot rifled musket, and the security provided by trenches and field fortifications combined to kill Grant's enthusiasm for infantry assaults (that of the troops had died much earlier). Grant began the slow process of squeezing the life out of Petersburg by cutting its communications with the south and west. With the fighting falling into a routine the interest of the Army and of Patrick turned to politics. Patrick, a lifelong Democrat, had no patience with Copperhead or antiwar sentiment and counted himself a loyal War Democrat. The state and federal elections of 1864 posed a very real dilemma for men of Patrick's feelings. McClellan, the Democratic candidate, remained a hero to much of the Army of the Potomac, but the stand of his party on the issue of the War was equivocal. Lincoln, on the other hand, seemed to be in the hands of the Abolitionists, and there wasn't much evidence that he cut much of a figure as a chief executive anyway. As Patrick's Diary shows, the Army was pulled into the center of the campaign by the fact that many states made very considerable efforts to poll the soldiers in the field, appointing special agents and, in some instances, urging that soldiers be furloughed home to vote.

Thursday, 4' August—— Camp, near Birchett's[.]

Yesterday Morning I was up early and prepared to go to City Point. . . . Went down to Forage Station & took the cars. . . . Affairs at City Point are a little Squally—— [Gen. U. S.] Grant has been sick—quite under the weather & yesterday, as soon as he was up, started for Washington, with his Staff. It seems that he had sent [Gen. Philip] Sheridan up to take command of Such troops as belong to the Army of Potomac[.] It is supposed that this has raised a row & that Grant has been obliged to go up to Washington to see about affairs there. . . .

Friday, 5' August[,] *1864*—— Same Camp, near Birchett's[.]

But a part of what I might have said, was written on the opposite page—— Grant left about 12' or 12'30" yesterday, soon after the Mail Boat passed Harrison's Landing where she had been shelled by 'Johnny,' at her first attempt. . . . Today—this morning—Meade sent over for me and I spent some two hours with him—— He keeps me pretty well posted—— It seems that there is trouble brewing—— [Gen. Henry W.] Halleck and [Edwin M.] Stanton are hostile to Grant and it appears that when we were in the neighbourhood of Hanover or rather, of Guinea [Guiney's] Station, Halleck advised Grant to hold on to that road for his line of Communication and to move by the *Right* Flank instead of the *Left,* as that would keep him between the Enemy and Washington, which if uncovered, would lead to disaster—— Halleck was overruled, & *now* retorts upon Grant that he warned him of invasion—— the necessity, now, for placing some one of rank to command all in Washington & about it, Caused Grant to recommend [Gen. William B.] Franklin—— This was returned disapproved, as Franklin was not acceptable—— The

Same proposition of Consolidation was urged in behalf of
[Gen. George B.] McClellan by very strong Republicans for
two reasons—One, that by giving him Military position it
would dispose of him politically—the Other, that his name
would bring forward a host of Volunteers—— The plan was
rejected at Washington—— Then Grant Suggested the name
of Meade, which caused the call for an interview with the
President, who asked if Meade desired it—— Grant said he
had not spoken to him as to whether it would be agreeable or
not, and that Meade was a man to obey orders without
questions—— It was then decided, that as there had been a
clamor some time ago about his removal, which he (Old Abe)
opposed, it would look as if he had yielded and *displaced*
Meade for Cause—— So the thing Stood and Grant came
home & Sent Sheridan merely to command the Troops, not
the Departments—— Meade wants to go but thinks the
Administration & Grant *fear* him. He certainly has a very high
opinion of himself—— He is now, very inimical to McClellan
& every body above him—— He has put charges against
Burnside and insists that they shall be tried—— He is very
hard & unfeeling—— There is no sympathy in his disposition
[Gen. Joseph] Hooker quarrels with operations in the West,
because he is not placed in [Gen. James B.] McPherson's
Command, instead of giving it to [Gen. Oliver O.] Howard,
So [Gen. W. T.] Sherman relieved him & Sent him North——[1]
It seems now to be tacitly, or openly acknowledged, that the
time for carrying Richmond by ordinary Army operations
ceased with the Peninsular Campaign of McClellan—— That
the time for carrying it by assault ended with the Burnside
failure of last Saturday; and that all we can do now, is to
begin a regular system of works around both cities, so strong

---

[1] Gen Hooker, commanding the Twentieth Army Corps, felt that he
should succeed to the command of the Army of the Tennessee upon the
death of Gen. McPherson, who was killed before Atlanta on July 22,
1864. Sherman chose Howard for the post and Hooker resigned his
command.

that a small body of men can hold them and wait for 100 or 150 thousand more men to blockade & starve out these cities—— This is now our only resource and the sooner it is put into operation the better—— To fight, now, except behind breastworks is nearly useless, and the Old Officers & Men are disgusted—— The Officers who are promoted, under the present ruling as to mustering in for 3 years from the date of the new Commission, refuse to muster & are going. . . .

Sunday Evening[,] 7' *Augt.* Same Camp——

Slept in new bed, or bunk, with Mosquito Bar. . . . Mr. [William] Bross[,] Editor Chicago Tribune, came with [John C.] Babcock, to see about the body of his brother, Col. Bross, killed at the assault of 9' Corps on 30' & (as it proves) buried within the Crater. . . . I talked with Burnside, fully, as to the probabilities in relation to the Court, meeting to investigate the Causes of Saturday's failures—— It is not *his* intention to appear before the Court as a party interested—— I have urged him to do it, in order that the *whole* matter may be understood; otherwise, the matter will only be investigated so far as the Carrying out of Genl. Meade's *Order* is concerned & Meade, himself, escapes—— I hope that Burnside will re-consider his decision. . . .

Monday Night, 8' August. Same Camp, near Birchett's[.]

. . . The Burnside Court is going on today, Meade is over there, but Burnside is not. Coburn, *our* Stenographer, is at Court, for Meade—— Revelations from Deserters show, that all of [Gen. James] Longstreet's Corps has left us; how disposed of, we do *not* know, whether *all* to [Gen. John B.] Hood, or part to [Gen. Jubal] Early——[2] Transportation is ordered *here*, by

---

[2] Gen. Hood was south of Atlanta, preparing to march northward to attack Sherman's supply lines. Gen. Early was still in the Shenandoah Valley.

[Quartermaster General] Meigs, for 30,000 Troops at a pop—— Grant is to be back here tonight—— Changes are the order of the day. . . .

Tuesday Night[,] *9' Augt*[.]—— Same Camp——

. . . The Court has been in session all day, over at [Gen. Winfield S.] Hancock's—— Sharpe writes me that Butler, as is supposed in Washington, relieves Stanton! That McClellan is to have a Command. That Sheridan takes the four Departments, and that nothing is known of a Command for Joe Hooker. The impression seems to be that Washington is not threatened. . . . At about 11'30" this morning I was sitting at my writing table & was startled by a tremendous explosion at City Point—— Telegrams and despatches soon came in, giving particulars—— A Barge loaded with Ordnance Stores, lying at the Wharf, blew up carrying with it the Ordnance Depot, another Barge lying alongside & whatever was near by, filling the air with Shot, Shells, chains, links—every thing, in fact. Many (the number unknown) were killed & more wounded——[3] The neighborhood of My Office is covered with debris and [Capt. Charles E.] Scoville was slightly struck in the leg—no others of mine hurt tho' the tents were pierced thro' with fragments—— Dr. [Fowler] Prentice was struck in the leg—— I do not know if badly[.]

Wednesday Night, 10' August—— Same Camp, Near
   Birchett's[.]

. . . The news of the day is, that [Admiral David G.] Farragut is succeeding well at Mobile. . . . The destruction at City Point

---

[3] The explosion was caused by a time bomb placed aboard a barge by John Maxwell, a Confederate Agent, and resulted in 43 dead and 126 wounded.

has been very great and not all the dead & wounded were in when Sharpe wrote. . . .

Thursday Night, 11' Augt. Same Camp——

. . . There has been a Court Martial over at Head Quarters, today, to try Meade's Steward, E. A. Paul for Selling Whiskey to Soldiers—— [Gen. Andrew A.] Humphreys[4] & Lyman have been in a great Stew, disbelieving in his Guilt, but there was some fun when it was found that the fellow made a practice of hiding it in Humphreys' Tent. . . .

Saturday Night, 13' August—— Same Camp——

This has been an intensely hot day and the night is hot—— Up in good time, utterly unable to sleep on account of the constant popping in front of the 9' Corps, which has kept me awake for 3 or 4 nights, last past. . . . Burnside has gone on 20 days['] leave of absence, under Charges—— It is supposed that he will not return. . . .

Monday Night, 15' August[,] *'64*—— Same Camp——

. . . A letter from Sharp[e] this P. M. says that Hancock, [Second Corps], at Deep Bottom & [Gen. David B.] Birney with the 10' Corps, have carried one line of the enemy's works; taken 8 brass guns, 2 howitzers & say, 200 prisoners; but that the Rebs. have "line upon line". . . . Burnside has gone home, on leave, under charges from Meade. [Gen. John G.] Parke is in command of the [Ninth] Corps, as I understand & ex[pects] it, soon to be ordered from this Army to Sheridan; Meade is said to be raving. . . .

---

[4] Gen. Humphreys was still Meade's Chief of Staff.

*Tuesday Night, 16' August, '64——— Same Camp, near
   Birchett's[.]*

. . . The Remitting of Darkies in the Army has been interfered
with sadly, by Butler, and I may have some collision with
him——— Have sent the papers to the Point, before seeing—or
referring them Officially. . . . I rode over to the 9' Corps this
morning, having understood that Genl. Parke had returned——— He got back only night before last and ought not
to have come at all———He was out yesterday, riding along
the lines and this morning it was evident that he was just about
to have a severe attack of Chills & Fever, again——— He feels
much dispirited. There is an idea abroad, that Burnside will
succeed in getting the 9' Corps withdrawn from this Army———
He will try it——— Meade is intensely angry with Grant for
allowing Burnside to take nearly all his Staff with him. . . .

*Wednesday Night, 17' Augt. Same Camp, near Bir-
   chett's[.]*

. . . My Shoulder gives me some trouble, both day & night and
I do not see that we are getting rid of it at all——— Dr. Parrish
of Philadelphia was here today and suggested that I should
apply "Electricity"——— I think I will go over to the Telegraph
Office and try it. . . .

*Thursday Night, 18' Augt. '64. Same Camp[,] near Bir-
   chett's[.]*

. . . Genl. [Thomas Francis] Meagher is lying in the Tent of
the Chaplain of the 20' as drunk as a Beast, & has been so
since Monday, sending out his Servant for liquor & keeping
his bed *wet* & *filthy*! I have directed Col. [Theodore B.] Gates

to ship him tomorrow if he does not clear out——— Grant is not
at all well, & there are fears that he is breaking down. . . .

Friday Night, 19' Augt. '64——— Same Camp———
    Birchett's

. . . I have had a call from [Col. Henry S.] Burton, today, who
returned from Sick leave last night——— He gave me some
information as to the plots etc. against Grant, by Butler———
It is said that Grant has been, *twice, drunk,* when the "Beast"
was present——— Once when at [Gen. W. F.] Baldy Smith's
and that the "Beast" will use this against him. [Gen. Henry J.]
Hunt & others have been over here, talking over the political
news——— It seems to be understood, distinctly, that Lincoln
has got frightened & is now endeavoring to Sound the public
mind as to proposals for Peace——— [John W.] Forney[5] is
taking the lead and his Editorials for the 16' & 17' are strongly
hinting at a peace, without the recognition of Emancipation
and on the basis of the Constitution——— The Chicago Convention will meet within ten days from this date, and the
matter of the nomination will, then, probably, be settled———
From all Sources I learn that there is universal depression in
the North, and a strong belief that the Draft will be resisted,
in many places, by riots. I confess that I fear the result of
pushing the people, overloaded, taxed and trampled upon, as
they now are, by a set of heartless political despots. . . .

Sunday Night, 21' Augt[.]——— Same Camp———

Slept pretty well last night, although there was a deal of firing
on the left, and all along the line, which continued this morning. The Rebels assaulted, but did not know what they were

---

[5] Forney retained his post as Secretary of the Senate and was the
publisher of both the Philadelphia *Press,* and the Washington *Chronicle,*

at, and were beaten off, with heavy loss, about 300 prisoners falling into our hands. These prisoners did not get in until quite along in the Afternoon and are here tonight—— We sent down to the Point (228) prisoners of War yesterday—— The Second Corps returned, last night, from the North Side of the James and resumed its old position. . . .

Tuesday Night, 23' Augt. Same Camp——

. . . I am expecting to go down to City Point tomorrow morning, if all continues quiet. . . . I am just back from a call on Genl. Meade who has been giving me a history of the causes of his demoralization—— It is the old Story—Grant recommended him & Sherman in May last, for Major Generals & Hancock for Brigadier—— *Why* he has been left out in the cold he does not know, and of course, is sore——

Wednesday Night, 24' August, Same Camp, Birchett's[.]

. . . At City Point I was very busy, especially in matters pertaining to Genl. Butler's interference with the Mail Boats—— I have prepared, and left for the examination of Ingal[l]s & [Theodore S.] Bowers,[6] before issuing it, an Order regulating this whole matter of Mail Boat Guards—— The recruiting of Colored persons within our lines is, virtually, abolished, by instructions received this morning from Genl. Grant, which I am glad of—— All appearances indicate, however, that Butler has his hand upon Grant's throat, and that Grant feels his gripe[sic]. . . .

---

[6] Ingalls was still Chief Quartermaster of the Armies Operating Against Richmond and Col. Bowers was an Assistant Adjutant General on Grant's staff.

Thursday Night, 25' Augt. '64—— Same Camp——
Birchett's[.]

. . . This evening Hancock is engaged at Reams Station——
There is a determination on the part of Lee to retake the Rail
Road & he is massing all his Troops down there. His losses on
Sunday were heavy—— Their repulse by Warren [Fifth
Corps] is regarded by them as the bloodiest they have had
recently[.] My Cavalry & Infantry are all out, to replace
[Gershom] Mott's men [3rd Division, Second Corps]. . . .

Friday Night, 26' Augt. '64—— Same Camp——
. . . There has been nothing of a Military Character of interest
today. . . . Sharpe writes me that Butler has gone to New
York, taking his Short hand man, to look out for the Chicago
Convention. I should be glad if he were never to return here
again. . . .

Sunday Night, 28['] August—— Same Camp——

. . . I have been reading some Criticisms on Renan's Life of
Jesus & searching the Mosaic Code with special reference to
the Sanitary Condition of its Military Camps. Cleanliness is
regarded as part of the Mosaic Law. . . . I learn that Genl.
Hancock's spirits are very low & that he says his [Second]
Corps behaved Shamefully the other night—that he now has
no confidence in the Corps—— His men would not rise from
behind their breastworks to fire—— He has many Companies
Comd. by noncomd. Officers.

Monday Night, 29' Augt. '64—— Same Camp—— Birchett's[.]

. . . I have suffered much pain in my Shoulder today, though
I adopted the course of painting it with Iodine this morn-

ing—— I am also taking a preparation of Iodine internally.
. . . Rev. [Dr. John] Van Ingen has been here several hours
today, and as he is just from New York, has posted me quite
thoroughly—— His idea is that McClellan will receive the
nomination on a War platform; or rather, upon a platform
referring all issues to the Constitution and the Undivided
Union. . . . He says that no fears are felt about riots in enforcing the draft, as the excitement will work off through the
ballot Box—— It is believed that a great political Revolution
is at hand, to be consummated this year. . . .

Wednesday Night, 31' August—— Same Camp, Birchett's[.]

. . . I drove to the Point reaching there before 9 o'clk—and
remaining until 5—when I drove home again in my own
waggon. . . . General Grant had gone down to Fortress Monroe, to take his Wife and Family, they having been visiting at
City Point for the last few days. . . . The 4 or 5 Officers, confined by Genl. Butler, as Citizens, left this morning—— Genl.
Grant[']s order to release them was positive. . . .

Thursday Night, 1' September—— Same Camp, near
Birchett's[.]

. . . Genl. Meade left, this evening, quite suddenly, on a seven
days['] Leave of Absence—— There is much Speculation
afloat as to the cause of the move, but I apprehend it is, partly,
to push his claim for a 2' Regular Star, and partly to see if he
can get another Command—— There is some hope that his
reign over this Army is at an end—— Genl. [Rufus] Ingal[l]s
has gone to Lake Superior on a Leave of Absence for Thirty
Days—— Genl. [John G.] Parke commands in the absence of
Genl. Meade——

Friday Night, 2' September—— Same Camp——

. . . I have suffered much today & am in agony much of the time with my shoulder; so I mounted & rode out, after dinner, as far as the Stiles['] House—— I did not go in, but seeing Mrs. Stiles near the fence, rode up & asked of their welfare—— She Said they were very little molested, as they have a Safe Guard—and she is now 'All Right'. . . .

Saturday Night, 3' September—— Same Camp——
Birchett's[.]

. . . Have had a call from Mr. [George H.] Stuart and the Christian Commission delegates this Afternoon. . . . The nomination of McClellan has opened the flood gates of abuse against him, as was to have been expected and his friends will have hard work to elect him; especially if any military Success attends our arms before election. . . .

Sunday Night, 4' September—— Same Camp——

. . . The report of the fall of Atlanta is confirmed & Gen. [William J.] Hardee reported killed—also Genl. [Pat] Cleburne——[7] No other particulars.

Monday Night, 5' September. Same Camp, near Birchett's[.]

Last night I fell asleep at about 10 o'clock, or soon after, but was routed out about 12 by a tremendous burst of Artillery

---

[7] The reports were a bit exaggerated. Both Hardee and Cleburne would live to fight again another day.

along the whole line——— Orders had been given to give one grand Salute for the Fall of Atlanta——— It was one continued roar of Guns for half an hour——— Bands playing and Drums beating. . . . I was at Genl. Grant's and had a long talk with [Col.] Bowers about Liquor (matters) in the Army, which is now making a great deal of disturbance. . . . I have a letter from my Wife. . . . They are crazy about McClellan's nomination——— There is much regret felt in the Army that Such a platform was adopted——— [Gen.] Hunt says, however, that it is not understood by those who talk of it as not meaning a vigorous prosecution of the War——— He understands that McClellan's Letter of acceptance will cover the whole ground, and leave no doubt of the policy of his administration, if elected——— I hope he will. We are now getting quite a number of recruits, convalescents etc. about 1000 daily, tho' many of the recruits, who are Substitutes, run away by the first opportunity, to the enemy——— The Rail Road is being run, quite rapidly, in the rear of our lines, and will, probably, be in condition to supply the Troops before the fall rains set in much. . . .

Thursday Evening, 8' September, '64. Camp near Birchett's[.]

Last night, late, I recd.. a note from Col. Sharpe, to the effect that the "enlisted men" of the 20' had purchased, some time ago, a very handsome sword & "fixings" to be presented to me, as they are about to leave for home——— I have written back to him, giving the reasons why it should not be done, and to defer it until we are out of Service——— I have got to receive it, however, as the thing has gone too far to stop, and Genl. Grant says if I were to decline it, the men would be chilled to death & would not re-enlist——— So it is settled that I go down on Saturday & receive it. . . .

Sunday Night, 11' September, 1864—— Camp near Birchett's[.]

This has been a dull and quiet day, with a little rain in the
Afternoon—— I have not been well at all. . . . I have written
a short letter to my wife & enclosed the Carte of Genl. Burnside, who will not, probably, return——

Wednesday Night, 14' Sept. '64. Camp near Birchett's[.]

. . . Went over to see Genl. Meade, on business, when he made
a point, with me on the Liquor Circular, and said he doubted
the right of Genl. Grant to so prohibit Liquor. Then, too, he
should join issue with him for issuing Orders through me etc.
etc. He may get himself into trouble about it—— I am preparing to leave here, in one way or another, before many days
are past. . . . I have commenced a registration of all Citizens
within our lines, through the Officers of 3d Penn. Cavy. with
reference to sending them out of the lines unless they take the
Oath. . . .

Friday Night, 16' Sept—'64—— Camp near Birchett's[.]

This has been a busy day. . . . was sent for by Genl. Meade,
who told me that the enemy had broken through our Cavalry
line & he feared for City Point—— I put the Telegraph at
work and gave the necessary instructions for the defence of the
Depot, sent out my Cavy. towards Jordans Point to hold a line
from there to the River to prevent the Stampeding of Trains
& sent Troops on Transports, to be sent to the relief of Fort
Powhatan if necessary—— Beckwith took charge in the River.
We were on the Qui vive all day, sending couriers, telegraphing
etc. etc. The whole result is this—The Cavalry of the enemy,

in large force, made a charge upon the Main herd of Cattle & drove off about 2600 head—— They escaped scot free—— . . .

Saturday Night[,] *17' September*—— Same Camp——

. . . I went down to the Point and spent the day. . . . Genl. Grant and all the others, nearly, are gone—— Grant went up to see what is the matter with Sheridan & [Col. Horace] Porter[8] has gone to See Sherman, out west—— All is hanging by the ears down here. . . .

Sunday Night, 18' September [,] *1864*—— Same Camp——

. . . I have had a great deal of business, all day—— Had a Company up for Counterfeiting—1' Penn. Cavy.[—] sent three of them to the Old Capitol, where the Captain is—— Have had to place on board the Prison Ship at City Point a Captain & Lieut. from Elmira for Swindling Substitutes. . . .

Tuesday Night, 20' September—— Same Camp——

. . . Col. Sharpe has applied to me for my decision in regard to a Leave of Absence, and I have given it fully, with my plans for the winter, if I can have my own way, both for myself and him—— I hope he will now cease plotting—at least so far as I am concerned. . . . We have good news from Sheridan tonight—— He says that he fought the enemy from 6 A. M. till 7 P. M. yesterday driving him from the Opequan thro'

---

[8] Col. Porter, an Aide-de-Camp on Grant's staff, was carrying a letter dated September 12 in which Grant described the situation on his front.

Winchester in haste, took from 2500 to 3000 prisoners, 5 pieces of Artillery, 9 Battle Flags, & all the Rebel wounded in Winchester, amounting to 3000. . . . Sheridan would pursue them up the Valley today—— This is glorious news—— The day has been mild & I am feeling more easy——

Wednesday Night, 21' September—— Same Camp——

. . . The night was noisy and, of course, I slept but little—— The "Hundred Guns" from Each Corps"[sic] blazed away for Sheridan's Victory over Early, which today's advices increased in magnitude and importance. . . . Sheridan was still pursuing. I have had a great many business calls today from Officers and others—— One from Genl. Meade of a Singular character, and which, but for the hint Beckwith gave me, might have upset me. . . .[9]

Thursday Night, 22' September, 1864—— Same Camp——

I went to bed last [night] in pretty good condition, after having been put through a course of Electricity by Dr. Cummins. I had comparatively little pain, but much numbness of the Arm & fingers. . . . This Evening I have had Rev. Mr. Burdick, Chaplain of the 61' New York here, for the 2d time, in regard to a gross outrage committed upon him by Capt. & Lieut. Ames of a Battery in the 1' N. Y. Artillery, in the 2' Corps—— They tied him up to a Battery Waggon & the trial seems to be a farce—— I have taken it over to [Col. Edmund] Schriver & [Gen. Henry J.] Hunt. . . .

---

[9] Probably a reference to the warning Beckwith had given Patrick that Col. Sharpe wanted Patrick to take a long leave "for his health" during which Sharpe would get things into his own hands.

Saturday Night, 24' September[,] '64. Same Camp——

Went to bed last night, about 9'30", and came near falling asleep, when a letter from Meade, written at a little after ten came over, on some ordinary matters, and closing by saying that Sheridan had won another victory over Early and was pursuing him in hot haste—— There has been another Salute this morning. . . . After attending to my business, most pressing, as it was raining hard, I concluded to come home in the Special Train, at 11 o'clock, with Genl. Grant. Had a pleasant run up with him & over here, to Genl. Meade's. . . .

Sunday[,] 25' September, 3 o'clock P. M. Same Camp——

I have just closed a letter to my wife and before I lie down may as well make a note—— I slept pretty well last night and felt pretty well this morning—— At 11 o'clock I went over to [Col.] Collis' Head Quarters, to attend service—— Rev. Mr. Waters (Episcopal) of Kingston [N. Y.], officiated[.] Preached from "the man who drew a bow at a venture & smote the king etc. etc." Applied it to Erikson's [sic] Monitor, after the consternation in regard to the Rebel Iron Clad. . . .

Tuesday Night, 27' September[,] '64—— Same Camp, Birchett's[.]

. . . After getting through my ordinary work I wrote a letter to Mary telling her that Beckwith would call for Brayton and to have him ready. . . .[10]

---

[10] Captain Beckwith was picking up the eldest Patrick boy, Brayton, at Geneva, and bringing him down to spend the winter with his father at City Point.

Wednesday Night, 26' September, '64—— Same
    Camp——

. . . Col. [T. B.] Gates came up at my call and I have had a
talk with them—*him,* I should say, in regard to Col.
Sharpe—— He tells me that the Colonel is known, at home,
and by *his* Regt[.], as a man on whom little reliance can be
placed—— Tricky and full of all sorts of Policy—— Sharpe
has written me to ask for *his* Regt.—I have not, *yet,* asked for
it—— There is an order out, tonight, for the movement of the
whole army, nearly—— Head Quarters to be ready to move
at 6 o'clock—— Only a thin line, in the Breastworks & Forts,
remain to guard our whole Lines. . . .

Thursday Night, 29' Sept. '64—— Same Camp, Bir-
    chett's[.]

There was very little sleep last night, growing out of the operations incident to a move at daylight—— I do not yet know
what our plans were, but Suppose the intention was, to have
Butler attack on the right, and then, if any troops were withdrawn from *our* front, for Meade's Army to pitch in—— We
have been packed up all day, but not any thing has been done
by Meade. . . .

Friday Night, 30' Sept. '64—— Same Camp, near
    Birchett's[.]

Well! After another day of discomfort, night has come and we
are preparing for bed on the same ground as last night. We
slept tolerably well, though there was some confusion. Genl.
Meade went off to the left, and spent the day mostly with
Warren— There was an assault made by [Charles] Griffin

[1st Division, Fifth Corps] on the Enemy's works, near the Peeble's Farm, & carried in "handsome style"—— [Romeyn B.] Ayres, [2nd Division, Fifth Corps] also, carried some works—— [Robert B.] Potter of the 9' [Corps] attempted something similar and failed—— We have taken only about 60 prisoners. . . .

Saturday Night, 1' October[,] *1864*—— City Point, Va[.]——

. . . Along about noon, I found that I must get into a dryer atmosphere, and as Genl. Meade had gone to the front, I wrote him a note, to the effect, that I proposed to leave [Capt. Alexander J.] Dallas in charge of the office & [Col. Charles H. T.] Collis in charge of the Troops, and go, myself, to City Point—— This he granted very handsomely. . . .

Sunday Night, 2' October—— City Point, Va[.]——

. . . The Head Quarters of Genl. Meade are removed to the Aiken House, near the Weldon Rail Road—— Our Troops seem to be pushing on the left, and Grant, with Butler, on the right—— So far all is well. . . .

Monday Night, October 3' 1864—— My Office, City Point——

. . . The Administration is sending its Agents to the field to Canvass & Electioneer for its own side of the House—— There will be nothing like fairness, or freedom of choice among the Soldiery, judging from present operations. . . . I took a ride this evening, with Col. Gates, to look at the police and other matters around the Point, within his command—— The character of the Troops stationed here, temporarily, makes a bad state of police all around us. . . .

> *Tuesday Night, 4' October, '64*—— My Office[,] City
>   Point——

. . . My Nephew, Columbus, now about 34 yrs. of age, arrived today, with a detachment of 17' Mich., Co. I. He came to see me, & has been over this evening again. It is probable that he will break down if he tries to do duty as a Soldier & I think of having him on duty as a Carpenter. . . .

> *Wednesday Night*—— *5' October*[,] *'64*—— My Office,
>   City Point——

This has been a busy day. . . . After Breakfast, took my seat, at 8'20" in the Car for the front, but we were delayed & I became very tired—— It must have been three hours before we reached Head Quarters—— I talked half an hour or more, with Meade, got all matters fixed, or in train, & then came home, reaching here about 3 o'clock. . . . It seems that the question is mooted—Why I am not a Major Genl. . . .

> *Thursday Night, 6' October, 1864*—— My Office(City
>   Point——

. . . Have spent a very busy day, though I have not accomplished a vast deal. . . . I was being sketched in colors, by [Ole Peter Hansen] Balling who has come down here to paint Genl. Grant & all the distinguished Officers of his Staff &

Army——He has made a very good head, & my long beard makes a patriarchal picture. . . ."[11]

Friday Night[,] 7' October, 1864—— My Office, City Point——

Slept tolerably well & rose early—— Col. Sharpe went down last night to meet and receive from the U. S. Ship Circassian some, say, 100 Naval prisoners, captured at Mobile. . . . I was over at Head Quarters this morning, but Grant went yesterday, to Washington. . . .

Sunday Night, 9' October[,] '64. My Office, City Point——

. . . It has been a day of great labor & vexation for me, as I have had to investigate the cases of a host of these Elmira Substitutes & Officers & Guards, taking up the most of my time. . . . Had a note from Rev. Dr. Adams this evening, enclosing a Letter from McClellan to Hunt—— He is more hopeful than I thought he would be and seems to hope for his election, yet—— He foots up the votes of States very differently from what they are counted by the Administration papers.

Monday Night, 10' October, 1864—— My Office, City Point——

. . . I have written, tonight, to my Wife . . . and one, [to] Lieut. Col. Pierce, Chief Quarter Master 9' Corps, asking of him, if he can do so, to have my Nephew, Columbus, detailed as a

---

[11] Balling, as he preferred to be known, was a Norwegian who had come to the United States in 1856. His painting of U. S. Grant and twenty-six Union generals is now owned by the Smithsonian Institution in Washington.

Carpenter & Joiner, as I have a letter from him saying that it is affecting his health to be exposed as he now is, to the weather. . . . 28 years ago this night I was married. . . .

Wednesday Night, 12' October, 1864—— My Office, City Point——

. . . The day has been pleasant, but it came on to rain at about 5 o'clock. . . . Capt. Webb, a [Confederate] naval officer & Senior of those now in the harbor, for exchange, was up and Spent some time here—— A companionable man. We have sent up, on a call from Gen. Butler, endorsed by Genl. Grant some 70, or 80 Rebel prisoners, to be put to work on the Dutch Gap Canal, to retaliate for our own prisoners at work on their fortifications. . . .

*Thursday Night, 13' October, 1864——*My Office, City Point——

. . . I was very agreeably surprised today, by the arrival of Capt. Beckwith and Brayton—— They are a day earlier than I looked for, but came through via Harrisburg, making good time and no delays—— Brayton has grown, but his manners are very boyish—childish even——[12] He has been so long with women & children that he talks incessantly and oftentimes foolishly—— He is affectionate and I hope to be able to change his habits Somewhat. . . .

*Friday Night, 14' October[,] 1864——*My Office[,] City Point[.]

Went to bed at my usual hour, with Brayton in my room, on the floor—— Slept tolerably well and rose early—— Had the

---

[12] Patrick's son, Brayton, or "Bucky," was fifteen years old at the time of this visit to his father.

privilege of prayers and reading the Scriptures with Brayton.
. . . I have been all day at hard work, in the office and had no
let up—— It has been rather a pleasant day and I have been
fixing up Brayton's Tent, so that he sleeps there tonight—— It
will be comfortable after I get a stove in there for him—— He
appears quite contented and although boyish, I have no doubt
he will get along quite well, after a while. . . .

Saturday Night, 15' October, 1864—— My Office[,]
    City Point——

. . . The Box of Brayton's Clothing etc. arrived this evening,
but in very bad condition, Julia having put in a lot of grapes
which crushed, and the juice ran into his clothing—— I have
got for him, today, Pants, Cap, Blouse, shirts & Drawers which
I have put in the hands of a Tailor to fit for him—— This
evening I have been over to Genl. Grant[']s on business.

Sunday Night, 16' October, 1864—— My Office[,] City
    Point——

This has been a pleasant day—— I slept well, rose early, had
Brayton in & prayers before Breakfast. . . . Came back to my
room & after a while took Brayton & went over to the Brick
Church where Chaplain Street, of the 20' [N. Y. Mil.] held
forth, using the Episcopal service—— Then he preached a
good sermon on "Idle words," but I am told, that his preaching
& his practice do not go together at all—— We came home
and I found that Secretary Stanton[,] Genls. [Montgomery C.]
Meigs, [Amos B.] Eaton & [Joseph K.] Barnes had arrived &
that I had been inquired for——[13] So, after lunch I went over
to Head Quarters but they had all gone up to Butler's. . . .

---

[13] Meigs was the Quartermaster General, Eaton the Commissary
General, and Barnes the Surgeon General of the Army.

Monday Night, 17' October, 1864—— My Office[,] City Point[.]

. . . I mounted, after Breakfast, and rode around the place, looking to see what is wanted—— Then I rode over to see the Secretary and his party, but they had gone to the front, which was very satisfactory to me. . . . This evening is mild and beautiful. . . . Brayton has been sitting here, reading the North British Review.

Tuesday Night, 18' October, 1864—— My Office, City Point——

Last night, after closing my Book, and as Brayton was about to leave me, the Band of the 120' came down to serenade me & remained quite a time. . . There has been nothing new today—— Some colored Troops arriving from the West. . . .

Friday Night, 21' October, 1864. My Office, City Point[.]

. . . I recd. a letter last night from Oliver C. Chapin, saying that he should ship Grapes & fruit etc. through his consignee, or would, perhaps, come to the Army himself. Tonight a Mr. Hope arrives, bringing a letter from Mr. Chapin, authorizing him to act as his Agent—— Accordingly I have given him the means of making quite a business, on which they will, about, double their money—— Election matters are absorbing a great deal of the public interest and I hope we shall have done with them before long. In the Army it is making a great deal of trouble, as some of our Officers refuse to act, unless the votes are as they wish, Genl. Hunt so informs me in relation to several Batteries—— I have had a box of documents sent to me and have turned them over to Mr. Dodge, who has the

matter in charge for the New York Democratic Committee—— This evening I have been over to Genl. Grant's Head
Quarters on business, & have had a talk with him about various
matters of my work and especially in regard to another Regt.
for duty here—— I shall, probably, be able to secure the order
before long—— . . .

> *Saturday Night*[,] *22' October, 1864*—— My Office,
> City Point——

. . . Cloudy most of the day & quite raw. . . . I have had,
yesterday & today, the Cavalry overhauling the Cars, at Cedar
Level & elsewhere, and taking out men and Officers by the
hundred, having no passes. . . . I have also had the case of one
J. Wilberforce Dennison, Election Agent for Connecticut, in
hand this evening—— He has been in confinement since Sunday last for a Simple expression of his opinions, in the 2'
Corps——

> *Monday Night, 24' October, 1864*—— My Office, City
> Point——

Last night I wrote a letter to my wife, quite late, and then
went to bed, to be Electrified. . . . I have been over to Genl.
Grant and had a talk with him about matters. . . . There is
to be a movement here, this week, probably an attempt on
Richmond—— I am getting all things into as good shape as
I can, to hold here with as few troops as possible. . . .

> *Tuesday Night, 25' October, 1864*—— My Office[,]
> City Point[.]

I took my dose of lightning last night and went to bed before
ten o'clock. . . . After Breakfast I mounted and rode out with

Capt. [Henry B.] Blood, and Capt. [Daniel D.] Wiley, to look at the Bake Houses just completed——[14] It will turn out 100,000 rations in 24 hours—— Every thing is on a grand scale and of the most convenient & economical character—— They make most excellent bread. . . . Election matters are prominent over all others & fill the papers. . . . Have had Col. [Jacob B.] Hardenberg & Capt. Scoville to identify my vote, which I have, this evening, enclosed to James O. Sheldon—for McClellan & Seymour—— I dislike [Horatio] Seymour, but dislike [Reuben E.] Fenton still more——[15] It is a choice of evils—— I vote for McClellan because I cannot vote for Lincoln—and because I believe it will most surely, bring to us peace—— There has been some little preparation today for a movement—ordering detailed men to be armed——It is expected that we make a rush for Richmond[.]

Wednesday Night, 26' October[,] '64—— My Office[,] City Point.

This has been a busy day—— I was up in good season and prepared for action—— After Breakfast I was all about & over the grounds, looking at the order of arrangement for Defences provided any thing should require my assistance—— I have, also, been making arrangements for keeping a Police Guard in active operation here, during the Front Movement[.] Genl. Meade moved his Head Quarters, this morning, to Poplar Spring Church, beyond the Weldon Rail Road and the Ball will open tomorrow—— Genl. Grant will go up at day-light—— Both Armies advance tomorrow. . . .

---

[14] Blood was an assistant quartermaster and Wiley was a commissary officer at City Point.

[15] New York Republicans nominated Fenton, a Chautauqua business-man, to try to unseat Horatio Seymour in the gubernatorial contest of 1864.

Thursday Evening, 27' October, 1864——— My Office,
    City Point[.]

. . . Gen. Grant went up at seven o'clock this morning, leaving
an Order here for me to take command in case any thing goes
wrong with Benham. . . . Mr. [William] Kelly writes in much
depression of low spirits, believing that the administration
agents are so manipulating the votes of the Soldiery, by every
dishonest trick, that McClellan will be defeated. . . .

Friday Night, 28' October, 1864——— My Office, City
    Point[.]

. . . After Breakfast I went back—went to see Gen. Grant. . . .
The result of the Operations [at the Front] has been a loss of
about 1500 killed & wounded, supposed to be about equal
to the loss of the enemy, and the Capture of about 900
Rebels— We are not holding the ground taken & come back to
our former position——— The Trains are ordered back to their
Corps. . . .

Saturday Night, 29' October, 1864——— My Office, City
    Point[.]

. . . After breakfast I went over to Genl. Grant's[.] Had some
talk with [Theodore S.] Bowers & [Ely S.] Parker.[16] Met Gen.
Halleck & Genl. [Lorenzo] Thomas. . . .

Sunday Night, 30' October, 1864——— My Office[,] City
    Point[.]

Last night I had a very extensive "Electrifying" from Dr.
Gates and I think it did me some good. . . . After Prayers &

---

[16] Lt. Col. Parker was a military secretary on Grant's staff.

breakfast I went out to look at the troops and around by the Office and Steam Boat. . . . I have had a tiresome day, winding up with a most insolent Telegram from [Charles A.] Dana, saying that I am charged with rendering assistance to the Democratic Agents that I would not give to Republicans etc. etc.

Monday Night, 31' October, 1864 —— My Office, City Point——

This has been a busy day—— I was up much earlier than usual and after prayers closed up the Statement I had made in regard to Certain matters, before breakfast. . . . [Capt. Henry P.] Clinton came down, in answer to my call, and after the Boat was off, came to my room—— He tells me that he thinks one "E. D. Webster" Private Secretary of Gov. Seward, has had some agency in these transactions—— This Webster is the man who telegraphed to me, for Hazard of Buffalo, that Clinton had the Ballots & Envelopes etc. Clinton has never received one, and has been warned that evil was intended him at the State Department—— I have drawn up a Statement for General Meade, as he requested me, covering all my transactions with State Agents, Election Commissioners etc. This paper will be sent, I presume, to the Secretary of War, and may make quite a fuss—— I hope it will—— The insolence of the Secretary, and of the Administration generally, is intolerable—— It has taken me all day to gather up material to answer the charges of the War Department. . . . There is much feeling in regard to the insult offered me by the War Department, and Col. [T. B.] Gates goes to Washington intending to have the matter inquired into by the administration officials. . . . Beckwith has received a cake of mammoth proportions from the Ice Cream Man[.]

Tuesday[,] *November 1' 1864*—— My Office, City
   Point, Va[.],

. . . I have been all day at work in the usual business of the
office, which seems to grow upon me so that I can get no time
to write for myself. . . . The papers still harp upon the Baltimore Frauds and also upon the arrest of Col. North, the State
Agent at Washington.

Wednesday Night, 2' November, 1864—— My Office,
   City Point——

Did not sleep as well last night as heretofore—— Although
pretty well filled with Electricity, sleep did not come soundly.
After Breakfast I took a pretty good shock, Brayton turning
the crank. . . . He is improving, some, in his general bearing,
conduct & Equestrianism—— I want to have him learn to
write well. . . .

Thursday Night, 3' November, 1864—— My Office, City
   Point——

This has been a day of hard work. . . . Gates writes me from
Washington, that Dana says he only telegraphed me what he
was ordered to telegraph, by the Secretary of War——
Several attempts were made by the Col. [Gates] and Col.
Thompson, Chief Agent of the Republican Party from New
York, to see Stanton in regard to it, but without effect—— I
have had a call from Jerry McKibbin, Genl. [William]
McCandless, and [Sid] Demming——[17] The latter came over

---

[17] Jeremiah McKibbin was an election commissioner from Pennsylvania,
assigned to the Army of the Potomac. A question about the vote in the
118th Pennsylvania had been raised by Seth Williams at Army headquarters. Gen. McCandless was the commander of the 2nd Pennsylvania
Reserves. Demming represented the Associated Press.

this evening and posted me fully in regard to the State [of] things in the North—— There is an awful state of affairs & we seem to be on the brink of Revolution in the North——

Friday Night[,] 4' November, 1864—— My Office, City Point——

. . . I was out until near 12 o'clock, giving directions about passengers on the Boat—— There were so many that we could not put them all on board—— Another Steamer soon after left, taking the remainder—— They are all going home to vote, if possible. . . . I was over at Genl. Grant's and had a short talk with him, then came home—— Large numbers of Troops are going from here to New York, and the papers say, that Genl. Butler has gone there to assume command—— Demming has placed me in possession of the plans of the Administration, they having been revealed to him by [Allen] Pinkerton, who got them from the President & Secretary of War—— I received a Letter from Mr. [William] Kelly this evening from Washington. . . . He says, there has been systematic action there, to prevent Officers from verifying the votes, or assisting the Election Agents——

Saturday Night[,] 5' November, 1864—— My Office, City Point[.]

. . . There has been nothing strange today or new—— The papers, tonight, are quite tame, and nothing but raids on the New York frontier, from Canada, seems to afford food for gapers. . . .

Monday Night, 7' November, '64—— My Office[,] City Point.

. . . Dr. [John] Van Ingen has just returned from New York— no—Washington—— He saw Messrs. [William] Kelly &

Allen—— There is no doubt, in my mind, that the object of [Col.] North's arrest was to prevent the votes of New York Soldiers from being sent home—— All possible obstacles were thrown in the way of a fair Soldier's vote——

Tuesday Night, 8' November, 1864—— My Office, City
    Point[,] Va[.]——

. . . [Adam] Badeau & [Col. Orville E.] Babcock (or some other of Grant's Staff) were over this afternoon, to tell me, that up to 2'20" P. M. today all was quiet in New York—— I do hope the Election in New York will pass off quietly—— This day is an important one in the destinies of our country——

Chapter XIV

A Winter of Waiting

NOVEMBER 9, 1864, THROUGH FEBRUARY 4, 1865

As PATRICK'S DIARY makes evident, the Army of the Potomac became increasingly absorbed in the routine of the siege of Petersburg during the winter of 1864-1865. Little effort was made by either Grant or Lee to break the military stalemate. General Butler amused himself by attempting to cut through a neck of land inside a loop of the James River with his Dutch Gap canal.

In the Shenandoah Valley Sheridan rode roughshod over Early's battered command. To the South Sherman moved out of Atlanta, headed for salt water, on November 16. In the West Hood's Confederate Army was checked at Franklin, Tennessee, on November 30 and destroyed at Nashville on December 15 and 16. On December 20 Sherman was able to offer the news of the capture of the city of Savannah to Lincoln and the North as a Christmas present.

Wednesday Night, 9' November, 1864—— My Office,
    City Point——

Slept tolerably well, but only tolerably. . . . Brayton, too, is
quite unwell and I feel somewhat uneasy about him—— He
does not appear to be [at] all recuperative & energetic——
He is dreamy & dull—very dull! Nothing practical about him,
nor can I, thus far, get any thing practical into him—— There
is still much excitement about election and although the
Presidential Vote is given to Seymo—to Lincoln, many believe
that New York has gone for [George B.] McClellan &
[Horatio] Seymour.[1] . . . We had news, by Telegraph, last
night, to Genl. Grant, but today, for some unexplained reason,
the Telegraph has not given us any news. . . . We are all on
the qui vive, as it is expected that many of us will have
"tickets of leave["] before the 30' Instant[.]

Thursday Night, 10' November, '64—— My Office,
    City Point.

. . . I was up and about my business as usual, but was over at
Genl. Grant's Head Quarters from about the time the Boat
went off for two hours—— I could not see the General alone,
but I had a talk with [Lt. Col. William L.] Duff,[2] from which
I found that Genl. Grant had no intention of leaving here
until the fall of Richmond—— Of course this brings to the
ground my calculations about Meade's being left in command
of both these Armies. . . . There is trouble at Head Quarters
about Election Agents and I understand that Stanton has
again telegraphed Meade in regard to me and my Department——[3]

---

[1] Fenton defeated Seymour by a vote of 368,557 to 361,264.

[2] Col. Duff was an Assistant Inspector General on Grant's staff.

[3] Stanton had telegraphed to Meade, in reference to the arrest of
McKibbin, "If General Patrick is your provost-marshal-general the
Department has not confidence in him; do not think that their safe
keeping should be left entirely to him."

Friday Night, 11' November, 1864[.] My Office, City
   Point[,] Virginia——

Last night I was turned out of my bed, about 12 o'clock, by
the arrival of [Lt.] Col. J.[oseph] H. Taylor, with a guard of
25 men, on a special Steamer, for the persons of Jere.[miah]
McKibbin and his two confreres—— I telegraphed up to have
them sent down here, but Genl. Meade decided that Col.
Taylor must go there—— So I sent him up in a special Train
this morning & Beckwith accompanied him—— They are all
sent forward to Washington—— Of course I got no more
sleep, after Taylor was here, as he staid an hour, talking over
home matters—— McKibbin wrote me a note before leaving.
I have been at work all day, as usual. Have had [Theodore S.]
Bowers over here, something like an hour, talking over these
matters of War Department operations, and this systematic
abuse of me—— I think he will now understand all about
matters. . . .

Saturday Night, 12' November, 1864, My Office, City
   Point, Va.

. . . I was engaged in my usual duties during the forenoon,
and of course had all I could attend to, including the calls of
female Secesh. . . . The papers are still doubtful as to the
Election of Gov. Seymour, or Mr. Fenton, as both sides claim
the Election. . . .

Sunday Night, 13' November, 1864—— My Office,
   City Point——

This morning we were turned out unusually early, Taylor's
watch being rather faster than usual. . . . Brayton and I

spent about an hour & a half, at our devotions. . . . Then we walked down to the Steamboat & remained until the refugees and prisoners were placed on board—— We then got into the Ambulance and rode up to the General Hospitals. . . .

Tuesday Night, 15' November, 1864—— My Office, City Point[.]

. . . Was Over at Head Quarters and, finally, got into the Ambulance, with Brayton, and went off to see the Hospital Steamer Connecticut. . . . The accommodations are very fine, indeed, for say 400 men. . . . The impression is strong in the North that Genl. Butler should be put in Stanton's place—— Unless something is done *here,* I am fearful that it may be done. . . .

Wednesday Night, 16' November, 1864—— My Office, City Point——

. . . I had a talk with Genl. Grant about Col. Sharpe, and have that matter all fixed right—— I think he is off for Washington this night, or tomorrow, with a view to head off Butler as Secretary of War—— He talked freely to me of matters and I am now ready to see Genl. Meade with reference to the Army of Potomac. . . .

Thursday Night, 17' November, 1864—— My Office, City Point——

. . . I saw Genl. Meade for an hour and have partially arranged matters with him but concluded to let Genl. Grant return before finally deciding upon the future, as Meade tells me that he & Grant have talked the matter over, of Stanton's fierce attacks & that Grant will call it up, at Washington. . . .

Friday Night, 18' November, 1864—— My Office, City Point.

. . . I sent up the resignation of Col. Sharpe this morning, but have not received any returns from it. . . . Mr. [John A.] Cole has been here to talk of Christian Commission. . . .

Monday Night, 21' November[,] 1864—— My own House—C.P.

. . . Genl. Meade declines to act on Col. Sharpe's resignation until Genl. [Grant] returns & he has conferred with him.

Tuesday Night, 22' Nov. '64—— My Quarters, City Point.

. . . I have been engaged much as usual today, and in one respect, have done quite a thing—— I have written a long letter to Mary [Patrick], and enclosed for her Autograph Letters from Abraham Lincoln, George B. McClellan & Mrs. Lincoln, having before sent one from Mrs. McClellan. . . .

Wednesday Night, 23' November, 1864—— My Quarters, City Point——

. . . I drove up to the Hospitals, taking Brayton with me, to see about some charges against the embalmers—which, by the way, are true. . . . The first instal[l]ment of Thanksgiving Turkies (?) came in at 6 o'clock this evening and is now being distributed.

Thanksgiving day, 24' November[,] 1864——— City Point[,] Va[.]———

. . . The "James T. Brady" with another load of Thanksgiving Truck for the Soldiers, ran aground at Jamestown, and has not yet come up——— The impression is strong that the Pilot grounded her intentionally and I am of the opinion that several of our Pilots, and Masters of Government Transports, are Secesh in their proclivities and ought not to be in our Service——— We had our Thanksgiving dinner today, at 5 o'clock——— Only our own Mess were present, and we had a very nice Turkey, very nicely cooked, with plenty of Vegetables——— I sent down a Box of claret, which Sharpe made into a "Bishop," so strong that [Capt.] Beckwith and I had to come back to the plain claret. It is about time for us to have Duke, our cider man down here, and Beckwith tells me that a pass has [been] Sent to him. . . .

Saturday Morning, 26' November 1864——— My Quarters, City Point[.]

. . . There was a meeting of the Officers of the 20' last night, to elect Officers, and there is a feeling, as appears in regard to the promotion of [Capt. J. R.] Leslie, [Capt. John] McEntee being preferred before him——— They referred it to me, but I have required them to make their own Selection. . . . I . . . investigated some matters in the 186' N. Y. Vols. proving conclusively that a greater set of Scoundrels are not found

outside the Penitentiary. . . . Hancock has been here this
P. M. to say Good Bye—— [Gen. Andrew A.] Humphreys
has taken the Second Corps. . . .

Sunday Night, 27' November, 1864—— My Quarters,
  City Point——

. . . There has been some firing in our front today, just to
make Johnny suppose we are going to attack him, with Gunboats, Monitors, etc. but I do not think there is any intention
of running a risk of repulse, until after Sherman is in
position——

Monday Night[,] 28' November, 1864—— My Office[,]
  City Point[.]

. . . Was at the Boat, and was at Genl. Grant's—— Had a
talk with the Genl. about Sherman and matters generally——
As for Butler, he assures me that he will not be made Secretary
of War—that he (Grant,) knows it, though he does not desire
me to speak of it. . . .

Wednesday Night, 30' November, 1864—— My
  Quarters, City Point[.]

. . . After breakfast and prayers I took a turn, with Brayton,
and went down through the Machine Shops, to give him a
chance to look at the operations—— I then started off, to see
about Steam Boats etc. Intended to have called on Genl. Grant,
but found that Gen. [John] Pope, whom I did *not* wish to
see, had just arrived, with some others, so I kept away—— My

day has been spent in hard work, of various kinds, in the usual way—— I have written a letter to Reuben E. Fenton, Governor Elect of New York, in relation to the appointment of Genl. [Chester A.] Arthur as the Inspector General on his Staff, Major [Silas W.] Burt having addressed me a letter on the Subject. . . .

Thursday Night, 1' December, 1864—— My Office, City Point, Va[.]

. . . Meade received his Commission as Major General U. S. Army some days ago—— Genl. [George H.] Thomas telegraphs that Genl. [John M.] Schofield has given [John B.] Hood a thrashing at Franklin, below Nashville. . . .

Friday Night, 2' December, 1864—— My Office, City Point——

. . . Meade came in here and staid an hour or more, mad as a March Hare about the Burgess Case and a great many others—that is to say, a most unreasonable man about various things—— However, I talked to him, after a while, about various things and finally got him into good humor. He has not, however, received any notice of his appointment as Major General U. S. Army. . . .

Saturday Night, 3' December, '64—— My Quarters, City Point[.]

This has been a warm and somewhat close day, giving promise of change of weather. . . . We have been hoping the fine weather might continue, until Sherman can reach a place of Security on the coast—— Nothing is going on here, *now,* excepting a heavy cannonading, much of the time, intended to keep Lee in the belief that we were ready to attack in case he should send off any men. . . .

Sunday Night, 4' December, '64[.] My Quarters, City Point.

. . . After Breakfast Brayton and I had our usual Sunday morning devotions, after which I was obliged to go down to the Wharves. I came back and we went up to Service in the Chapel of the Christian Commission—— It was very full, and we had several of the Delegates of the Commission with us, tho' there was a want of character and education, visible among them. . . . The Service was a queer one, combined of the Methodist, Episcopal and I know not what else. . . .

Monday Night, 5' December, '64—— My Quarters, City Point.

. . . I have been busy about many papers from the Army of Potomac some of them, from Meade, of rather an insolent character—— I have answered them, quite plainly, and expect another attack which will, probably, end in my leaving the Army of Potomac. . . .

Wednesday Night, 7' December, 1864. My Quarters, City Point.

. . . Up at the usual hour and after Breakfast and prayers, went out about my business— Then I had a talk with Cole and Mr. Patterson of Phil.[adelphia] in regard to the Christian Commission—— . . . I concluded to write to Rev. Dr. Adams, giving him some warning as to the downward course of the Commission as regarded men and tone—— This process of deterioration must be checked in some way. It is probable that there will be a move of the Troops very soon, as the preparatory Orders are now out—— The 10' & 18' Corps are consolidated—and the White Troops belonging to them constitute the 24' Corps, Genl. [Edward O. C.] Ord Commanding—— All the Colored Troops in Meade's & Butler's Armies are also consolidated as the 25' Corps, Genl. [Godfrey] Weitzel Commanding. . . .

Thursday Night, 8' December, 1864. My Quarters, City
Point.

This has been a cold, raw day, threatening to storm, but as yet it has not come on—— The night is windy, as has been, to some extent, the day. . . . There is a move going, Warren, with 25000 men [Fifth Corps], is moving down the Weldon Rail Road way, and all others preparing to follow except the 9' Corps—— All the Cavalry has been withdrawn from our front, and I am now sending out my own. . . . to look out for our lines—— I am also patrolling here, night and day, to guard against incendiaries. . . .

Friday Night, 9' December, 1864—— My Quarters,
City Point——

. . . The day has been cold and windy—tonight is stormy—rain, hail and Sleet—the worst kind of storm for our Troops, the greater portion of which are on the move—— Some 6000,

or 7000 of Butler's Troops have Sailed for Wilmington——
Many of Early['s] Troops—2 Divisions have left the Valley, &
Grant has telegraphed Sherman [Sheridan?] to wipe out the
remnant. . . .

Monday Night, 12, November [December], '64—— My
   Quarters, City Point.

. . . Has been clear and cold all day, with some high wind
early in the morning. . . . We had a case either of Suicide,
or very great indifference to life on the part of a Soldier of the
184' N.Y.[,] a man from Canastota—— He seemed to have
laid himself down, intentionally, about 50 feet in front of the
locomotive—— He was terribly mashed to pieces of course.
. . . Warren is supposed to be in his old Camp tonight &
reports says [sic], has been badly handled—— I have no
particulars. . . .

Wednesday Night, 14' December[,] 1864—— New
   Quarters——

. . . I have had a great many calls of all sorts, during the
day, and the early part of the evening; but as I had been
Specially notified that I was expected to go down and see Mrs.
Grant I determined to go. So I went down at 8 to the Steamer
Martin, and there I found all Sorts of music, banjoes & singing
etc. etc. Well, I found Mrs. Grant, a Miss Hyde, Mrs. Dent
and Miss Steele—a daughter of John B. Steele——[4] I made
quite merry and came home. . . .

---

[4] Mrs. Dent was the wife of Frederick T. Dent, Gen. Grant's brother-
in-law who served on his staff. John B. Steele was a Democratic Congressman from Kingston, New York,

Thursday Night, 15' December, 1864—— New Quarters,
   Ciyt Point.

. . . I have had the fitting up of new Barracks on hand, for
the men, examining in relation to the escape of two Rebel
Scouts from the Guard House, last night by cutting thro' the
floor. . . . After I left the Steam Boat last night Genl. Grant,
very unexpectedly, started for Washington——- He recd.
despatches from Sherman, in cipher, to the effect that he had
invested the City of Savannah, that his Troops had plenty of
Supplies, and he had communicated with Genl. [John G.]
Foster & Admiral [John A.] Dahlgren on the coast. . . .

Friday Night, 16' December, 1864—— New Quarters,
   City Point[.]

. . . [Capt.] Leslie has done just as [Capt.] Scoville did—
let one of his prisoners escape—— I am perfectly disgusted
with this neglect of duty—— Genl. Meade may well find fault
with me for it. . . . It is very encouraging. There is news from
[George H.] Thomas, that he has attacked & routed Hood
completely [at Nashville]—— Also that Gen. Sherman is in
Savannah, with 30,000 Contrabands—— This I can scarcely
credit, but he has, certainly reached the Coast. . . .

Saturday Night, 17' December, 1864—— New Quarters,
   City Point[.]

. . . Had a very busy time until about 3 o'clock, when I
mounted, and, with Brayton, rode out to see Dr. [John C.]
Dalton[,] the Hospital Steamers and the Sutlers of the Cavalry
Corps Hospitals—— I called to see Mrs. Mackay, as she was

The type of stockade and sutler's hut that were part of the daily life of General Patrick and his friends at the Head-quarters of the Army of the Potomac. This one belonged to the 50th New York Engineers which was assigned to Army headquarters during the campaigns of 1864–65. (From the Prints and Photographs Division of the Library of Congress.)

running about when I rode through, & wanted me to look at her new diet kitchen.[5] . . .

Sunday Night, 18' December[,] 1864—— New Quarters, City Point——

. . . We ran up to Dutch Gap in a little over two hours, on

---

[5] These "Diet Kitchens" were the result of long efforts by the U.S. Christian Commission to provide suitable diets for the sick and wounded in Northern military hospitals.

the Washington Irving or rather, to Aiken's Landing, whence we . . . walked a mile to the Gap—— It is not so large or important a work as a person would Suppose, from the time employed upon it—— The Howlett House Batteries were quiet and not a shot was fired while we were there—— I do not know when they intend to blow up the Bulkhead. . . .

Monday Night, 19' December, 1864. New Quarters[,]... City Point[.]

. . . I have been employed much as usual today. . . . From Richmond we hear, directly & indirectly, that Jeff. Davis is very ill, having attempted a second time, to poison himself——

Saturday Night, 24' December, 1864. New Quarters, City Point——

. . . The news is, thro' a Telegraph Operator, who deserted from Richmond, that a Telegram was received from [P. G. T.] Beauregard at Charleston, that Savannah had Surrendered, unconditionally, on the 20' with from 15000 to 18000 Troops under Lieut. General [William J.] Hardee—— Also that Fort Fisher, commanding the entrance to Wilmington, had been taken by Admiral [David D.] Porter. Jeff. Davis still continues very ill and the minds of the citizens are very much depressed. . . . After Breakfast I went over to the Bull Ring and brought a number of cases over for examination, which took me until, say, one o'clock—— Plenty of work all day & suffered a great deal from pain. . . . There will be no mail tonight, the Potomac being closed. . . . The day has been pleasant, but cold, and the Potomac is frozen over, as well as the harbor of Baltimore. . . .

Sunday Night, (Christmas) 25' Dec. 1864——— New Quarters, City Point[.]

. . . After Breakfast Brayton and I had our usual Sunday morning prayers & recitations. . . . After dinner we had rather busy times, in consequence of some two or three matters coming up——— Terence Boyle, the prisoner who escaped from Leslie in New York, enlisted in the [blank] Artillery, came to the Army, deserted, crossed the River and was accidentally picked up . . . by some men of the 20' and brought in——— He is now in irons, on the Wallkill——— The other is the case of a man by the name of Alley, a Refugee, claiming the privileges of a deserter—a bad man any way——— Genl. Grant has the case in hand. . . .

Monday Night, 26' December, 1864——— New Quarters, City Point.

Another good sleep, after a rubbing with Chloroform, and having another when I arose——— We were all very late this morning, as it was dark and rainy———So it has continued not a heavy rain, but a Scotch mist——— Just before going to bed an Official telegram from Sherman arrived giving notice of the fall of Savannah; but Hardee & his Troops had escaped— 32000 Bales of cotton were captured. . . .

Tuesday Night, 27' December, 1864——— New Quarters, City Point———

. . . I have found time to write a letter to my wife, as this is her 52' birthday——— She has completed her 51' year——— The day has been mild, but heavy, and I do not feel very keen——— Went out to the Evening Parade of the 20'. . . .

Wednesday Night, 28' December, 1864—— New
   Quarters[,] City Point.

. . . Genl. Butler has returned today—— The Expedition to
Wilmington has been a perfect failure—— Fort Fisher was
not taken and nothing really, was done—— Matters are in
Train to oust Butler, but I fear the President's weakness. . . .

Friday Night, 30' December, 1864—— New Quarters,
   City Point.

. . . Was notified that Montgomery Blair was at Head
Quarters & went to see him—— Sat a while with him & his
Father [Francis P. Blair, Sr.] & Gen. Grant, then Blair and I
went off to a Tent and had a talk of an hour—— We will give
it to Stanton some day. . . . I was very glad that I went over
and Saw Blair—— We had a long & interesting conversation
about the Cabinet—— He says that [Sec. of War Edwin M.]
Stanton is a tool of [Sec. of State William H.] Seward, who
appointed him, and that all their apparent hostility to each
other is for effect—— He wanted McClellan to ask that
[Senator] Ben Wade Should be the Successor of [Simon]
Cameron [as Sec. of War]—— Thence arose Blair's outfall
with Mac[Clellan]. Blair expects to be Senator from Maryland,
if Seward & Co. don't buy out his friends.

Saturday Night[,] 31' December, 1864—— New
   Quarters, City Point——

. . . Yesterday, at Genl. Grant's, I met [Benson J.] Lossing,
the Military Biographical Writer, whom I last met, as he
reminded me at Capt. [Josiah] Tatnall's. . . . The Report
of Admiral Porter is published and embodies a letter of Genl.
Butler, which is very damaging to the writer—— The report,

& letter, leave the failure at Butler's door, entirely, and I judge that it will be difficult for Butler to evade the responsibility. . . . The order from Genl. Grant, tonight, is, to cease all firing & endeavor to have as quiet a New Year's Day, tomorrow, as possible. . . . So winds up the last evening of 1864—— God Grant that the 31 day of December, 1865 may find us all at Home!

Sunday Night[,] 1' Jany. 1865[.] City Point[,] Va[.]

. . . I was up at an early hour—— The rain & snow & sleet of yesterday had given way to severe cold freezing the earth to rock-like hardness, accompanied by the most cutting wind of the season. . . . Just after 12 there came calls from the Staff of Genl. Grant and others—— I concluded that as we were likely to be overrun by a set of men whom I do not care to know, that we would take a turn ourselves—— So we brought out the 4 in hand and started off, [Capt.] Beckwith[,] Brayton and myself—— We rode up to [the] Hospital. . . .

Monday Night, 2' January, 1865—— City Point, Virginia——

. . . This morning was up early and have worked hard all day. . . . Capt. [Alfred] Ransom has been "dismissed the Service for conduct unbecoming an Officer and Gentleman"— probably for throwing a Pitcher at the head of a person who told him, that any man who would vote for McClellan was a Traitor. . . . Butler's Dutch Gap blew up yesterday & mad[e] a perfect Fizzle![6]

---

[6] Gen. Butler had been building a canal through a bend in the James River, at Dutch Gap just above City Point, in order to shorten the channel and open it to Federal gunboats. When the plug at the upper end of the canal was blown out on January 1, 1865, in an effort to open it to the river, the dirt fell back into place and had to be dug out by hand and by dredge. Of no military benefit, Butler's canal became, in time, the normal channel for shipping on the James River.

Tuesday Night[,] *3' January, 1865*—— City Point,
    Virginia——

. . . [Capt. Henry P.] Clinton writes me, tonight, that the
Army is out of Forage, in consequence of Ice in the
Potomac—— So I have been obliged to order the Horses here
on Short Allowance. . . .

Wednesday Night, 4' Jany. 1865. City Point, Va[.]——

. . . Have spent the day in much the same manner as usual——
have been engaged in ferreting out some leaks in the way
of passes—— There has been a great deal of money made out
of the Sale of Genl. Grant's Passes, at from $100, to $125.
each—— Also money made among the Quarter Masters[']
employees by hiding deserters. . . .

Friday Night, 6' Jany—1865—— City Point,
    Virginia——

. . . Spent some time in the morning running about in the
mud, and this afternoon, in the Rain, went over to Genl.
Grant's on a Telegram from Col. [James A.] Hardie, about
Cider—— We have not, before, prohibited it, but Genl. Grant
decides against it, which is very foolish and will cause men to
drink Commissary Whiskey. . . .

Saturday Night, 7' Jany. 1865—— City Point,
    Virginia——

. . . This Morning a Telegram came down from the
President, directing that a certain man's case should be

referred to him, instead of trial & sentences——— My reply, after telegraphing to Genl. [Charles] Griffin was, "The man was hanged Yesterday"——— These are sad cases. . . .[7]

Sunday Night, 8' January, 1865——— City Point,
  Va[.]———

This has been a very quiet day—unusually so. . . . The news of the day is, that Major General Butler has been relieved, by the President, from the command of the Department of Virginia and North Carolina and ordered to Lowell, where he will report by Letter to the Adjt. General—Hurrah for Ben!

Monday Night, 9' January, 1865——— City Point,
  Va[.]———

. . . After Breakfast Dr. [John C.] Dalton came, and then I had Genl. [John] Gibbon here, everybody perfectly delighted at Butler's being relieved. . . .

Tuesday Night, 10' January, 1865. City Point, Va[.]———

. . . We have had a most lugubrious day, and the mud is very deep——— We have been tied to our Offices today, excepting while I thought to see Grant alone, as no one would be out Such a day; but it seems that he had taken his leave after breakfast, and ran up, with Col. [John E.] Mulford,[8] to see

---

[7] Lincoln's inquiry concerned Waterman Thornton of the 179th New York Volunteers. Gen. Griffin commanded the 2nd Division of the Ninth Army Corps.

[8] Col. Mulford worked with the flag of truce boat and conducted prisoner exchanges on the James River.

the Operations up in the Army of the James. . . . Yesterday Genl. Hunt was down here and read me a paper on the Organization of the Artillery. . . .

Thursday Night, 12' Jany. 1865. City Point, Va[.]——

. . . After the early morning work and getting the Boat off, I went over to Genl. Grant's; met him on the way and went over to his Quarters to talk—— Got well at it and then Seth Williams came in—— So I left a Memorandum for him to look at tonight and came home—— The Army of Potomac has lost its Adjt. General—— Seth Williams reported here as Acting Inspector General on Grant's Staff—— He goes off, in the morning, to Nashville. . . . We have made a large number of arrests today, of Soldiers engaged in selling passes—— They are Stolen from [Col. Theodore S.] Bowers. . . .

Friday Night, 13' Jany. 1865. City Point, Va[.]——

. . . I have had a busy day, having arrested another lot of the Reserve Corps, for robbing the Recruits they guarded—— We are not yet through with the investigation—— Capt. [Paul A.] Oliver went up, today, with the "Silver Star" to see Colonel Mulford & take up two women who have been here some time, to go through the lines, with the President's pass—— There is a great deal of interest and excitement, about affairs in Richmond—— It is generally believed in Richmond that the City will be evacuated—— Again, there are strong symptoms of a peace element making itself felt. . . .

Sunday Night, 15' Jany—1865—— City Point[,]
Virginia——

. . . After Breakfast I had to fit out Brayton and then to do
considerable business, as I was desirous of going up to the
Chris.[tian] Com.[mission] Services. . . . Went up to Church
at 10'30". . . . Then went to the Steamer Connecticut, where
I staid an hour and a half, with Mrs. Hood and Mrs. Case——
It was a pleasant visit, but, as both these ladies—especially
Mrs. Case, are intensely bitter against the South, I enjoyed
their conversation less than I would if they had less
bitterness.. . . .

Tuesday Night, 17' Jany. 1865. City Point[,] Va[.]——

. . . The news of the morning was a Telegram from Fort
Monroe, that Fort Fisher had been surrendered. . . . This
will settle all matters for Maj. Gen. Butler and place Genl.
Grant on the right foundation at Washn. The newspapers
give us the information that Edward Everett died last Sunday
Morning of Apoplexy. . ., .

Wednesday, 18' Jany. 1865—— City Point[,] Virginia
(10 o'clk[.] P. M.)

. . . Have been on Office work all day—— Have had an
unusual variety of work—— An Old man of Oswego County,
74 years Old, who came to get help to go home, having been
down here to see his sons in the Army—— When I returned
from Dinner I found two Confederate Lieutenants—Deserters
—from Virginia & Georgia Regiments—— Then I had to
examine a woman, dressed in our Uniform—Charley (or

Charlotte) Anderson, of Cleaveland [sic], Ohio, who is, or has been, with the 60' Ohio—— She has told me the truth I think, about herself. . . .

Friday Night, 20' Jany. 1865—— City Point, Va[.]——

. . . The usual Office work has kept me very busy & I have had not time for any thing else. . . . I have had some more rascals from Trenton in hand, for robbing Substitutes and Recruits—— Have drawn up a paper, through Col. [Gen.] Sharpe, on the Subject. . . .

Saturday Night, 21' Jany. 1865—— City Point, Va[.]——

We have important information today from Richmond—— [Sec. of War James A.] Seddon is replaced by [Gen. John C.] Breckinridge, and there are other changes in the Cabinet—— Lee is Generalissimo of the Confederacy. . . .

Sunday Night, 22' Jany. 1865—— City Point, Va[.]——

. . . This evening I have been over to the Chris. Com. Tent, to hear Bishop [E. S.] Janes—— Nothing Striking, but a Sermon of love & peace & good will. . . . I have also sent off Several persons, including my woman dressed in men's clothing, for Cleveland. . . .

Monday Night, 23' Jany. 1865—— City Point[,] Va[.]——

Another Miserable sort of day. . . . Bishop Janes called to see me about 8'30", then Came Bishop Lee, than Mr. Jones of

Ex[ecutive] com[mittee] C.[hristian] C.[ommission.] They talked and conferred about their matters of the Chris. Com. very freely and I too, talked freely with them. . . . I have, this evening, ordered another of Andy Hepburn's Store[s] to be closed and have sent the papers in the case to General [John A.] Rawlins. . . . The Boats in the Potomac are ice bound, and no Mail Boat left there this morning——

Tuesday Night, 24' Jany—1865—— City Point, Va[.]——

. . . This morning at a little before 4 o'clock Dunn of Grant's Staff turned me out, to Say that the Rebel Rams had started and were past the Obstructions, en route for City Point—— I sent over to have the long Roll beaten and all the Troops turned out—— They were under Arms & ready for a fight long before we could see anything—— When Daylight came, there was nothing to be seen and Beckwith came back from Gen. Grant's to Say the Rams had stopped above, & my men were returned to their command. . . . I went over to see Genl. Grant, whose first words to me were, "If Providence had not Shown us more favor than the Navy we Should have gone up——" It seems that 4 rams started about 12 o'clock and ran down through the obstructions, within 2 miles or 3 of Aiken's landing, at Sight of which Capt. [Commander William A·] Parker ran away with the Onondaga, without firing a Shot—— From Some unknown cause the Rams turned around and Started to go back, but 2 of them ran aground and a third blew up—— [John] Gibbon pounded them with his field pieces, without effect, and Grant could not get Parker up to the Scratch, with his 15 inch Gun & $14\frac{1}{2}$ Rifled piece—— Had these guns been brought to bear upon the Rams while aground, it is believed they would have been destroyed—— With the high tide however the Rams got off & returned to their former anchorage. . . .

Wednesday Night 25' Jany—1865—— City Point, Va[.]——

. . . Have had some men who were with the fleet of the Rebels, that ran aground—— If Parker had done anything at all, they would have been all Captured, or destroyed[.] I was over at Genl. Grant[']s this Afternoon and he told me that he had had Parker relieved and sent to Fort Monroe. . . .

Thursday Night—26' Jany—1865—— Fort Monroe—— On State of Maine[.]

Was up very early this morning. Got things packed up before Breakfast. . . . We got off at ten and ran down the river, very pleasantly, reaching here at 4 o'clock. . . . When we reached here we went on Shore, to get orders for Coal. . . . We found that we could not get Coal and so returned to the Boat and are now off for Annapolis——

Friday Night—27' Jany—1865—— Washington—— Mr. Oppenheimer's——

. . . We had a slow & icy passage to Annapolis, reaching there at 10'30"—— Were obliged to remain until 2'30" before we could get away—— I had trouble to get my prisoners & those who came here with the Webster off—— Had all sorts of a time coming over, and reached here after dark. . . .

Saturday[,] 4'15" P. M., 28' Jany—[']65—— Washington, 305 Pa. Avenue[.]

. . . It was about 9'15" when I got out this morning—— Went first to take my large picture over to [Mathew] Brady——

no; [Alexander] Gardner[']s new establishment—the best I ever saw—— He wanted me to sit again for him, and to have Brayton taken with me—— So I sat—— I sat also for a Vignette—— Went out and found the rooms of the Chris. Com. . . . Then had an interview with Dr. [Charles] Demond of Boston relative to [John A.] Cole—— Came down here to this house and then went to the War Department— Brayton with me—— Saw John Potts, Sharpe and all of them—— Had a long talk with Dana—— He is frank & out-spoken and Says he will aid me in any manner he possibly can[.]

——12 o'clock P. M. After dinner I went over to the 7' Street Rail Road and rode up to the Campbell Hospital. . . . Staid there and took tea—staid until 9 o'clock & came down to the Seton House, where were the Executive Committee of the [Christian] Commission—— We had all sorts of consultation and a very pleasant time indeed. . . . I am to go, tomorrow, to the War Department & meet the Secretary. . . .

Monday Night, 30' Jany—'65—— Washington, 305 Penn. Avenue——

Yesterday morning I slept late, . . . and as I was to be at the War Office at 10'30" I took Buck up to Dr. [Phineas D.] Gurley's [New York Ave. Presbyterian] Church[.] Finding Mr. Cole there I turned Brayton over to him and left for Stanton's[.] After staying there half or ¾ of an hour, found he would not see me and came home. . . . At 6 o'clock Mr. Demond came for us and off we went—— Took in Dr. [S. H.] Cox and Mr. [George H.] Stuart and drove to the Capitol—— Such a jam I never Saw—— It was difficult to get in— very—— Mr. [William H.] Seward presided[.] The meeting was not what I like—too much anxiety for effect—too much

claptrap—— There was *some* good speaking—not much——
Chaplain [C. C.] McCabe & General [Clinton B.] Fisk told
stories, but were, nevertheless, eloquent—— I got through
very well—as well as I expected at least—— Certainly I had
no reason to be dissatisfied with its reception[.] As the house
began to thin out, I went on the floor to meet Mrs. Beck &
Judge [Robert C.] Grier [of the Supreme Court]. Met
[Admiral] Farragut and many others. . . . It was late this
[Monday] morning when we rose and [Capt.] Dallas and
others came in before I got through breakfast—— I went up
Street to Maj. [Wliliam B.] Rochester's. . . . From Rochester
I went to the War Office—— After a half hour Saw Mr.
Stanton in the outer room and demanded an interview——
In half an hour we were in his private room and the door
locked—— I never talked more plainly to any man in my
life—— I will do him the justice to Say, that he behaved
well—— He heard me patiently, said what he had to Say and
gave me the key to much of the mischief that has been going
on—— I have not time to write it out, but enough to Say—he
appeared as much interested as I was and expressed his great
Satisfaction at the interview, saying that he wished me to
come to the City never without seeing him—— Dana and
[James A.] Hardie were as much delighted at the result
as I could be—— They were very much interested——
Monday—— From the War Department I went to see [Genl.
[Amos B.] Eaton and then to see [Christopher C.] Augur. . . .

Tuesday Night, 31' Jany 1865—— Washington, D. C.

Up in pretty good season. . . . I went over to Gardner's to
get Photographs, but they were not made, except Specimens[.]
Went to see Senator [Henry] Wilson, but he had gone. . . .
I then went to see Senator Wilson again, (I should have said

that I was finally Summoned yesterday—no—today, but it was put off until tomorrow) about the Senate Committee, but he was off. . . .

Wednesday Night, 1' February, 1865——
Washington— Oppenheimer's[.]

This has been a pleasant day—— After Breakfast had Dallas here & then went to the Senate—— Was before the Committee about half an hour then looked around, meeting acquaintances, until Mary Chapin came—— We had long and very pleasant talks of old times—— She is perfectly frank and outspoken—— Very intelligent & very radical——

Thursday Night, 2' February, 1865—— Washington——
Oppenheimer's[.]

This has been a very busy day and I am very tired tonight—— Was up quite early and after a while went out to the picture Gallery of Mr. Slagel, and also at Gardner's again—sitting at both places. . . . Professor Eben N. Horsford of Yale [Harvard], and James S. Tryon, of First National Bank, Hartford, came to see me and Spent some time——

Saturday Night, 4' February, Annapolis, Steamer State of Maine[.]

. . . We spent our day on the Boat, which could not coal yesterday and is only taking coals on tonight[.] This is a one horse town and a one horse rail Road—— There is not coal enough brought over the road for coaling even the Mail

Steamers—— We get off tonight, however—— Genl. Ingal[l]s
has come and Started up business here in a hurry—— We
have Spent our time on board very pleasantly, reading
Ivanhoe, Music, conversation etc. . . . The President is now
in Washington, having come up in the night from his interview
with the [Confederate] Commissioners at Fort Monroe——
Messrs. [Alexander] Stephens, [R. M. T.] Hunter & [John
A.] Campbell—— Many think there will be no more blood-
shed, but I am not yet quite So Sanguine as all that.

Chapter XV

End of the Siege

FEBRUARY 5, 1865, THROUGH APRIL 5, 1865

THE RETURN OF SPRING AND the inexorable weakening of Lee's forces as Grant stretched his lines farther and farther westward produced a quickening tempo at the Headquarters of the Armies Operating against Richmond. Patrick's time was more and more absorbed with receiving and forwarding prisoners of war. There seems to have been little awareness, however, of how close the end really was. Clearly, Lee's defensive skill, was never underestimated at Grant's Headquarters.

On April 1, Sheridan attacked Confederate forces under Pickett at Five Forks, turning Lee's extreme right flank. Petersburg fell on April 2 and Richmond on April 3. Lincoln walked the streets of Richmond on April 4.

Lee sought safety by moving west along the Richmond and Danville Railroad. Grant sought to head him off by moving along the Southside Railroad toward Lynchburg. Rear guard actions on April 6 and 7 further weakened Lee and on April 9 Grant and Lee met in the McLean house in the crossroads village of Appomattox Court House to arrange the surrender of the Army of Northern Virginia.

Sunday Night, 5' February, 1865—— My Quarters[,]
   City Point.

Got up this morning & found myself just opposite Newport
News—— We were engaged all the way until our arrival here
in Melodeon Music, Singing, reading and talking—— When
we were opposite our place here, I waved my handkerchief &
Started an Ambulance for the Hospital Wharf, which I found
there, with [Capt.] Beckwith, almost as soon as ourselves——
I took it, with Beckwith, and came home . . . & then reported to
Genl. Grant—— Found his Wife with him, staid 15 or 20
minutes and came home—— There is a move of the 2' & 5'
Corps, to the left to break up the Rebel Train & Corduroy
Road, between Bellfield & Petersburg[.] Everybody has left
Head Quarters A. of P.—on the raid. . . .

Monday Night—— I have been hard at work all the
day—— There has been a constant run upon me, and I am
not through nor any thing like it. . . . It is said that our Troops
were repulsed in an assault yesterday, though Successful the
day before. . . . The weather is cold again tonight and I fear
that the Potomac will soon be closed again——

Tuesday Night, 7' February, '65—— My Quarters, City
   Point——

This has been a Stormy day—Sleet all day—— I do not
know what has been the Condition of the Troops at the Front
today—— The reports are unsatisfactory. . . . [Col. Theodore
S.] Bowers has been here Some hours, talking over matters of
duty & future arrangement—— We are to have some trouble,
I fear, in arranging our affairs with Genl. Meade. . . . The

papers are full of the Peace Commission & fully Sustain the President's Action at Fortress Monroe——[1]. . .

Thursday Night, 9' February, 1865—— My Quarters, City Point[.]

This has been a pleasant day, but cold—— [Capt. Alexander J.] Dallas telegraphs that no Steamer leaves Washington today, on account of ice. . . . The report of the Committee on the Conduct of the War, in relation to the "Mine" has been published and is very severe on Meade, with more justice than is usually shown—— If it would have gone further, and inquired what Meade was doing all that Morning, the truth would have been known—— I do not think the end has yet appeared—— . . .

Saturday Night, 11' Feby. 1865—— My Quarters, City Point——

. . . This evening, by the Boat, Prof. [Eben. S.] Horsford,[2] arrived and has taken up his Quarters with me for tonight and I wanted to talk with him, but [Col. John T.] Sprague came and spent the evening here, leaving me no chance to work, or to talk—— I have received a Letter from Mr. [Packer] Prentice, congratulating me upon my promotion, (wonder when it was,) & saying all Sorts of kind things. . . .

---

[1] This is the Hampton Roads Conference which took place on February 3, 1865 aboard the *River Queen* anchored off Fortress Monroe. Abraham Lincoln and Secretary of State Seward met with the three Confederate Commissioners, Alexander Stephens, R. M. T. Hunter, and John A. Campbell. But the Commissioners were unable to meet Lincoln's minimum terms of Union and Emancipation.

[2] Prof. Horsford, Professor of Chemistry at Harvard, was trying to interest the Army in his concentrated rations.

Sunday Night, 12' Feby. 1865—— My Quarters, City
   Point, Va[.]——

Went to bed rather late last night, after a long talk with Prof.
Horsford, who, after breakfast this morning, or at 10′15″ was
sent up to Genl. Humphreys [Second Corps]. . . . The reports
from Richmond are favorable—— Every thing there is in
great agitation, and they hear that Sheridan is moving upon
some point—— Lee's Cavalry is ordered to meet him—— The
Wind, tonight, is very high & very cold—— Tom [Chambers]
& [Eben] McGee [Magee] are drunk tonight and want overhauling.[3]

Monday Night, 13' Feby—1865—— My Quarters, City
   Point——

. . . I have had the usual amount of work today & about as
busy as usual—— I have taken time, however, to give my
Report, for [Gen. George W.] Cullum's forthcoming work, at
West Point.[4] . . . [Capt. John C.] Babcock left here Yesterday
morning, for home, on 20 days['] leave, and Capt. [Paul A.]
Oliver was sent up to take his place—— This Afternoon Capt.
Oliver was sent back by Genl. Meade, with an insolent letter
from Meade to [Gen. George] Sharpe—— The Arrangement
was made by Sharpe, with Meade, in a perfectly Satisfactory
Manner & this comes like a thunderbolt—— He (Sharpe) will
pay him off. . . .

Wednesday Night, 15' Feby. 1865—— My Quarters[,]
   City Point[,]

This morning I was up in my usual good Season, had our
devotions, went to Breakfast, came back and found here Genl.

---

[3] Tom Chambers was an orderly and Eben Magee a scout at Patrick's
headquarters.
   [4] George Washington Cullum, *Biographical Register of the Officers and
Graduates of the U. S. M. A. at West Point. . . .*

Humphreys and Professor Horsford—— Humphreys left on
the Boat, but Horsford Staid and has had an interview with
Grant, backed by letters from Meade and Others—— Grant
has given him a Letter from the Sec—no, *to* the Secretary of
War, asking him to Order 500,000 of these Concentrated
Rations—— I have written to [James A.] Hardie, privately,
and also to [Charles A.] Dana, on the Subject, and Sincerely
hope the Experiment will be made—— This System *should* be
severely tested, and Grant is disposed to give it a trial. . . .

Friday Night, 17' Feby. 1865—— My Quarters[,] City
   Point——

. . . Today we have had some rain & some hail—a raw,
uncomfortable sort of a day—— We are having a great many
deserters come in, of late—today we have had 89—yesterday
54—and it is Said that still more are going daily to the
rear—— Our communications from Richmond go to show
that they are preparing to move from there at any moment——
They are in great distress about Sherman's operations. . . . We
are all feeling discouraged about the character of the re-
inforcements we are receiving—they being bounty jumpers &
. . . Scallowags generally—— We have as much as we can, by
any possibility attend to, in the way of watching them. . . .

Saturday Night, 18' Feby—1865—— My Quarters[,]
   City Point——

. . . Wrote to Senators [Samuel C.] Pomeroy [Kans.] and [Ira]
Harris [N. Y.], in relation to the Resolution of the former as to
furnishing of Liquor to Officers & men. . . . The Rebel Flag
of Truce Boat ran into one of its own Torpedoes & blew up,
yesterday—none of *our* people on board—— Two Transports

from Baltimore, with exchanged Rebel prisoners on board, arrived this P. M. and evening. . . .

Monday Night, 20' Feby. 1865—— My Quarters, City
   Point.

Another very beautiful day, which has been drying up the mud very fast. . . . Tonight we are in *Barracks,* with our 2000 men—— Richmond papers of Saturday, announce the occupation of Columbia, S. C. by our Troops, and within half an hour after, we received from [Col.] Bowers, the announcement that Charleston was evacuated last Tuesday, by [Gen. William T.] Hardee & co. . . .

Tuesday Night, 21' Feby—1865—— My Quarters, City
   Point[.]

. . . After lunch I took the Saddle, and Brayton rode out with me, to look at things around the Point, and Hospitals etc. The day was beautiful, and *some* of the mud was dried up. . . . I had been back but a Short time when the Mail Steamer arrived, and brought Admiral [Franklin] Buchanan here, a prisoner, under a Capt. Wilson of the 17' Infy. to be forwarded for exchange—— He staid here an hour, or an hour & a half while we were getting matters fixed to send him up—— We had to put him on board the little Tug, Burnside—— He talked very well and we parted very pleasantly.[5]. . . I have a letter from Professor Horsford this evening, saying that the Secretary of War had ordered the Commissary General [Eaton] to carry out Grant's instructions. He feels very well and very grateful. . . .

---

[5] Admiral Buchanan had commanded the Confederate ram, Tennessee, in the battle of Mobile Bay on August 5, 1864.

Wednesday Night, 22' Feby. 1865—— My Quarters,
  City Point[,] Va[.]——

I rose at the usual hour this morning, had prayers and went
to my Breakfast. . . . Went to the Boat and found [Capt.]
George Meade, there on his way home, saying that his Brother
Sergeant was very low—— A few hours after Meade came
down, himself, & left for Philadelphia, on a Telegram that
reported the death of Sergeant.[6]. . .

Thursday Night, 23' Feby—1865—— My Quarters[,]
  City Point——

. . . The day has been somewhat rainy, though not altogether
so. . . . Brayton did not get home from the Front until towards
9 o'clock and says he had a grand time—— Rode about the
lines in all directions, and saw Rebels behind their breastworks— --

Friday Night, 24' Feby. 1865—— My Quarters, City
  Point——

. . . There has been much exultation over the evacuation of
Wilmington, of which we received the news this morning, thro'
Genl. Grant—— The Rebs. are getting very much depressed
and within the last 24 hours 192 have come into my hands as
deserters—Good men too. . . .

Saturday Night, 25' Feby. 1865—— My Quarters, City
  Point——

I slept well again last night, and rose in our usual time this
morning. . . . I have had to overhaul a Soldier of the 5' U. S.

---

[5] George Meade was an Aide-de-Camp on his father's staff. John
Sergeant Meade, who died on February 21, was Gen. Meade's younger
son.

Cavy. for attempting to marry a girl when he has a wife
already living at Falmouth. . . .

Tuesday Night, 28' February[,] *'65*—— My Quarters,
   City Point[.]

Left at 3 o'clock with Hunt. . . . Went over to see [Gen. John
G.] Parke, [Gen. Alexander] Webb and all the fellows—— I
was overhauled and Shaken nearly to pieces—— [Col. George
D.] Ruggles too, [Maj. James C.] Duane, [Col. Simon F.]
Barstow, [Col. Edmund] Schriver, [Col. Thomas] Wilson &
[Dr. Thomas A.] M[a]cParlin—all of them were on hand——
Webb gave me a long talk about matters and posted me well
in regard to Meade's views——[7] I was with him an hour——
It was about 11 o'clock when I left & went to bed in Schuyler's
fancy house. . . . Was up early, had a cup of Coffee and came
over to the Train, with [Capt. Henry P.] Clinton, at 7
o'clock—— It was raining—not heavily—from sometime in
the night until 10 o'clock this morning—— I reached here at
8'30" and went about my work. . . . A letter from Mr.
[William] Kelly & a long one, relative to the Ithaca and Ovid
Colleges——[8] They behave very unwisely in Ovid, of course,
and require Cornell's College to make a new Organization. . . .

Wednesday, 1' March, 1865—— My Quarters, City
   Point, Va[.]——

. . . I have had a busy day, tho' there has been nothing extraordinary going on what I know of—— I had a long call from

---

[7] Gen. Webb was now Meade's Chief of Staff in place of Gen. Andrew
A. Humphreys.

[8] Hon. William Kelly was a member of the Board of Trustees of the
New York State Agricultural College at Ovid over which Patrick had
presided.

Mrs. [Annie] Wittenmeyer[9] and Mr. Smith, in order to Satisfy me of their Status—— Of course I have to cave in before an Order of the War Department, and acknowledge her right to be here, and to do her work—— I will do her the justice to say, that she behaved remarkably well, and, on the whole, I was as well pleased with her as I well could be with a woman who had come here under Such circumstances. . . .

Thursday Night, 2' March[,] *'65*——My Quarters, City Point——

. . . There was an arrival this evening, in the Boat, of a large number of the Members of the Christian Commission, and I sent my Waggon for them, to take them from the Boat to the Commission Quarters—— I suppose they will be down upon me in a body, as is their wont, where nothing can be done—a Town Meeting! . . .

Friday Night, 3' March, 1865—— My Quarters[,] City Point——

. . . Was about usual duties, until about 9 o'clock, when a deputation, headed by George H. Stuart, called upon me—— Mr. Holden & Morris K. Jesup came with letters from Bishop [E. S.] Janes & Dr. Adams—— Mr. [John V.] Farewell [Farwell] of Chicago—Rev. Drs. Scudder and [J. L.] Duryea of New York with other gentlemen of the [U. S. Christian] Commission[.] They staid about $\frac{3}{4}$ of an hour and I made arrangements for them to go up to Point of Rocks—— At 1'30" I

[9] Mrs. Annie Wittenmeyer was with the Army under the auspices of the U. S. Christian Commission. She had developed the "Diet Kitchen" idea in the western armies and was now supervising their installation in the eastern hospitals.

took the Boat with them at the Hospital Wharf and ran up to Broadway Landing, thence rode in Waggons to the Station, Chapels, Diet Kitchens etc. . . .

Saturday Night, 4' March[,] *'65*—— My Quarters, City
     Point, Va[.]——

. . . It was rainy and dirty for a while—in fact, until about 11 or 12 o'clock. . . . I am telegraphed to go up to see Genl. Meade at my earliest convenience, which will be, I think, on Monday—— What he wants I don't know, but the presumption is, that he wishes to arrange matters for the future in my Department—— It will not be a pleasant business[.] . . .

Monday Night, 6' March[,] *'65*—— My Quarters at City
     Point——

. . . Busy until 9 o'clock & went to the Cars. . . . I went directly to Genl. Meade's and had a long interview with him—— It was, in the main, Satisfactory—and he is adopting the Course that I would advise him—— It has resulted in just this— General [George N.] Macy will return in the course of the Week, and will report to me for the purpose of acquainting himself with the duties of the Department down here—— I will post him as well as I am able, in all things, and will then turn over to him the duties of Provost Marshal General of the Army of Potomac—— I was surprised at Genl. Meade's careful manner towards me, and hope he will maintain it. . . .

Tuesday Night, 7' March, 1865—— My Quarters[,] City
     Point——

. . . Was at Genl. Grant's & told him of the change—— He says, All right, and that he wants me to stay with him—— I have been looking about the prisons etc. . . . There is a Dance on board the River Queen, which brought down the party from Washington. They have beset me to go, but I cannot mix with that gathering. . . .

Wednesday Night, 8' March, 1865—— My Quarters, City Point.

Rose in good time, but did not have a very good sleep. . . . Drew up Memoranda for Genl. Macy etc. The Mail did not bring anything of consequence, but Genl. Sharpe returned, bringing with him his Brother in law James Hasbrouck—also Rufus K. Delafield of New York——[10] Of course they have been with me—— I took them up to the Hospitals, let them see what was to be seen, & Came back, in mud & rain. . . . My shoulder is a little Sore tonight, probably owing to my having knocked a man down, this evening, who was insolent to [Lt. J. H.] Winfield.

Thursday Night, 9' March, 1865—— My Own Quarters, City Point——

. . . After Breakfast I was with the Gentlemen at the Cars, at 8'30″ as a party of Ladies & Gentlemen were to go up to the Front—— After they went off I went to work and have been at it quite regularly—— I have examined prisoners, and assigned persons to Regiments——Have done much irregular outside work besides this. . . . Stiles, the husband of the woman who was victimized last summer, is now here, a deserter, and I am intending to send him home. His wife wrote me Yesterday, and I shall try to help her in this. . . .

---

[10] Mr. Delafield, an old friend of Patrick's, was also a member of the Board of Trustees of the New York Agricultural College at Ovid.

Friday Night, 10' March[,] 1865—— My Quarters, City
    Point, Va[.]——

Rainy Night, Misty morning, Showery day. . . . I went up with
Mr. [Philip] Schuyler [Sr.] to call on Genl. Grant, just as they
were going to lunch[.] So we lunched with them. . . . I came
home and went to work, but when the Boat came, it brought
Dr. Rose to me a prisoner, taken on this last raid for
tobacco—— He is staying with me & I have sent up to Richmond for certain papers in his case—— Have also seen Genl.
Grant in relation to him, and his tobacco business——

Saturday Night, 11' March, '65—— My Quarters, City
    Point, Va[.]——

. . . I have been a very busy man ever Since breakfast, doing
the current business of the Office—— We are examining now
with reference to assignment of unassigned & unknown
men—— We had a party of deserters broken up, 8 in number
who have been staying in the woods, encamped, for Several
months—— Some of the Commissaries and Sutlers, must have
known who they were, and supplied them. . . .

Sunday Night, 12' March[,] '65—— My Quarters, City
    Point—Va.

This has been a very pleasant day again. . . . Sheridan has
Sent two of his Scouts through—— He has destroyed James
River Canal, thoroughly, he thinks—— The papers of this
evening announce that Capt. Paul A. Oliver of My Staff is
Brevetted a Brigadier General! What next?

Monday Night 13' March, 1865—— My Quarters, City
    Point——

. . . In the morning I was turned out early, as the Carpenters
were at work on my piazza. . . . In the middle of the day—

about 11 o'clock—I went over with John [Potts] to see Genl. Grant—— Well, we had a good talk—— Sheridan has ripped up all the Central Rail Road & James River Canal—— He will be at White House, probably, tomorrow. He is doing a great work. . . .

Tuesday Night, 14' March, 1865—— My Quarters, City Point——

. . . Genl. Macy came down this morning and Spent the day—— We have given him all Sorts of information, and he has deliberately set himself about learning—— He says that he has had as much put into him today as he can stand, but he will go to [Capt. Philip] Schuyler tomorrow and get posted there; then come down here again—— He seems determined to take hold of this thing understandingly. . . . And So has passed away the last day of my 54' Year—— My days are swifter than a weaver's shuttle.

Wednesday Night, 15' March, 1865—— My Quarters[,] City Point.

My own Birthday! 54 years of my life passed away—— I rose in good season, but had to Sit down and prepare the necessary papers for Dr. Rose, So that he could go to Washington, this morning, with John Potts. . . . As soon as Breakfast was over, [Col. Edmund] Schriver came in—— He is going on duty for the War Department, Somewhere, for 4 or 6 weeks. . . . To night I have had to talk with [Gen. George H.] Sharpe very unpleasantly, for meddling with matters that do not belong, at all to him—— And just now, Tom [Chambers] has come and wants to go away, after having been with me 3 Years——

> *Thursday   Night,   16'   March,   1865*—— My   Own
>   Quarters[,] City Point[.]

. . . Was out and about my business, for Some hours during the
day—including inspection of Barracks of Prisoners & Convalescents[.] I have, also, been looking over "Statements of
Prisoners," and such kinds of work—— There is every preparation going on for a "Move" in the Army of Potomac—— All
baggage & every sort of Stuff has been sent down here for
present Storage—— Schuyler is in great distress, fearing to be
kept with Meade. . . .

> *Friday Night, 17' March*[,] *'65*—— My Own Quarters,
>   City Point, Va[,]——

. . . I was engaged about Office Matters until One o'clock when
the Order came down relieving me from duty in the Army of
Potomac & appointing Bvt. Brig. Genl. Macy my Successor. It
relieves [Capts. William W.] Beckwith, [Charles E.] Scoville,
Potter & [Lt. J. H.] Winfield also from duty there, but does
not relieve [Capts.] Schuyler nor Clinton. It erects an independent Command of the City Point Garrison, placing [Gen.
Charles H. T.] Collis in Command, with the 20' New York,
61' Mass[.], 68' and 114' Penn[.], and 1' Mass. Vols. as the
Troops of Garrison.

> *Saturday Night, 18' March, '65*—— My Quarters, City
>   Point, Va[.]——

This Morning I was up in good time and after the usual duties
of the Morning, until about 10'30" mounted, with [John V.]
Bouvier & Brayton, and rode out to see the 3d Penn. Cavy.
off—— Then took a turn with him about the establishments

of the Qr. Masters and Hospitals, stopping a few minutes with Dr. [John C.] Dalton, & then rode up to the execution—— It was well conducted until the firing—— They fired at the word Aim, but the men both fell in their coffins dead—— Baker, the bad one, seemed very penitent, prayed & talked very long & fervently—— I have never before seen a person executed by Musketry—— There was a large concourse of Spectators present—— The day has been very pleasant and the wind, as well as Sun, has dried up the roads wonderfully. . . . I have received a letter from Gen. Meade, Saying that I do not leave the Army by his Act, and that it was not initiated by him. It is a Singular letter, and perfectly characteristic. . . .

Tuesday Night, 21' Feby—No March—1865——
Quarters[,] City Point——

The night was warm, very warm, and I slept very little. . . . Then I went over to Genl. Grant's and attended to morning business until 11 or 12 o'clock—— I read the President's Proclamation to the Prisoners in No[.] 2, and gave them an opportunity of owning up as to their names etc. . . .

Wednesday Night, 22' March, '65—— My Quarters, City Point——

. . . Macy (there is no use in denying it) is acting like a Swell, and I have asked that the Point here may be placed under my jurisdiction, So far as Trade, afloat and ashore are concerned—— If it is not conceded, I must get out of this, Some way. . . .

Friday Night, 24' March, 1865—— My Quarters, City
     Point——

. . . I have got my work pretty well out of the way and have
put some curb upon either Macy or Meade, I don't yet know
which—— If Genl. Grant sustains me, all well—— If not, I
can only resign and go home—— That is quite easy—— I was
over at Grant's nearly an hour this Afternoon—— All were
there, none of *our* people having gone up the river with Genl.
Meade's party, which is a large one. . . .

Saturday Night, 25' March, '65—— My Quarters, City
     Point——

This has been a busy day—— I was up & after our morning
devotions, had our breakfast early, when [Gen. Frederick T.]
Dent came over to me, with a call for all Troops to the Breast
Works—— There was a Rebel attack upon the 9' Corps, just
at daylight, breaking our lines at first, but in the end resulting
in a loss of a very large number of killed & wounded Rebs,
and about 104 Officers & 2467 Enlisted men, taken prisoners—— Our own loss, Total, not 500 men—— This is very
Significant. . . . President Lincoln, Wife & Tad, have been at
the Front, I believe, today—— They arrived about 8 o'clock
last night——

Sunday Night, 26' March[,] *1865*—— My Quarters, City
     Point[,] Va[.]——

Slept pretty well last night, tho' aroused several times by the
coming in of prisoners & the sending out of a detachment of our
Scouts, as they were driven back yesterday. . . . Rose in the
morning in time for prayers before Breakfast—— Directly

after I went to the Barracks and talked to the Deserters, notifying them that the Union Societies in New York & Philadelphia would assist them—— Came back and went over to Genl. Grant's to see him about allowing certain of the prisoners to be counted as Deserters, if they desired—— He and the President, and party went up the River today—— Came here & found a Mr. Hewitt of New York, Agent for the New York Union Association for Refugees & Deserters—— Took him up to Church with us, and heard Dr. Vincent again—— He preached well—— Came down and made the appeal to the Rebel Prisoners, which caused over a hundred to come out, and ask to take the Oath of Allegiance. . . .

Monday Night, 27' Mch. '65—— City Point, My Quarters——

After the Boat was off I was here and all about on business, until about 3 o'clock, when I went over to See Mrs. Webb and found her in a great State, because Meade had done with her as he usually does with every one—insulted her—— And all for the reason that she thought proper to act as Mrs. Grant and the General advised—— Then I went over to Grant's place where I had a talk with him and Genl. [Mortimer D.] Leggett —then I went down to the River Queen with them and spent half an hour or three quarters, with the President—— He was very happy and talked very freely about many persons in high position; as freely as I would talk of them in my own family—— Grant and I bore our full share in the conversation—— As we were coming out he thanked us for calling upon him—— Grant said that Sherman would be there at Six o'clock, which appeared to astonish him greatly—— I came home at about 5'30" and by the time we came out from dinner, (6'20") the Blackbird went by and the Malvern poured forth a Salute—— After I thought they were through with

their dinner, I went over and Sat awhile with Sherman——
He looks remarkably well, better than he did when he was
about Washington in 1861—so full of fun and cracking jokes,
especially with Admiral [David D.] Porter—— Porter, Grant,
[Gen. George L.] Hartsuff & some one or two Naval Captains
were there—— I went out & stepped in to See Mrs. Grant &
Mrs. Rawlins—— Then went over to the Engineer Camp to
See Mrs. Webb, who walked over to Mrs. Grant's with me,
and there arranged to be off tomorrow, fully determined never
more to accept any thing from Genl. Meade. . . .

Tuesday Night, 28' March, 1865—— My Quarters, City
Point——

Up at the usual hour. . . . Then was about business, here &
over at Genl. Grant's—— Sherman & Sheridan were here all
night—Meade came down this morning, & Staid a couple of
hours—— [Gen.] Sharpe has gone with Sherman as far as Fort
Monroe, to talk with him—— The Army of Potomac & a part
of the Army of . . . the James move early in the morning. . . .
Grant and his Staff go up this evening to be all in readiness——
Sheridan will launch out with his Cavalry on the left. . . .

Wednesday Night, 29' March, 1865—— My Quarters,
City Point——

. . . Genl. Grant did not go to the front until 9'30" this morn-
ing. . . . With the arrival of the Boat came Archy Campbell &
Hull Adams, then Genl. [John P.] Slough & Capt. Church,
then [William A.] Nichols & [Col. Louis H.] Pelouze——
They came down knowing that the Army had moved, or was
about to move, and wanted to see the performance—— Well!
I went over to Bowers with them, and found a lot of Governors,
Senators & others. . . .

Thursday Night, 30' March, 1865—— My Quarters, City Point——

Last night, after going to bed, there was a most terrific cannonading opened, (no one knows how) on the 9' Corps lines & continued over an hour—— All our Troops were ordered into the outer breastworks, and remained there, in the rain, all night—— It has rained all day, seriously interfering, I fear with movements at the front, of which we hear nothing, except that we have recd. here 120 prisoners. . . . It is reported by Nichols that Mr. [William H.] Seward has arrived here and joined the President—— What means this?

Friday Night, 31' March, 1865—— My Quarters, City Point——

. . . Gen. Grant telegraphed for Sharpe to go up, and he went at 12 o'clock—— I was about my office business until 3 o'clock, when I went over to Bowers, on business—— There I met the President and Admiral Porter again—— Sat with them half an hour and came home. . . . Mr. Seward has come down here for Something; what, I do not know. . . .

Saturday Night, 1' April[,] 1865—— My Quarters, City Point——

. . . Over at Prisons and all about until 10—— Over at Grant's to see Bowers—— President there and arranged to send his wife up on the Monohansett at 12. . . . Went out to the Hospitals towards night and coming home fell in with Mrs. Grant[,] Mrs. Rawlins and Col. Bowers. . . . Came back and George Meade came in to see me—— He came down with his Uncle, Col. Sargent [John Sergeant], wounded, & returns to his Father tomorrow—— He, and all others, tell me that the Army of Potomac is not doing well at all—— . . .

> *Sunday*[,] *2' April*[,] *1865*—— *3 o'clock P. M.* My
>   Quarters, City Point——

. . . At 2 o'clock a despatch came to Bowers & thence to me—that Sheridan and the 5' Corps were having a big fight with the Enemy at 11'25″—an hour later, that Sheridan was driving every thing before him, had captured 3 Brigades of Infy. & a Waggon Train—— Several Batteries captured & several thousand prisoners—— At 7'30″ this A. M. another Telegram that the 6' & 9' Corps had carried the enemy's lines at various places, had taken many prisoners and turned the guns of the captured forts on the Enemy—— Later Still that all was going on well etc. etc. At *this* hour, about 3'30″ P. M. we hold all the way *around* Petersburg, from the Appomattox to the Appomattox[.] This carries with it, Genl. Grant thinks about 10,000 prisoners—— I have been sending them, one load, on board the Matamora, under the charge of a Marine Guard—— My Troops are all at the front, at the Head Quarters of Genl. Parke—— They have been engaged, as I understand, and behaved very handsomely——

> *Sunday Night, 2' April, 1865*—— My Quarters, City
>   Point——

This has been a very busy day, as may be seen from the last page—— It has been a very lovely day in its brightness and temperature—— I did manage to slip off long enough in the morning to go up to Church. . . . Prof. Barrows of Andover preached—good but prosy—— The guns were booming, but he made no allusions to the circumstances of the occasion——

Just as the meeting was about to close, I felt that prayer—
special prayer should be offered up for the Success of our
Arms if so be that God would bless us with Peace—— So I
Said a few words & read the Telegrams of the last night & this
morning[.] Dr. Vincent was called upon to pray, but it fell on
me to lead and on him to follow. It was a time of His own
presence, I verily believe—— Then we Sang America &
separated. . . .

Monday Night, 3' April[,] *1865*—— My Quarters, City
    Point——

This has been a very busy day—— At ten o'clock last night I
left the President & Admiral Porter, Staid a few minutes with
Mrs. Grant & Mrs. Rawlins, came home & went to bed——
This Morning at daylight, Our Troops entered Petersburg,
which was evacuated during the night, and [Godfrey]
Weitzel[11] entered Richmond between 8 and 9 A. M. the Enemy
having left at daylight—— No *heavy* fighting, as we learn,
during the day, but the enemy have been pushed back
Strongly—— [Capt.] Scoville has gone into Richmond with
[Lt. Ely S.] Parker this Afternoon—— I have been busy
attending to prisoners—— We have received some 7000 today.
. . . Every thing is all agog and we Scarcely realize that we are
in possession of the Rebel Capital—— What will be the immediate consequences no one, as yet, can possibly foresee——

Tuesday Night, 4' April[,] *'65*—— My own Quarters[,]
    City Point——

Was routed out last night to send forward to Sharpe—— They
all put off this morning for Burk[e]sville, in pursuit of the

---

[11] Gen. Weitzel commanded the Twenty-Fifth Army Corps, manned
entirely by colored troops.

enemy—and I have just heard that Grant has Telegraphed
2000 more prisoners in the flight—— I was very busy all the
morning. The President & Admiral Porter went up to Richmond this morning. . . .

Wednesday Night, 5' April, 1865—— My Own Quarters,
    City Point——

Up early tho' I did not go to bed until midnight—— [Col.
William] Hoffman [Commissary of Prisoners] leaving at that
time, for Fort Monroe—— Horses on board my Boat at 8'30"
but [Assist. Sec. Charles A.] Dana, Wife, Son & Roscoe Conkling[12] were here to go & delayed us till ten o'clock—— Had a
fine run up the River—— Found that with care & the pilots of
the Gunboats to help us, we could run up—— We reached
Richmond & landed at 1'30", then rode up to the Capitol,
where I found [Lt. Col. Frederick L.] Manning, & thence, with
Halleck, to Jeff. Davis['] House, where [Gen.] Weitzel
quarters—— Staid there a while & rode to the Van Lieu
[Van Lew] house, which was full of people liberated——[13]
Thence to the Boat & ran down through the Obstructions
before dark—— Got home, had dinner about 8'30'", and
spent about an hour afterwards, with the President. Talked
fully and freely of Richmond Matters which appear to be in a
bad State. . . . Richmond is one great mob—— There does
not appear to be any Military control—— The works along the
River are of astonishing Strength and there are quantities of
Torpedoes on the banks fished out by our Navy.

---

[12] A long-time member of the House of Representatives from New York,
and married to the sister of ex-Governor Seymour, Conkling did not, at
this time, hold any public office.

[13] The Home of Besty Van Lew. Known locally as "Crazy Betsy,"
Elizabeth Van Lew was a New Yorker, from near Ovid, whose family
had moved to Richmond prior to the war. The Van Lews had prospered
in Richmond and "Crazy Betsy" was tolerated in spite of her avowed
abolitionist and unionist sympathies.

Chapter XVI

Appomattox and After

APRIL 6, 1865, THROUGH JUNE 16, 1865

RICHMOND QUICKLY BECAME the greatest attraction in America. Every Northern officer, government official, or private citizen who could wangle a pass and find transportation was soon on his way there. From Lincoln down to the lowliest camp-follower, they gazed at the "Burnt District," wandered through Jefferson Davis' house, and visited friends and relatives in the huge hospitals ringing the city.

Union authority, as Patrick attests, was slow in coming and confused when it arrived. It was several weeks before the duties and responsibilities of various troop commanders, department heads, bureau chiefs were untangled. Patrick's sympathy for the defeated enemy was widely shared by the Army. The assassination of Lincoln, however, produced a noticeable hardening of sentiment against ex-Confederates and Lincoln's successor lacked his magnanimity. It was General Grant, who had shown little evidence of a personal animosity toward Southerners, who suggested Patrick's removal from the post of Provost Marshal of Richmond because Patrick's "well known kindness of heart" might "interfere with the proper government of the city."

Thursday Night, 6' April, 1865. My Quarters, City Point,
Va[.]——

Woke up this morning and found [Gen. William] Hoffman in
my room, just back from Monroe—— He was here to breakfast and then went to Richmond at 9—— I had quite a time
in getting off, or withholding women from going up to
Richmond—— It was my intention to have sent [Capt.
William] Beckwith up to day, but [Col. Theodore S.] Bowers
came home this morning, thoroughly disgusted, and after a
long confab, we have decided to go up to see Genl. Grant
tomorrow before we remove to Richmond—— We propose
to leave early tomorrow morning, by Cars to Petersburg——
Thus far we have no news today from Grant. . . . [Ex-
Senator] Preston King and [Vice President] Andy Johnson,
with some others, came down this Afternoon & will go to
Richmond tomorrow. . . . Mr. [Joseph] Patterson has been
here quite a while this evening, talking of our Christian
Commission matters—— Genl. Meade, as it seems, has taken
some dislike to the Commission, mainly as I believe, because I
have taken an interest in it myself. . . . I have just returned
from seeing Bowers—— Found the President there—— He did
not go up with his Wife, to Richmond, but sent her up, in
his Boat and is now the Guest of [Admiral David D.]
Porter—— Mrs. Grant & Mrs. Rawlins have also gone up in
their Boat. . . .

Sunday[,] *9' April*[,] *1865*—— In my own Quarters, at
City Point, Va[.]——

On Friday morning we were up, & breakfasted by 4'30'' ready
to start at 5, on the Train—— We ran slowly as far as
Sutherland's, took out our horses & mounted at 8 o'clock. . . .

We made one halt at Blacks & Whites and fed our horses, lunched, and rode to Nottoway Court House, where we halted a half hour with Genl. [John G.] Parke, then rode on to Burk[e]sville[.] The Head Quarters of Genl. Grant were there and he was expected to return that night, but did not. . . . It was just at dark that we arrived there & I did not feel like waiting very long for any body—— So I arranged to have Clinton come for me, as he was not over half a mile away & then went to see the Rebel Generals, [Richard S.] Ewell, [Joseph B.] Kershaw, [G. W.] Custis Lee, [Montgomery D.] Corse, [Dudley M.] Dubose, [Eppa] Huntoon [Hunton], [James P.] Sims [Simms] & [Seth M.] Barton—— Kershaw I knew well & Ewell recognized me at once, though I had not seen him since Mexico. Barton & Lee I talked with freely and I think they were glad to see me. . . . On Saturday morning I went to see Genl. Grant, but found he had not returned—— He had sent orders to remove Head Quarters to Prince Edward's Court House—& to send prisoners down to the Rail Road, at Wilson's under a guard of the 9' Corps—— As it was very necessary for me to get here before these, & some 2000 other prisoners, arrived, it was agreed that Bowers should go on & see Genl. Grant, that Oliver should take charge of the prisoners until they should reach the Rail and that I should come home. . . .

Sunday Night[,] [*blank*] *o'clock*[,] *9' Apl. '65*—— My
   Quarters[,] City Point——

. . . I have had no time to write home today, and perhaps it is as well, for there is little doubt that Lee has surrendered and that the only force now loose is Joe Johnston's[.][1] I called, at

---

[1] Gen. Johnston was facing Gen. Sherman, whose army was catching its breath in Goldsboro, North Carolina.

Hoffman's request, on Genl. Grant's Wife & Mrs. Rawlins, and then went over to the Telegraph Office[.] I think there is no doubt that a Cipher Telegraph went through this evening to the War Department, that Gen. Lee has surrendered, with all his forces, to Genl. Grant. . . .

Monday Night, 10' April[,] *'65*—— My Own Quarters, City Point——

Last night, when the news of the Capture of Lee was made Official, I was serenaded by Band & Glee Club etc. etc. until it was very late. . . . I can hear nothing of any prisoners on the way, trains are off the track and all sorts of obstacles to rapid movement. . . . The Officers & men of Lee's Command are to be paroled and return to their homes—— This is all right—— Genl. Grant and Staff are to take train at Wilson[']s at 2 o'clock P. M. tomorrow for home—— The Order & despatch are dated at Appomattox Court House. . . . I am feeling much troubled about Matters in Richmond, but I suppose my Services can no longer be useful. . . .

Tuesday Night, 11' April[,] *1865*—— My Quarters, City Point——

I am weary tonight, and altho' it is only 8 o'clock, I would be glad to go to bed—— For two days I have [been] watching the arrival of prisoners which are not yet in—— I have been waiting for some instructions in regard to business, and about the Richmond Government etc. All ending in perfect ignorance of every thing future—— Genl. Grant is expected tonight, and I shall hope, by tomorrow, to do a little Something in the way of clearing out my prisons, preparatory to a break up. . . .

The "Grand Photograph" of General Grant and his staff taken by Mathew Brady on April 12, 1865, at City Point, Virginia. Grant and all but three of the officers pictured here had just returned from the surrender ceremonies at Appomattox Court House and Grant left almost immediately after this picture was taken for Washington. The Patriarch on Grant's left is General Patrick. The others are, from left to right, Col. Horace Porter, Col. Michael R. Morgan, Col. T. S. Bowers, Col. J. D. Webster [or Col. Frederick T. Dent], Gen. John G. Barnard, Gen. John A. Rawlins, Gen. Grant, Gen. Patrick, Gen. Seth Williams, Gen. Rufus Ingalls, Col. Adam Badeau, Col. Ely S. Parker, Capt. Henry C. Robinette [in front]. The man behind Capt. Robinette and the blurred figure on the extreme right have not been identified. [Photographs from the Brady Collection at the National Archives.)

Thursday Night, 13' April, 1865——My Quarters, City
    Point——

. . . Genl. Grant and Staff arrived Yesterday morning at
daylight—— I saw him for a half hour—— [Asst. Sec.
Charles A.] Dana had told me that I was to go to Richmond
& Grant told me that the Army of Potomac would be broken
into Corps, probably, as soon as Genl. Joe Johnston should
be cared for—— That [Gen. Edward O. C.] Ord would
command the Department of Virginia, and that if I were
willing, he would like very much to have me go with Ord, as
Marshal of the Department—— That instructions would be
given him to give the control of Richmond to me—and to send
the Troops, Military Governors etc. out of the City—— The
20' N. Y. to go with me—— He wished me to see Ord at
once & I agreed to go up at once—at 2 o'clock, but was
delayed in various ways, by [Mathew] Brady taking a Grand
Photograph, by Dana & [Gen. Seth] Williams lunching with
me, and by waiting for Custis Lee to come with me. . . . It
all delayed us until 4 o'clk, and of course we got into the
Obstructions in the dark, and did not See Richmond till
9 o'clock—— We sent Custis Lee home, & ourselves (Beckwith
& I,) staid on board——

Thursday Night—— *13' April,* [']*65*—— City Point[,]
    Virginia——

. . . We turned out & had a cup of coffee at about 6'30" &
at 7 commenced hunting the city, in an Ambulance, for Genl.
Ord—— There was no one who knew where he was to be
found, and we chased all over the town until 8'30" before we
found him at a Mr. Bacon's—— Talked with him a little
there and went to the Custom House, where I was to meet him

in an hour, at the end of which time I was put in possession of
his views, fully, and Col. [John] Coughlin was ordered to
turn over to me—— I did not wish to have him relieved, but,
Ord wanted to use him for other purposes, about which no
time could be lost.[2] . . . There is, evidently, a world of work
to do, and I hardly know where to begin—— I met Rev. Dr.
Moore, of the city, whom I knew at Dr. Finley's, at Fort
Monroe, in '47—— He Says there is a very kind feeling
towards me, personally, and the people are anxious to have me
go there. . . . I have been telegraphing to Meade about Sending prisoners up to the front by [Gen.] Collis—— He has
finally agreed to authorize the movement—— There are 6 or
7 thousand men to go forward. . . .

Friday Night, 14' April, 1865. City of Richmond
  (Stephens House)[.]

Quartered in Richmond at last! We were up early & breakfasted by 5'40" but we did not get the Offices etc. packed &
all on board, until after 9 o'clock. . . . I have directed the
20' New York to prepare for moving to Richmond[.] We
reached here about one o'clock, but had a great deal of
difficulty in finding a place to unload horses, Waggons & a
very great quantity of Stuff—— It was after 8 o'clock before
we had our dinner, and we are only temporarily arranged for
this night, so as to get some of the desks open, tables out, and
a chance to do a little writing—— I went to the Office as soon
as I arrived, and find things in great confusion—— Genl. Ord
is anxious to do every thing that can be done, and is therefore
with Such a temperament as his, getting things mixed. . . .

---

[2] On April 25, 1865, Lt. Col. Coughlin, 10th N. H. Vols., was placed
in charge of the "labor district between the James and Appomattox
Rivers," to have charge of all matters "relating to negro affairs."

Sunday Night, 16' April—— My Quarters[,]
    Richmond——

. . . The great rush yesterday (in the rain) was for Passports
& I had all hands at it—— Just at 5 o'clock I recd. a
telegram (or read it) from Maj. [Thomas T.] Eckert saying
that President Lincoln was assassinated at Ford's Theatre on
Friday Night, & that a pistol ball was put thro' his head——
He could not Survive—— Also that Sec. Seward & [his son]
Fred. were assassinated at their own residence—— The thing
was kept perfectly quiet until today, when Marshal [Ward
Hill] Lamon, who was here, made a fool of himself by *opening*
in presence of several Rebel Officers—— Of course the whole
thing is now blown & Custis Lee has just been in here to talk
of it—— I was busy last night in ordering in Troops for the
city Marshals & for a reserve force, to be held in readiness for
any thing desired during [the] night—— All was quiet,
however, and this morning rose bright & beautiful—the
morning prayer was offered, breakfast out of the way and to
town Custom House etc. we went. . . . I have had various
calls this afternoon and evening—— One from Custic Lee,
who will leave on Tuesday Morning, and who has given me
much valuable information. . . .

Monday Night, 17' April, 1865—— My Office, City
    Point[,] Va[.]—— [Richmond ?]

This has been a very busy day and I am very tired tonight.
. . . I have been overwhelmed with work and so has every one
of the Officers of my Department—— Since I came up from
dinner, at 6 o'clock say, my house has been thronged with
callers—— I am followed by all the old Officers of the Army
and tonight have had [Col.] Ben. [S.] Ewell, Genl. Joe [R.]

Anderson, Dr. [Robert H.] Archer and Maj. [George H.] Chandler here at one time. . . . They are very much disposed to claim me as an Old Friend here in Richmond. . . .

Tuesday Night, 18' April, '65—— My Quarters, Richmond[.]

This has been a very busy day, I was up early and intended to have done a deal more, today, than I have done, but the fact is, I have again been overrun with business, the entire day—— I have had any number of persons calling upon me, and have had the Shacklefords of Culpepper, the Burtons of Henrico, and various others—— We have been less crowded today, than yesterday, but I have been less good natured, for Mrs. Hooe of Frederic[k]sburg has been to bore me—— Mrs. Jones (Beck. Taylor) came with the Rebel Gen. [Joseph R.] Davis to see me tonight—— She is an arrant Rebel—— She goes home in the morning and I send my carriage for her—— The orders have been more intelligible today & we are getting into business habits a little more than heretofore. . . . There is to be a closing up of business Offices tomorrow, growing out of the recent calamities——

Wednesday Night, 19' April[,] '65—— My Quarters[,] City [of] Richmond[.]

Was roused at one o'clock by Telegram, to prohibit Paroled prisoners from going North of Fort Monroe & had to send off guards to the morning Boat—— Got no sleep afterwards—— It has raised the mischief here, our not permitting Rebels to go North—— I went to the Office and worked until after 12 o'clock, when the Offices were closed for the President & all flags half masted. . . . Am sorry to say, that Ord is

relieved from Command here, and ordered to Charleston——
Halleck is to relieve him, which I very much disapprove——
[Frederick T.] Dent—now a Bvt. Brig. Genl.[3] is here tonight
and is to assume Command in the City—so he tells me——
There is likely to be very little comfort in serving here, so far
as I can judge and I am disgusted——

Thursday Night, 20' April, '65—— My Quarters,
  Richmond——

Another very busy day. . . . I got home and attended to some
business, then remounted and rode by the Libby & Castle
Thunder——[4] Did not go in, as it was too dark—— There
will be a great deal of work for [Gen. George H.] Sharpe and
others in the settlement of many matters of rent, lease etc. as
well as these Tobacco claims etc. etc. There will also be a
system of detective Police taken up——

Friday Night, 21' April, 1865—— My Quarters, City
  of Richmond——

This is a warm, close night—tried to rain, and may rain
before morning. . . . I came home soon after 4, or before 5,
and soon after 6, took a long ride, about the upper part of
the City—— After my return I went over to see Genl. [Robert
E.] Lee, as he had expressed a desire to see me, and spent about
an hour and a half with him—— It has made me feel very

---

[3] Gen. Dent, Grant's brother-in-law, graduated from West Point in
1843.

[4] Castle Thunder was a Richmond Prison. Less well known than Libby,
it had originally been called Castle Godwin when organized in 1862,
but the name was changed by its heavy-handed jailer, Dick Turner. The
Confederate government had normally housed state prisoners, rather
than prisoners of war, in Castle Thunder.

sad, as I expected—— We had a very full and free interchange
of opinions and views, after the restraint of our first conversation had passed away, and he seemed to me, as much gratified
in Seeing me, as any one I have met with—— He is feeling
sadly at the prospect before us, and the delay in regard to
passports for the Northern Cities—— On the whole I almost
feel that our troubles are to come.

Saturday Night, 22' April[,] *'65*—— My Quarters, City
  of Richmond——

. . . Every body is commanding, all to pieces—— Genl. Ord
is giving Some Orders, not of himself, I think, which will
operate very badly indeed—— Such as giving facilities for
the removal to our Northern Cities of all Mechanics with their
families etc. etc. . . .

Sunday Night, 23' April, 1865—— My House,
  Richmond[.]

. . . Went to Church. . . . Dr. Moore preached a strong
Sermon, on the crime of murdering the President—— "Mad-
ness is in their hearts while they live etc[.]" He preached to a
crowded house & Said all that he could Say—— Tonight he
has been here and Says the women are all after him, but I
know the *thinking* men & women are all with him—— Judge
[John A.] Campbell[5] came home with me and talked a long
while on public matters. . . .

---

⁵ John A. Campbell, a former Associate Justice of the United States
Supreme Court and an Assistant Secretary of War in the Confederate
government, had taken the lead in attempting to get Lincoln to recognize and treat with a restored state legislature in Virginia.

Monday Night . . . 24' April[,] '65——— My Quarters———

I am feeling rather badly tonight—I find that Sherman has been playing the fool and that Johnston is likely to get away from him——— Like a fool he has halted, in order to negotiate, and the result is, the probable escape of the Rebels———[6] It is perfectly astonishing and humiliating——— Sherman must be crazy——— Grant has gone forward to join him, it is said, and is, probably, true. . . . I feel disheartened by Sherman's folly in negotiating, and letting this opportunity for crushing out Johns[t]on and the whole tribe of Rebels slip by——— Every thing is looking rather badly for us, we think—and I shall begin to think our affairs are in a worse condition than before Lee's Surrender——— However, Grant having gone down there, *may* retrieve the error before it is too late——— We cannot conceive how Sherman could be guilty of such great folly———

Tuesday Night, 25' April[,] '65——— My House, Richmond———

. . . There are many things being done which annoy me exceedingly, but at present I am not able to reach any definite understanding of the policy to be adopted——— It is said that Halleck has an Order in press that will define very many things, but I do not know——— There is universal surprise at the course of Sherman, and no one seems able to account for it——— This evening I came home by way of a Shoe Shop, to get a pair of Shoes made for Brayton. . . .

---

[6] Sherman had halted his armies and agreed to a truce with General Johnston, during which he negotiated a conditional surrender of Johnston's Army. The conditional surrender was disavowed by Grant, Stanton, and President Johnson, and Grant ordered neighboring troops under Halleck's command to ignore Sherman's truce. Sherman's anger at Halleck and Stanton knew no bounds and was soon revealed in studied insults to both.

Wednesday Night, 26' April, 1865—— My House[,]
Richmond——

. . . Genl. Ord has gone down to Fort Monroe, and left
[John] Gibbon in command of Troops here today. . . . After
dinner I went over to see and talk with Genl. Halleck for a
while relative to the policy to be pursued in very many
respects—— He has, in General terms, given the Outline and
published an Order making this a free Port, for Every thing
except what is, contraband of war and Liquors—— It will
take in all the States, in the Same way, except Alabama &
N. Carolina. He Says that Sherman is ordered forward by
Grant, and that [Gen. Horatio G.] Wright [Sixth Corps] is
ordered to pay no attention to any order he may receive from
Sherman, but go ahead. . . .

Thursday Night, 27' April, 1865—— My House,
Richmond[.]

. . . I am happy to learn, thro' a telegram received . . . [by]
General Halleck, that Booth, the murderer of the President
was shot by his pursuers while attempting to escape across the
Rappahannock—— [David E.] Harold [Herold], his associate,
was taken and with the body of Booth, is now in Washington—— The hope now is, that the public mind will become
quiet and the paroled Officers be allowed to go home, via
Baltimore and New York. . . . Band playing at Genl.
Halleck's Door. . . .

Saturday Night, 29' April[,] 1865—— My House[,]
Richmond——

. . . Mayor Slaughter is up from Fredericksburg and has spent
an hour or more in posting me about the State of affairs down

there—— He brings up a set of Resolutions, of the Common
Council in regard to a return to their Allegiance to the United
States etc. etc.—— All very well, and I was, on the whole,
glad to see him . . . I have had quite a time here with the
new Commissioner of Internal Revenue, who comes clothed
with curious powers——

Sunday Night, 30' April, 1865—— My House,
    Richmond.

. . . Spent an hour at the Office—— Ord came & at
11 o'clock we went to Church—— Dr. Moore did not do as
I hoped and expected he would, in his prayer & Sermon——
He Said nothing of our Government, but of "those in authority" only—— Ord was there and took notice of it, I know. . . .
There has been an Order issued withdrawing Troops, dividing
the Country into Districts & putting a Stop to all unnecessary
expenditures—— It is a virtual announcement that the War
is closed. . . .

Monday Night, 1' May, 1865—— My House,
    Richmond——

. . . I worked here, after Breakfast, until almost 9 o'clock
before I went to the Office, where I have run my usual day's
race—— All matters are mixed and muddy, very muddy——
I know not what we are to do, inasmuch as there are So many
contradictory orders—— From present appearances, the
Treasury Department is being run by a set of sharpers, for their
own emolument— —I came home at a little after four o'clock,
and after dinner was intending to call and talk with Halleck,
but he went off. . . .

Tuesday Night, 2' May, 1865—— My House,
    Richmond——

This morning was very cool—almost cold. . . . I went to
the Office this morning, and after a while came back to see
Genl. Halleck, in regard to business. . . . He does not understand that [J. S.] Loomis'' idea will be carried out at all; but
that all persons complying with Treasury requirements will
be allowed to do business—— . . .

Wednesday Night, 3' May, 1865—— My House,
    Richmond——

. . . Have had several persons in to take the Oath—— Have
administered it to Colonel Taliaferro of Culpepper and Maj.
[D. B.] Bridgford, Genl. Lee's Prov. Marshal[.] Genl. Davis
is in great tribulation, and I hardly know what to advise
him—— Genl. Meade came to see me this afternoon &
behaved very well—— We had a talk as to the future policy
of the Government etc. etc. . . . Many of Meade's Officers
have been to see us and [Capt.] George [Meade] dined with
us—— Genl. [Alexander S.] Webb and Col. [James C.]
Biddle have been here tonight. I am happy to Say that Col.
[James W.] Walsh, 3' Pa. Cavy, is again ordered to report to
me, and Capt. [Philip] Schuyler rejoins me. . . .

Thursday Night, 4' May, 1865—— My House,
    Richmond——

. . . The Army of Potomac is to march through Richmond
tomorrow, and I have been hoping to join it until tonight,

S. Loomis was a Special Agent of the Treasury Department, sent to
Richmond to take charge of the Treasury Department's Office there.

when work for tomorrow has burst upon me. . . . I was sent for by Halleck tonight, to tell me that he had seen a Telegram, to the effect, that proof is in the hands of the Government that the Canada Junta [Clement C.] Clay, [George N.] Saunders, Beverly Tucker & one Clary [William C. Cleary], were accessories to the murder, and Jeff Davis, also—— I am sending out this night, for [Gen. Ranald S.] M[a]ckenzie to furnish 200 men & send off to Burk[e]sville en route for Lynchburg, where Saunders resides, to search all parties & bring Mrs. Saunders here—— The house of Mrs. Tucker down here is to be searched tomorrow morning——

Friday Night, 5' May, 1865—— My House,
    Richmond——

This has been a very warm day. . . . I was quite busy last night until a late hour, with these Lynchburg operations. . . . The Army of Potomac did not march today but will leave tomorrow morning—— Have had a great many calls from Potomackers and Meade's Staff generally. Halleck just sent for me, for the purpose of continuing this Lynchburg hunt. . . .

Saturday Night, 6' May, '63[65]—— My House,
    Richmond——

This has been a very warm day—hot, hot, hot! I was up early and at work before breakfast quite a while after prayers—— There have been two or three of Meade's Staff here for 3 or 4 days—— George [Meade] is a good fellow, and I like him, but can't stand [Maj. Francis M.] Bache—— At their request I rode through town to see that all was right, and as I had prevailed on Meade himself to ride through at the head of

Column, I rode down and met him at the Bridge, and accompanied him to the Main Street—— Then, after he took a position at the Cap.—City Hall joined him and Halleck—— There we staid three hours. Saw the Fifth Corps pass & the head of the 2d. . . . It took about 6 hours for all to pass, but the troops did not appear as well as I expected. . . . The 24' Corps was drawn up to receive the Army of Potomac & passed entirely through the City, drawn up in two ranks—— . . .

Monday Night, 8' May, 1865—— My House[,]
    Richmond——

This has been a very warm day, and I have been Suffering from heat all day—— Was at the Office at the usual hour and soon after went down to call upon the Schuyler party, consisting of Messrs. Schuyler and Hoyt, Alex. Hamilton's wife, Mrs. Blacthford [sic], Miss Hamilton, two Misses Hoyt (I believe,) & Schuyler's two Sisters—— Then worked until about one, came up to lunch and get some papers, was overtaken on my way by the Schuyler party, taken into the carriage and driven to the Libby and Castle Thunder—— Looked through the two prisons, came up and went to work at my Office until 4 o'clock—— Came home and cleaned up, and, at 4'30" was waited upon again by the party, in two carriages, who took me in and we drove across the River to Belle Isle, where we looked about for a half hour, then recrossed & drove out to the Jackson Hospital, as the Schuylers are all on the "Sanitary" [Commission]—— Johnson of the Sanitary was along and I believe Phil. gave him an overhauling for traducing Lee—— We got back after dark and I found a Lady in arrest for wearing a Secesh Flag in her hair—— I gave here [sic] a talking and as she was very penitent, & much frightened, sent her home—— . . .

Wednesday Night, 10' May, 1865—— My House,
Rcihmond[.]

. . . After breakfast we rode down to the Office, intending
to see Sherman's Army go through the lower part of town——
The carriages were filled with the Schuyler party—and we
drove down to the bridges[,] drove over and went to Sherman's
Quarters, where we found him & [Gens. Oliver O.] Howard,
[Henry W.] Slocum and [John A.] Logan and [Andrew D.]
Baird—— We staid some time with them, said Good Bye,
drove up through the Camps, took a flying Review of the
3' Pa. Cavy. and came home well pleased. Sherman has had a
Row with Halleck and refuses to allow his Army to be reviewed
by Halleck, but will march through Richmond tomorrow. . . .
[John] McEntee has returned, with the person of R. M. T.
Hunter a prisoner— —He is now a prisoner on board the
Monohansett. . . .

Thursday Night, 11' May[,] 1865—— My House,
Richmond[.]

I have had a day of Official rest, but of personal unrest——
we have been obliged to remove from the Custom House and
have taken Offices in the Female Institute, with Ord and all
his Staff—— The rooms are not as pleasant as at the Custom
House, but far more convenient—— We are not so far from
business—— The 14' & 20' Corps passed through today, and
the Schuyler party were at the City Hall to see it—— We were
there in full force. . . .

Friday Night, 12' May, 1865—— My House,
Richmond——

. . . I am happy to Say, that an Order will be out in the
morning permitting all paroled prisoners to go to their homes,

in any of the States that have been in Rebellion, on taking the Oath of Allegiance—— This is all right. . . .

Saturday Night, 13' May, 1865—— My House, Richmond——

. . . Ord has turned over to me the control of Negro affairs hereabouts, and of Suffering Inhabitants, in order to check the issues of Subsistence to destitute persons—— I have accordingly sent for Capt. [George] Gibson and placed him in charge of the Organization of that Bureau, and have had the parties in charge of Penitentiary and Alms House here tonight in consultation. . . .

Sunday Night, 14' May, 1865—— My House, Richmond[.]

. . . On my way home [from Church] fell in with General Lee and his daughter Agnes and walked Some distance with them. . . . Jeff. Davis is a prisoner in our hands—taken near Macon [Ga.]. . . .

Monday Night, 15' May, 1865—— My House, Richmond[.]

. . . Have been trying to get rooms and get the Nigger Bureau organized, but am not yet out of the woods—— Schuyler returned this evening, and I will have the Order out tomorrow. . . . I never can love these people very strongly, who are so bitter against the South. . . .

Tuesday Night, 16' May, 1865—— My House, Richmond——

. . . I have been over to see Genl. Lee, at his request, to talk over several matters tonight—especially in regard to [John S.]

Mosby's parole, etc. leading to quite a talk in regard to Mosby—— We discussed State affairs pretty freely—— [Gen. George H.] Sharpe came in, tonight, with [John V.] Bouvier and Tappan—— We are all in a muddle here, and Sharpe tells me we are in a muddle there—at Washintgon—— He Says, that [Benjamin F.] Butler is at work, taking advantage of this excitement in regard to the Assassination of Lincoln, and that he will, probably, be Successful in driving Stanton out of the War Department—— What is to be the result of present movements no one can tell. . . .

Wednesday Night, 17' May, 1865—— My Office, Richmond[.]

. . . I had a call from McLane, formerly of 2' Infy. afterwards on [Gen. John E.] Wool's Staff[.] He married [Gen. Edwin V.] Sumner's Daughter—— He has been Inspector in the Rebel Army and being paroled, goes over to see Edwin Sumner [Jr.], at Frederic[k]sburg—— Bishop [John] Johns[8] has also been over here and had a long talk about the affairs of the Church generally, and of the Episcopal especially. . . .

Thursday Night, 19' May, 1865—— My Quarters, Richmond.

. . . I have had the usual amount of Office work this day, at noon Rev. Dr. Hoge came up here, to talk with me, at my house and I administered the Oath to him—— He is a Strong man and I wish he would do what is right—— He can do good, or evil, as he thinks. . . .

---

[8] Bishop John Johns was the head of the Protestant Episcopal Church of Virginia.

Sunday Night, 20' May[,] '65——· My Quarters,
Richmond[.]

. . . I went to Dr. Hoge's Church this morning and heard a
pretty good Sermon—— The Staff went with me. . . . Gen.
Ord has been over and had one of his rambling talks—
Especially about diseases among women of the Town. . . .
The day has been very warm, but the rain cools us off[.]

Monday Night, 22' May, 1865——— My House,
Richmond——

A very warm Night, last night, with heavy rain—*very* heavy,
washing away by the docks & markets, and doing a deal of
damage. . . . Tonight I have had a discussion with Mr.
[John A.] Cole, on the subject of Colored Schools, and
opposed a plan for having Geo. H. Stuart, [O. C.] Thompson
& others obtain a charter to establish a Colored Normal School,
before the question has been fully discussed[.] Judge Campbell
is below Stairs, a prisoner, by Washington Orders.

Wednesday Night, 24' May, 1865——— My House,
Richmond——

I have had two very busy days—— Yesterday I was very full
of business from morning until night—— At night I went
down to the Gun Boat, to see Messrs. [John A.] Campbell,
[James A.] Seddon & [R. M. T.] Hunter, and spent some time
with them. They feel very badly and of course I feel for
them myself—— Mrs. Seddon came to see me today, not
having been able to come down with her husband—— She

was denied by Genl. Halleck the privilege of Seeing her husband. . . . Have recd. from Secretary of War, of 13' March, a Brevet of Major General—— I do not think the honor can be borne——

Thursday Night, 25' May, 1865—— My House, Richmond[.]

. . . We had invitations to join the grand display for the reception of Gov. Pierpont, but as I did not wish to see it, concluded not to go—— We were, however, finally ordered to do so and closed our Offices, came home, dined at 4 o'clock and then went over to Genl. Ord's where we mounted and about 5 o'clock started for the Boat—— We found no boat there, but a great many people—— So we went off to Chimborazo Hospital—then off to the Race Course and had all sorts of a jolly time. Returning again to the Boat just at dark, we found no Signs of his coming. . . .

Friday Night, 26' May, 1865—— My House, Richmond——

. . . I have had a great many calls today, from Northern Sight Seers. . . . Well—They all came expecting me to furnish them with horses and Ambulances etc. etc. [Col.] Sheppard announced his desire to Speak to an Audience of colored persons, and I suppose expected me to get up a meeting for that purpose—— I gave him some pretty strong advice. . . . Went up & called on Governor Pierpont, for a few minutes—A Slim reception. . . .

Saturday Night, 27' May, 1865—— My Quarters,
   Richmond——

. . . Streets and all other places in Richmond have been full
of Strangers, who will be off tomorrow. . . . Mrs. Beverly
Tucker and party were arrested in Baltimore, by order of the
Secretary of War and reached here tonight, under the direction
of an Officer of Provost Marshal [Lt. Col. John] Woolley.

Sunday Night, 28' May, 1865—— My Quarters[,]
   Richmond[.]

This has been a lovely day. . . . [I] attended to various
things before Church. . . . We came home, after contributing
to the Church fund, and a few minutes after Gen. Lorenzo
Thomas [The Adjutant General] came in, having arrived here
to look into Indian Affairs, confiscated lands, and inspection of
Colored Troops—— Had a half or three fourths of an hour's
conversation on all sorts of subjects of a public character, when
he left. . . .

Tuesday Night[,] 30' May—'65—— My House[,]
   Richmond[.]

. . . After dinner I rode out to the Oakwood Cemetery and
thereabouts—— In coming home I heard Singing at the
African Church and went in. . . . About 2000 darkies were
there, and Dudley of the Freedmen's Association was there,
telling them all about what Government and the people would
do for them—— A mess of Stuff! I was disgusted—— The
darkies called for me and I said a few words to them, followed
by a Massachusetts Darky, Educated, who endorsed me——

A deal of Mischief is being done by these demagogues who are filling our Streets. . . .

Wednesday Night, 31' May, 1865—— My Of—House—
Rich——

. . . I have had a pretty hard day's work, and did not ride out this evening, as I some expected to go over to Halleck's, to meet Gov. Pierpont, with Ord, as Pierpont had sent me a note to that effect, but I found that a lot of blatherskites, including [J. S.] Loomis & Treasury Officials had gone there, making a regular Town Meeting— an assemblage that I do not propose to frequent. . . . I had a call from Miss [Elizabeth] Van Lew today, and quite a talk—— She has been mourning over my Secession proclivities, and told me that I was understood to be on the most intimate terms with the Rebel Society & She had mourned over my fall from grace terribly—— It was really funny to see her when she found out her mistake. . . . I have had long talks today with Genls. [James L.] Kemper and [Harry] Heth, who would like mighty well to be Union men—— Kemper has been making Union Speeches at home. The position of affairs in Virginia is very unsatisfactory to say the least of it—— It seems that the best of the men are excluded from action in forming or carrying out the State Government—— By the Amnesty Proclamation of the President, received this evening, I see that a very unwise money clause has been inserted excepting from Amnesty all Such persons as are in possession of property to the amount of more than $20,000—direct premium on meanness and rascality, for, if *all* that class remain outside, the Government will be in the hands of the rabble—— If they take the prescribed Oath, as Union Men always, they will perjure themselves, and cannot be trusted.

Thursday Night, 1' June, 1865—— My House,
Richmond——

. . . Ord came over this morning and Said he was going to
Washington, but comes in again tonight and Says, Genl. [O.
O.] Howard telegraphs that he will be here tomorrow and
wants very much to see him, So Ord remains and will not
go up until Howard has been here—— It is now settled that
Genl. Thomas⁹ comes here to relieve Halleck, who goes to
California again, to relieve Genl. McDowell, who is to return
to the Atlantic States—— I went out to ride this evening and
called to see Miss Van Lew, but she, too, was out riding with
McEntee——

Saturday Night, 3' June, 1865. My Quarters,
Richmond——

Hot weather—almost melting—— There has been nothing
today of much consequence, save that the Mayor has entered
upon the discharge of his duties and I have begun to send
the cases over to him—— This will relieve me very greatly——
I was [with] him a long time today, marking out the work
to be done. . . .

Monday Night, 5' June, 1865. My Quarters,
Richmond——

. . . I had a call this morning from Dr. Broaddus and the
two Taylors, of Staunton and Richmond—father and Son——
I have also had a long interview with Mr. Kent, who is, in

---

⁹ Gen. A. H. Terry was actually ordered to command in the Department of Virginia.

my estimation the best specimen of an honest gentleman I have met in Richmond[.] I am half inclined to settle down and live here——

Tuesday Night, 10 o'clock, 6' June, 1865—— My Quarters, Richmond[.]

. . . I have had some prisoners (released) from Point Lookout —300 and more, which I am sending off tomorrow morning—— Have had a great many applications to get prisoners released and tonight had a call from Rev. Dr. Burrows and his daughter, Mrs. Fontaine, to get her husband released. . . .

Wednesday Night, 7' June, [']65—— My Quarters, Richmond[.]

. . . Genl. Ord arrived at home this morning, but I can get no news from him—— Many of his Orders have been revoked, causing me much care and trouble—— I have given away 50 horses by his order and now he wants them to be gathered up and returned[.] I have had trouble to day with the carrying out of the Order in relation to the negroes, by the interference of the Northern people—— The Tribune Correspondent has been getting up a row and has sent a parcel of Stuff to his paper, which was stopped in Washington and sent back here for investigation—— Halleck has been sent for to have a report made—— I am disgusted and propose to resign very soon.

Thursday Night, 8' June, 1865—— My Quarters[,] Richmond——

. . . I have sent forward my resignation and shall hope to be at home by this time next week. . . . I have just come back

from Halleck's—— He gave me a good one in answering the
Telegram of Stanton—— He said more than I should have
said in my own favor——

Friday Night, 9' June, '65—— My Quarters, Richmond,
  Va[.]

. . . General [John W.] Turner has been designated as the
Officer to relieve me in command of the District, and the
Order is issued, but no one has been assigned to relieve me as
Marshal of the Department—— I shall not, however, do any
more duty. . . . I now expect and intend, to get off on
Monday Morning—— Tom [Chambers] will go with me, as
far as Elmira, if not beyond——

Saturday Night, 10' June, 1865—— My Quarters[,]
  Richmond——

. . . I was at the Offices for some time closing up and have
been hunted down here. Frank G. Ruffin, Dr. Minnegerode,
Ben. Ewell and last but not least, Maj. Genl. Dan. Ruggles
[C. S. A.], whose beard is longer than mine—— He is living
in King George County, and was here for help about mules,
horses etc. He looks old enough. . . . I went off to see Gov.
Pierpont and staid over an hour—— From there I went to
see Genl. Lee and had a half hour with him, coming home
at a little after 10 o'clock[.]

Sunday Night, 11' June, 1865—— My Quarters[,]
  Richmond[.]

. . . Came home & went to say Good Bye to the 20' & talked
to the Regt. Said Adieu to the Van Lieus [Lew]. . . . More
calls but I am going to pack and clear out——

(From my Pocket Notes, en route for Geneva etc.)

Monday, 12' June—— Rose early and got things started off, so as to Breakfast at 5—— Said Good Bye to the Staff, Eddy & Winfield accompany me to the Boat. . . . Soon we were off, on the City Point and ran down the River. . . . We had a pleasant trip to Fort Monroe, unbroken by incident and filled up with conversation—— I had a long conversation with a Lady from Maine, who had been employed as a Teacher by the Christian Commission—— She was going to Yorktown—— Said there was no System in the operations of the Schools, or of the Commission. At Fort Monroe we changed to the Leary, Capt. Blakeman, for Baltimore—— On the Georgeanna there was a Richmond Delegation, en route for Washington, with John Minor Botts, R. J. Anderson (Tredegar) and other celebrities—— Botts kept clear of me and I of him—— We had a delightful run down—or up the Bay, the evening being very calm, bright and beautiful—— *Tuesday*[,] *13' June.* I arose after a night without sleep and at 5'30" came to the wharf in Baltimore. . . . I expected to have found Waggons there on my arrival, to take my traps to the Depot, as I had telegraphed for them, but they did not come until 7 o'clock—— I hoped to have had my car hitched to the Mail Train, at 9'20", but found it against orders. So I had to wait until 4 o'clock before putting my horses on board & loading the Box Car set apart for me. . . . At 5 we hauled out, in order to Start at 6, but through some mismanagement we only ran out a short distance, where Troops were taken . . . up, were delayed there Some hours and Morning found us a little more than half way to Harrisburg—— I had a hammock swung in the Cars, and a lunch basket, so that we managed to keep ourselves quite comfortable[.] *Wednesday*[,] *14' June.* Was spent in delays along the road So that we reached Sunbury only at a late hour and [on] *Thursday*

Morning[,] *15' June* Started for Williamsport, which place we reached in good Season, wandered about the town looking at every thing until 6 P. M. *Friday Morning, 17' (16') June,* found us in Elmira after a rough & rapid night ride from Williamsport—— The 50' N. Y. Engineers were with us—— Col. [Ira] Spaulding & Major [William W.] Folwell were both in my car a good part of the way—— On arriving at Elmira, after much trouble I succeeded in getting my traps transferred to a broad gauge Car & hitched to the 7 o'clock train for Jefferson—— I paid off Tom [Chambers], sent him back to New York and *we* came over to the head of the Lake [Seneca] —where horses and traps were put on board the Field, a good breakfast awaited us and we came home most agreeably. . . . We arrived Safely and found all well and waiting for us. . . .

Epilogue

THE RETURNING SOLDIER APPARENTLY MADE a ready adjustment to civilian life. General Patrick's loyalty to the Democratic Party, so apparent in his Diary, and his disgust with the Radical Republicans impelled him to enter politics in a small way. He was defeated, however, in his first try for public office and turned his attentions to his first love, scientific farming. By 1867 he was President of the New York State Agricultural Society and making speeches all over the state to both county agricultural societies and veterans' groups. In 1870 the census taker found him a prosperous farmer, living near Manlius, New York, surrounded by his entire family except for his daughter, Mary.

Upon the death of his wife in 1880, Patrick accepted an appointment as Governor of the Central Branch, National Home for Disabled Volunteer Soldiers in Dayton, Ohio, where he again established a reputation for stern discipline and tight administration. He died while still in harness at Dayton on July 27, 1888, at the age of 77.

Index

521

J